サイレントメビウス［完全版］

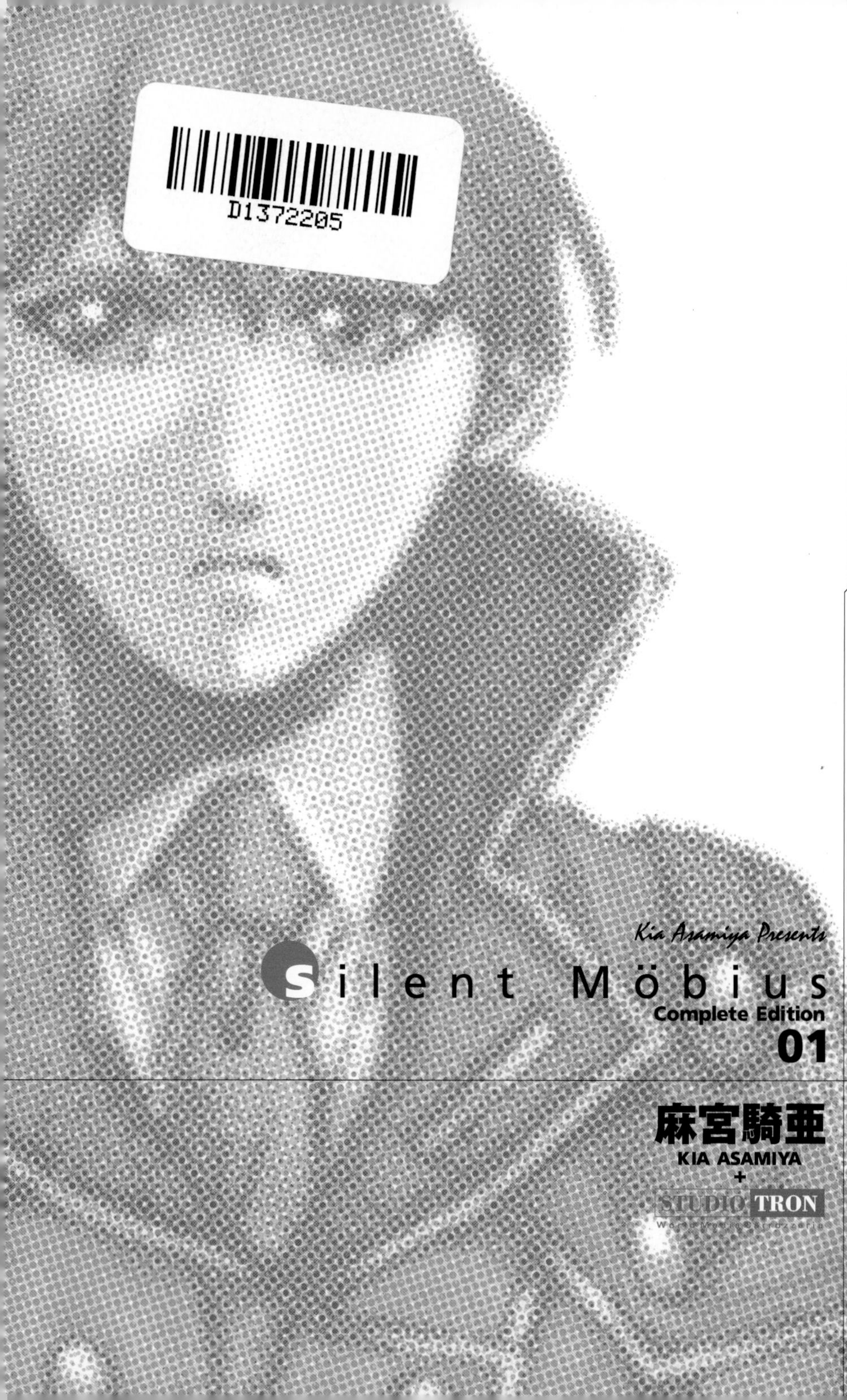

Kia Asamiya Presents

Silent Möbius

Complete Edition

01

麻宮騎亜
KIA ASAMIYA
+
STUDIO TRON

Silent Möbius

Complete Edition
01

✡

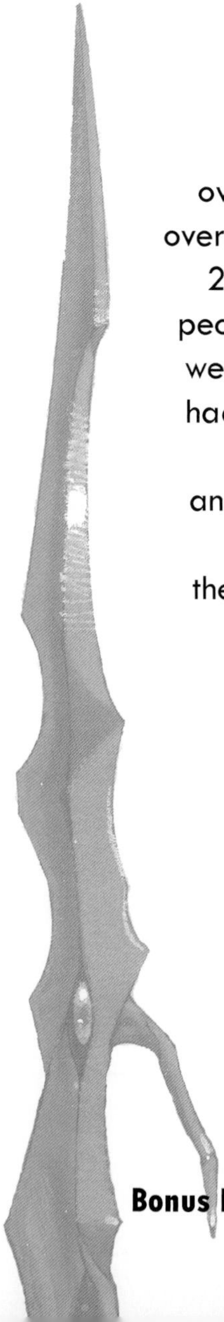

In Tokyo, the mega-city,

the acid rain fell in torrents. Its population was overflowing, and the environmental pollution was overwhelming. To make things worse, since the year 2000 many strange murders have occurred. The people were horrified to learn that these incidents were caused by other-dimensional monsters which had begun to inhabit the Earth. The police named this series of cases "The Creatures' Trap", and decided they needed a special organization to handle the growing menace. In 2023, the Attacked Mystification Police Dept. was born.

C O N T E N T S

サイレントメビウス［完全版］

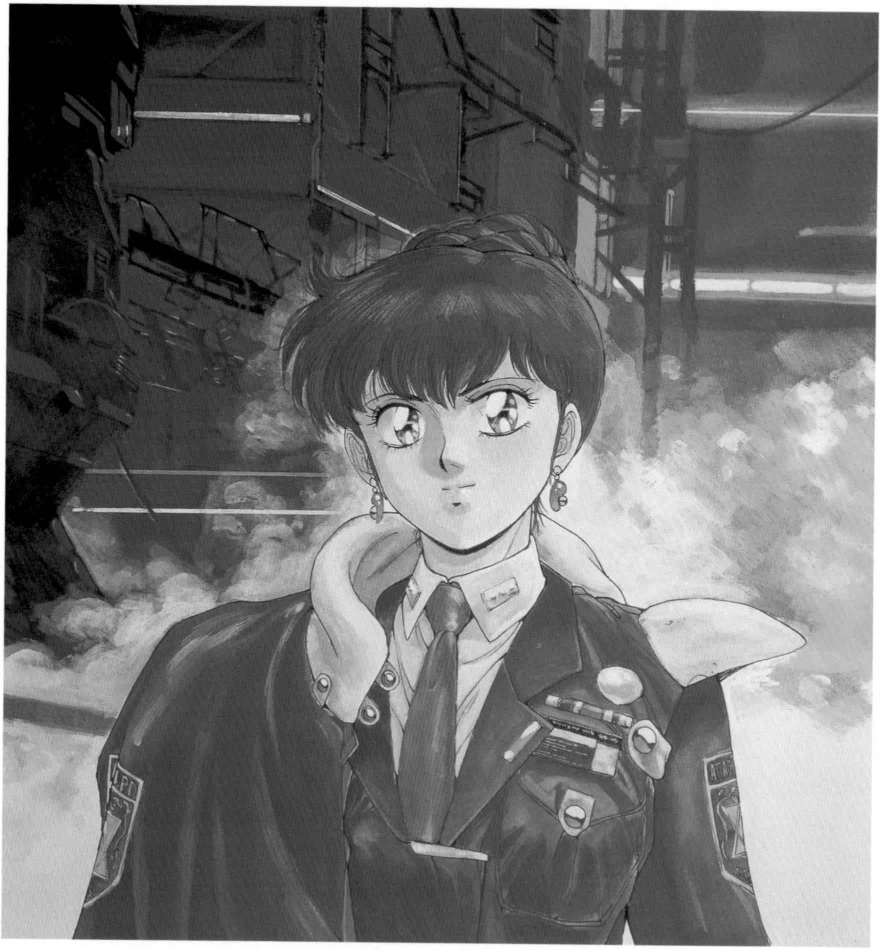

Illustration Data
Source: Comic book
Character: Katsumi Liqueur
Painting materials: Acrylic color / Illustration board

Silent Möbius
Illustration Gallery I
サイレントメビウス[完全版]●イラストギャラリー

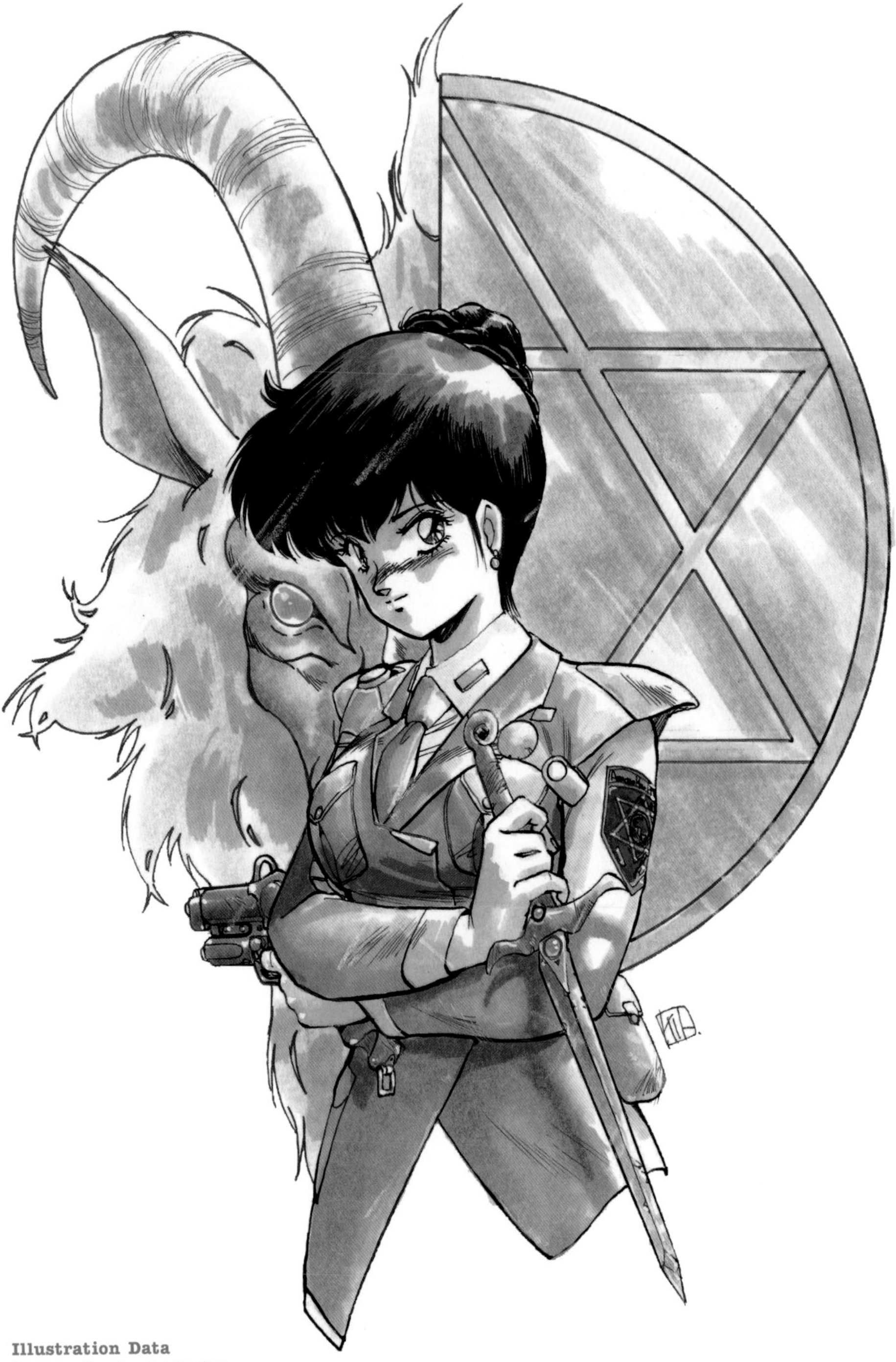

Illustration Data
Source:Comic magazine
Character:Katsumi Liqueur
Painting materials:PIGMA·Alcoholic marker/Copy paper

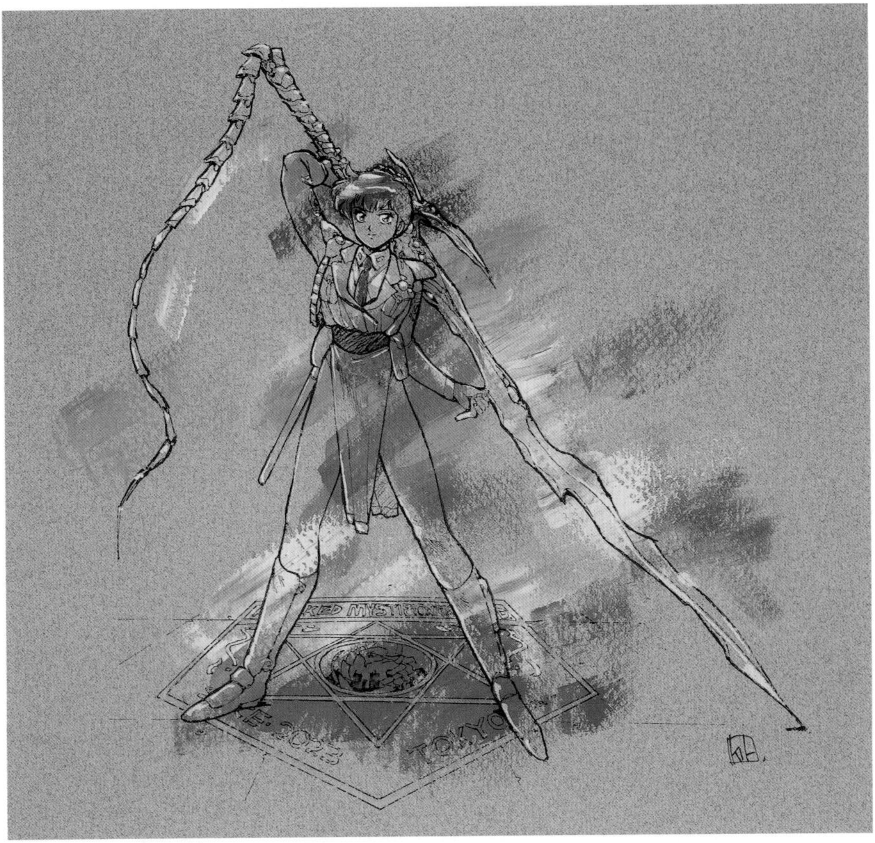
TOKYO

Illustration Data
Source:Present goods
Character:Katsumi Liqueur
Painting materials:Acrylic color / MUSE (Watercolor paper)

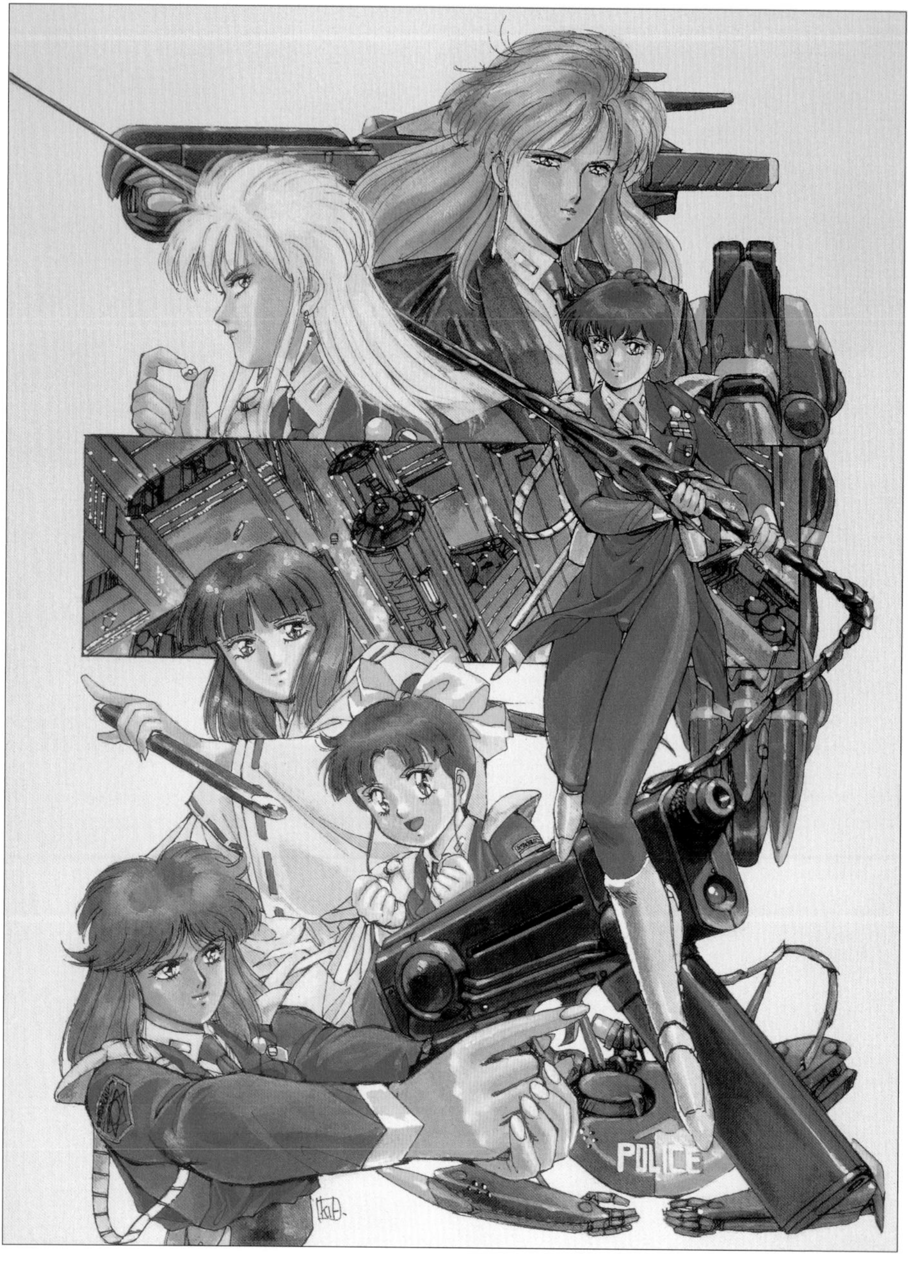
POLICE

Illustration Data
Source:Figure package
Character:Katsumi Liqueur/Rally Cheyenne
Lebia Maverick/Nami Yamigumo
Yuki Saiko/Kiddy Phenil
Painting materials:Acrylic color
/Arches Aquarelle(Cold Pressed)

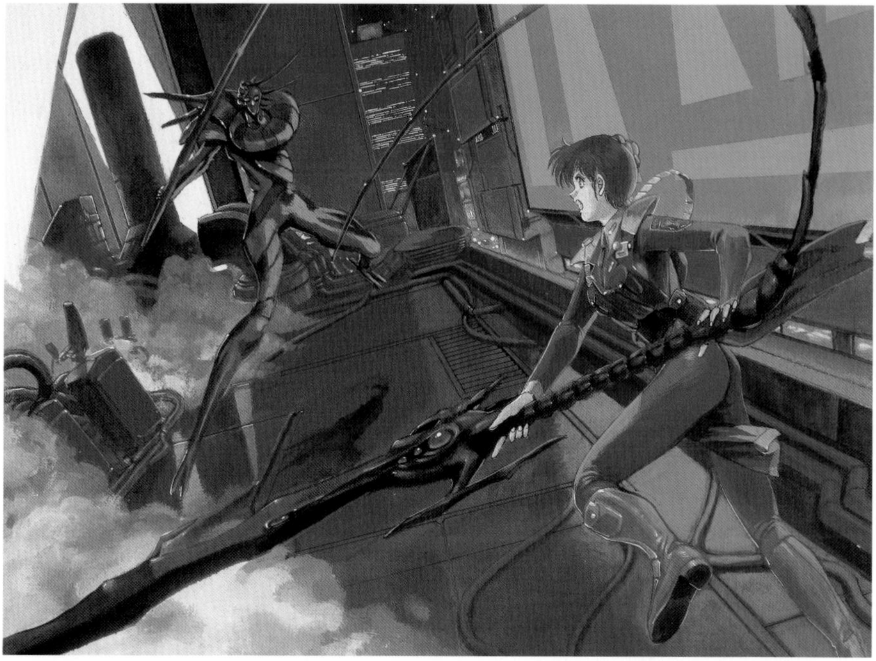

Illustration Data
Source:Comic magazine
Character:Katsumi Liqueur
Painting materials:Acrylic color
/Arches Aquarelle(Cold Pressed)

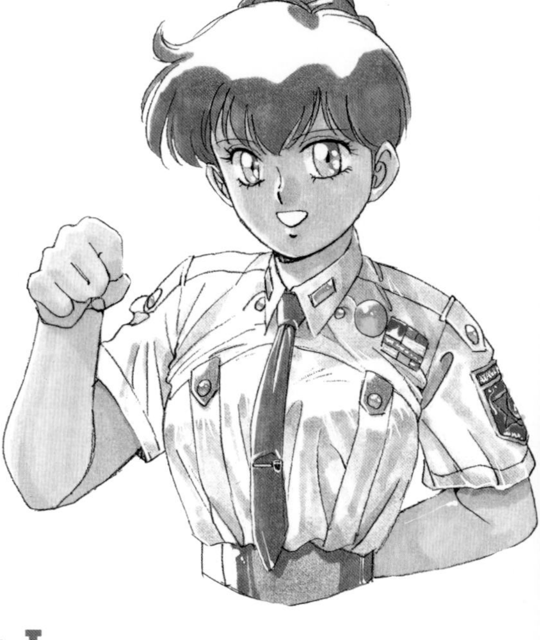

Illustration Data
Source:Contents for Comic magazine
Character:Katsumi liqueur
Painting materials:PIGMA
·Alcoholic marker/Copy paper

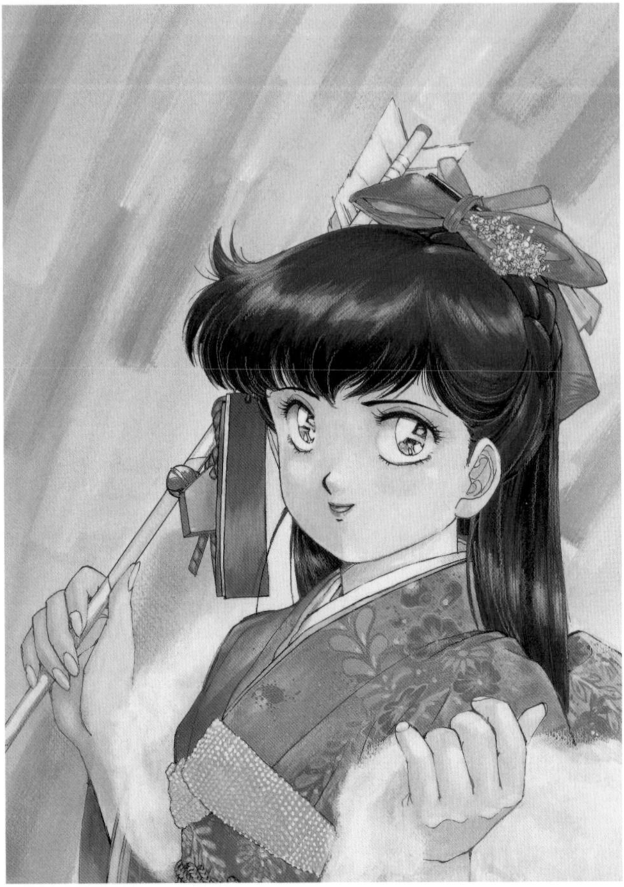

Illustration Data
Source:Greeting card
Character:Katsumi Liqueur
Painting materials:Acrylic color
/Arches Aquarelle(Cold Pressed)

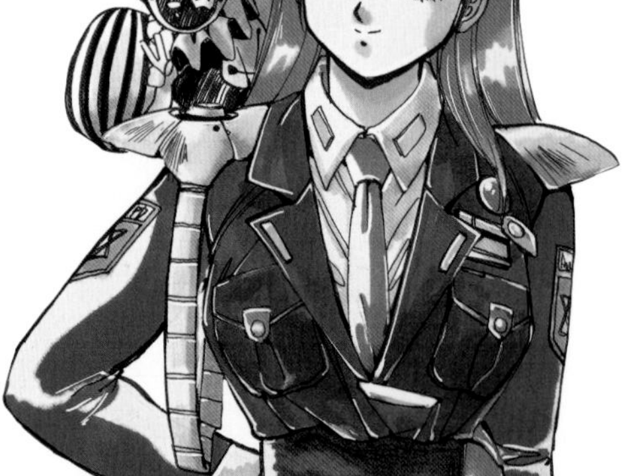

Illustration Data
Source:Contents for Comic magazine
Character:Katsumi Liqueur
Painting materials:PIGMA·Alcoholic marker/Copy paper

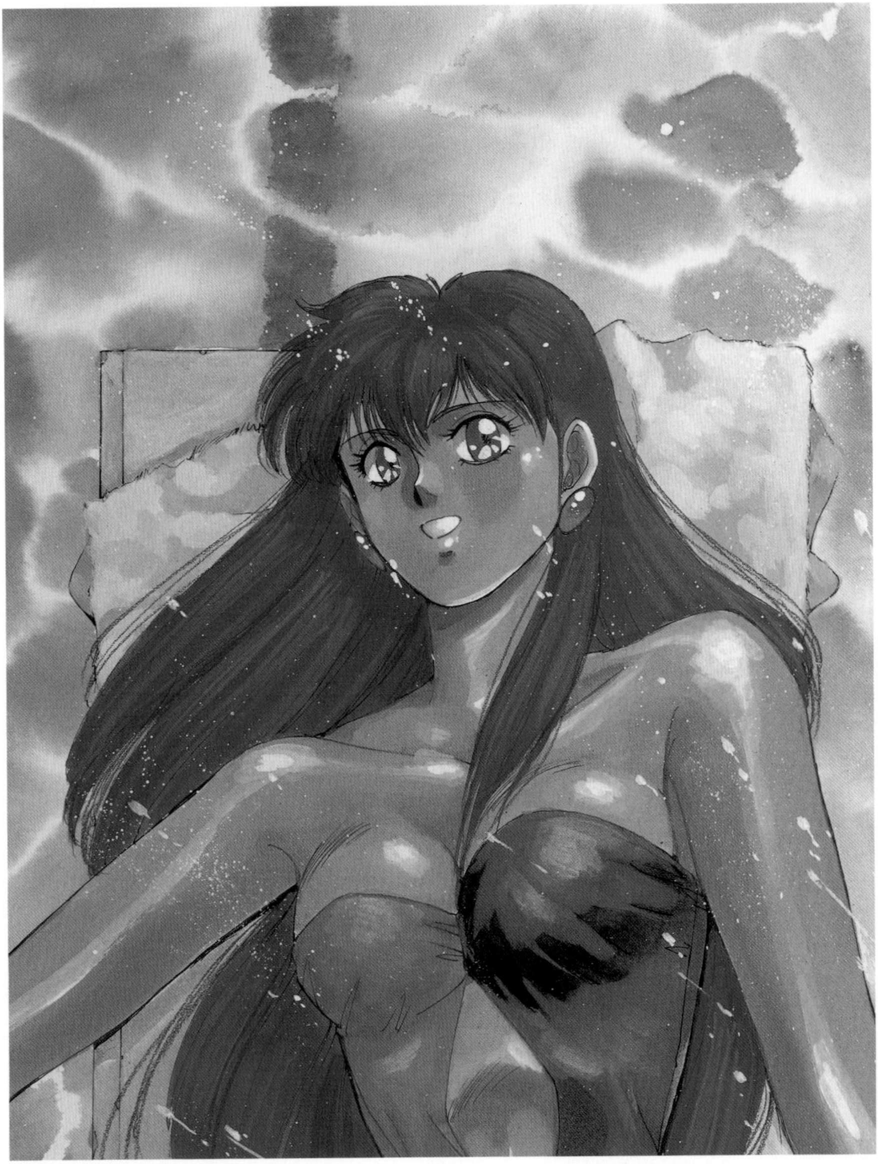

Illustration Data
Source:Comic magazine
Character:Katsumi Liqueur
Painting materials:Acrylic color/Arches Aquarelle(Cold Pressed)

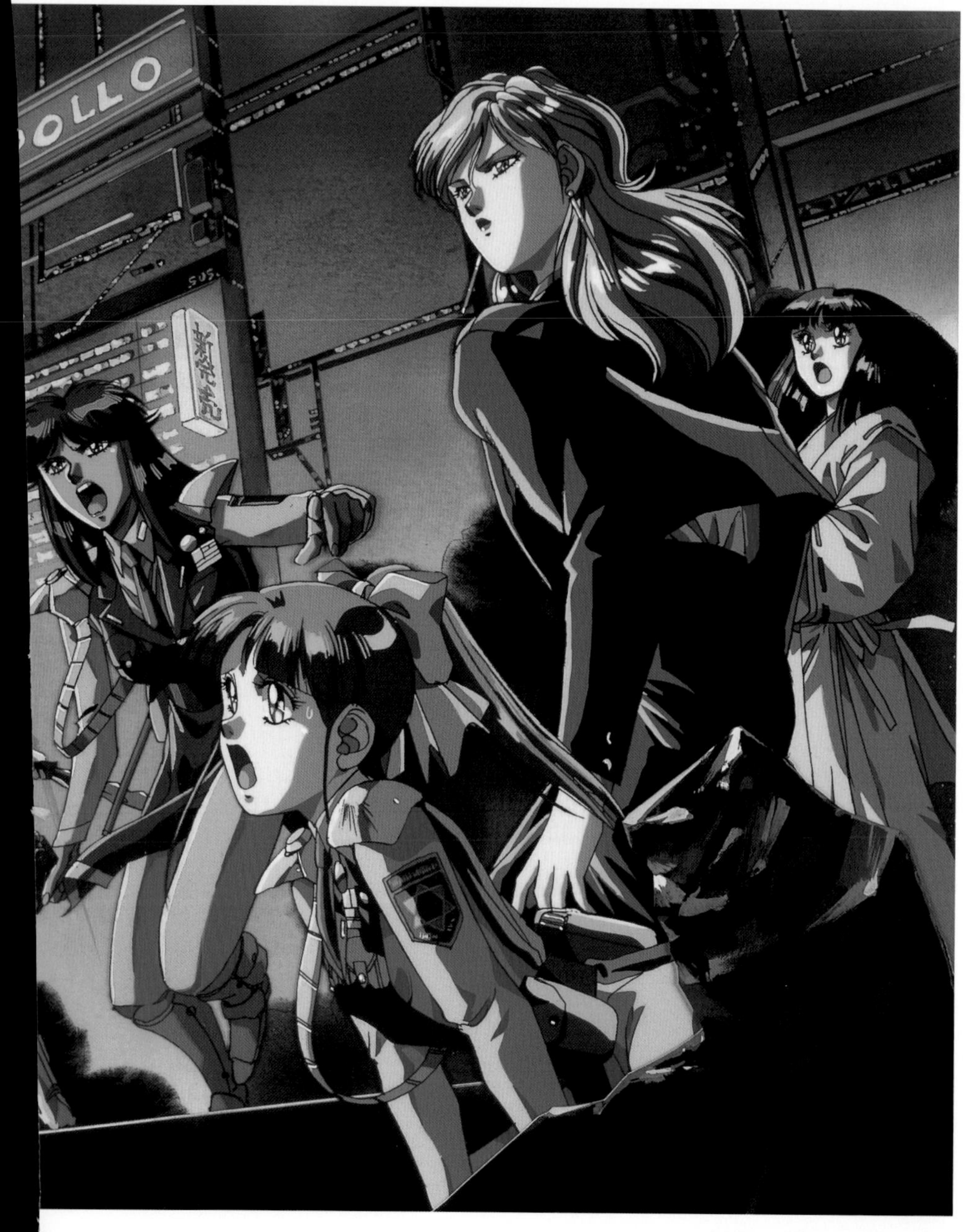
OLLO
SUS.
新発売

Illustration Data
Source:Calendar for 1991
Character:Lebia Maverick/Katsumi Liqueur/Kiddy Phenil
Yuki Saiko/Rally Cheyenne/Nami Yamigumo
Painting materials:Cell work

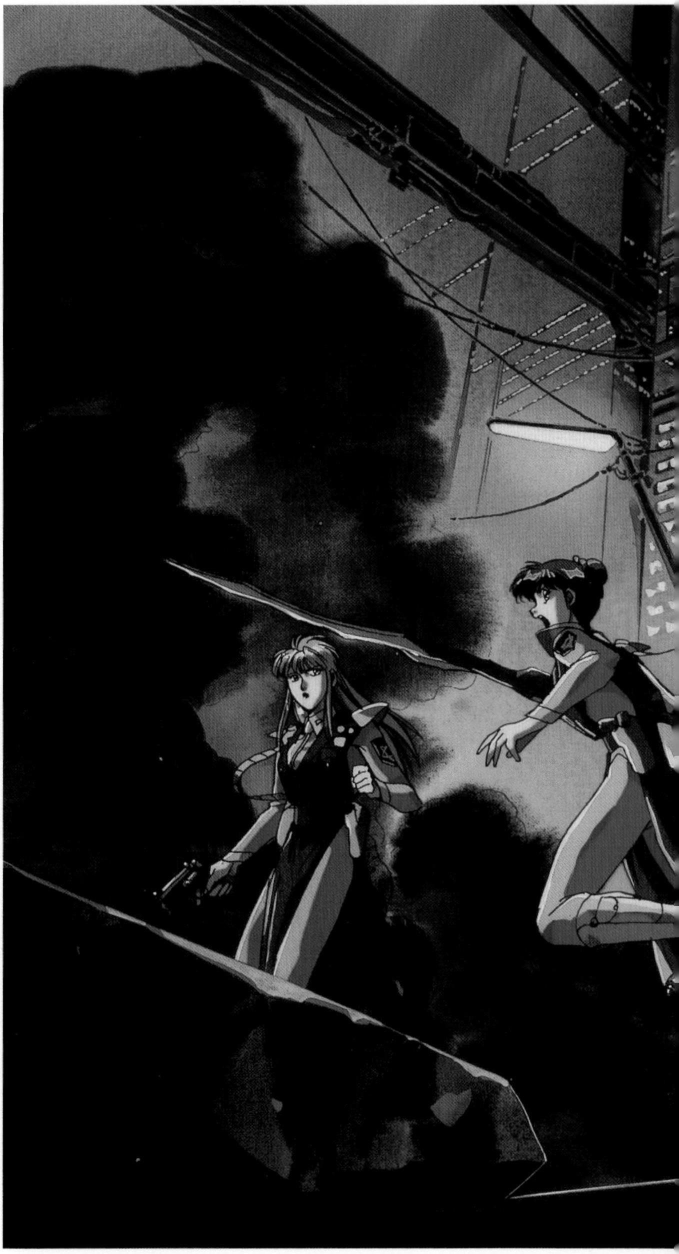

Silent Möbius
Illustration Gallery I
サイレントメビウス［完全版］●イラストギャラリー

Illustration Data
Source:Comic magazine
Character:Katsumi Liqueur
Painting materials:Acrylic color /Illustration board

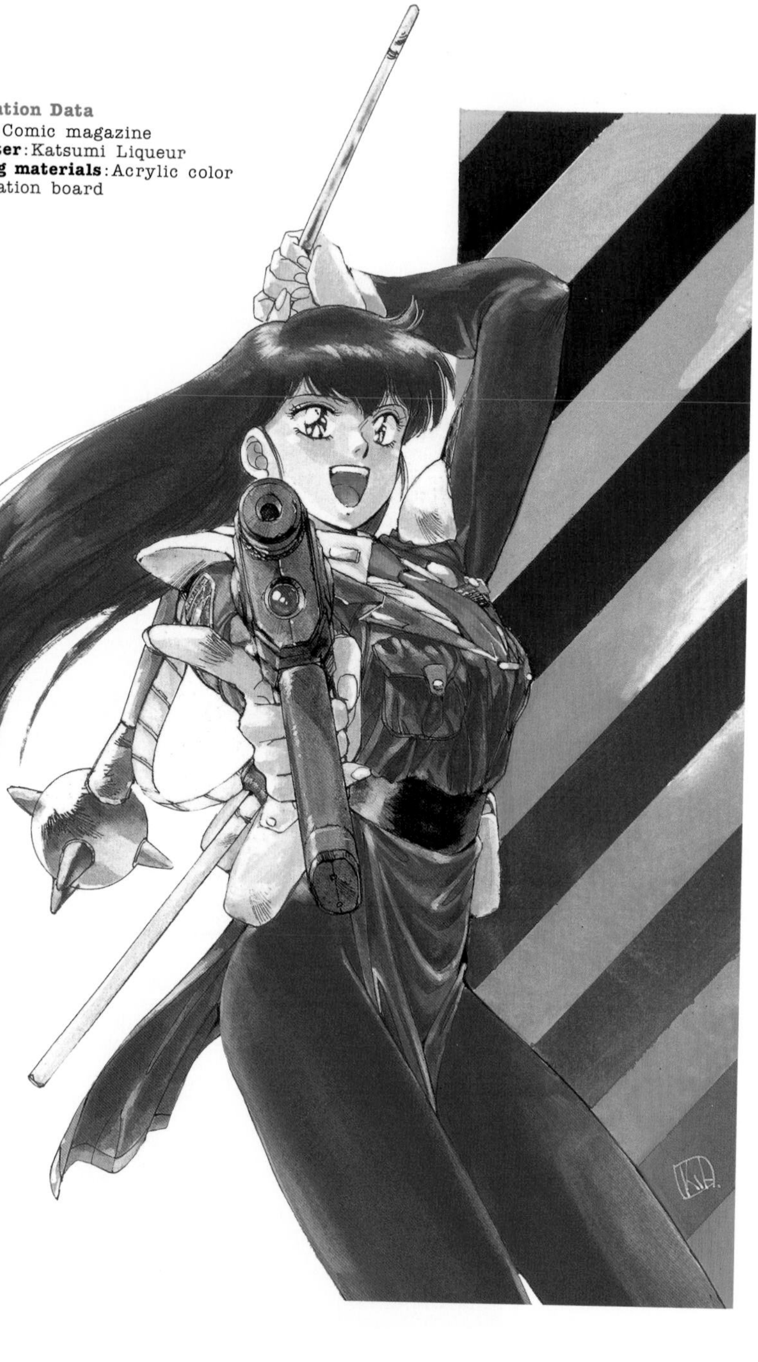

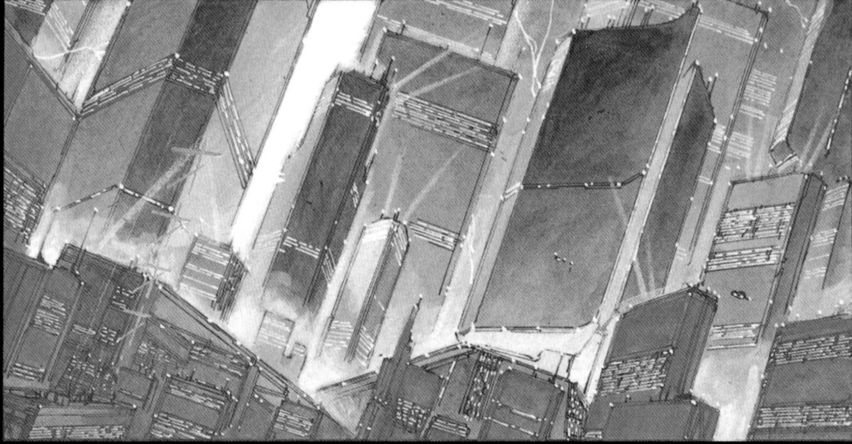

KIA ASAMIYA + STUDIO TRON

PRESENTS

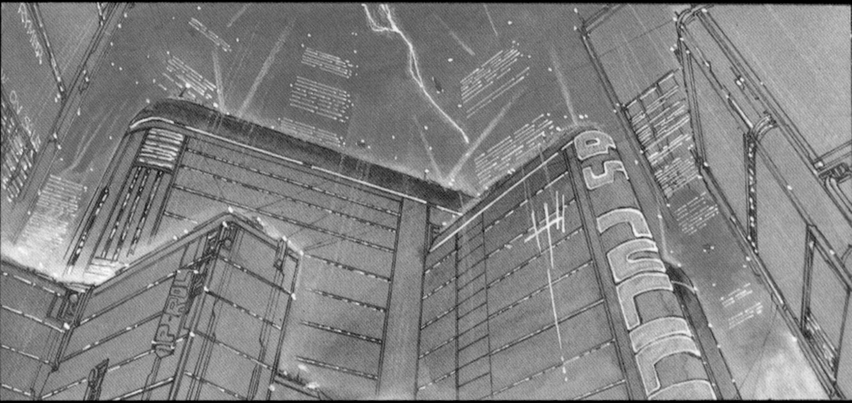

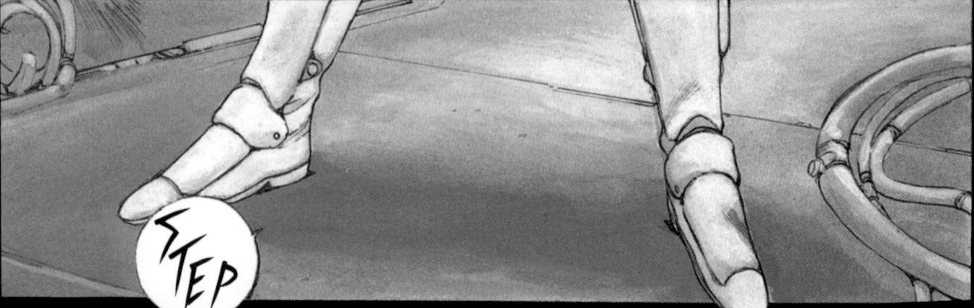
STEP

STARRING

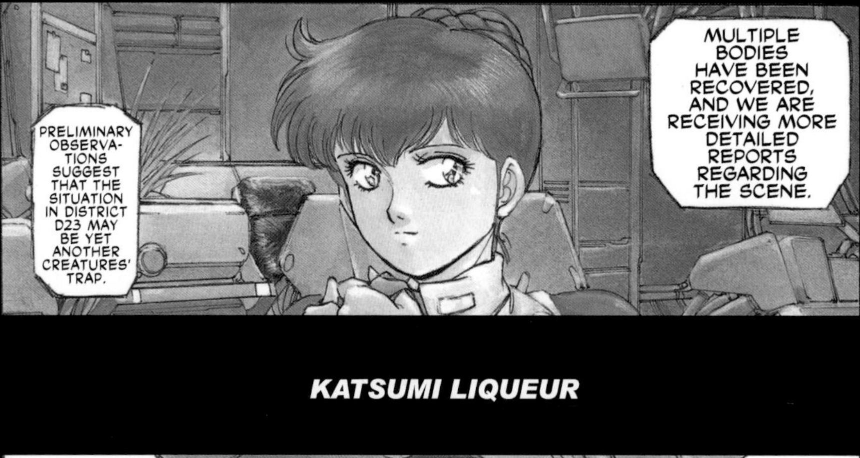
MULTIPLE BODIES HAVE BEEN RECOVERED, AND WE ARE RECEIVING MORE DETAILED REPORTS REGARDING THE SCENE.
PRELIMINARY OBSERVA-TIONS SUGGEST THAT THE SITUATION IN DISTRICT D23 MAY BE YET ANOTHER CREATURES' TRAP.

KATSUMI LIQUEUR

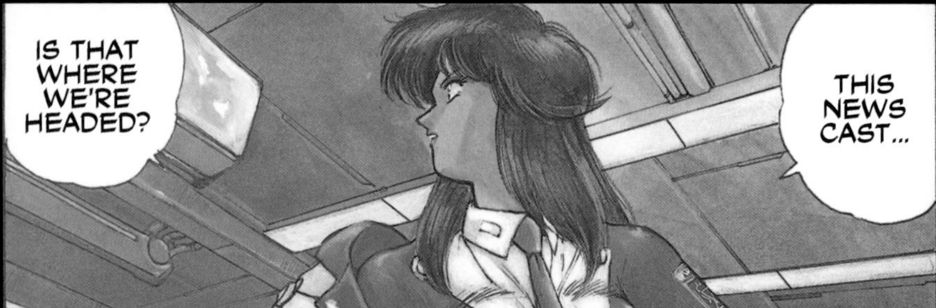
THIS NEWS CAST...
IS THAT WHERE WE'RE HEADED?

KIDDY PHENIL

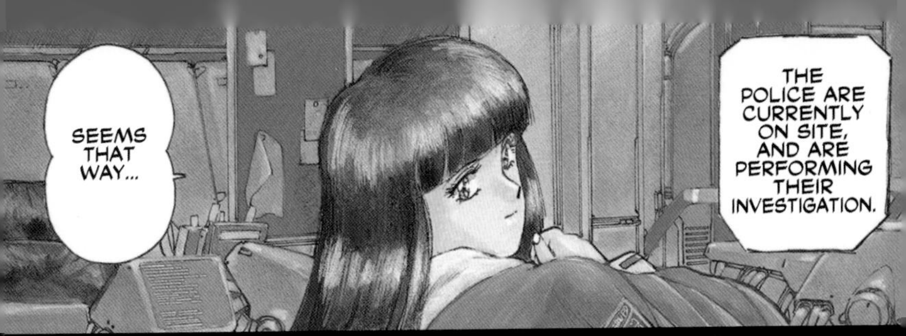
THE POLICE ARE CURRENTLY ON SITE, AND ARE PERFORMING THEIR INVESTIGATION.
SEEMS THAT WAY...

NAMI YAMIGUMO

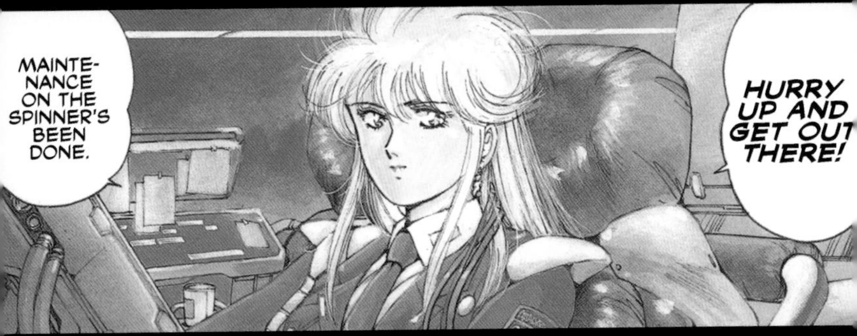
HURRY UP AND GET OUT THERE!
MAINTE-NANCE ON THE SPINNER'S BEEN DONE.

LEBIA MAVERICK

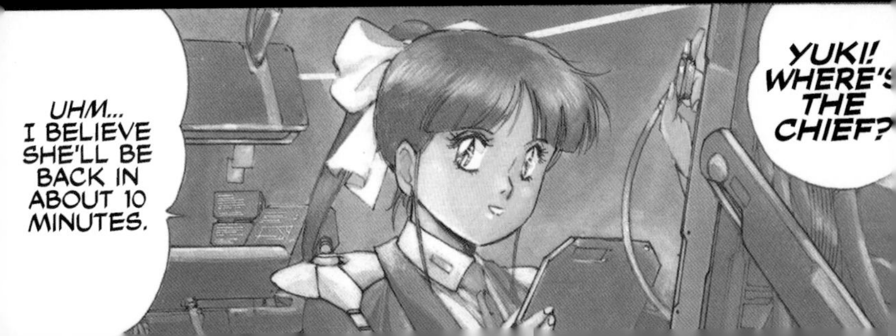
YUKI! WHERE'S THE CHIEF?
UHM... I BELIEVE SHE'LL BE BACK IN ABOUT 10 MINUTES.

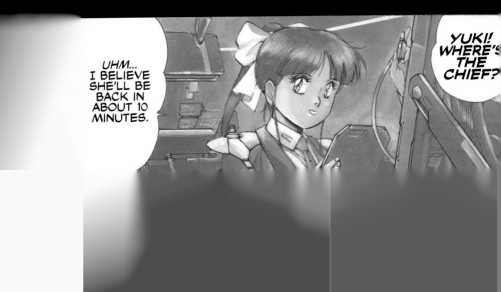

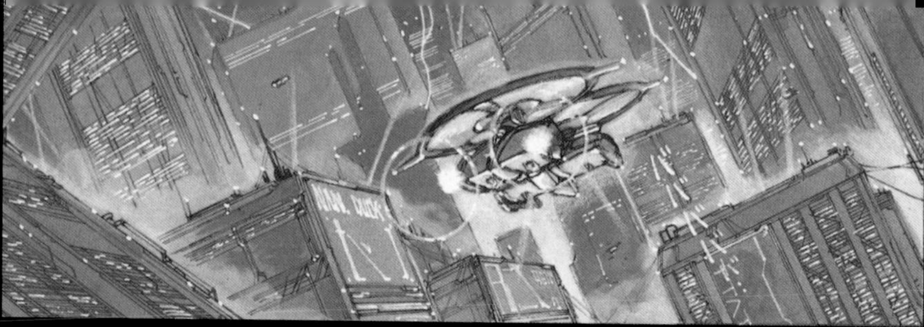

AND

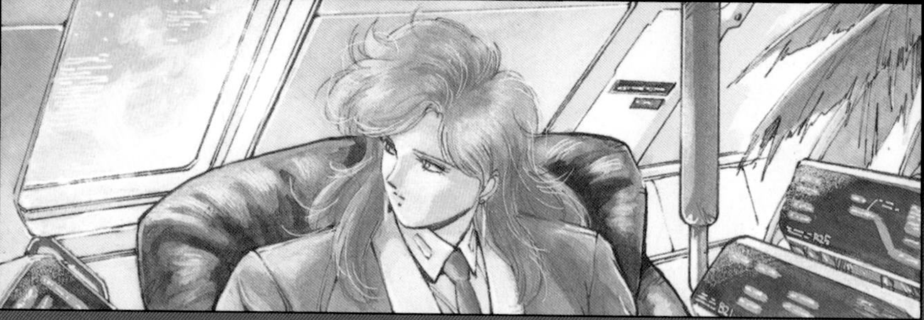

RALLY CHEYENNE

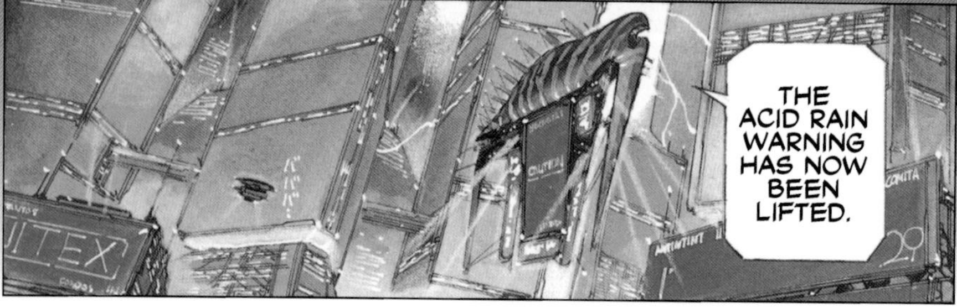
THE ACID RAIN WARNING HAS NOW BEEN LIFTED.

01: Cyber Psychic City

魔法陣都市

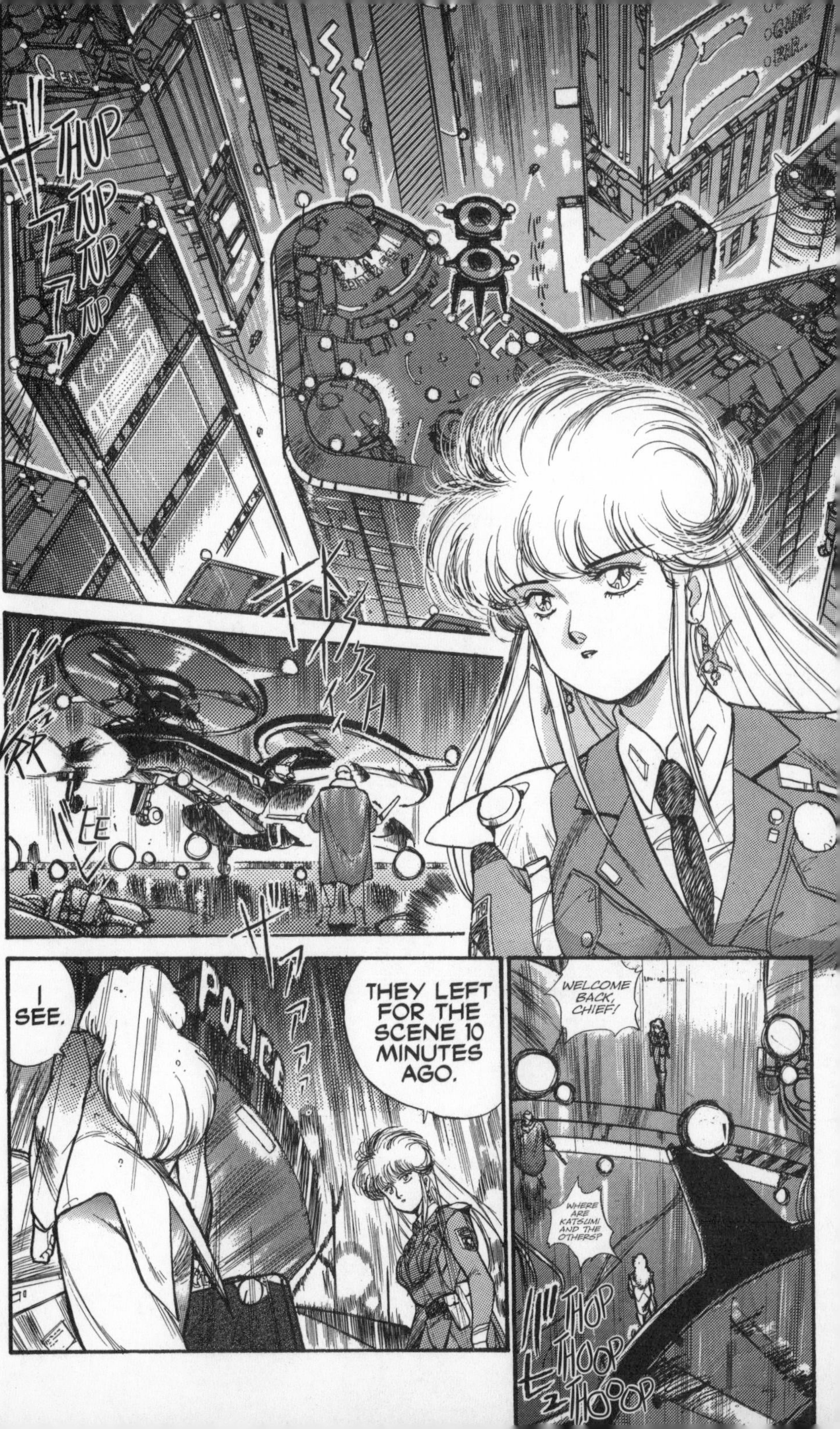
THUP
TUP
TUP
TUP
WELCOME BACK, CHIEF!
WHERE ARE KATSUMI AND THE OTHERS?
THOP
THOOP
THOOOP
THEY LEFT FOR THE SCENE 10 MINUTES AGO.
I SEE.

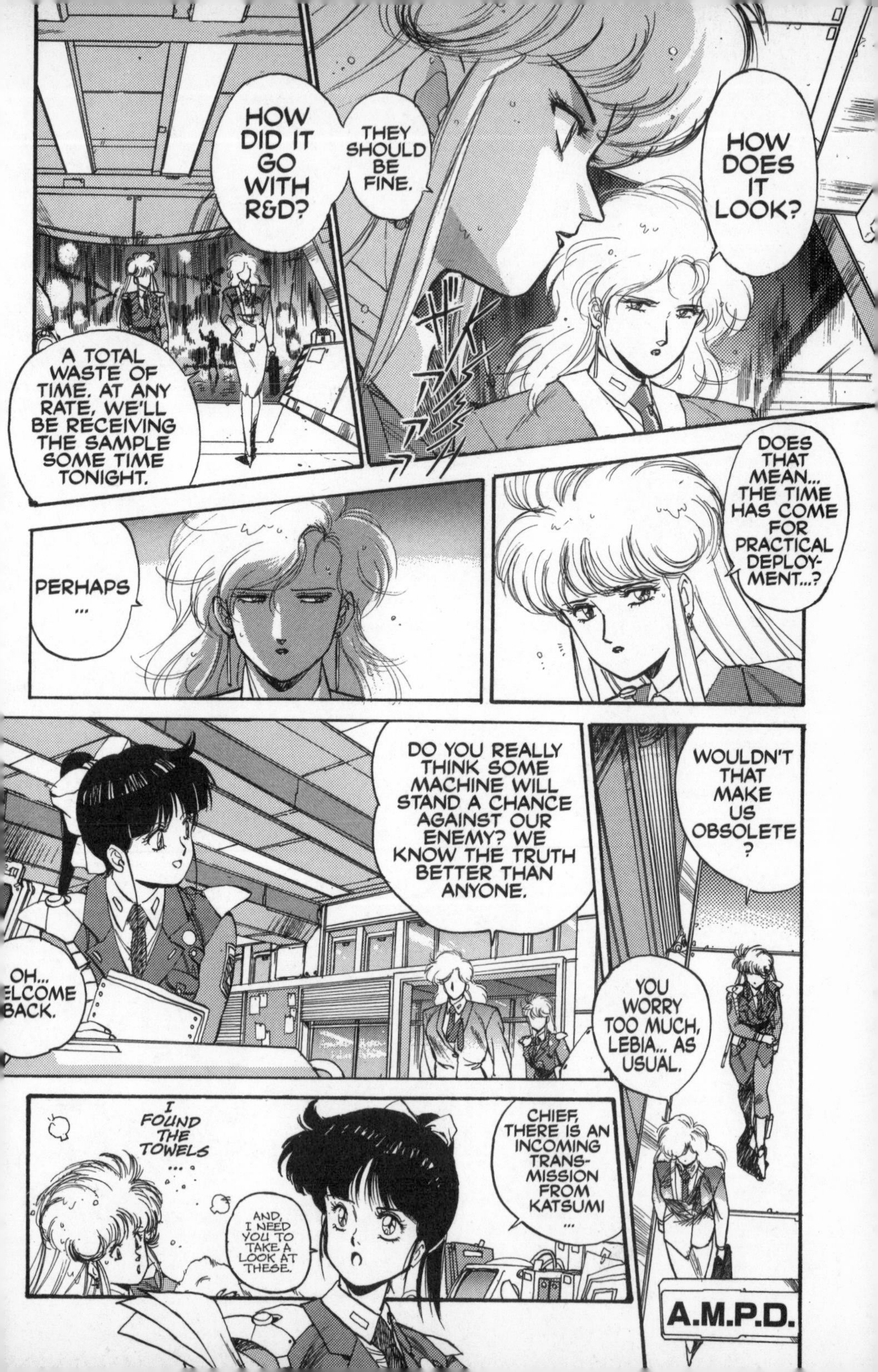
HOW DOES IT LOOK?
THEY SHOULD BE FINE.
HOW DID IT GO WITH R&D?
A TOTAL WASTE OF TIME. AT ANY RATE, WE'LL BE RECEIVING THE SAMPLE SOME TIME TONIGHT.
DOES THAT MEAN... THE TIME HAS COME FOR PRACTICAL DEPLOY-MENT...?
PERHAPS...
WOULDN'T THAT MAKE US OBSOLETE?
DO YOU REALLY THINK SOME MACHINE WILL STAND A CHANCE AGAINST OUR ENEMY? WE KNOW THE TRUTH BETTER THAN ANYONE.
YOU WORRY TOO MUCH, LEBIA... AS USUAL.
A.M.P.D.
OH... ELCOME BACK.
CHIEF, THERE IS AN INCOMING TRANS-MISSION FROM KATSUMI...
AND, I NEED YOU TO TAKE A LOOK AT THESE.
I FOUND THE TOWELS...

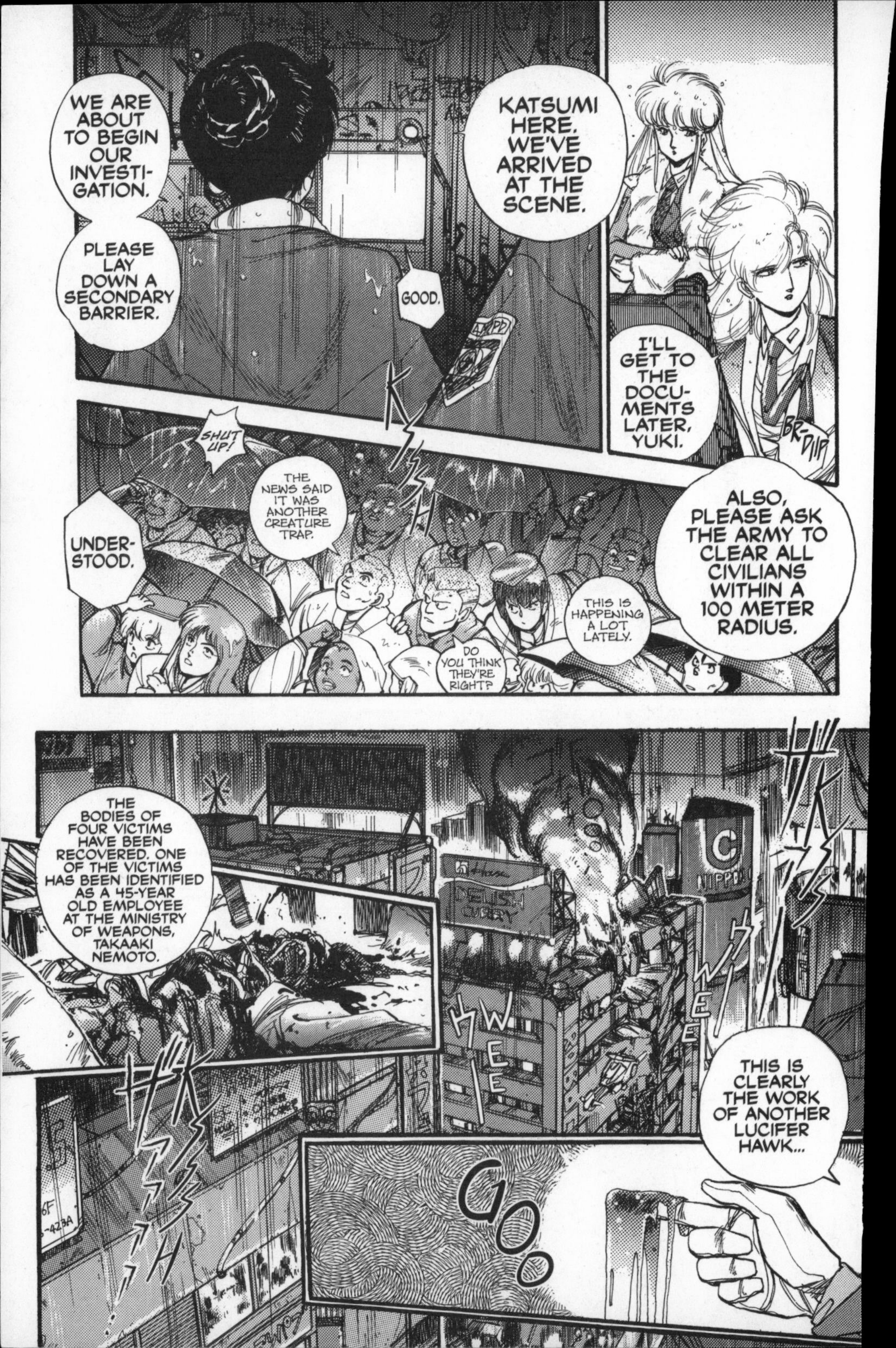
BR-DIIP
I'LL GET TO THE DOCUMENTS LATER, YUKI.
KATSUMI HERE. WE'VE ARRIVED AT THE SCENE.
WE ARE ABOUT TO BEGIN OUR INVESTIGATION.
GOOD.
PLEASE LAY DOWN A SECONDARY BARRIER.
KSSSH
ALSO, PLEASE ASK THE ARMY TO CLEAR ALL CIVILIANS WITHIN A 100 METER RADIUS.
THIS IS HAPPENING A LOT LATELY.
DO YOU THINK THEY'RE RIGHT?
THE NEWS SAID IT WAS ANOTHER CREATURE TRAP.
SHUT UP!
UNDERSTOOD.
KSSH
WEEE
HWEE
THE BODIES OF FOUR VICTIMS HAVE BEEN RECOVERED. ONE OF THE VICTIMS HAS BEEN IDENTIFIED AS A 45-YEAR OLD EMPLOYEE AT THE MINISTRY OF WEAPONS, TAKAAKI NEMOTO.
THIS IS CLEARLY THE WORK OF ANOTHER LUCIFER HAWK...
GOO
KSSSHHH

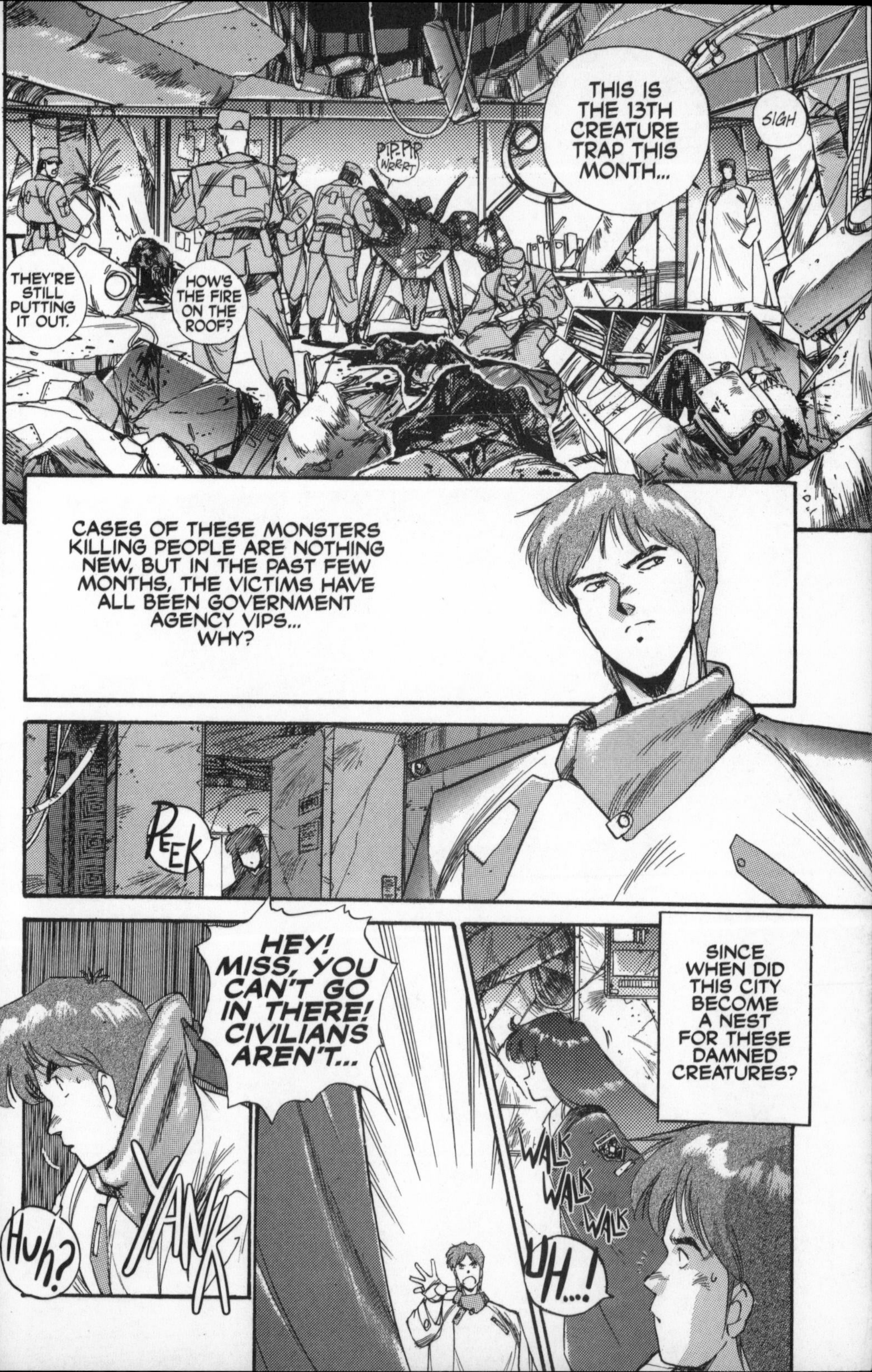
SIGH
THIS IS THE 13TH CREATURE TRAP THIS MONTH...
PIP PIP WRRRT
HOW'S THE FIRE ON THE ROOF?
THEY'RE STILL PUTTING IT OUT.
CASES OF THESE MONSTERS KILLING PEOPLE ARE NOTHING NEW, BUT IN THE PAST FEW MONTHS, THE VICTIMS HAVE ALL BEEN GOVERNMENT AGENCY VIPS... WHY?
PEEK
SINCE WHEN DID THIS CITY BECOME A NEST FOR THESE DAMNED CREATURES?
WALK WALK WALK
UH...!
HEY! MISS, YOU CAN'T GO IN THERE! CIVILIANS AREN'T...
YANK
Huh?

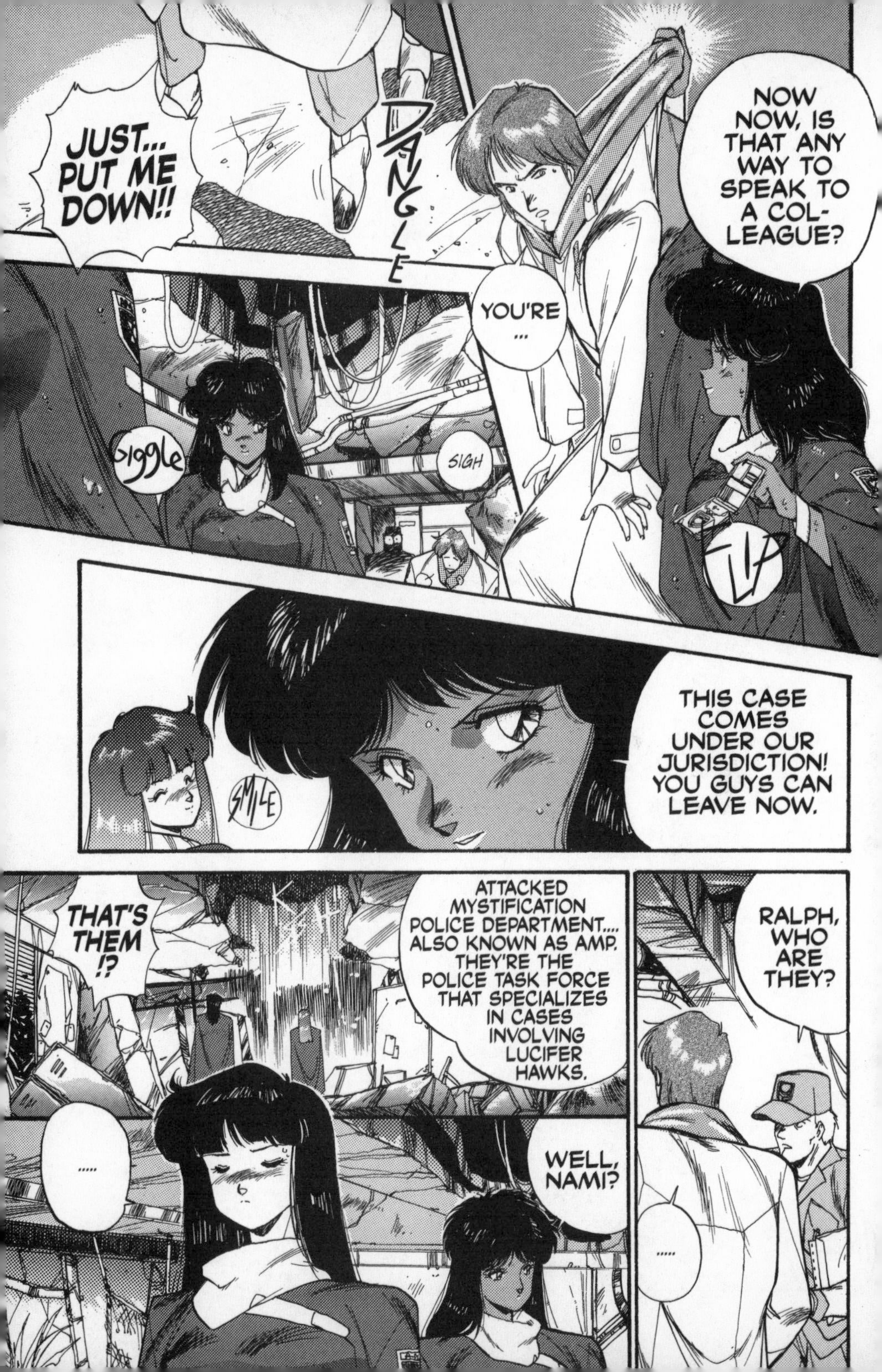
NOW NOW, IS THAT ANY WAY TO SPEAK TO A COL-LEAGUE?
JUST... PUT ME DOWN!!
DANGLE
YOU'RE ...
FLIP
SIGH
Giggle
THIS CASE COMES UNDER OUR JURISDICTION! YOU GUYS CAN LEAVE NOW.
SMILE
RALPH, WHO ARE THEY?
.....
ATTACKED MYSTIFICATION POLICE DEPARTMENT.... ALSO KNOWN AS AMP. THEY'RE THE POLICE TASK FORCE THAT SPECIALIZES IN CASES INVOLVING LUCIFER HAWKS.
THAT'S THEM !?
WELL, NAMI?
.....

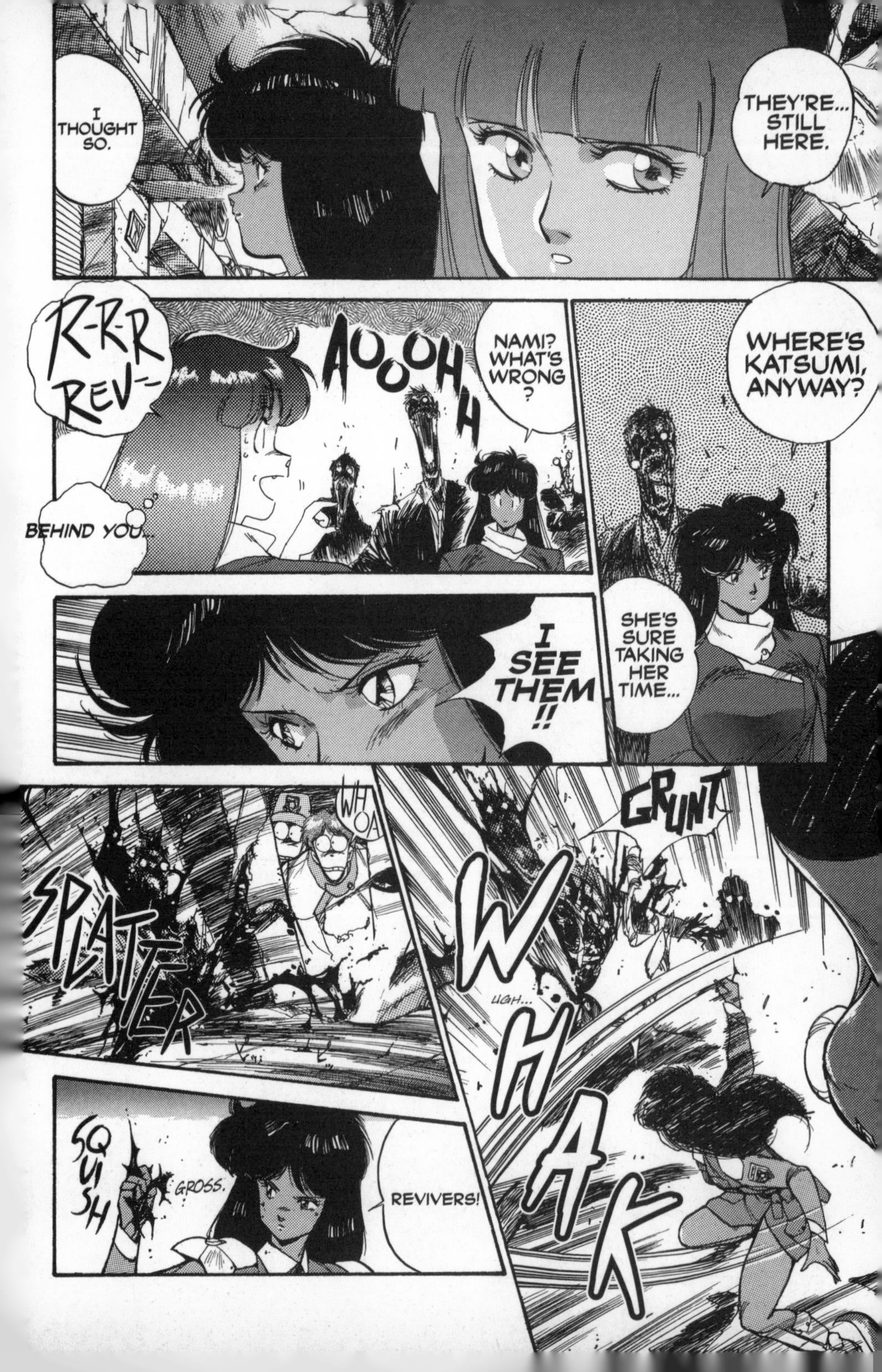
THEY'RE... STILL HERE.
I THOUGHT SO.
WHERE'S KATSUMI, ANYWAY?
NAMI? WHAT'S WRONG?
AOOOHH
R-R-R REV--
BEHIND YOU...
SHE'S SURE TAKING HER TIME...
I SEE THEM!!
GRUNT
WHAK
UGH...
WHOA
SPLATTER
REVIVERS!
GROSS.
SQUISH

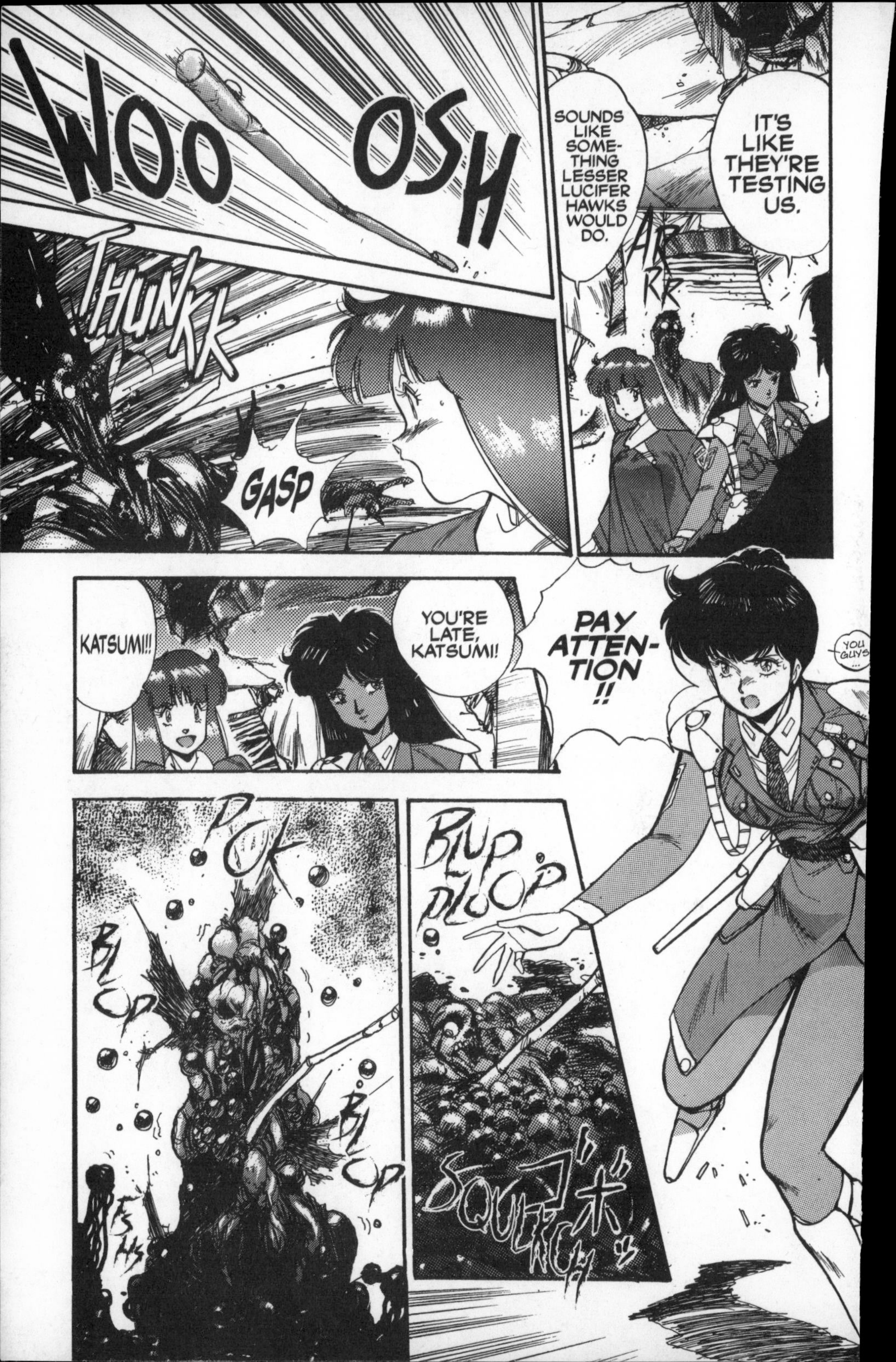
IT'S LIKE THEY'RE TESTING US.
SOUNDS LIKE SOME-THING LESSER LUCIFER HAWKS WOULD DO.
WOO OSH
THUNKK
GASP
YOU GUYS...
PAY ATTEN-TION!!
YOU'RE LATE, KATSUMI!
KATSUMI!!
BLUP DLOOP
SQUELCH
ゴボ

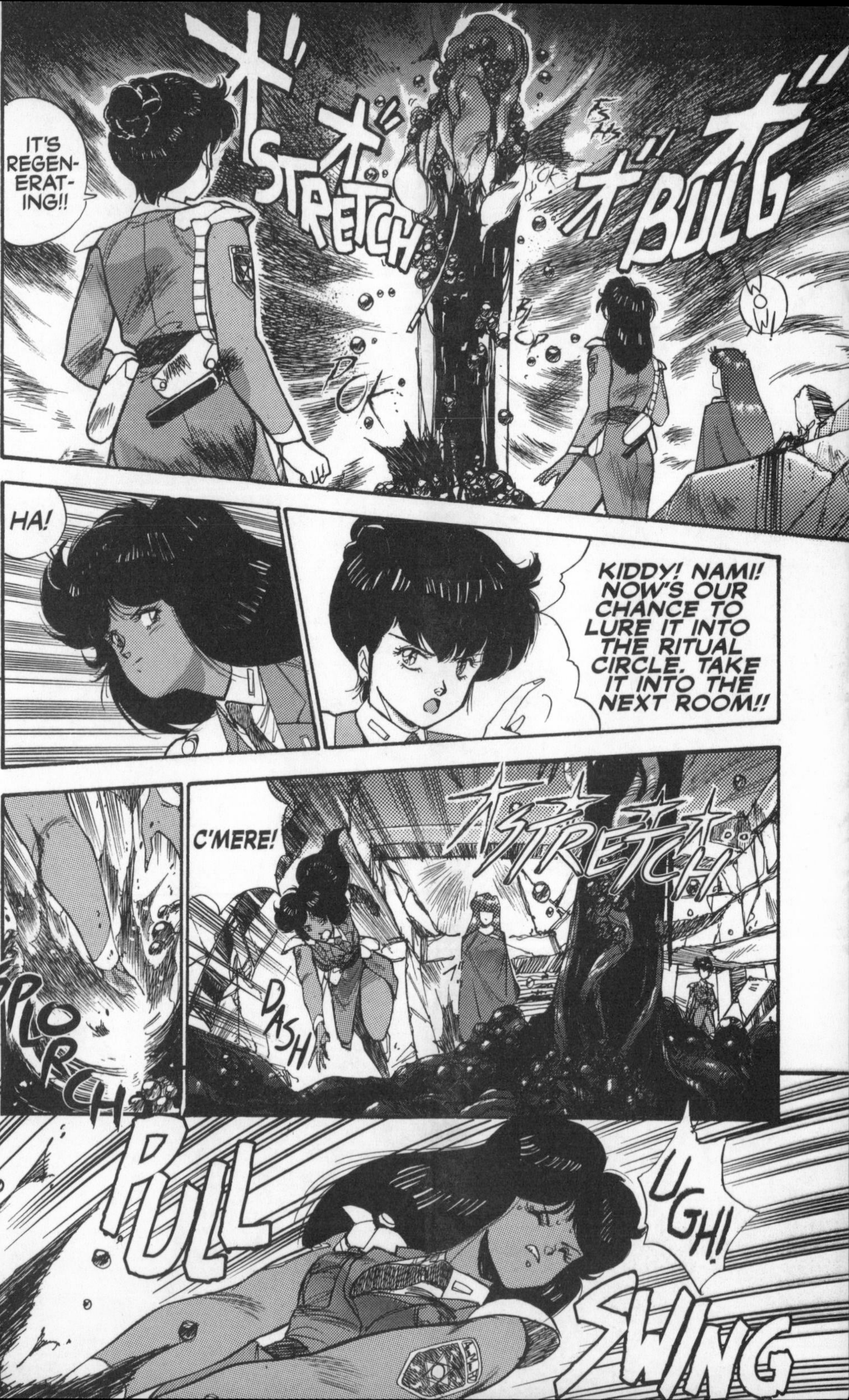
BULG
STRETCH
IT'S REGENERATING!!
KIDDY! NAMI! NOW'S OUR CHANCE TO LURE IT INTO THE RITUAL CIRCLE. TAKE IT INTO THE NEXT ROOM!!
HA!
STRETCH
C'MERE!
DASH
SPLORCH
UGH!
PULL
SWING

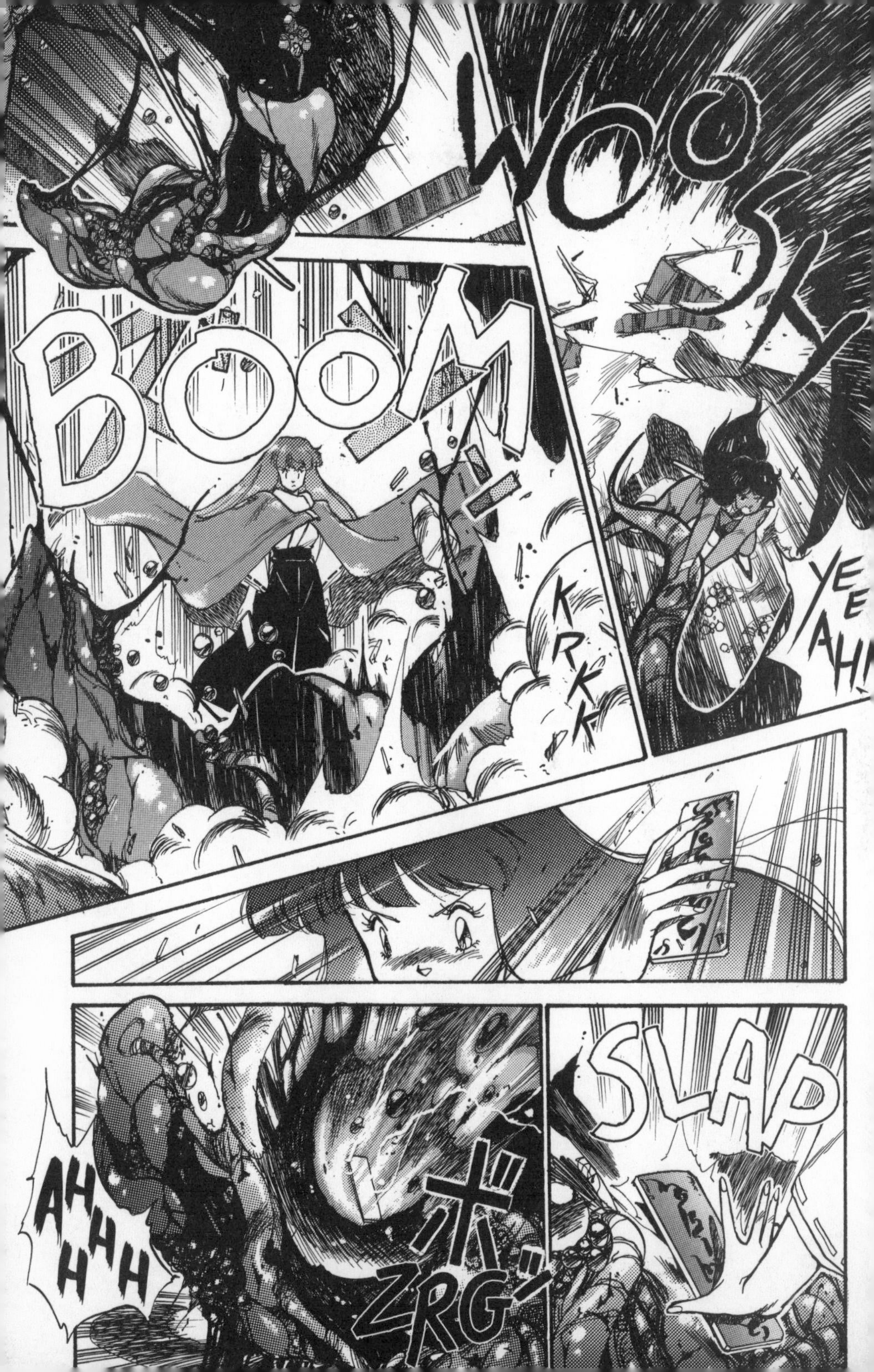
WOOSH
YEEAH!
BOOM
KRKKK
SLAP
AHHHHH
ZRG

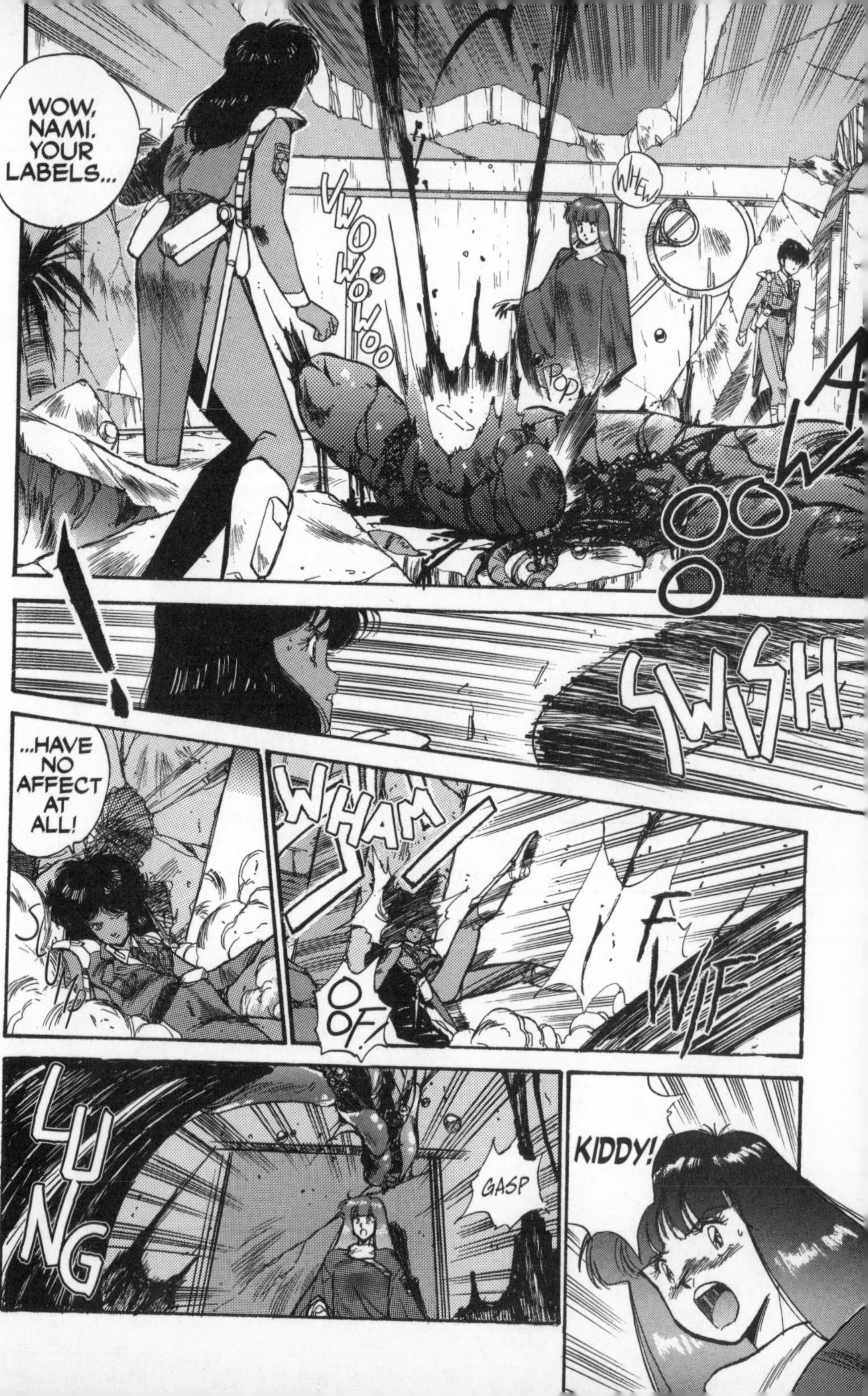
AWOOOO
WHEW
POP
VWOWOWOWOO
WOW, NAMI. YOUR LABELS...
SWISH
!
WHAM
FWF
OOF!
...HAVE NO AFFECT AT ALL!
KIDDY!
GASP
LUNG

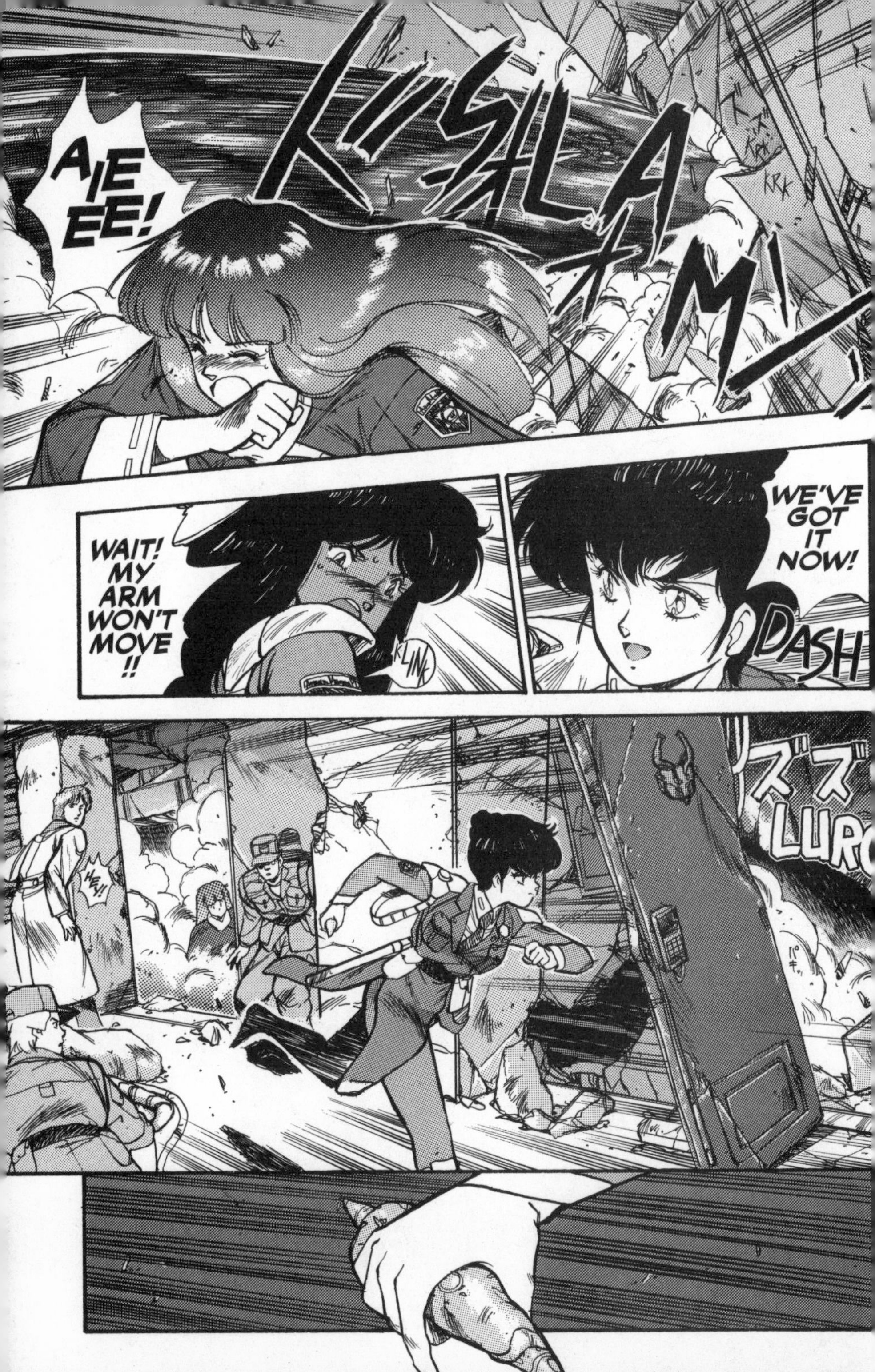
KRK
KRK
KU-SLAM
AIEEE!
WE'VE GOT IT NOW!
DASH
WAIT! MY ARM WON'T MOVE!!
KLINK
ズズ
LURC
HEY!!

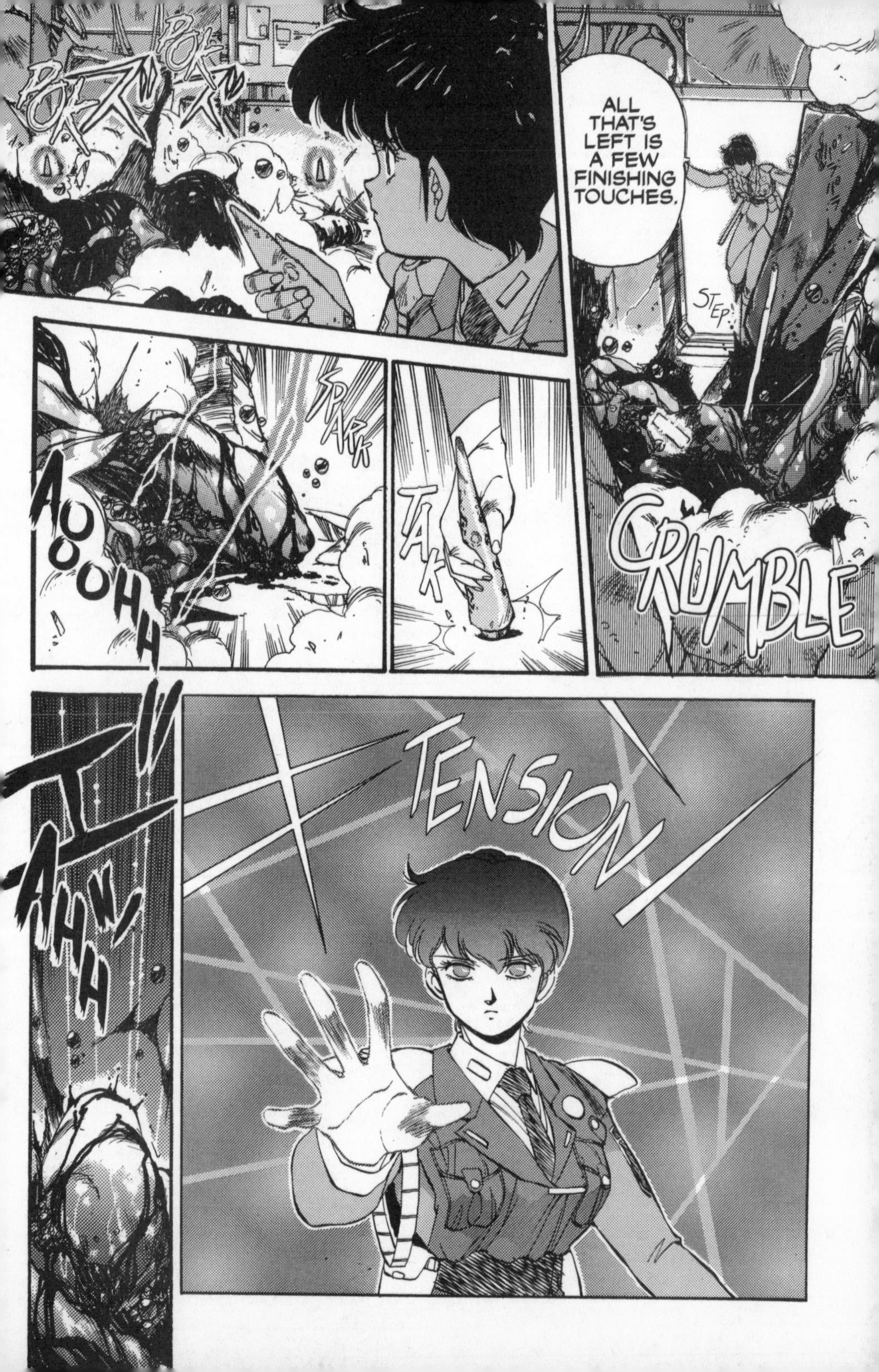
ALL THAT'S LEFT IS A FEW FINISHING TOUCHES.
STEP
CRUMBLE
POKE
POKE
TAK
SPARK
AUOOHHH
TENSION
AHHH

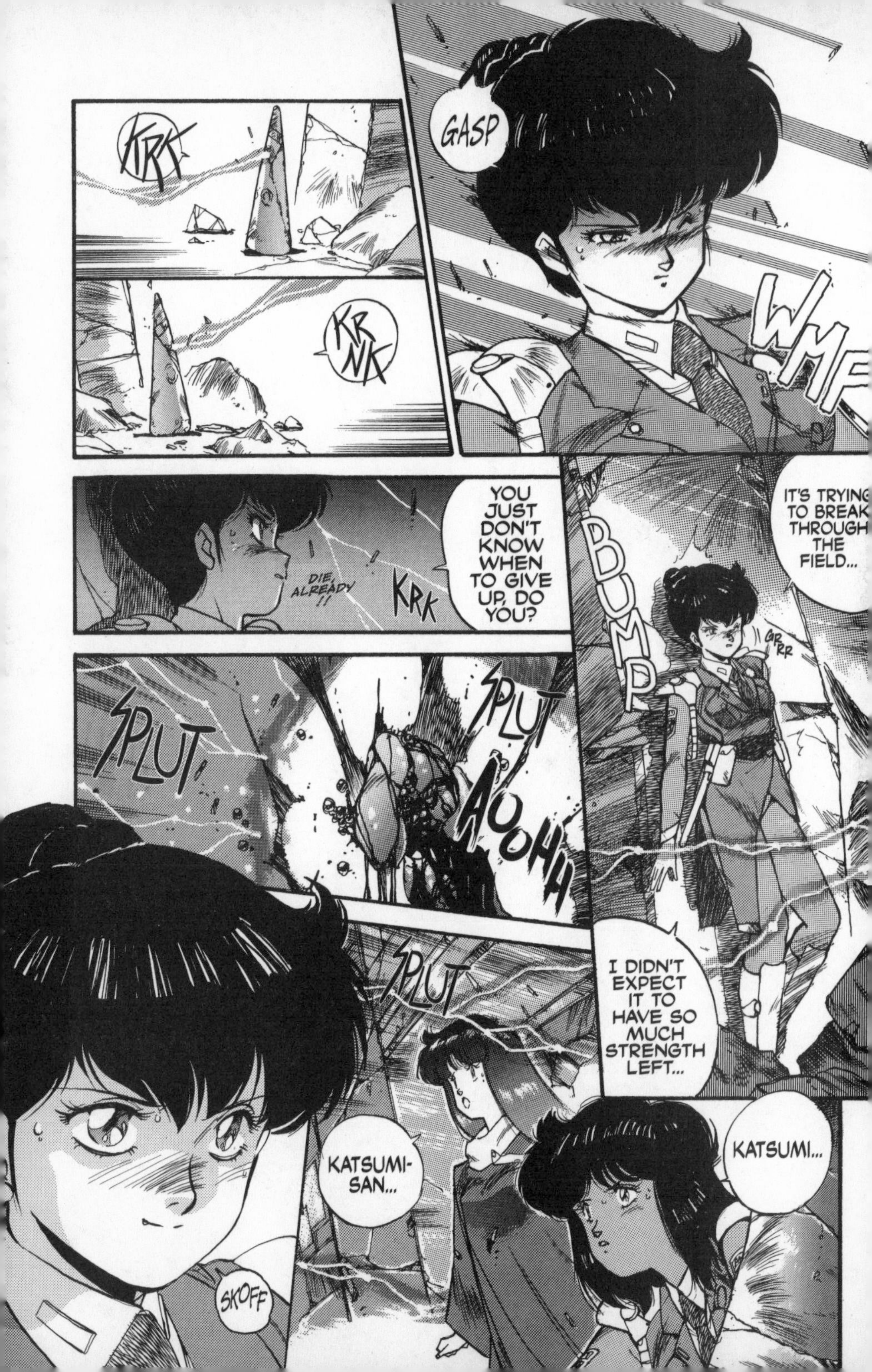
GASP
WMF
KRK
KRNK
IT'S TRYING TO BREAK THROUGH THE FIELD...
BUMP
GRRR
I DIDN'T EXPECT IT TO HAVE SO MUCH STRENGTH LEFT...
YOU JUST DON'T KNOW WHEN TO GIVE UP, DO YOU?
KRK
DIE ALREADY!!
SPLUT
SPLUT
AOOHH
KATSUMI...
KATSUMI-SAN...
SPLUT
SKOFF

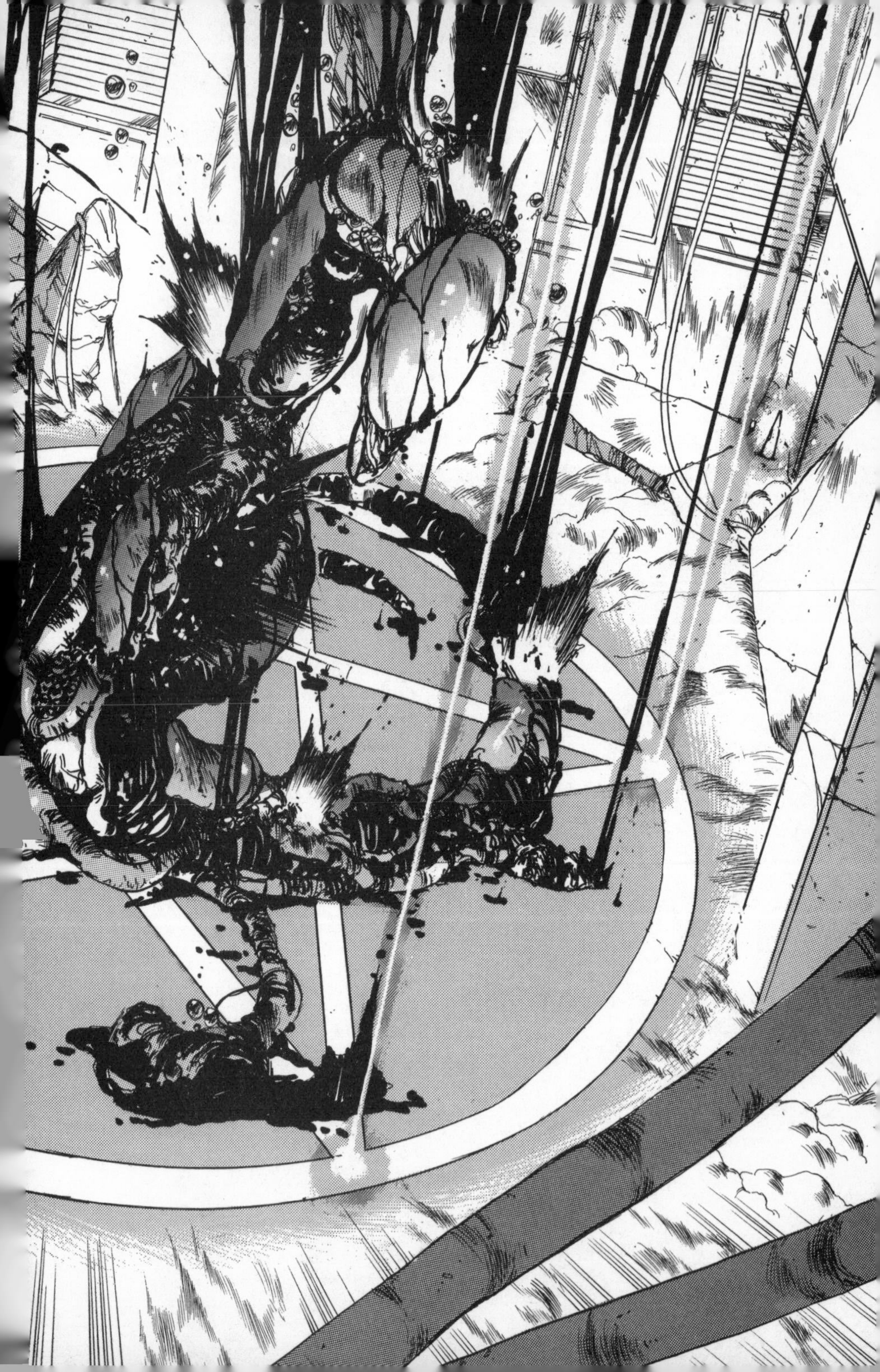

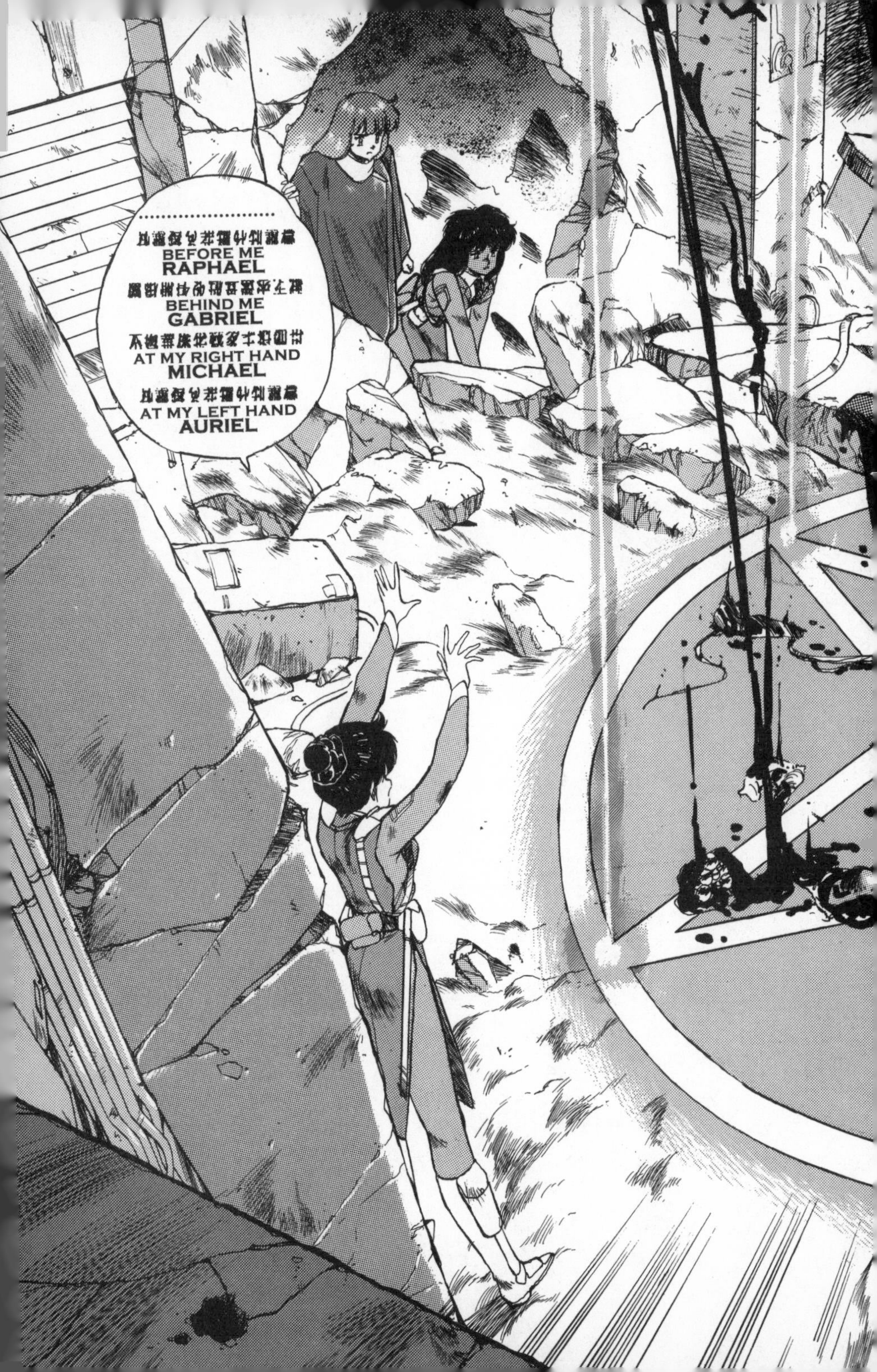
....
BEFORE ME
RAPHAEL
BEHIND ME
GABRIEL
AT MY RIGHT HAND
MICHAEL
AT MY LEFT HAND
AURIEL

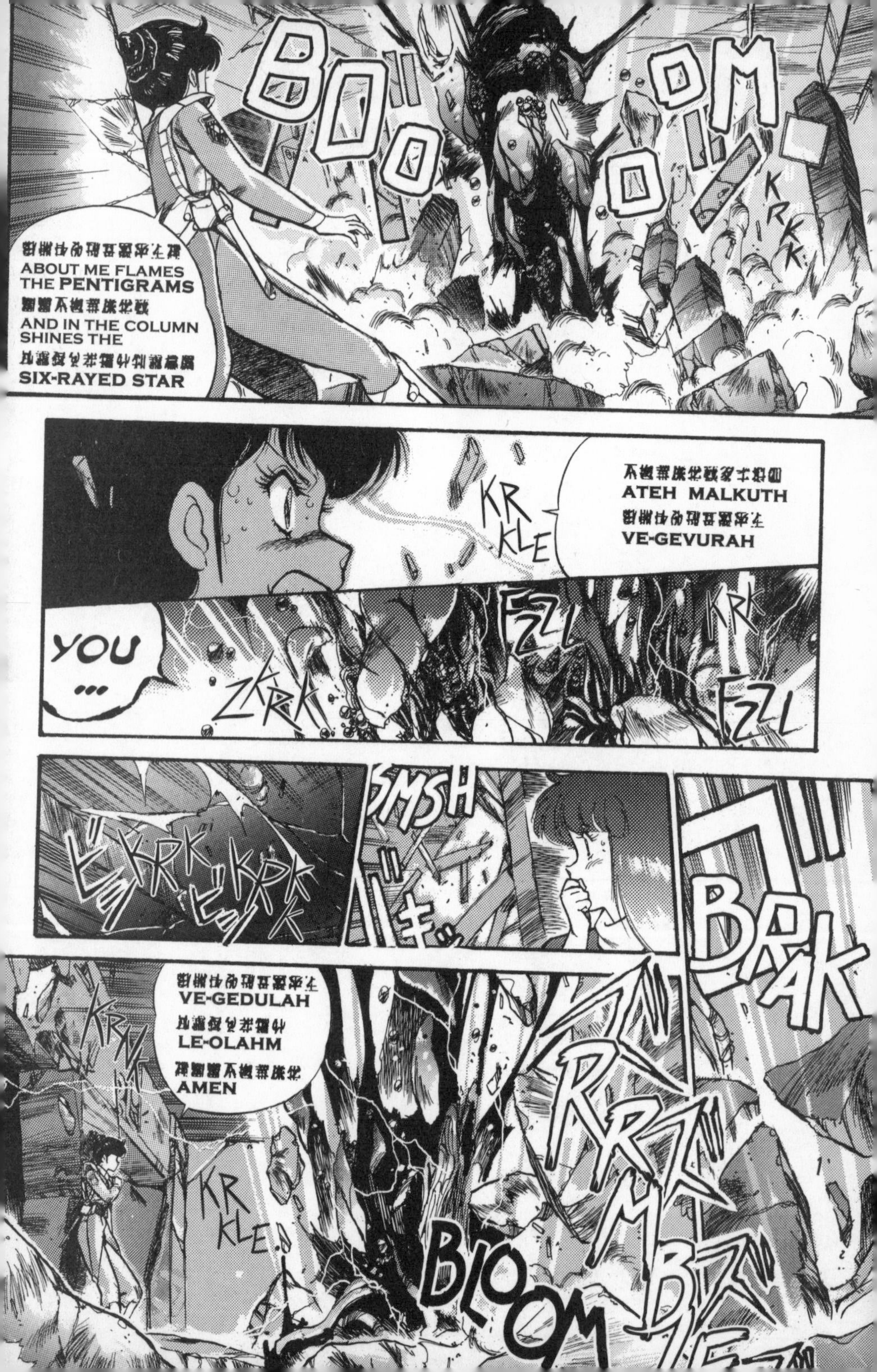
BOOOOM
KRKKK
ABOUT ME FLAMES THE PENTIGRAMS AND IN THE COLUMN SHINES THE SIX-RAYED STAR
ATEH MALKUTH VE-GEVURAH
KRKLE
KRK
FZZL
FZZL
ZKRKK
YOU ...
BRAK
SMSH
KRK KRK
VE-GEDULAH LE-OLAHM AMEN
KRAK
KRKLE
RRRMBL
BLOOM

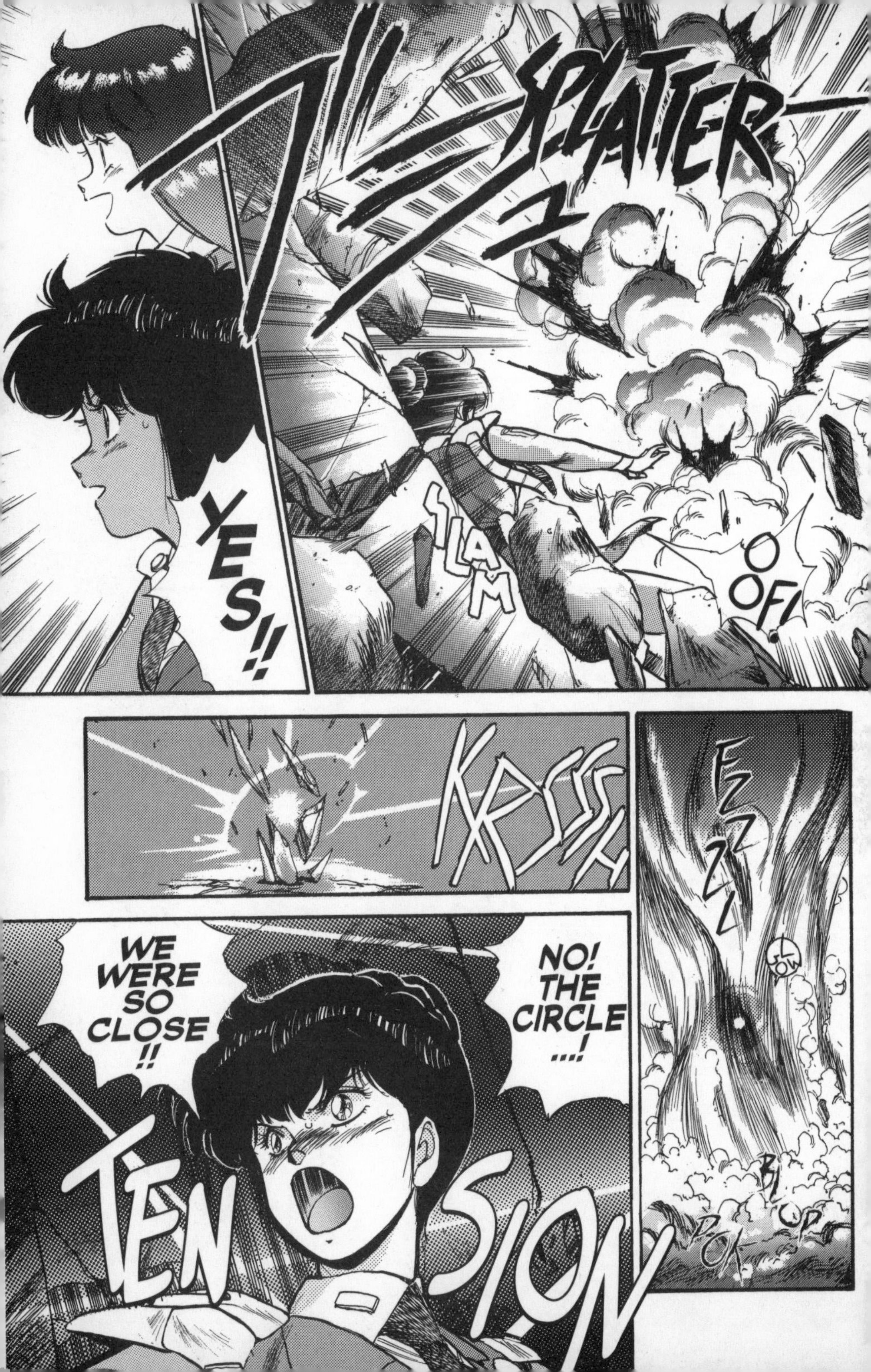
SPLATTER
SLAM
OOF!
YES!!
FZZZ
GLOW
KRSSSH
NO! THE CIRCLE ...!
WE WERE SO CLOSE !!
TENSION

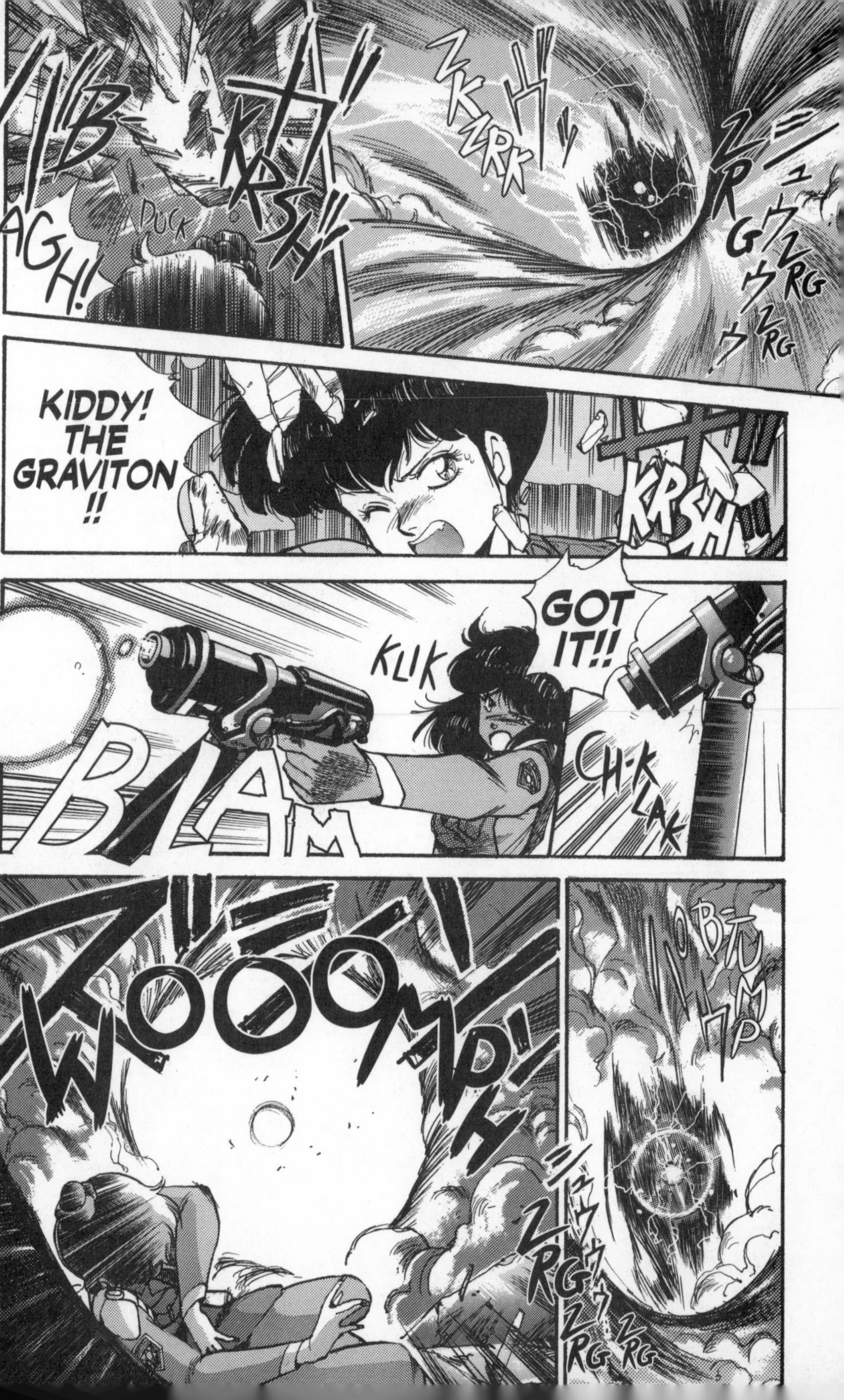
ZRG
ZRG
ZRG
ZKRK ZRK
B-KRSH!!
DUCK
AGH!
KRSH
KIDDY! THE GRAVITON!!
GOT IT!!
CH-KLAK
KLIK
BLAM
B-TUMP
ZRG
ZRG
ZRG
WOOOMPH!
ZRG
ZRG

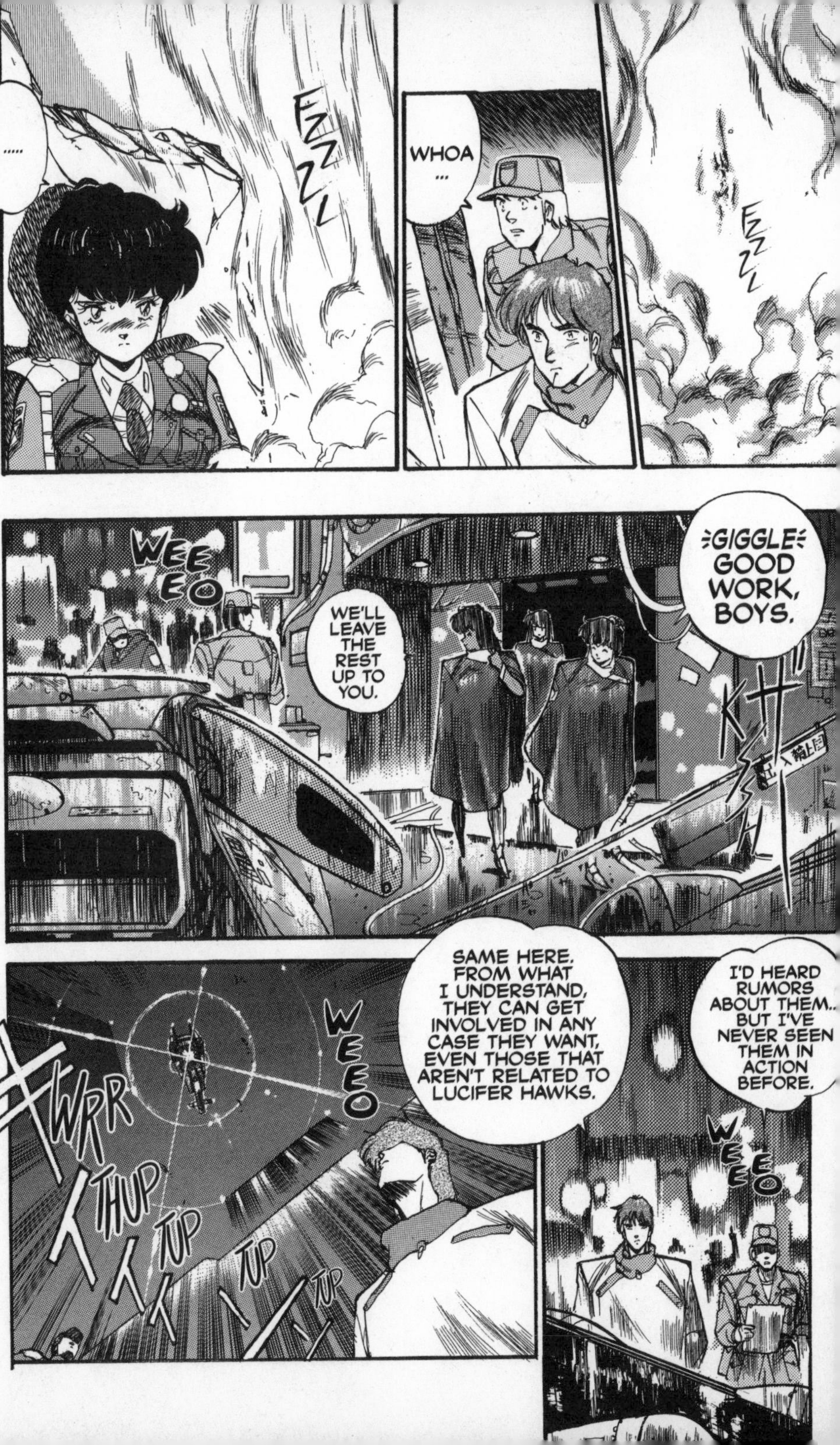
FZZZ
WHOA ...
.....
FZZZZ
GIGGLE GOOD WORK, BOYS.
WE'LL LEAVE THE REST UP TO YOU.
WEE EO
I'D HEARD RUMORS ABOUT THEM.. BUT I'VE NEVER SEEN THEM IN ACTION BEFORE.
WEEO
SAME HERE. FROM WHAT I UNDERSTAND, THEY CAN GET INVOLVED IN ANY CASE THEY WANT, EVEN THOSE THAT AREN'T RELATED TO LUCIFER HAWKS.
WEEO
WRR
THUP
TUP
TUP
TUP

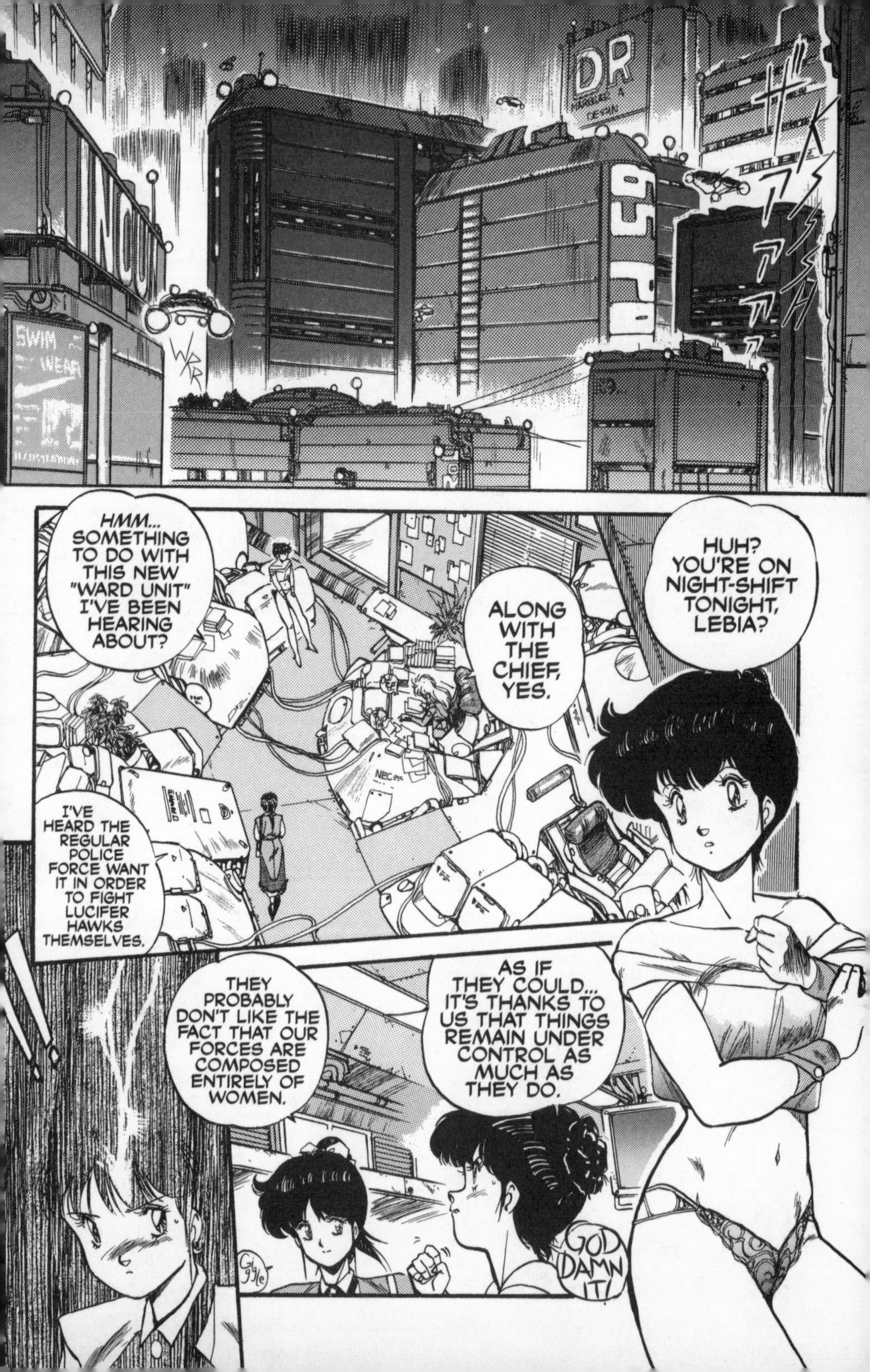
DR
KSSSH
WRR
SWIM WEAR
HUH? YOU'RE ON NIGHT-SHIFT TONIGHT, LEBIA?
ALONG WITH THE CHIEF, YES.
HMM... SOMETHING TO DO WITH THIS NEW "WARD UNIT" I'VE BEEN HEARING ABOUT?
I'VE HEARD THE REGULAR POLICE FORCE WANT IT IN ORDER TO FIGHT LUCIFER HAWKS THEMSELVES.
AS IF THEY COULD... IT'S THANKS TO US THAT THINGS REMAIN UNDER CONTROL AS MUCH AS THEY DO.
THEY PROBABLY DON'T LIKE THE FACT THAT OUR FORCES ARE COMPOSED ENTIRELY OF WOMEN.
GOD DAMN IT!
Giggle

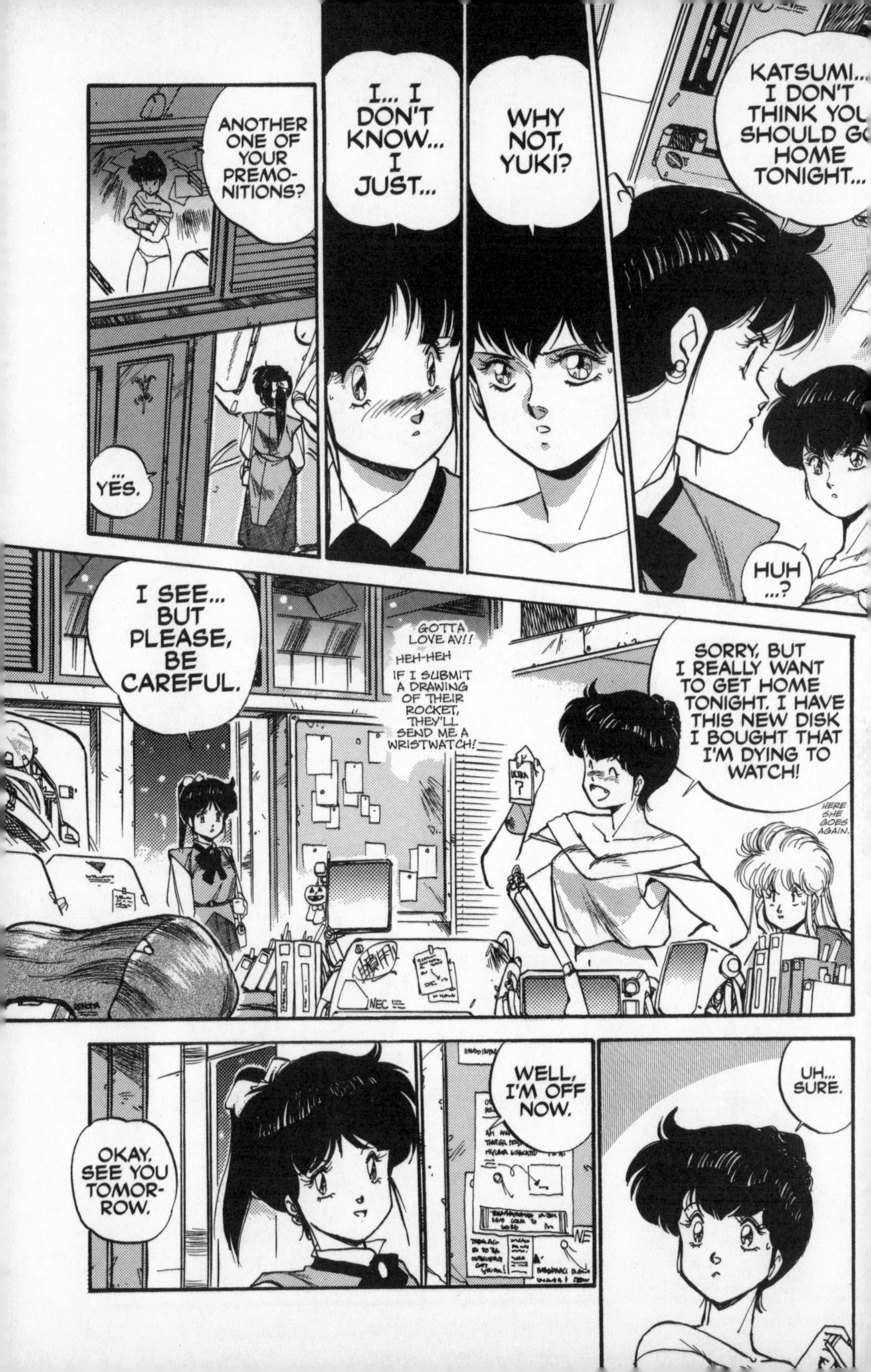
KATSUMI... I DON'T THINK YOU SHOULD GO HOME TONIGHT...
HUH ...?
WHY NOT, YUKI?
I... I DON'T KNOW... I JUST...
ANOTHER ONE OF YOUR PREMONITIONS?
... YES.
SORRY, BUT I REALLY WANT TO GET HOME TONIGHT. I HAVE THIS NEW DISK I BOUGHT THAT I'M DYING TO WATCH!
HERE SHE GOES AGAIN.
GOTTA LOVE AV!!
HEH-HEH
IF I SUBMIT A DRAWING OF THEIR ROCKET, THEY'LL SEND ME A WRISTWATCH!
I SEE... BUT PLEASE, BE CAREFUL.
UH... SURE.
WELL, I'M OFF NOW.
OKAY. SEE YOU TOMORROW.

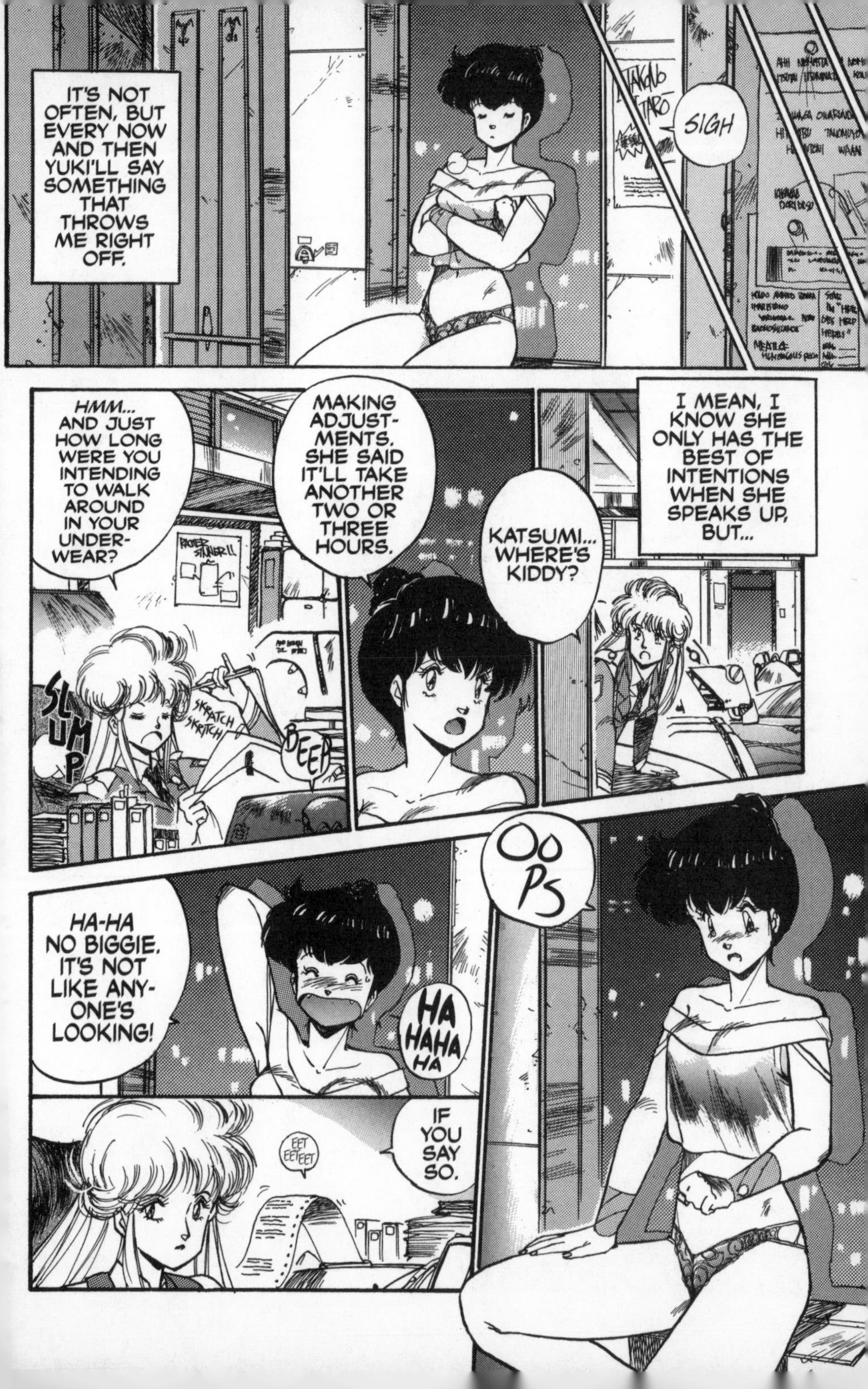
SIGH
IT'S NOT OFTEN, BUT EVERY NOW AND THEN YUKI'LL SAY SOMETHING THAT THROWS ME RIGHT OFF.
I MEAN, I KNOW SHE ONLY HAS THE BEST OF INTENTIONS WHEN SHE SPEAKS UP, BUT...
KATSUMI... WHERE'S KIDDY?
MAKING ADJUST-MENTS. SHE SAID IT'LL TAKE ANOTHER TWO OR THREE HOURS.
HMM... AND JUST HOW LONG WERE YOU INTENDING TO WALK AROUND IN YOUR UNDER-WEAR?
BEEP
SKRATCH SKRITCH
SLUMP
OOPS
HA-HA NO BIGGIE. IT'S NOT LIKE ANY-ONE'S LOOKING!
HA HAHA HA
IF YOU SAY SO.
EET EET EET

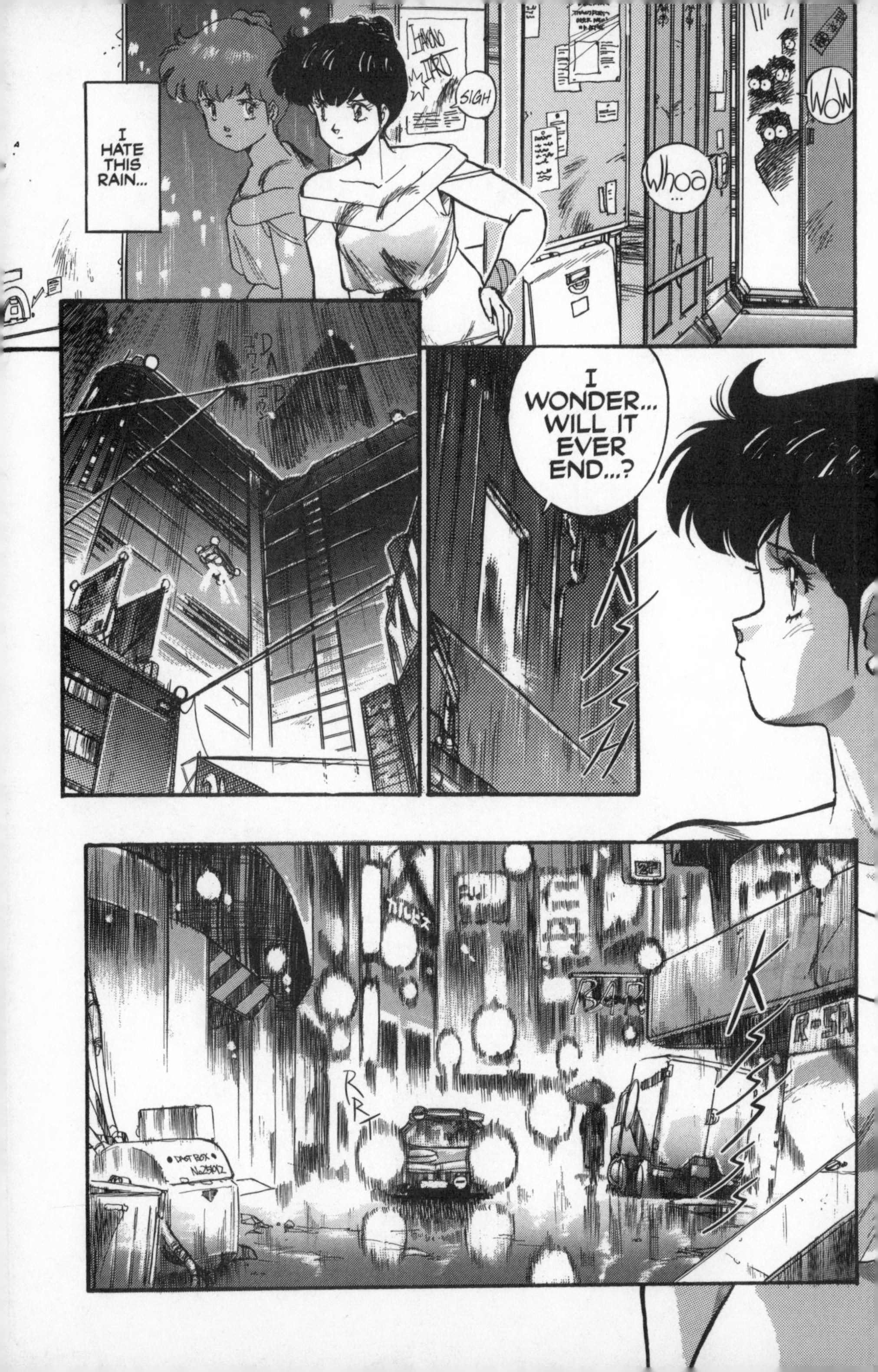
WOW
Whoa ...
SIGH
I HATE THIS RAIN...
I WONDER... WILL IT EVER END...?
KSSSSSH
BAR
KSSSSSSSH

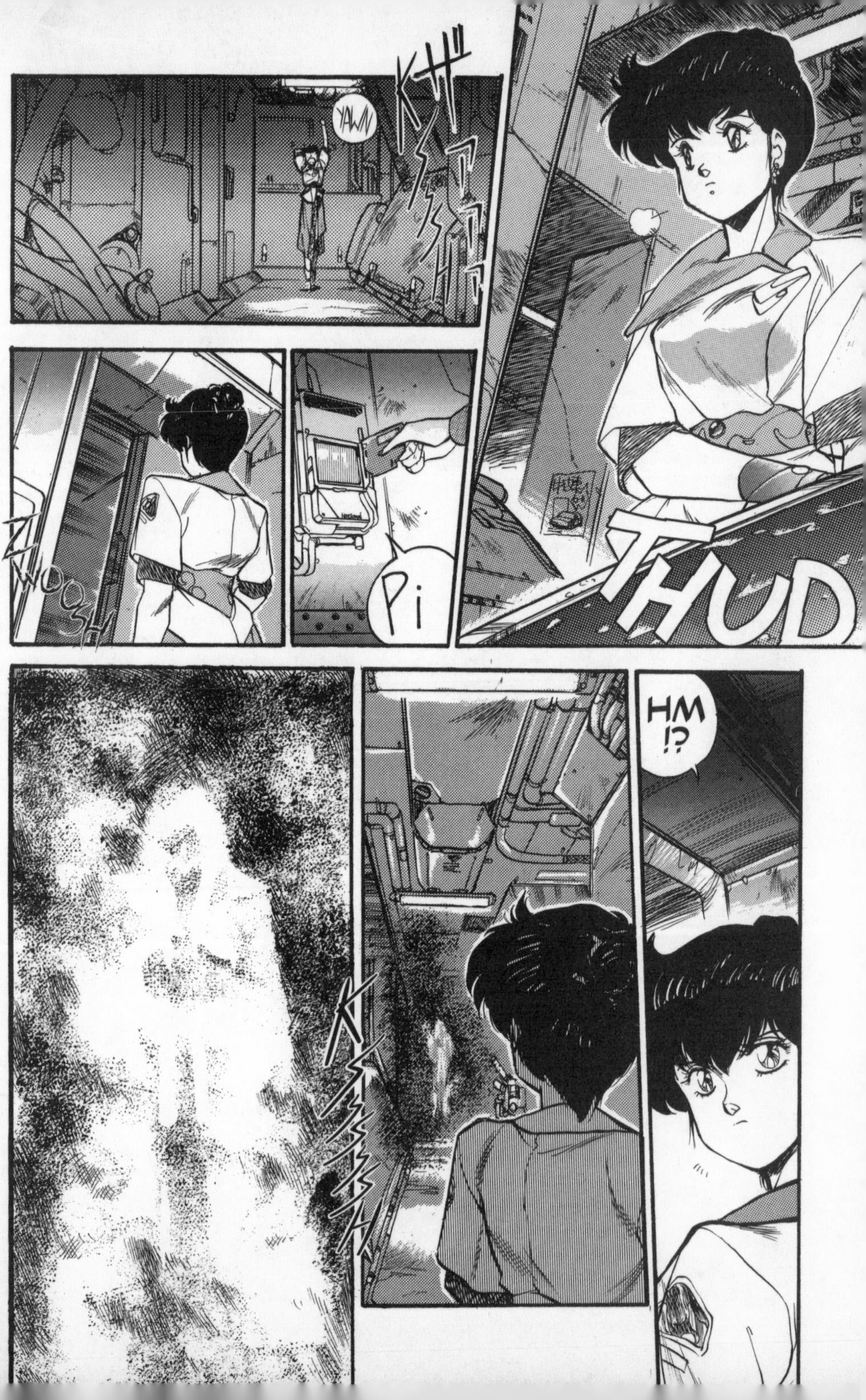
THUD
YAWN
KSSSH
ザアアア
Pi
ZWOOSH
HM!?
KSSSSSH

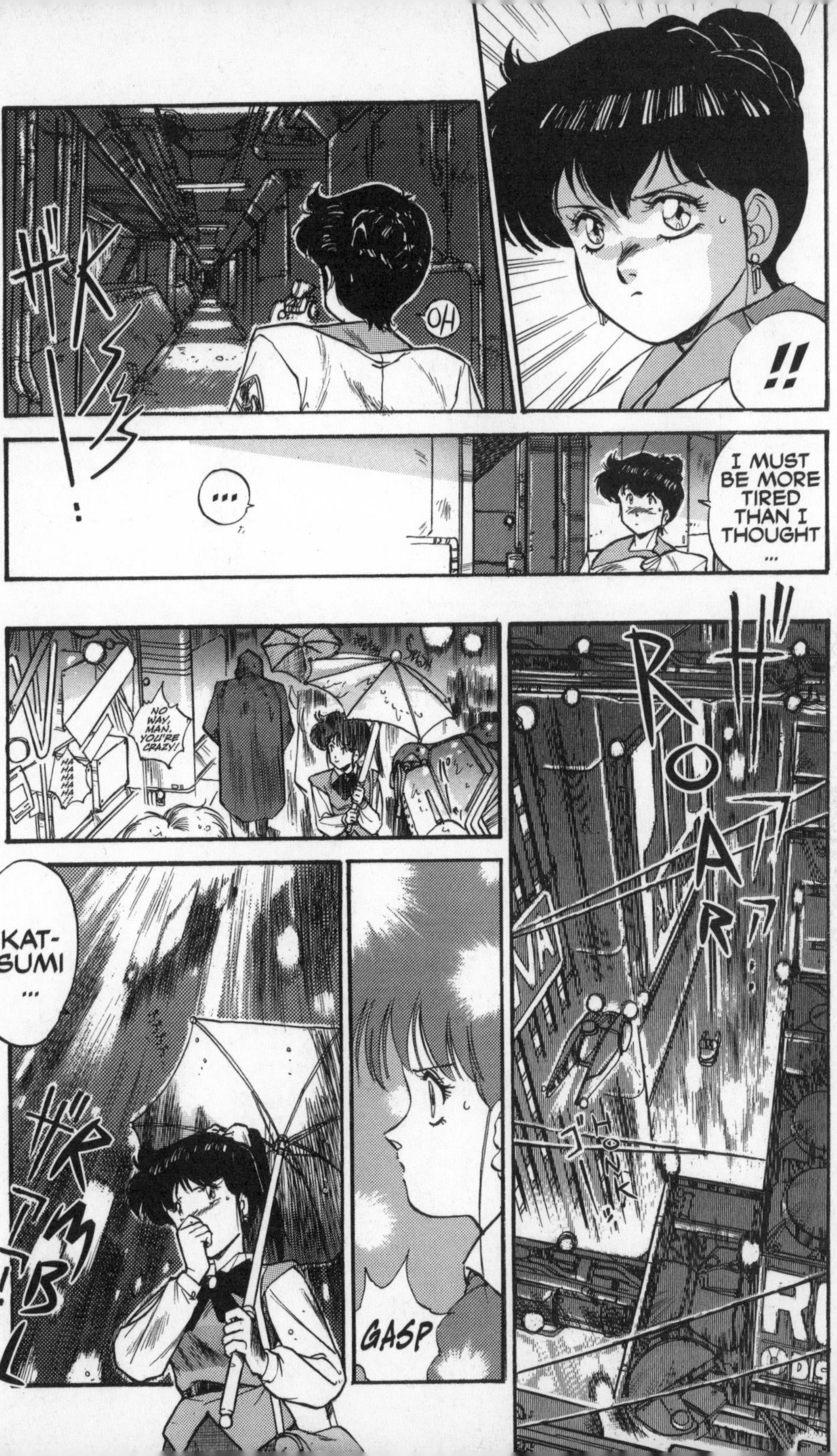
!!
OH
I MUST BE MORE TIRED THAN I THOUGHT ...
...
ROAR
HONK
NO WAY, MAN, YOU'RE CRAZY!
HA HA HA HA HA
GASP
KAT-SUMI ...
RMBL

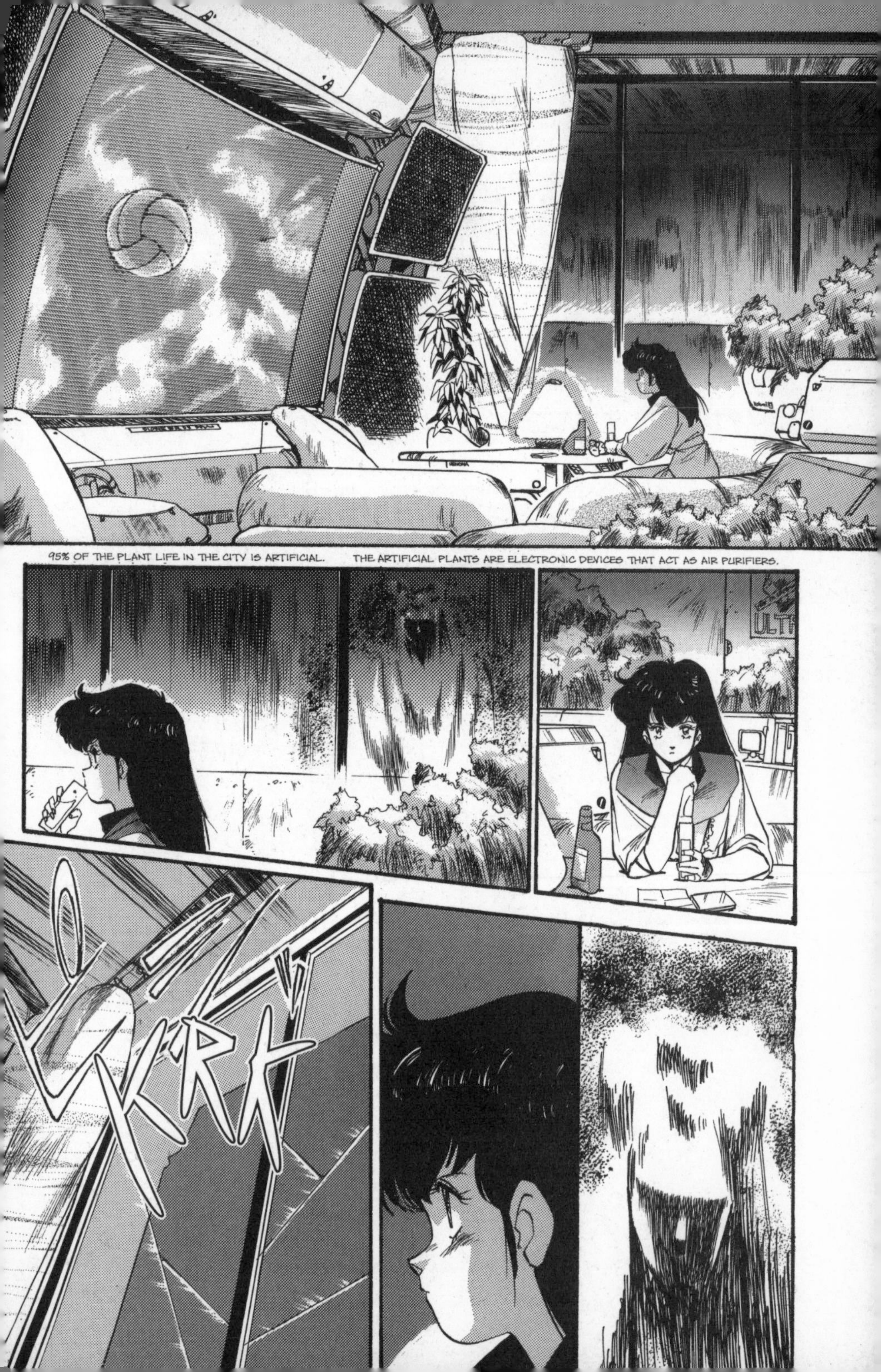
95% OF THE PLANT LIFE IN THE CITY IS ARTIFICIAL.
THE ARTIFICIAL PLANTS ARE ELECTRONIC DEVICES THAT ACT AS AIR PURIFIERS.

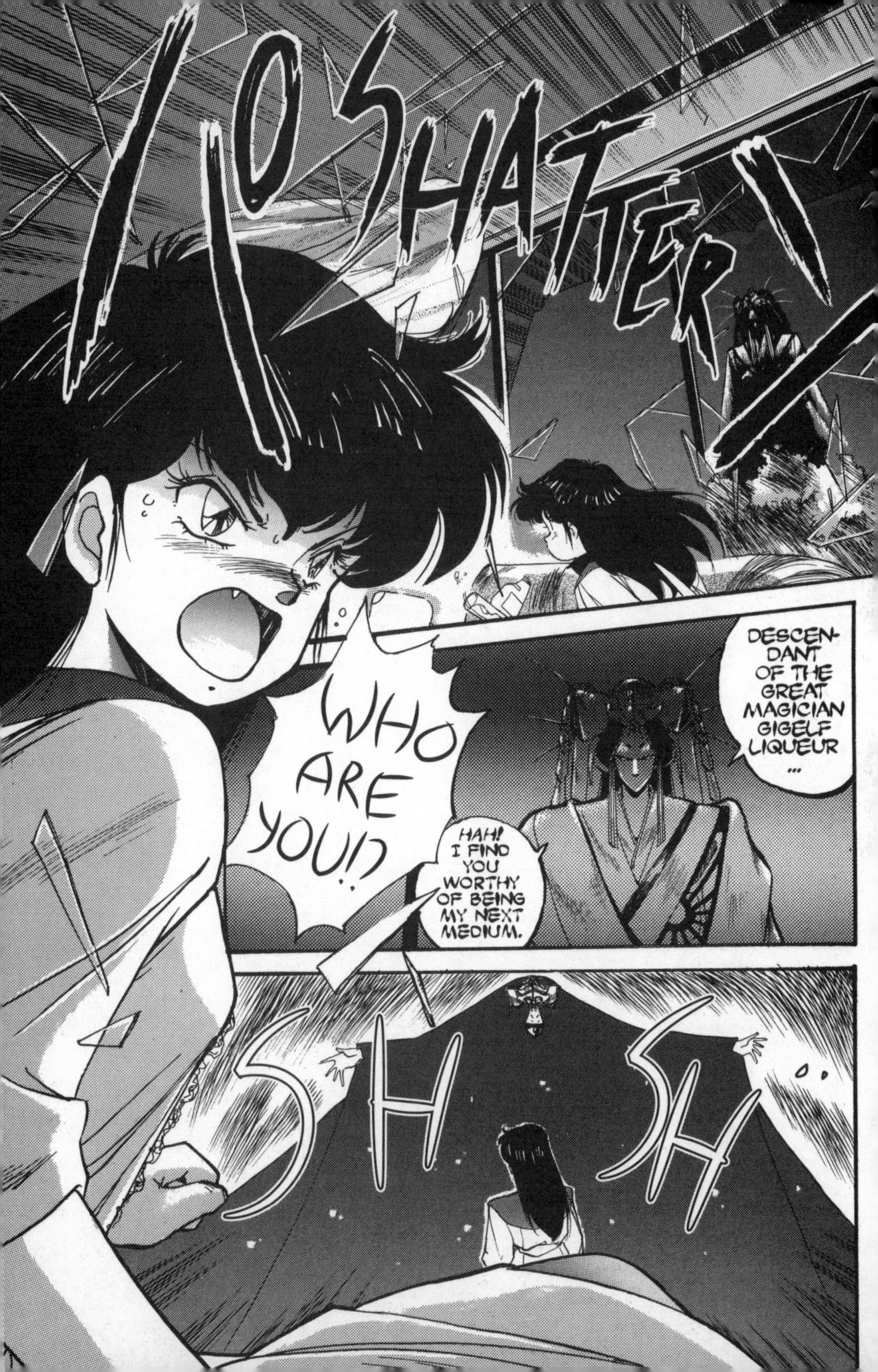
SHATTER
DESCEN-DANT OF THE GREAT MAGICIAN GIGELF LIQUEUR ...
HAH! I FIND YOU WORTHY OF BEING MY NEXT MEDIUM.
WHO ARE YOU!?
SH SH

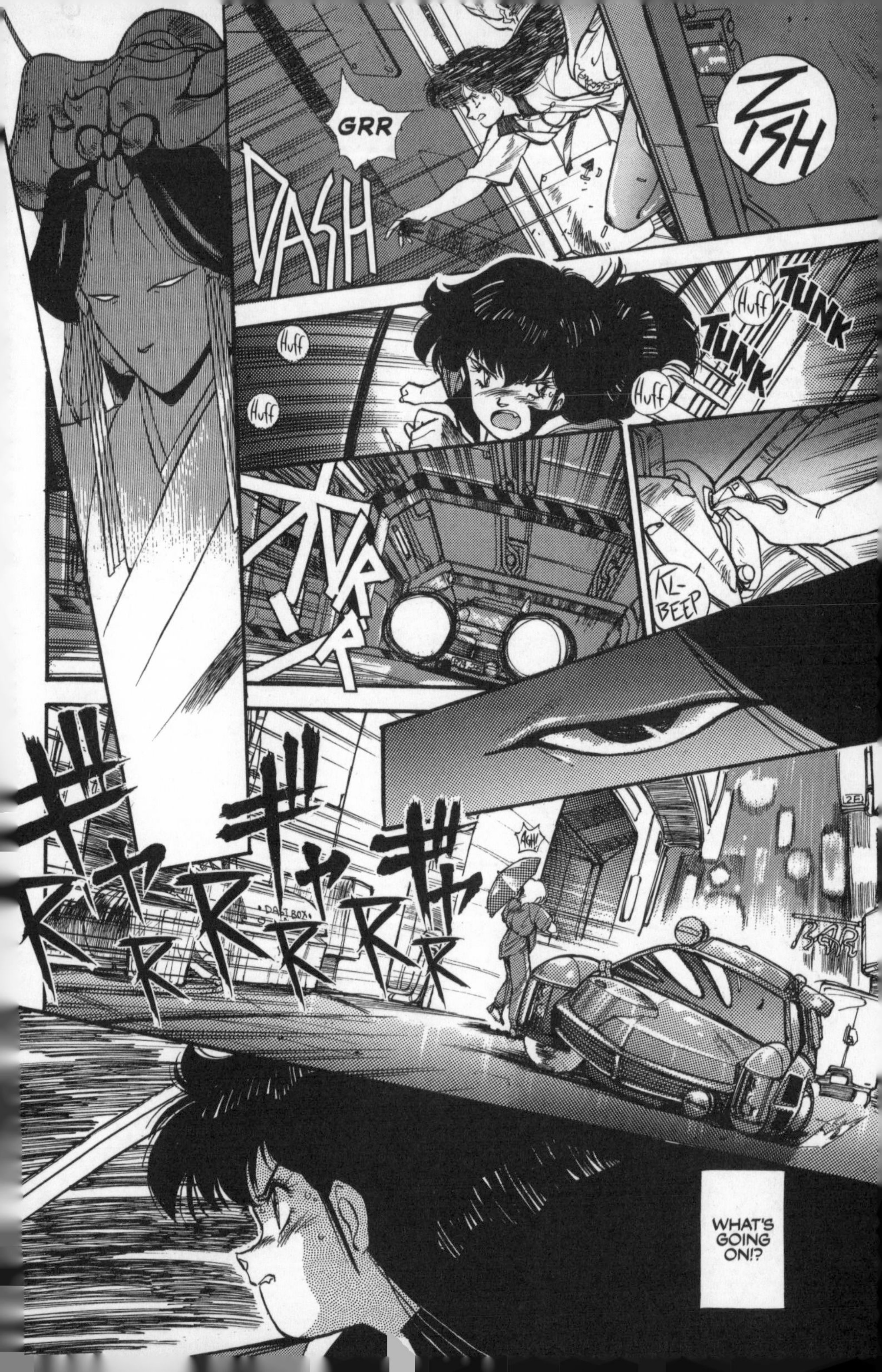
ZISH
GRR
DASH
Huff
TUNK
TUNK
Huff
Huff
Huff
KL-BEEP
VRRR
AGH!
BAR
DAST BOX
WHAT'S GOING ON!?

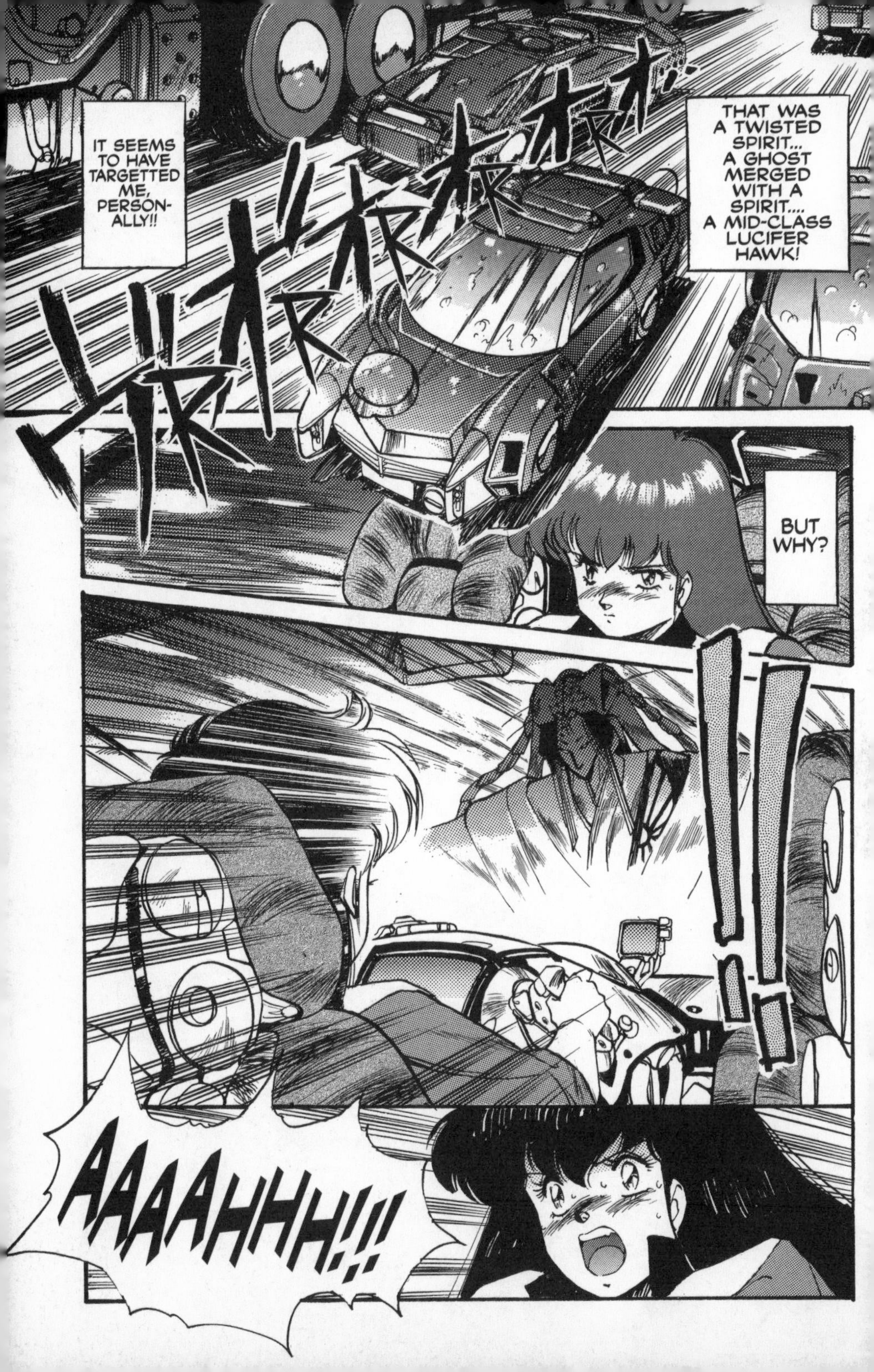
THAT WAS A TWISTED SPIRIT... A GHOST MERGED WITH A SPIRIT.... A MID-CLASS LUCIFER HAWK!
IT SEEMS TO HAVE TARGETTED ME, PERSON-ALLY!!
BUT WHY?
AAAAHHH!!!

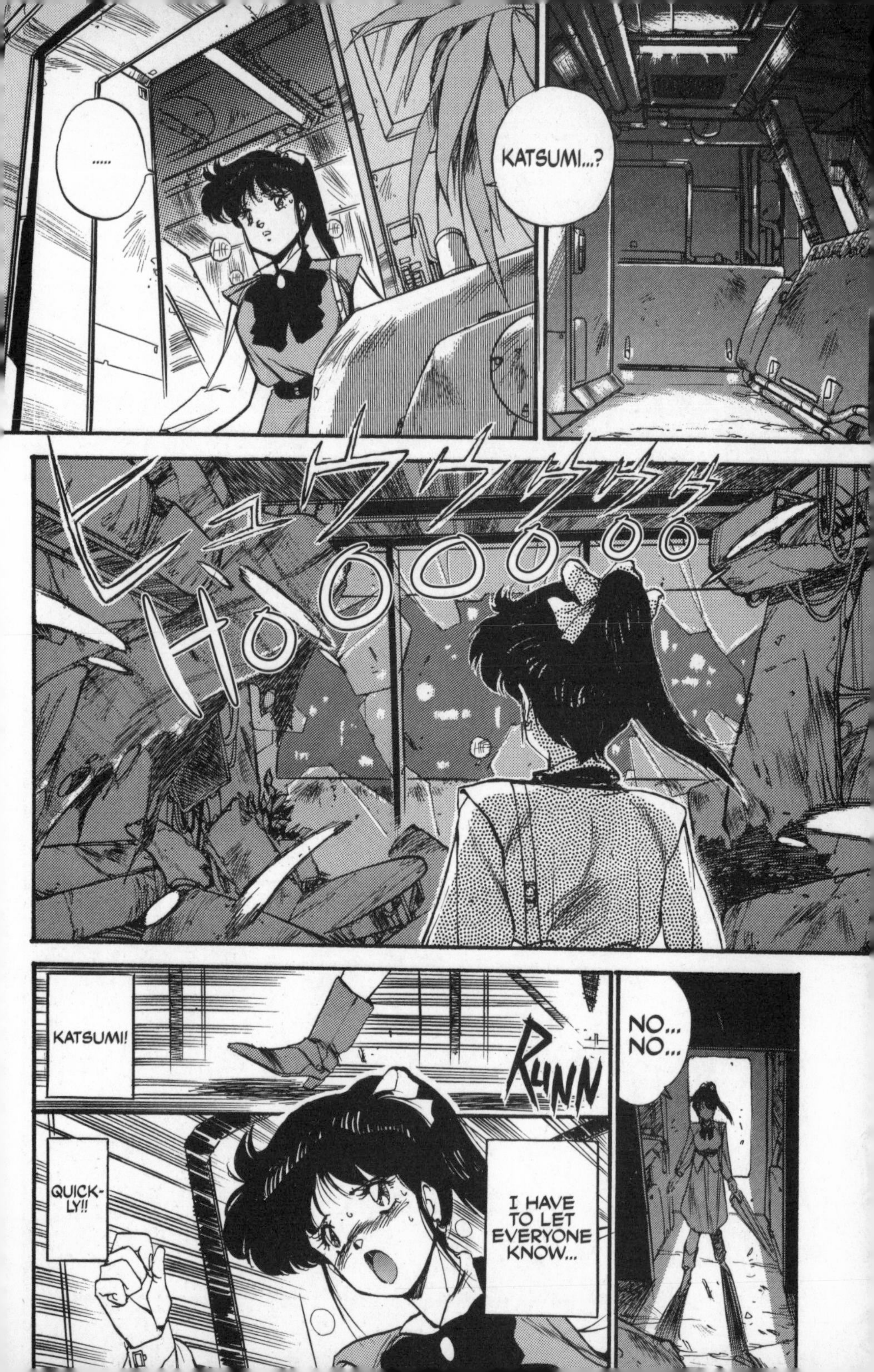
KATSUMI...?
.....
Hff
Hff
Hff
ヒュウウウウウウ
HOOOOOOO
Hff
NO... NO...
KATSUMI!
RUNN
I HAVE TO LET EVERYONE KNOW...
QUICKLY!!

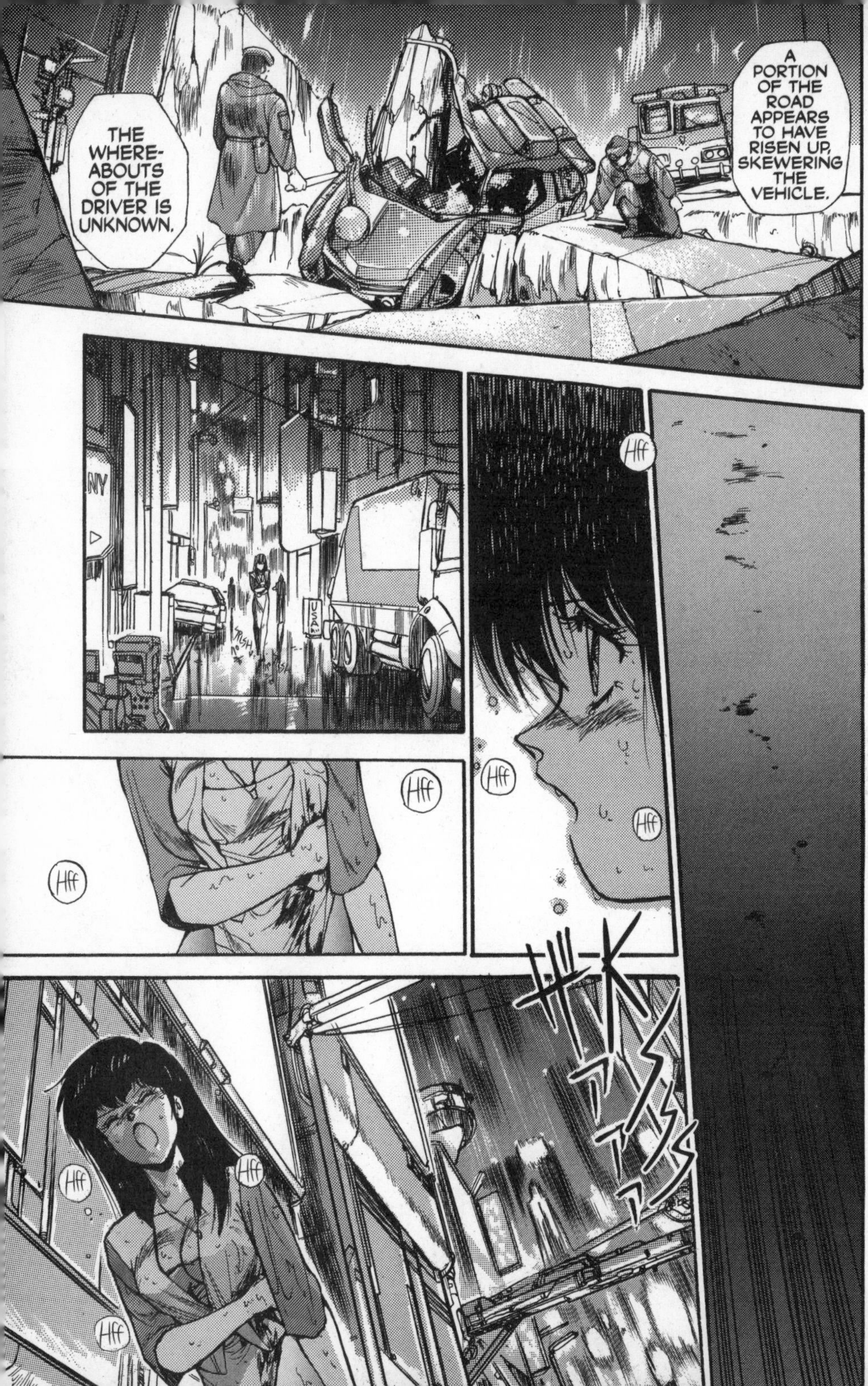
A PORTION OF THE ROAD APPEARS TO HAVE RISEN UP, SKEWERING THE VEHICLE.
THE WHEREABOUTS OF THE DRIVER IS UNKNOWN.
Hff
Hff
Hff
Hff
Hff
Hff
Hff
Hff

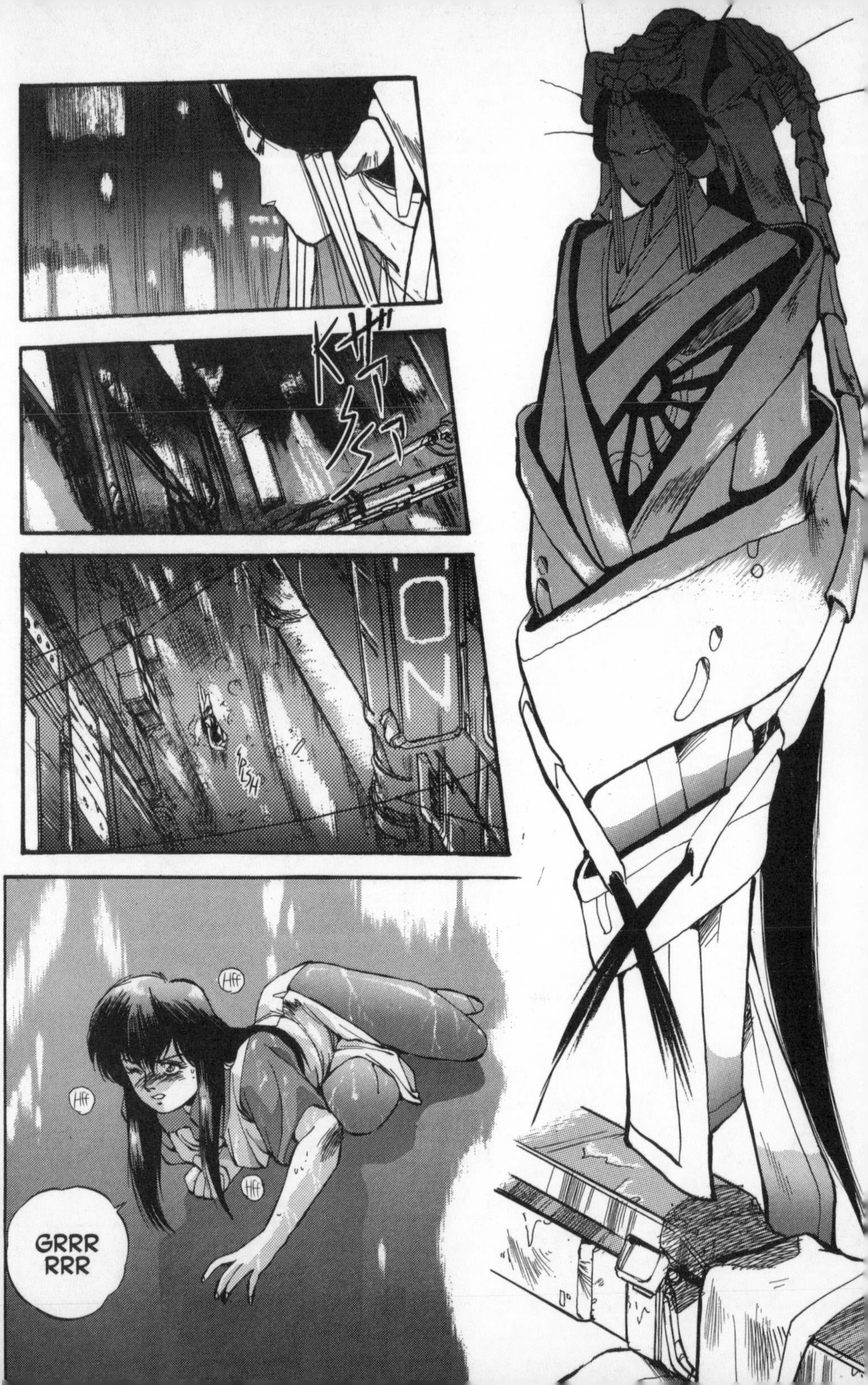
ザァァ
KSS
PLSH
Hff
Hff
Hff
GRRR
RRR

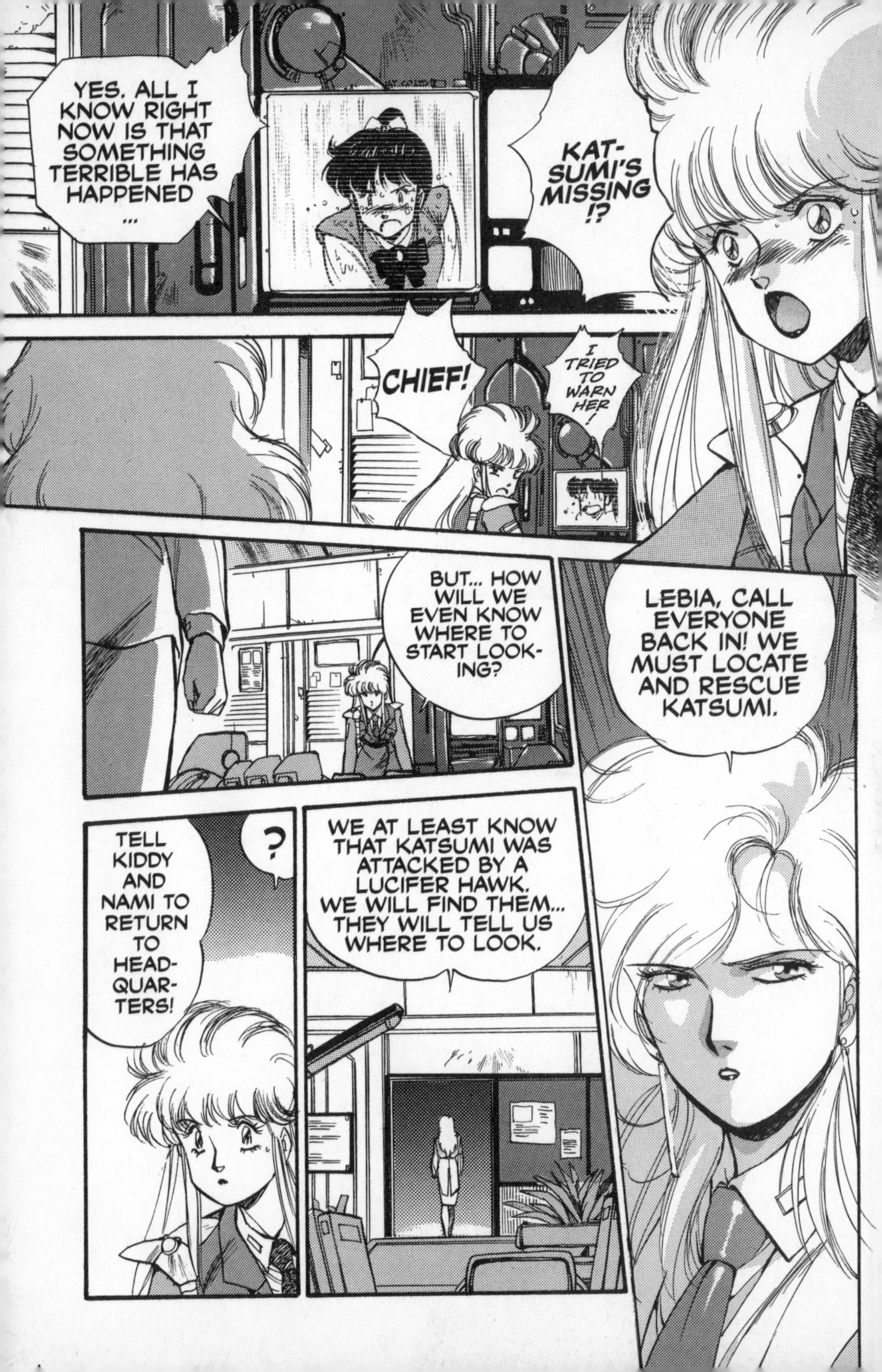
KAT-SUMI'S MISSING !?
YES. ALL I KNOW RIGHT NOW IS THAT SOMETHING TERRIBLE HAS HAPPENED ...
I TRIED TO WARN HER!
CHIEF!
LEBIA, CALL EVERYONE BACK IN! WE MUST LOCATE AND RESCUE KATSUMI.
BUT... HOW WILL WE EVEN KNOW WHERE TO START LOOK-ING?
WE AT LEAST KNOW THAT KATSUMI WAS ATTACKED BY A LUCIFER HAWK. WE WILL FIND THEM... THEY WILL TELL US WHERE TO LOOK.
?
TELL KIDDY AND NAMI TO RETURN TO HEAD-QUAR-TERS!

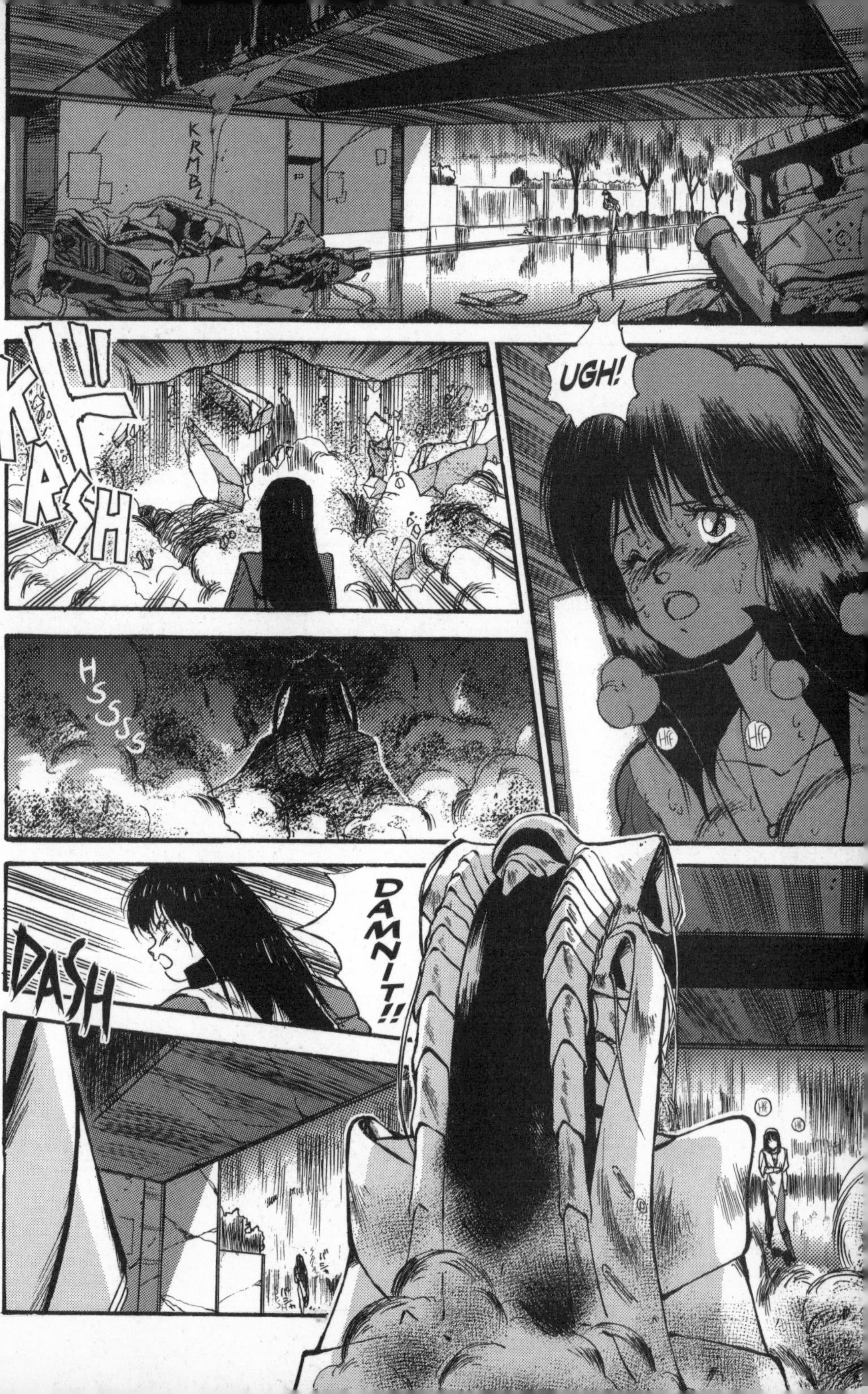
KRMBL
UGH!
HFF
HFF
KLASH
HSSSSS
HFF
HFF
DAMNIT!!
DASH

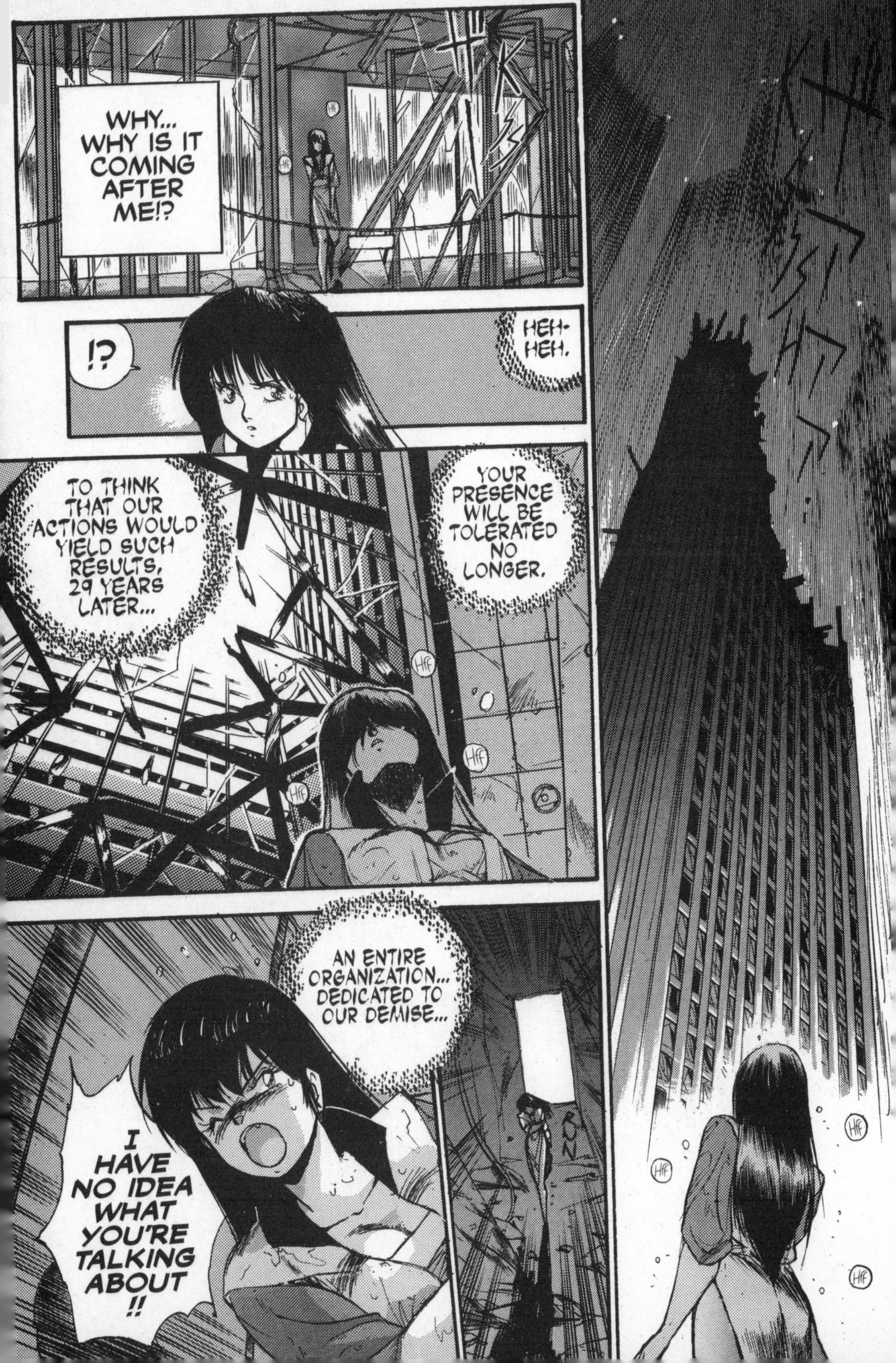
HFF
HFF
HFF
WHY... WHY IS IT COMING AFTER ME!?
HEH-HEH.
!?
YOUR PRESENCE WILL BE TOLERATED NO LONGER.
TO THINK THAT OUR ACTIONS WOULD YIELD SUCH RESULTS, 29 YEARS LATER...
HFF
HFF
HFF
AN ENTIRE ORGANIZATION... DEDICATED TO OUR DEMISE...
I HAVE NO IDEA WHAT YOU'RE TALKING ABOUT!!

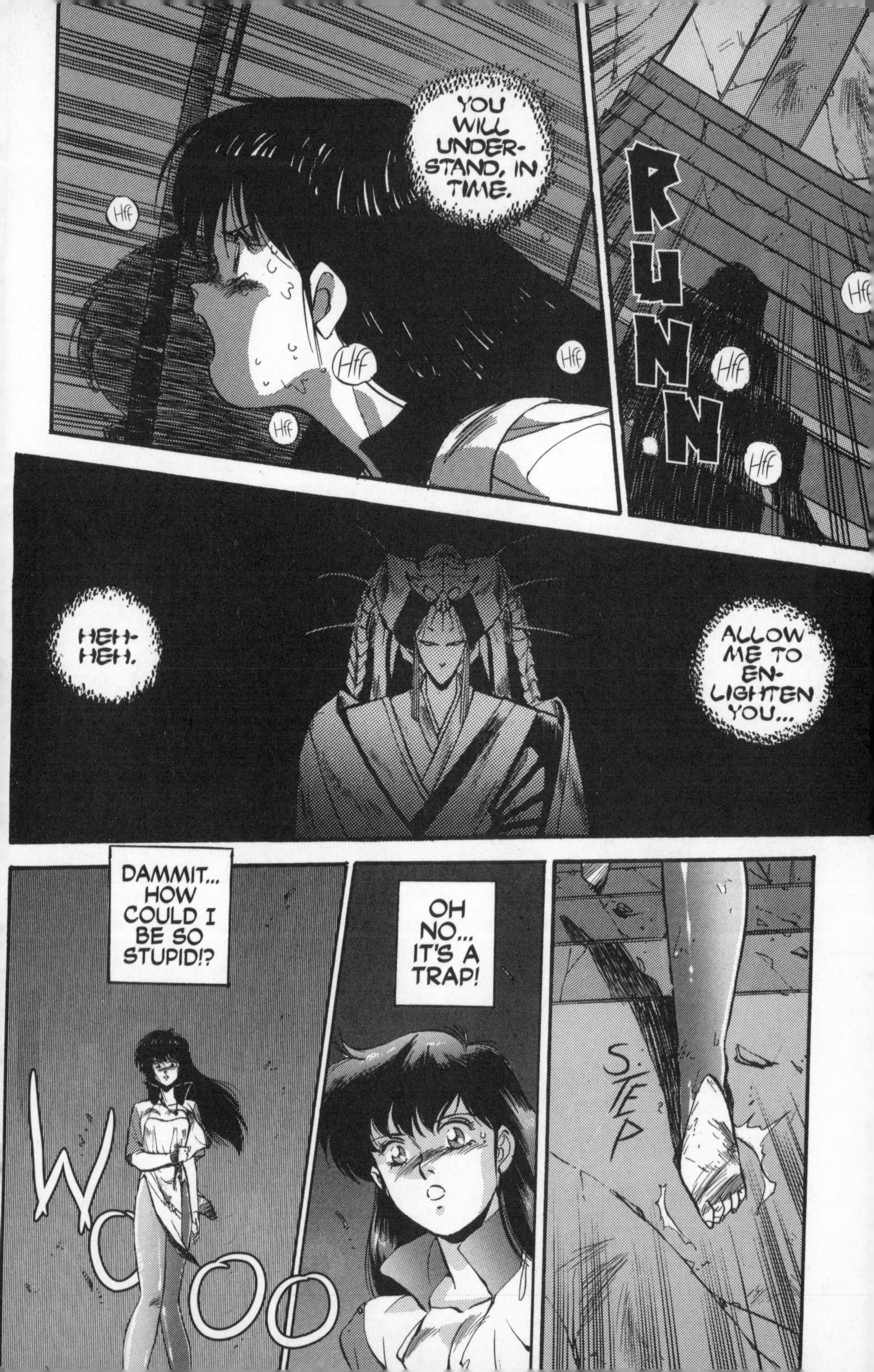
Hff
RUNN
Hff
Hff
YOU WILL UNDER-STAND, IN TIME.
Hff
Hff
Hff
Hff
ALLOW ME TO EN-LIGHTEN YOU...
HEH-HEH.
STEP
OH NO... IT'S A TRAP!
DAMMIT... HOW COULD I BE SO STUPID!?
WOOOO

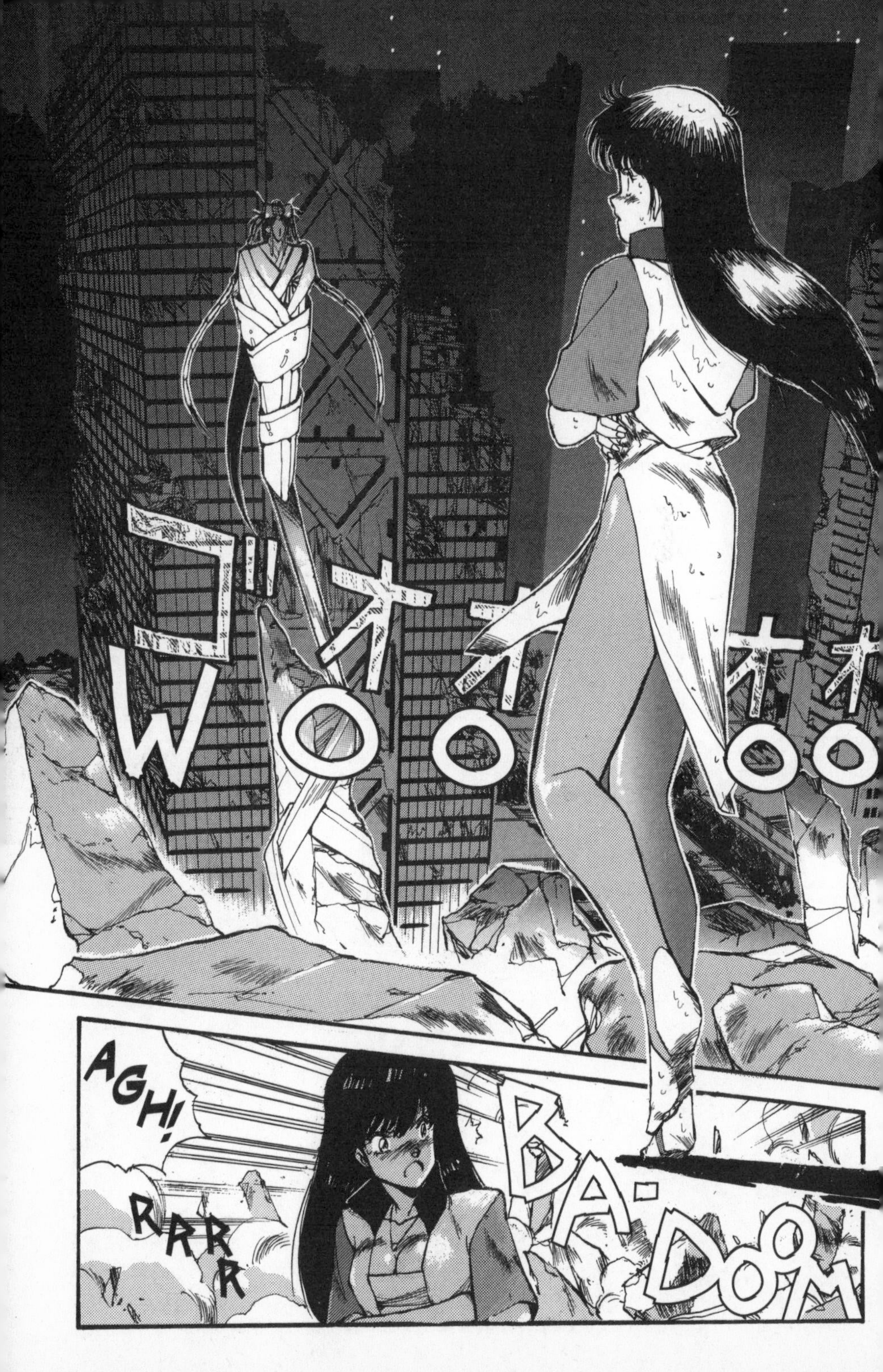
ゴオオオオ
WOOOO
BA-DOOM
AGH!
RRRR

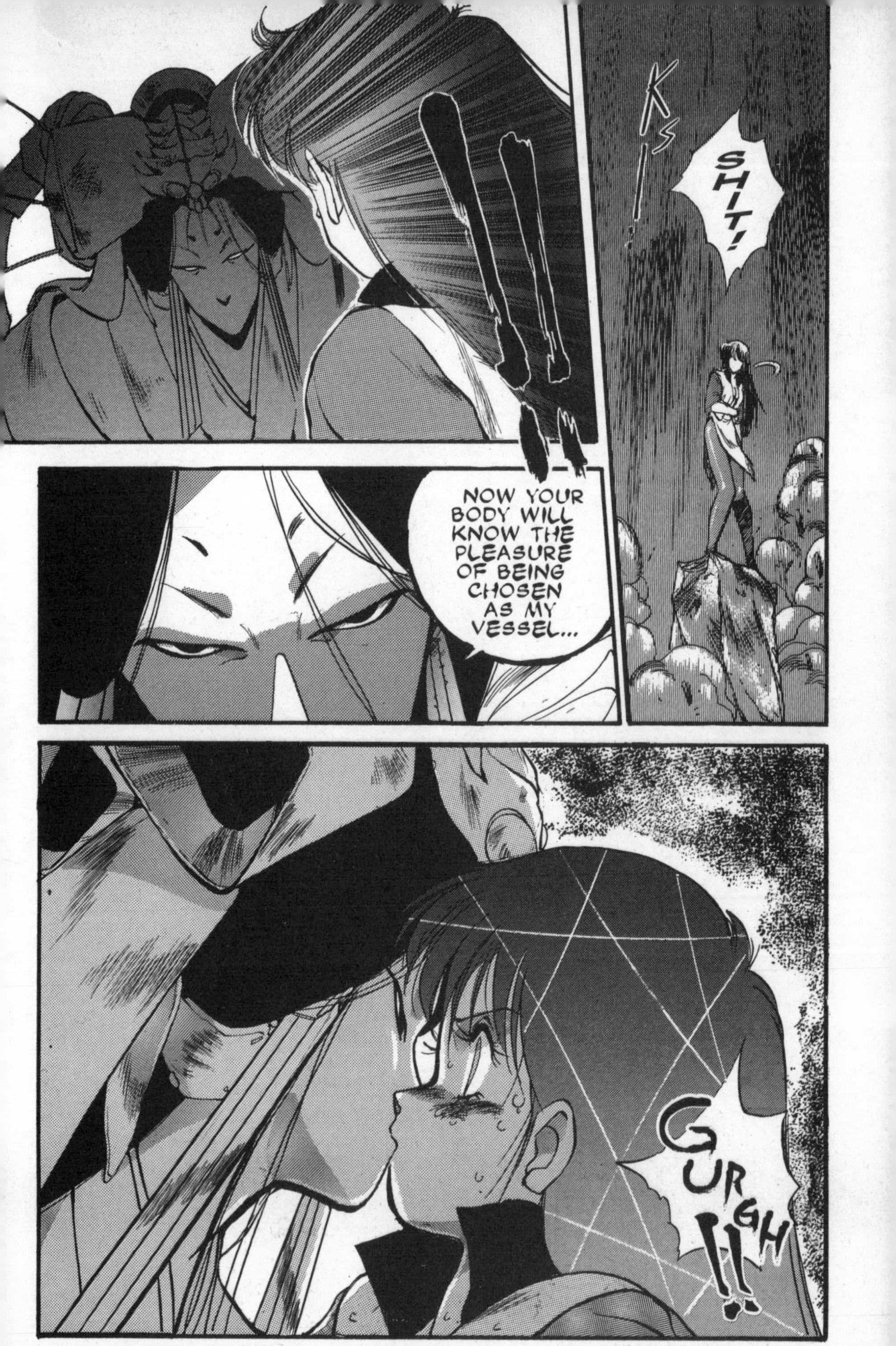
KSI!
SHIT!
NOW YOUR BODY WILL KNOW THE PLEASURE OF BEING CHOSEN AS MY VESSEL...
GURGH!!

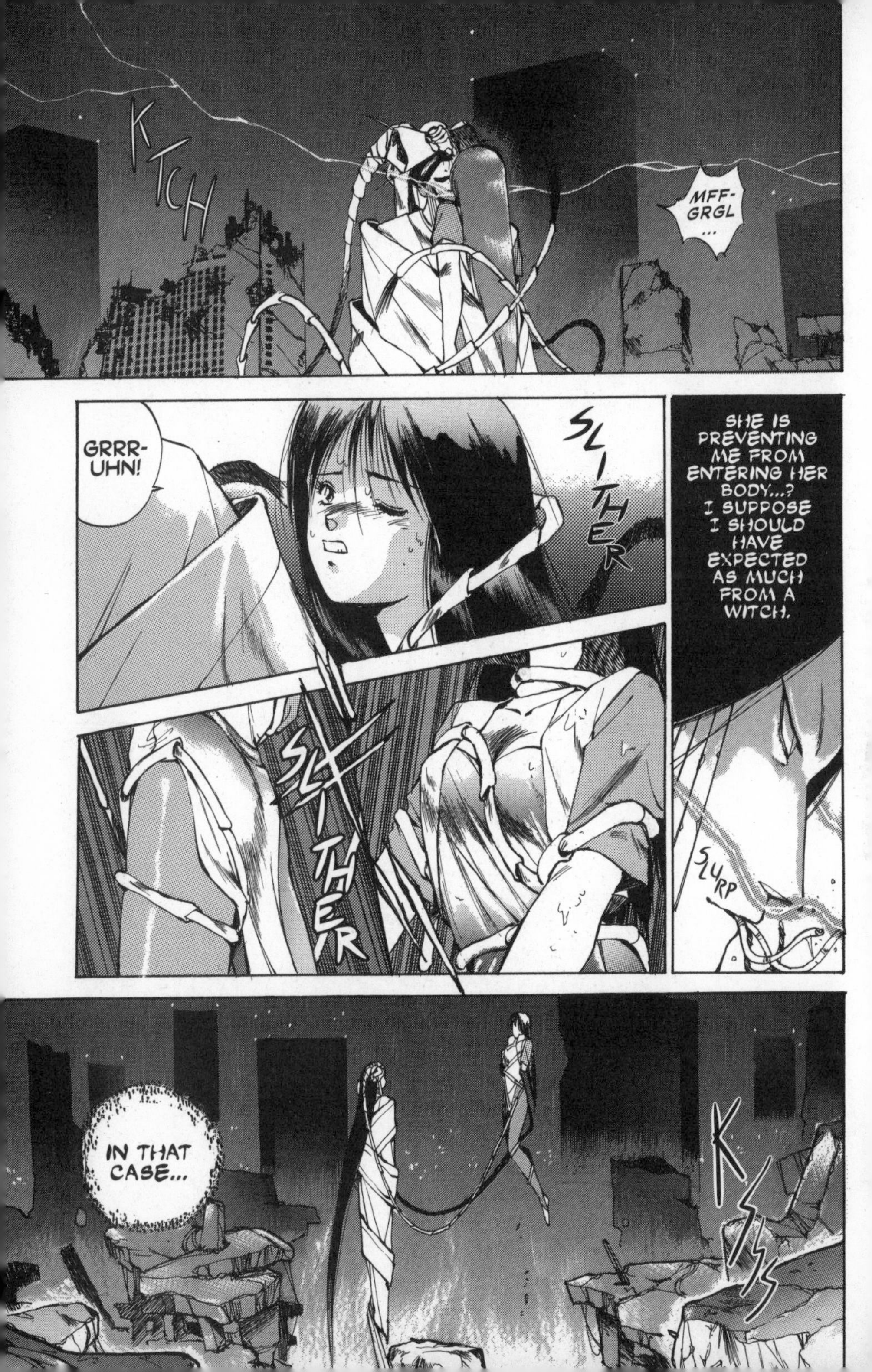
MFF-GRGL ...
KTCH
SHE IS PREVENTING ME FROM ENTERING HER BODY...? I SUPPOSE I SHOULD HAVE EXPECTED AS MUCH FROM A WITCH.
SLURP
SLITHER
GRRR-UHN!
SLITHER
KISS
IN THAT CASE...

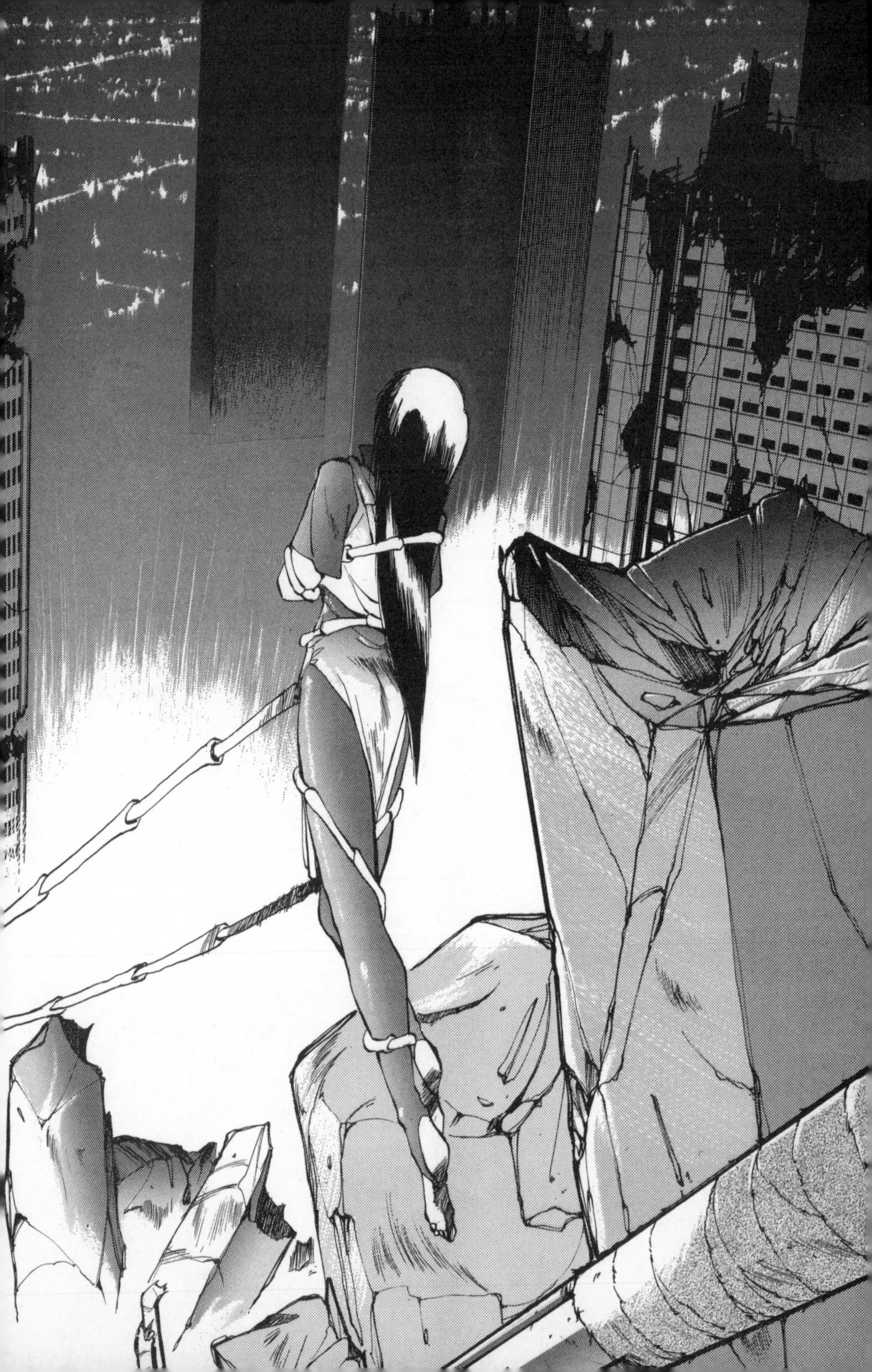

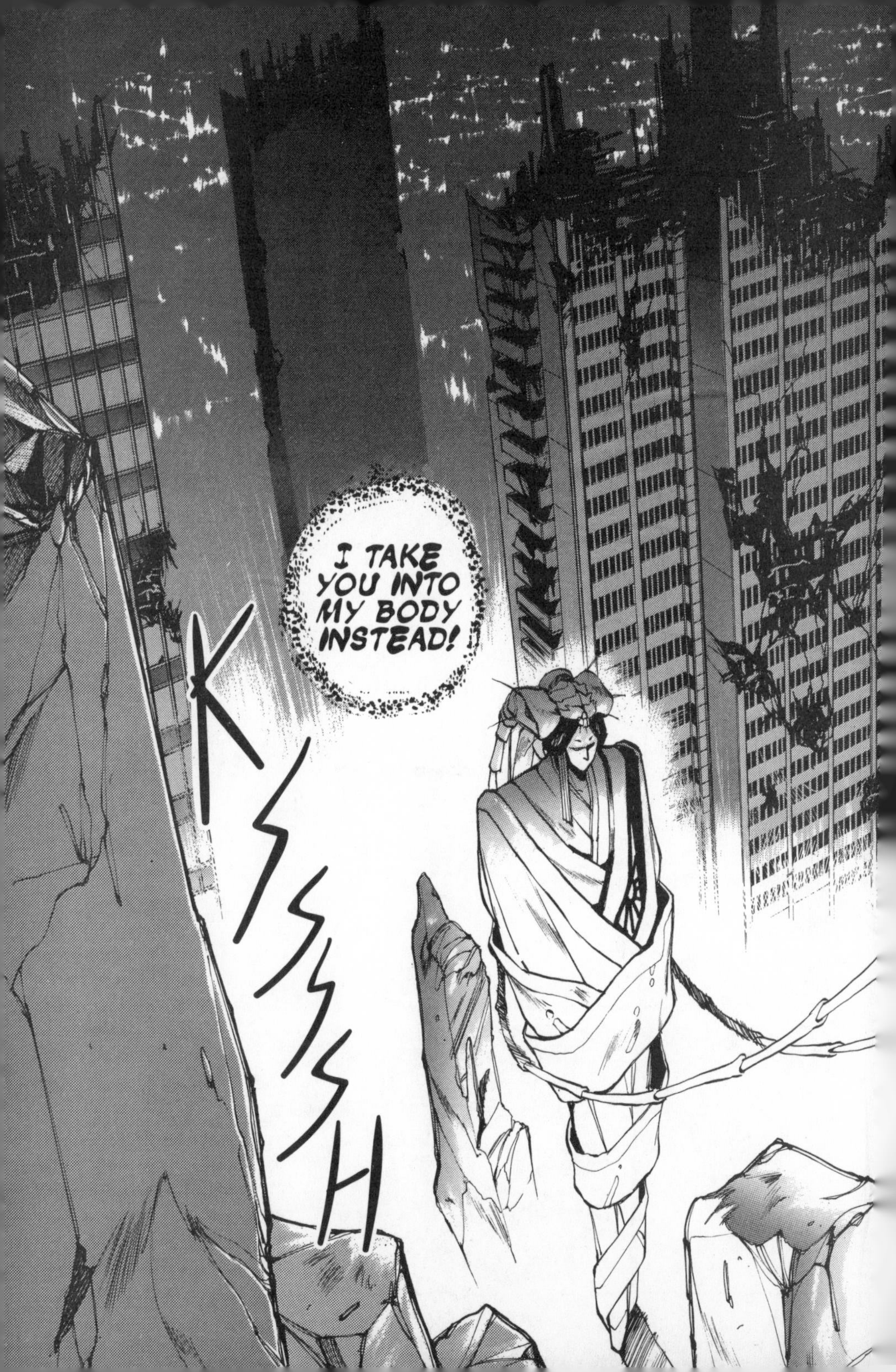
I TAKE YOU INTO MY BODY INSTEAD!
KISSSSH

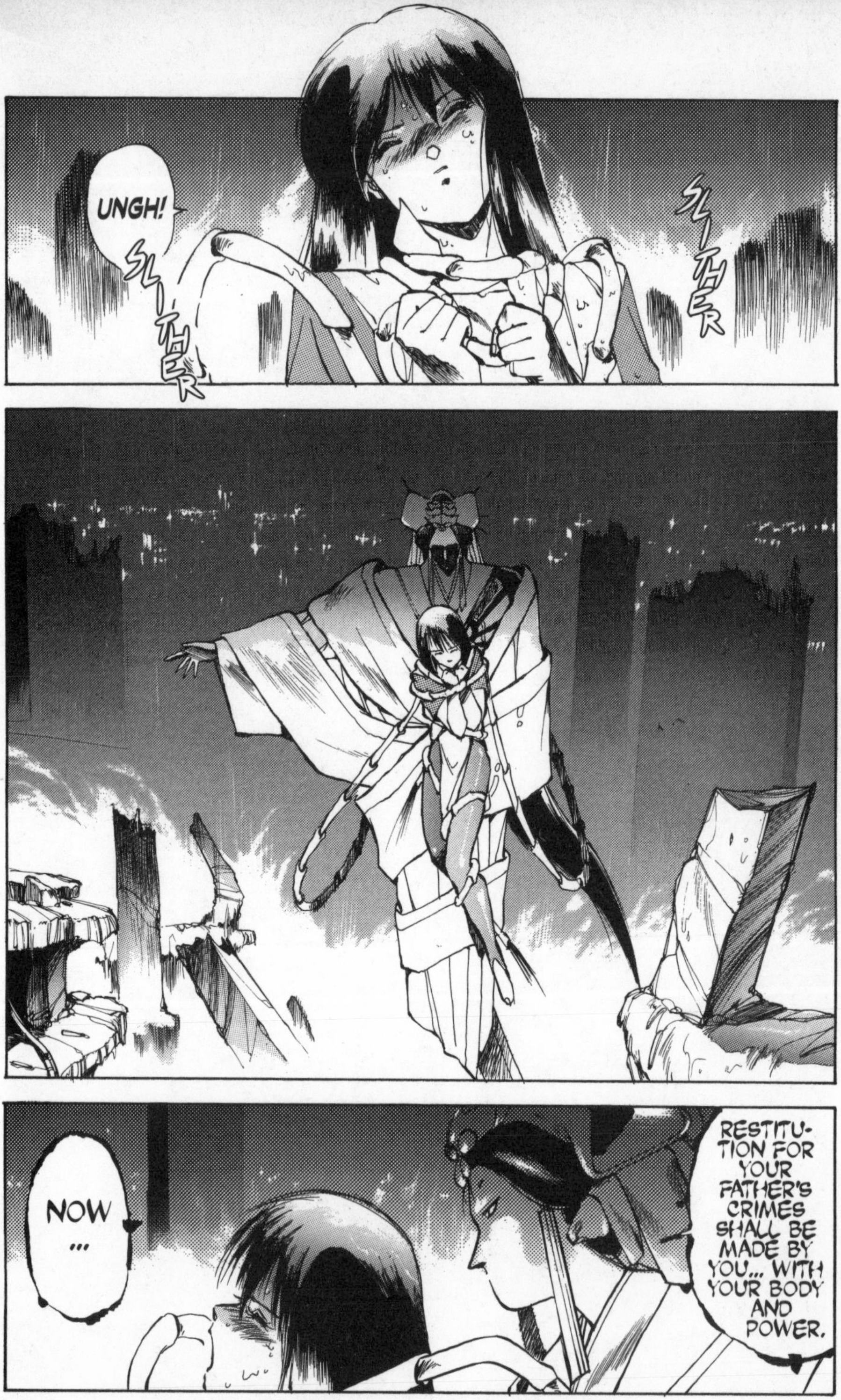
SLITHER
UNGH!
SLITHER
RESTITU-TION FOR YOUR FATHER'S CRIMES SHALL BE MADE BY YOU... WITH YOUR BODY AND POWER.
NOW ...

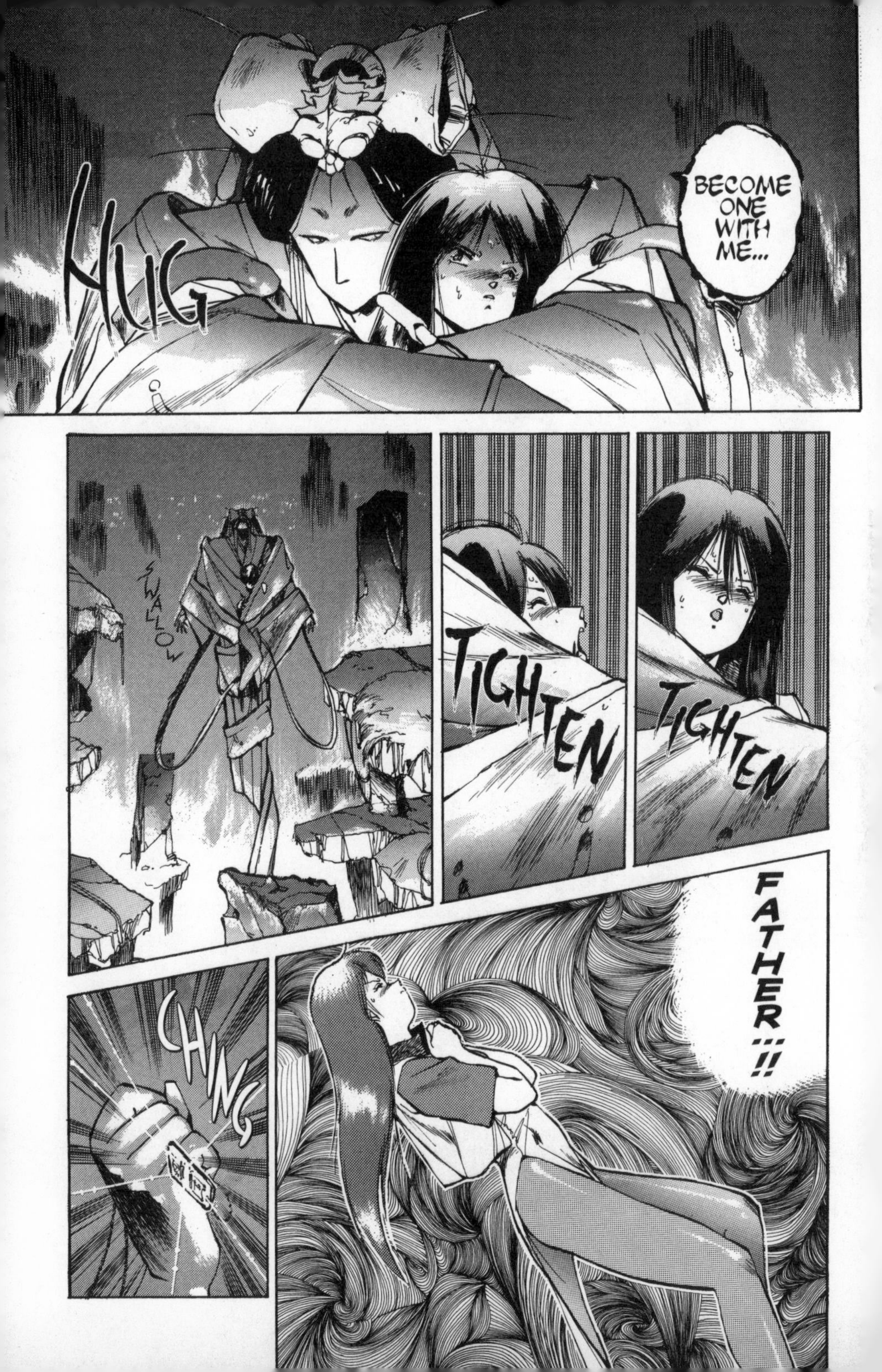
BECOME ONE WITH ME...
HUG
TIGHTEN
TIGHTEN
SWALLOW
FATHER!!
CHING

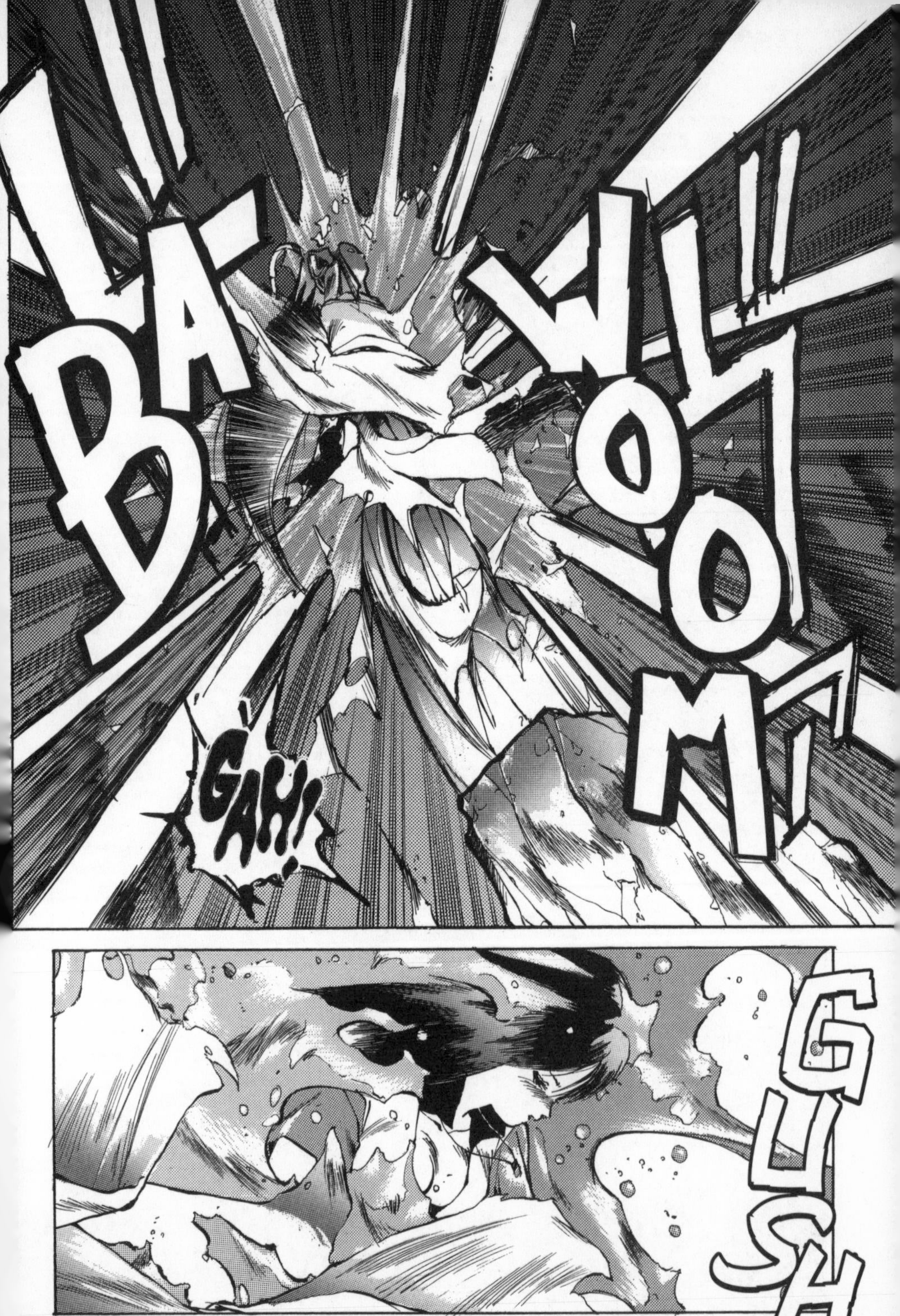
BAWOOOM!!
GAH!!
GUSH

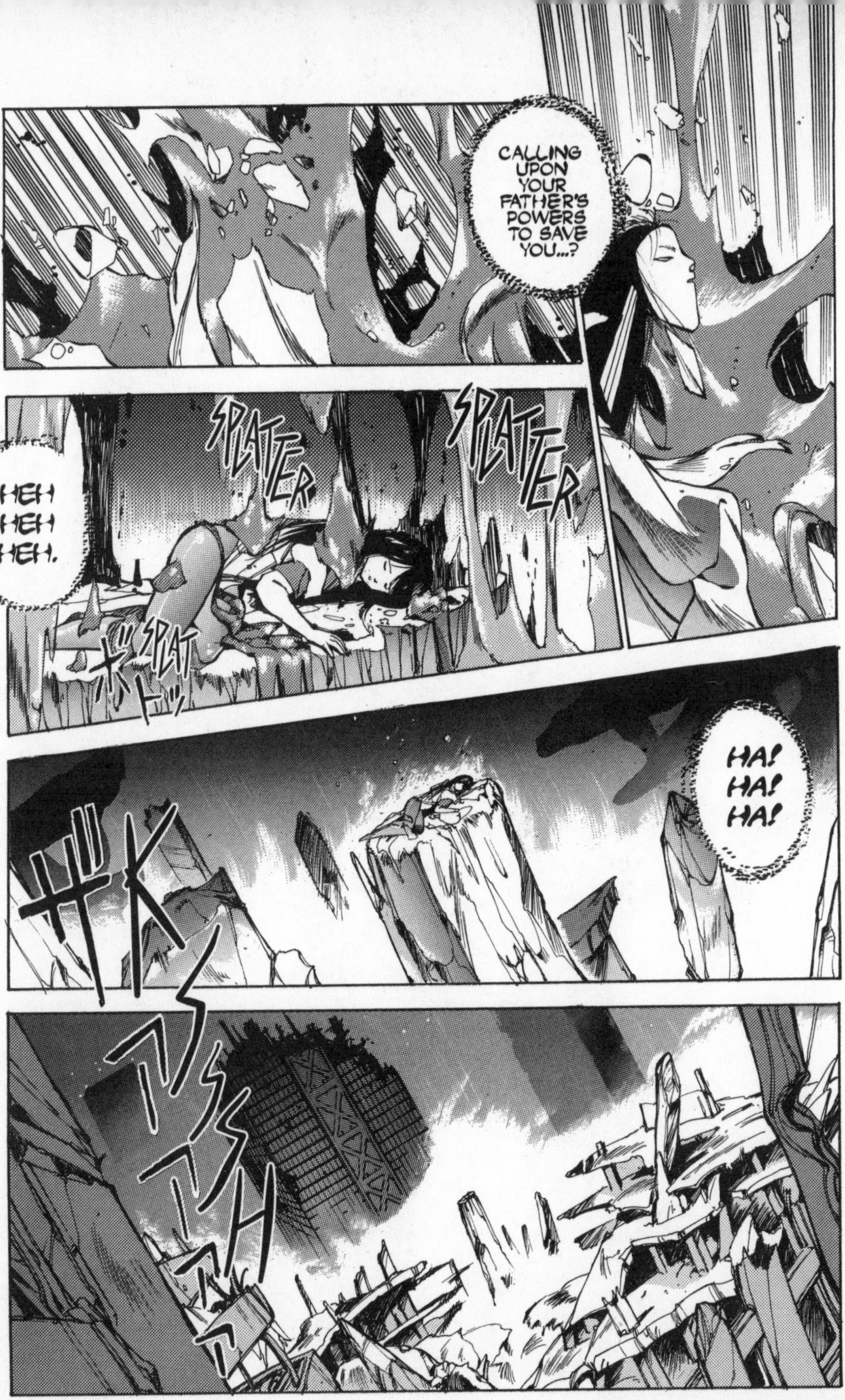
CALLING UPON YOUR FATHER'S POWERS TO SAVE YOU...?
SPLATTER
SPLATTER
HEH HEH HEH.
SPLAT
ボトッ
HA! HA! HA!

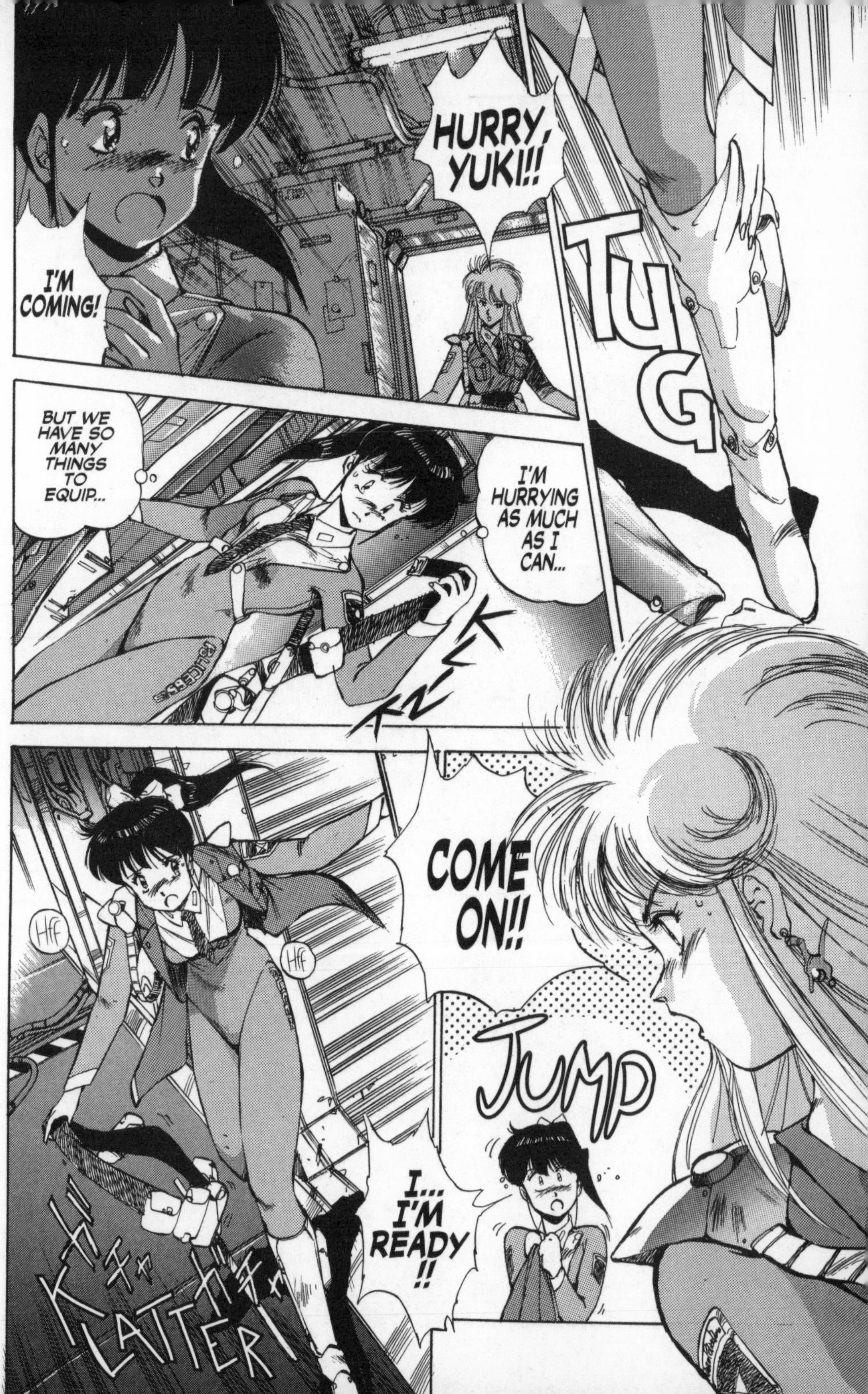
TUG
HURRY, YUKI!!
I'M COMING!
I'M HURRYING AS MUCH AS I CAN...
BUT WE HAVE SO MANY THINGS TO EQUIP...
KLIK
COME ON!!
JUMP
I... I'M READY!!
Hff
Hff
KLATTER!

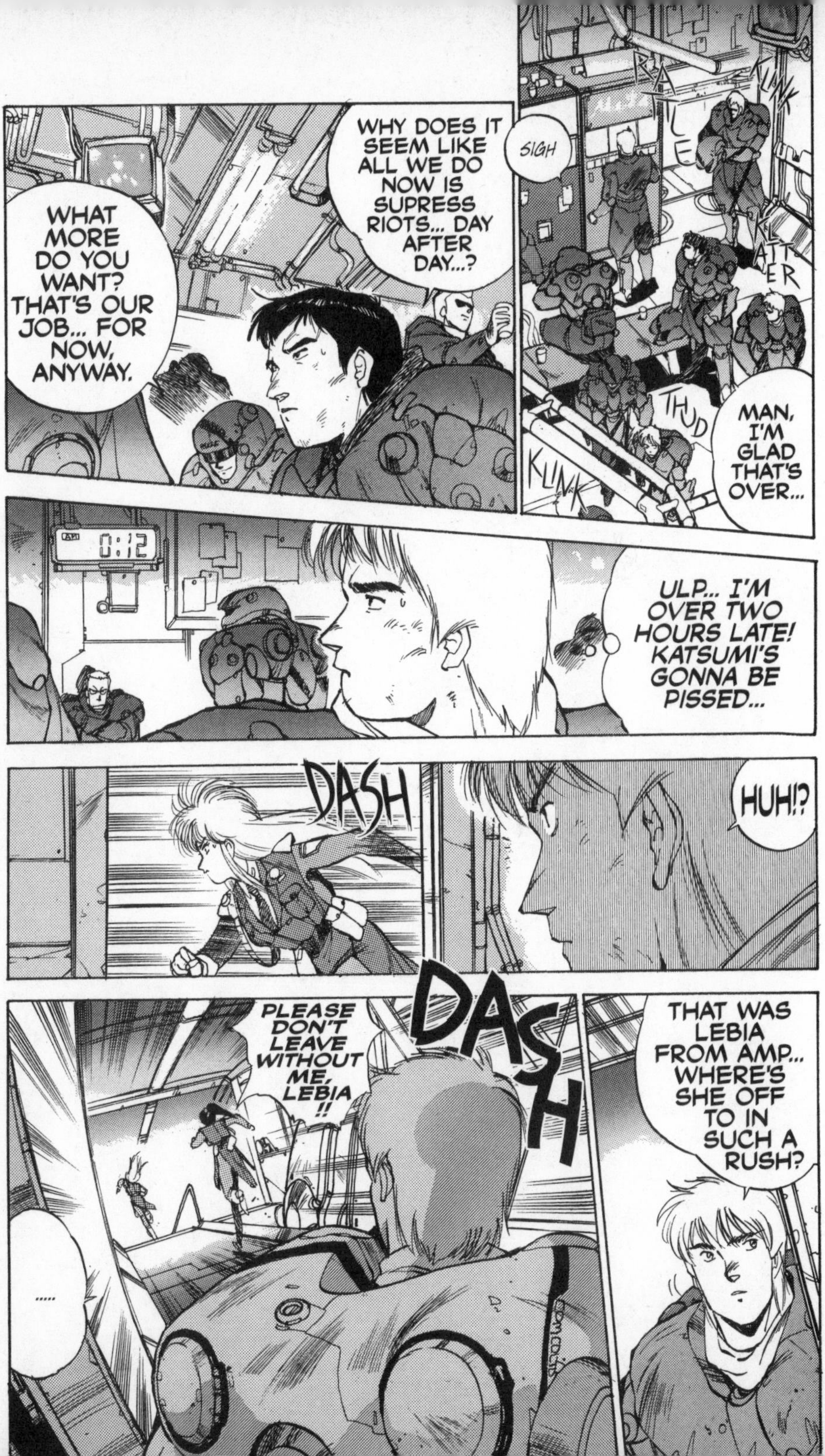
SIGH
RATTLE
KLINK
KLATTER
THUD
KLINK
MAN, I'M GLAD THAT'S OVER...
WHY DOES IT SEEM LIKE ALL WE DO NOW IS SUPRESS RIOTS... DAY AFTER DAY...?
WHAT MORE DO YOU WANT? THAT'S OUR JOB... FOR NOW, ANYWAY.
ULP... I'M OVER TWO HOURS LATE! KATSUMI'S GONNA BE PISSED...
0:12
HUH!?
DASH
THAT WAS LEBIA FROM AMP... WHERE'S SHE OFF TO IN SUCH A RUSH?
DASH
PLEASE DON'T LEAVE WITHOUT ME, LEBIA!!
......

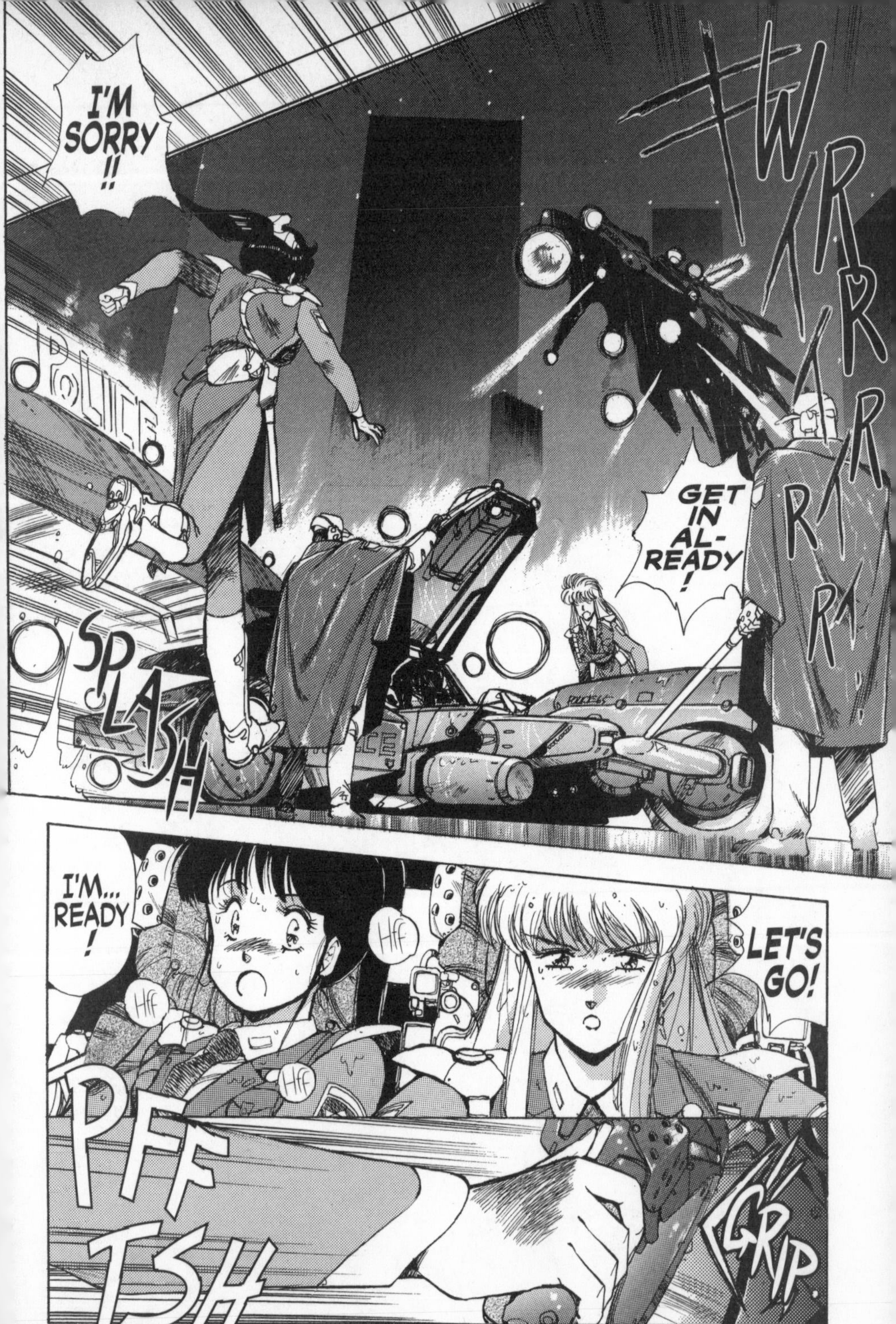
WRRRRRR
GET IN AL-READY!
I'M SORRY!!
SPLASH
LET'S GO!
Hff
I'M... READY!
Hff
Hff
GRIP
PFF TSH

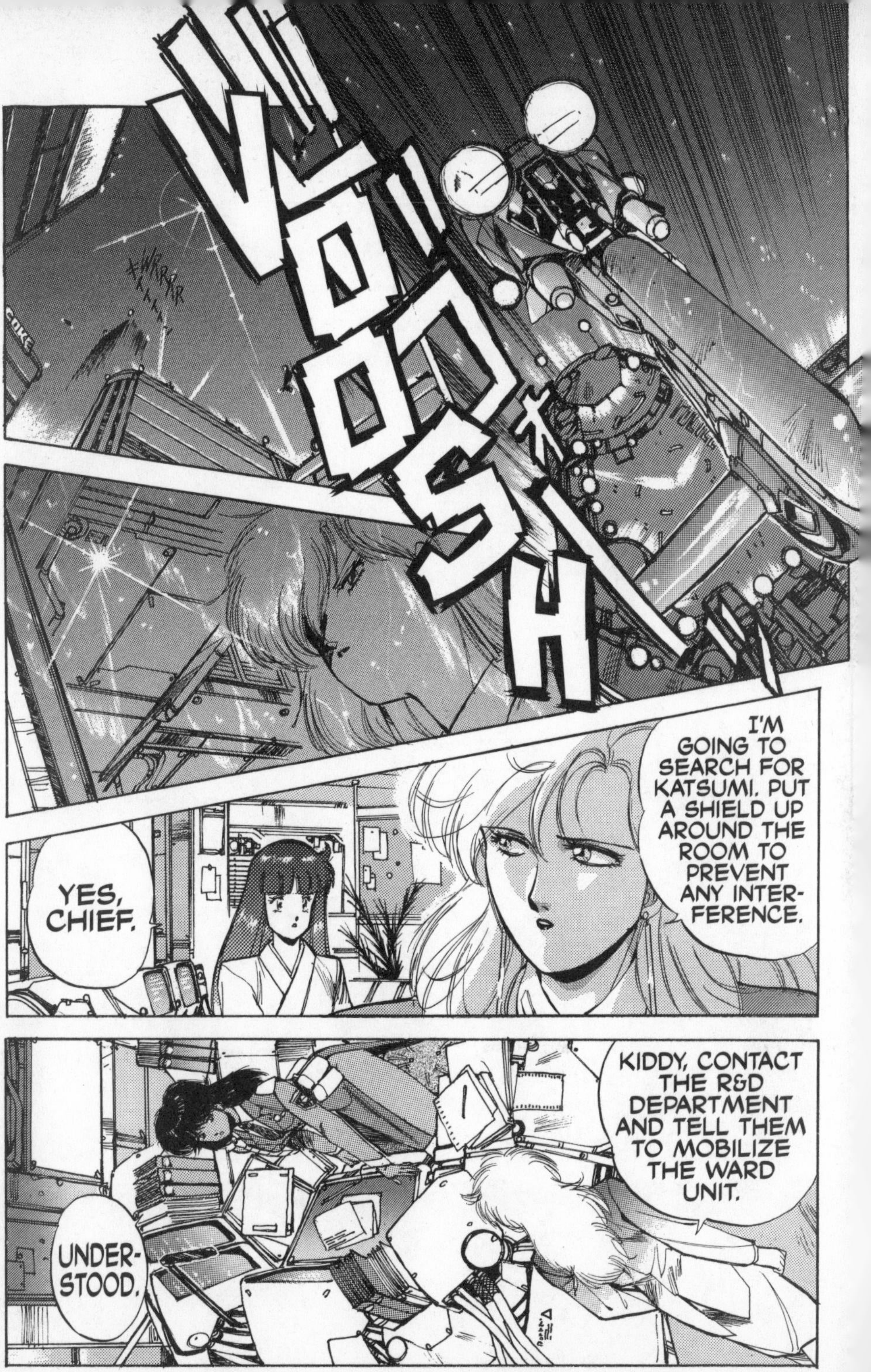
VROOSH
I'M GOING TO SEARCH FOR KATSUMI. PUT A SHIELD UP AROUND THE ROOM TO PREVENT ANY INTER-FERENCE.
YES, CHIEF.
KIDDY, CONTACT THE R&D DEPARTMENT AND TELL THEM TO MOBILIZE THE WARD UNIT.
UNDER-STOOD.

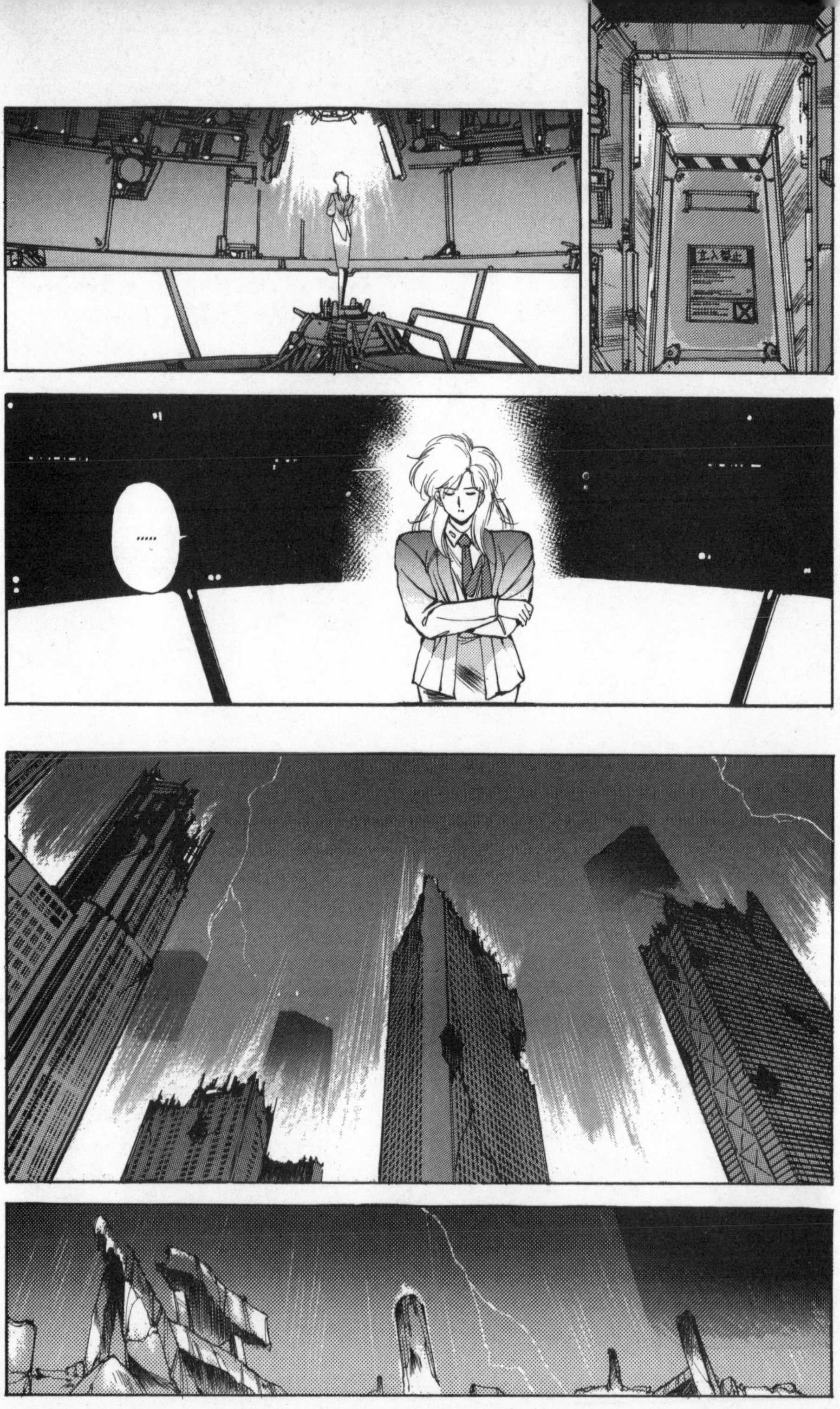
立入禁止
......

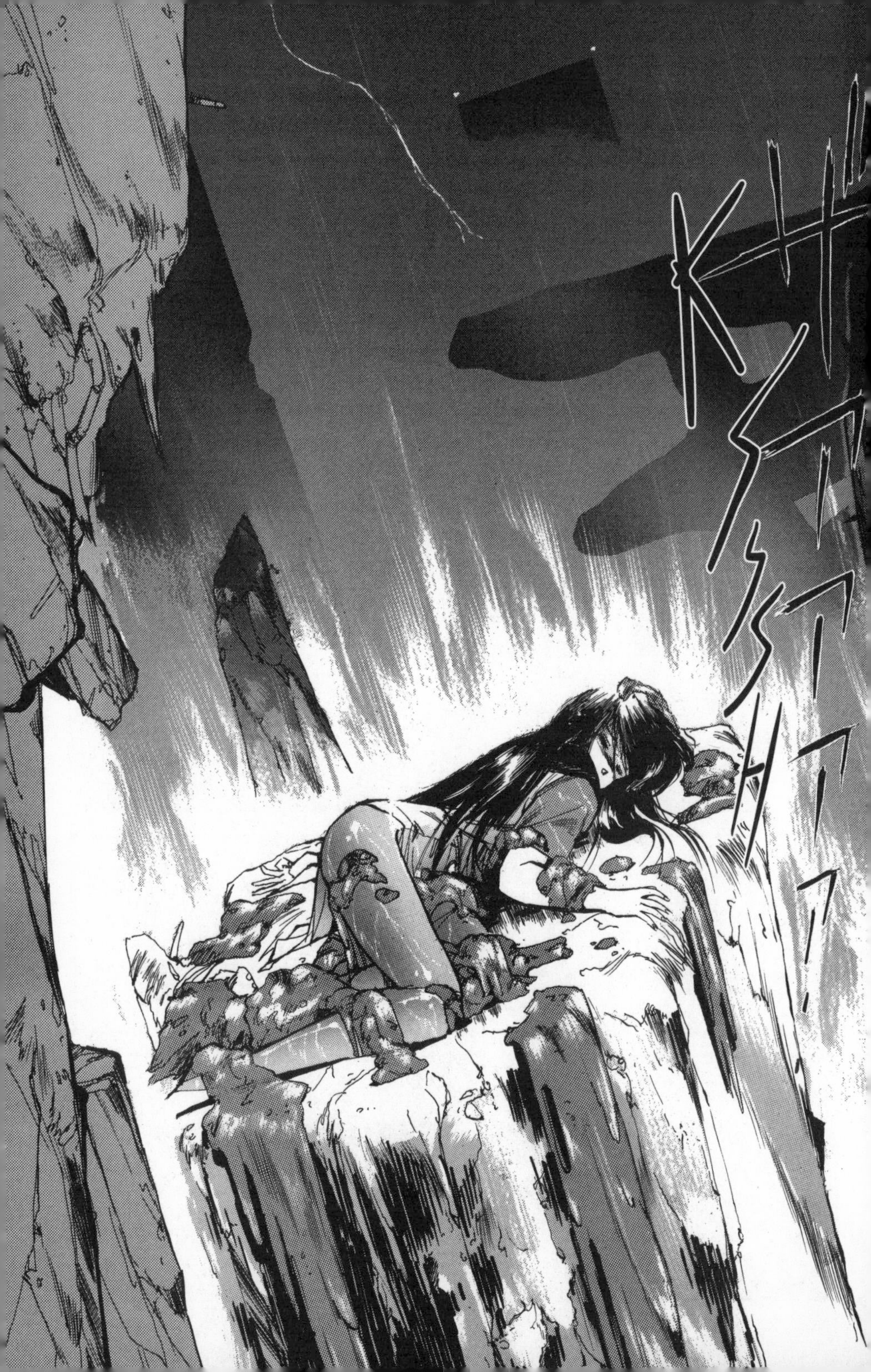
KSSH

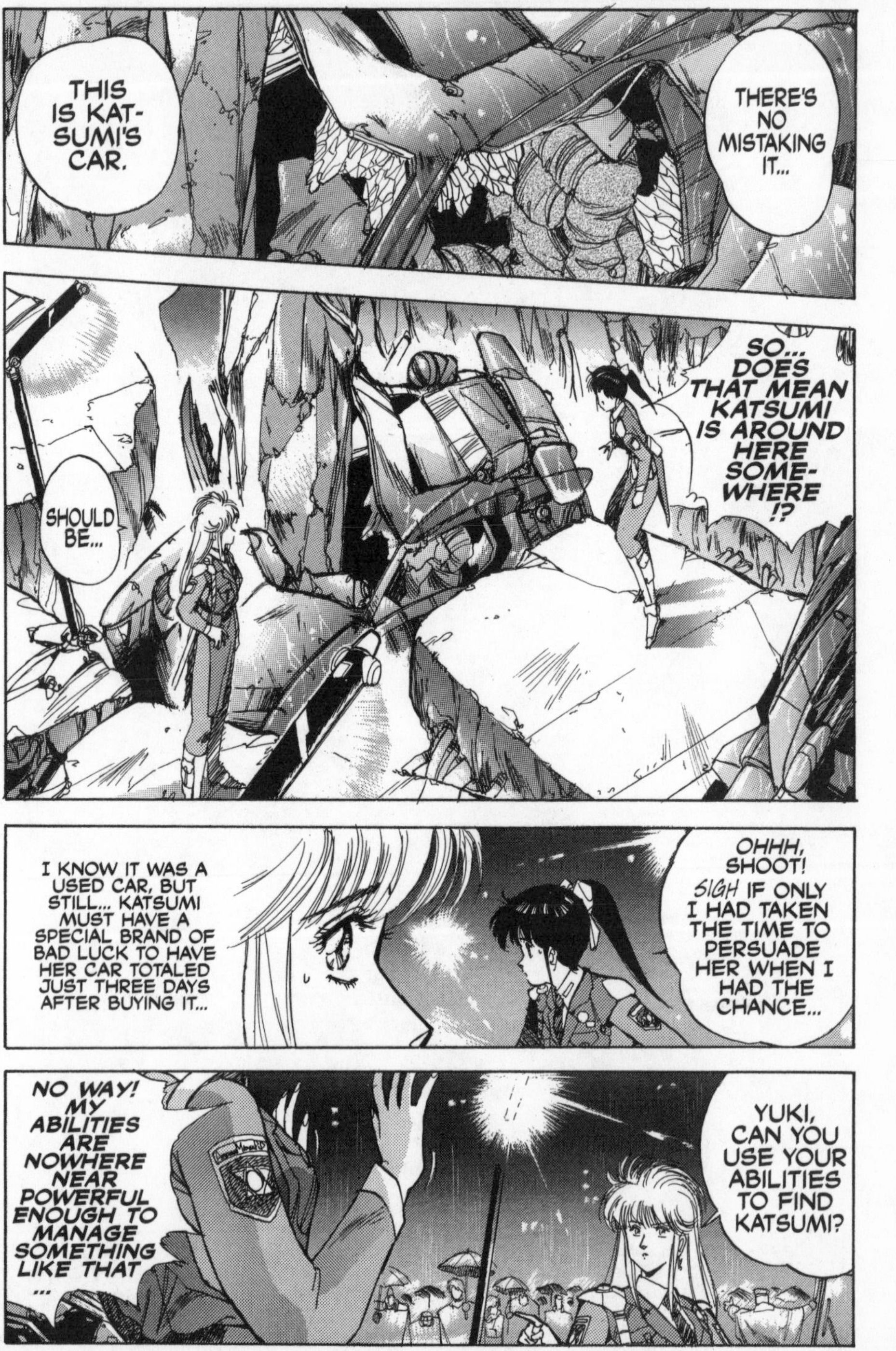
THERE'S NO MISTAKING IT...
THIS IS KAT-SUMI'S CAR.
SO... DOES THAT MEAN KATSUMI IS AROUND HERE SOME-WHERE !?
SHOULD BE...
OHHH, SHOOT! *SIGH* IF ONLY I HAD TAKEN THE TIME TO PERSUADE HER WHEN I HAD THE CHANCE...
I KNOW IT WAS A USED CAR, BUT STILL... KATSUMI MUST HAVE A SPECIAL BRAND OF BAD LUCK TO HAVE HER CAR TOTALED JUST THREE DAYS AFTER BUYING IT...
YUKI, CAN YOU USE YOUR ABILITIES TO FIND KATSUMI?
NO WAY! MY ABILITIES ARE NOWHERE NEAR POWERFUL ENOUGH TO MANAGE SOMETHING LIKE THAT ...

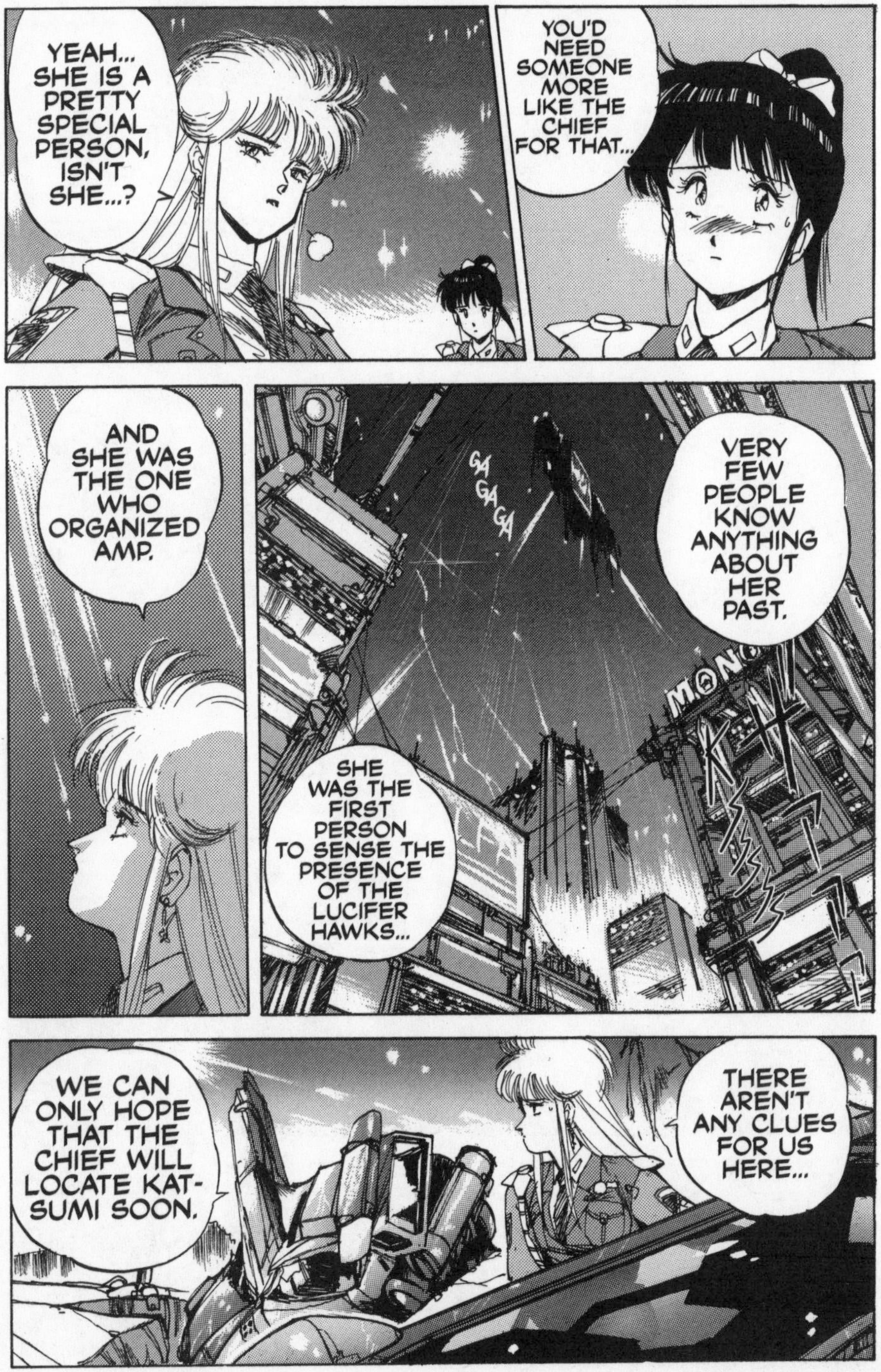
YOU'D NEED SOMEONE MORE LIKE THE CHIEF FOR THAT...
YEAH... SHE IS A PRETTY SPECIAL PERSON, ISN'T SHE...?
GA GA GA
VERY FEW PEOPLE KNOW ANYTHING ABOUT HER PAST.
SHE WAS THE FIRST PERSON TO SENSE THE PRESENCE OF THE LUCIFER HAWKS...
AND SHE WAS THE ONE WHO ORGANIZED AMP.
THERE AREN'T ANY CLUES FOR US HERE...
WE CAN ONLY HOPE THAT THE CHIEF WILL LOCATE KAT-SUMI SOON.

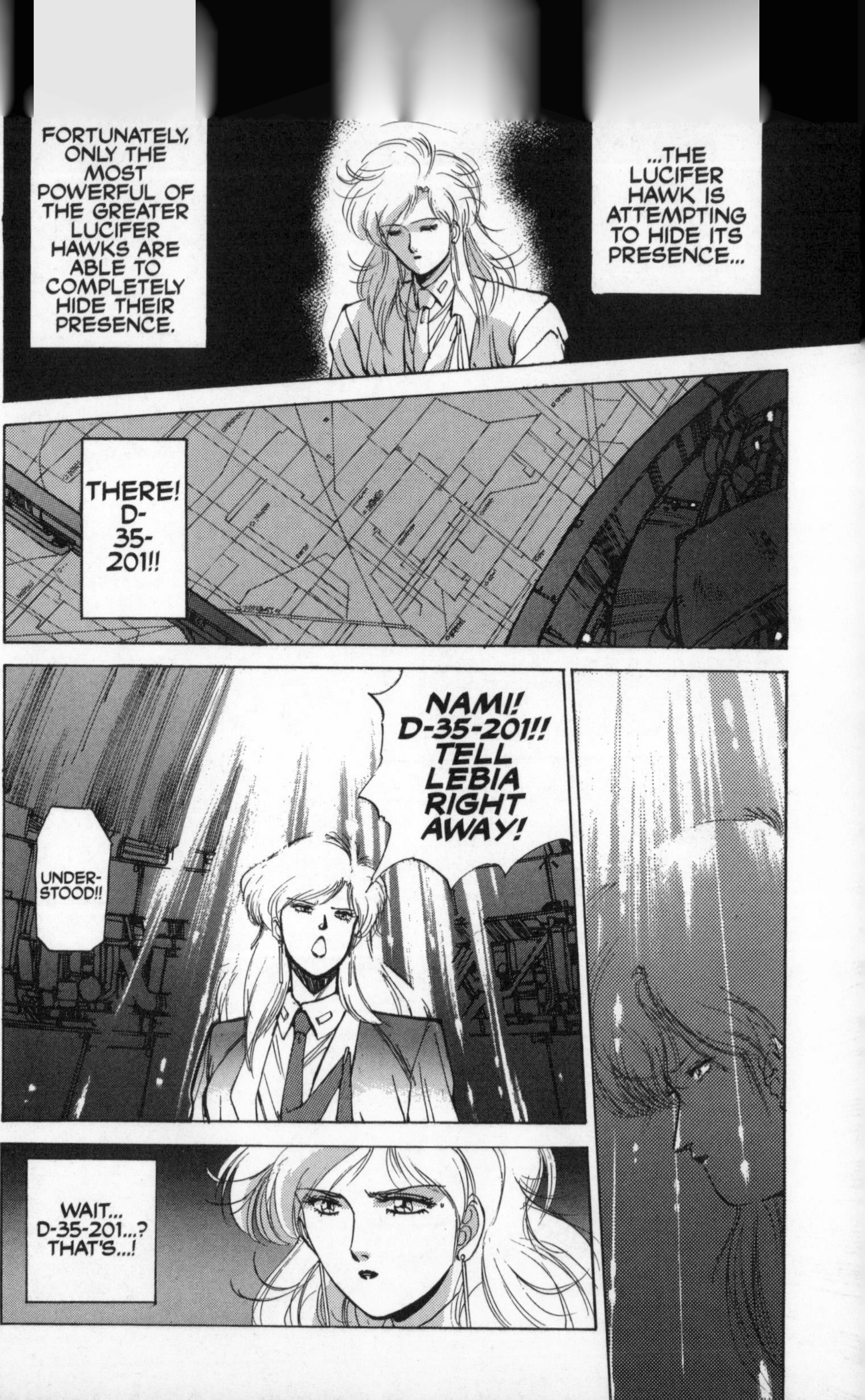
...THE LUCIFER HAWK IS ATTEMPTING TO HIDE ITS PRESENCE...
FORTUNATELY, ONLY THE MOST POWERFUL OF THE GREATER LUCIFER HAWKS ARE ABLE TO COMPLETELY HIDE THEIR PRESENCE.
THERE! D-35-201!!
NAMI! D-35-201!! TELL LEBIA RIGHT AWAY!
UNDER-STOOD!!
WAIT... D-35-201...? THAT'S...!

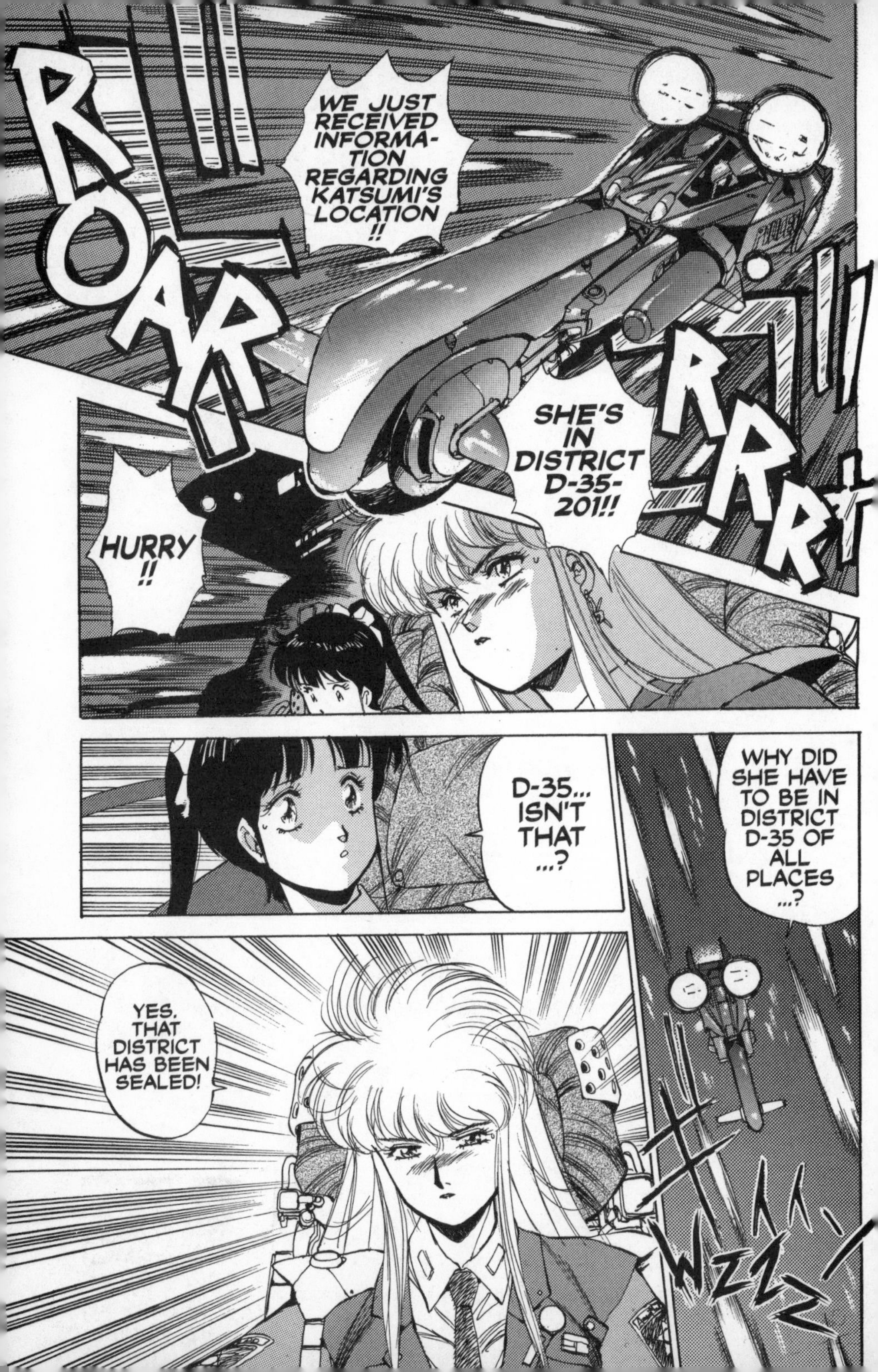
WE JUST RECEIVED INFORMATION REGARDING KATSUMI'S LOCATION !!
ROAR!!
RRRRT!!
SHE'S IN DISTRICT D-35-201!!
HURRY !!
WHY DID SHE HAVE TO BE IN DISTRICT D-35 OF ALL PLACES ...?
WZZZ
D-35... ISN'T THAT ...?
YES. THAT DISTRICT HAS BEEN SEALED!

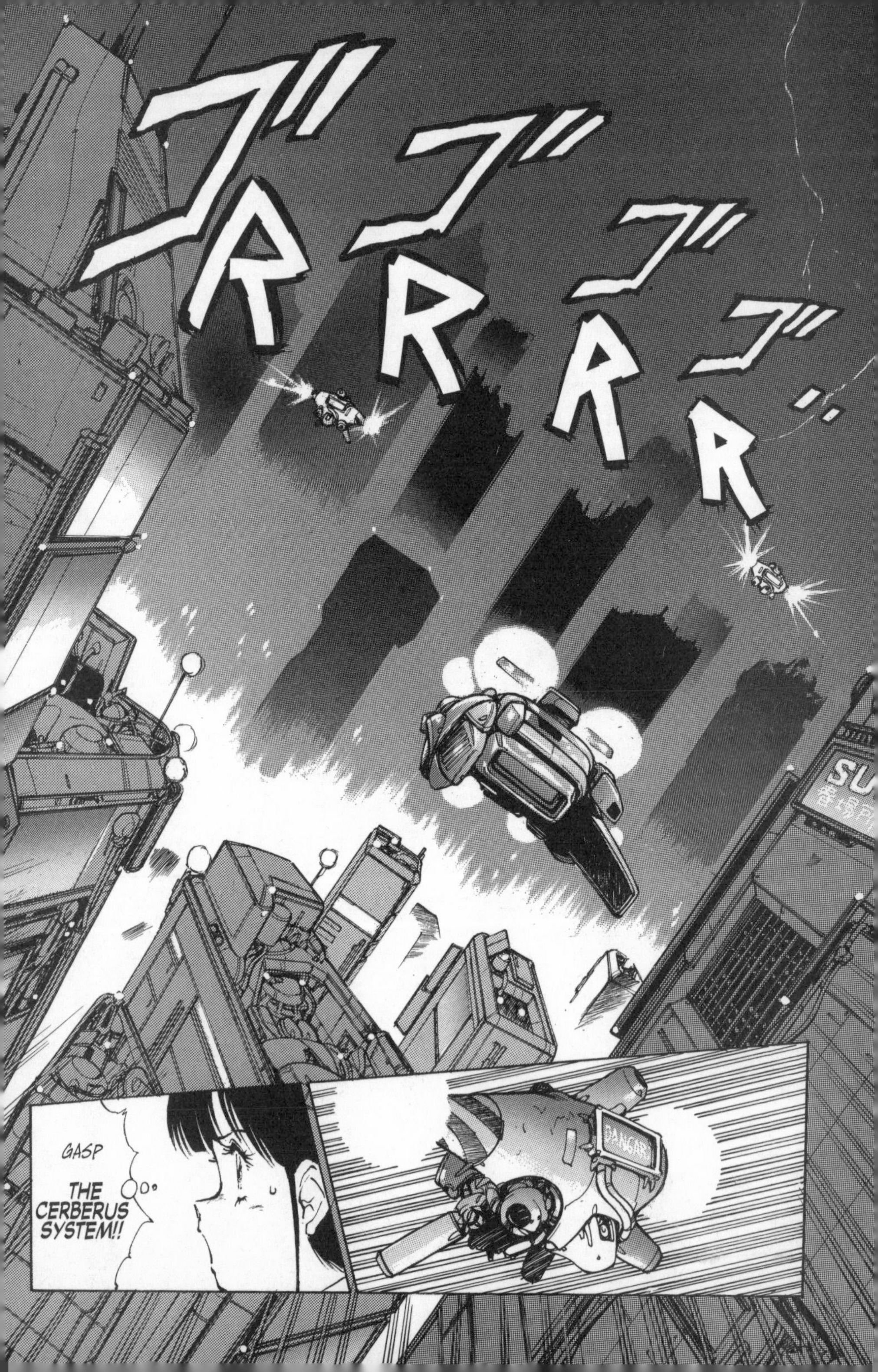
ゴRゴRゴRゴR..
GASP
THE CERBERUS SYSTEM!!

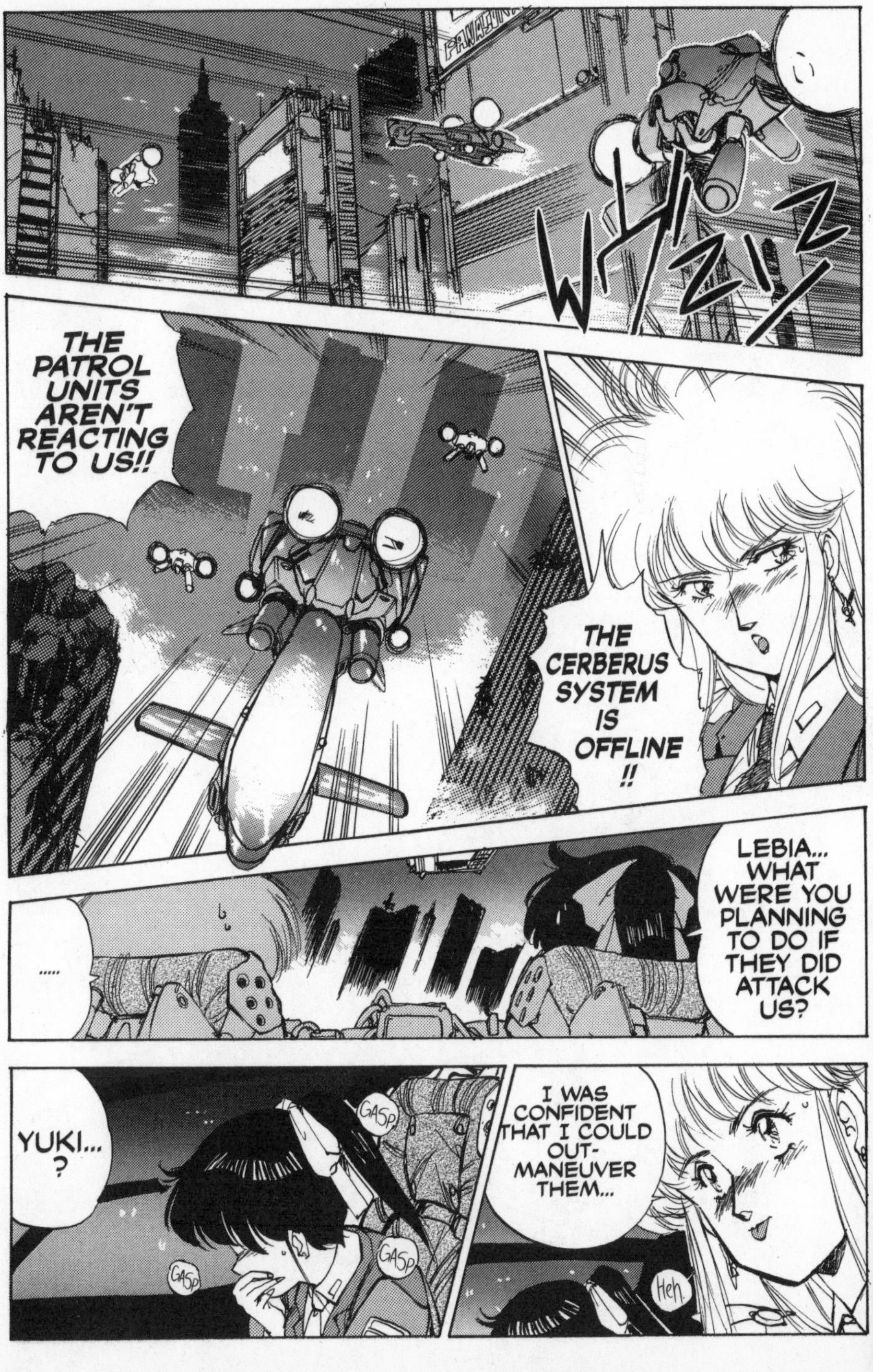
THE CERBERUS SYSTEM IS OFFLINE !!
THE PATROL UNITS AREN'T REACTING TO US!!
LEBIA... WHAT WERE YOU PLANNING TO DO IF THEY DID ATTACK US?
.....
I WAS CONFIDENT THAT I COULD OUT-MANEUVER THEM...
Heh.
GASP
GASP
GASP
YUKI... ?

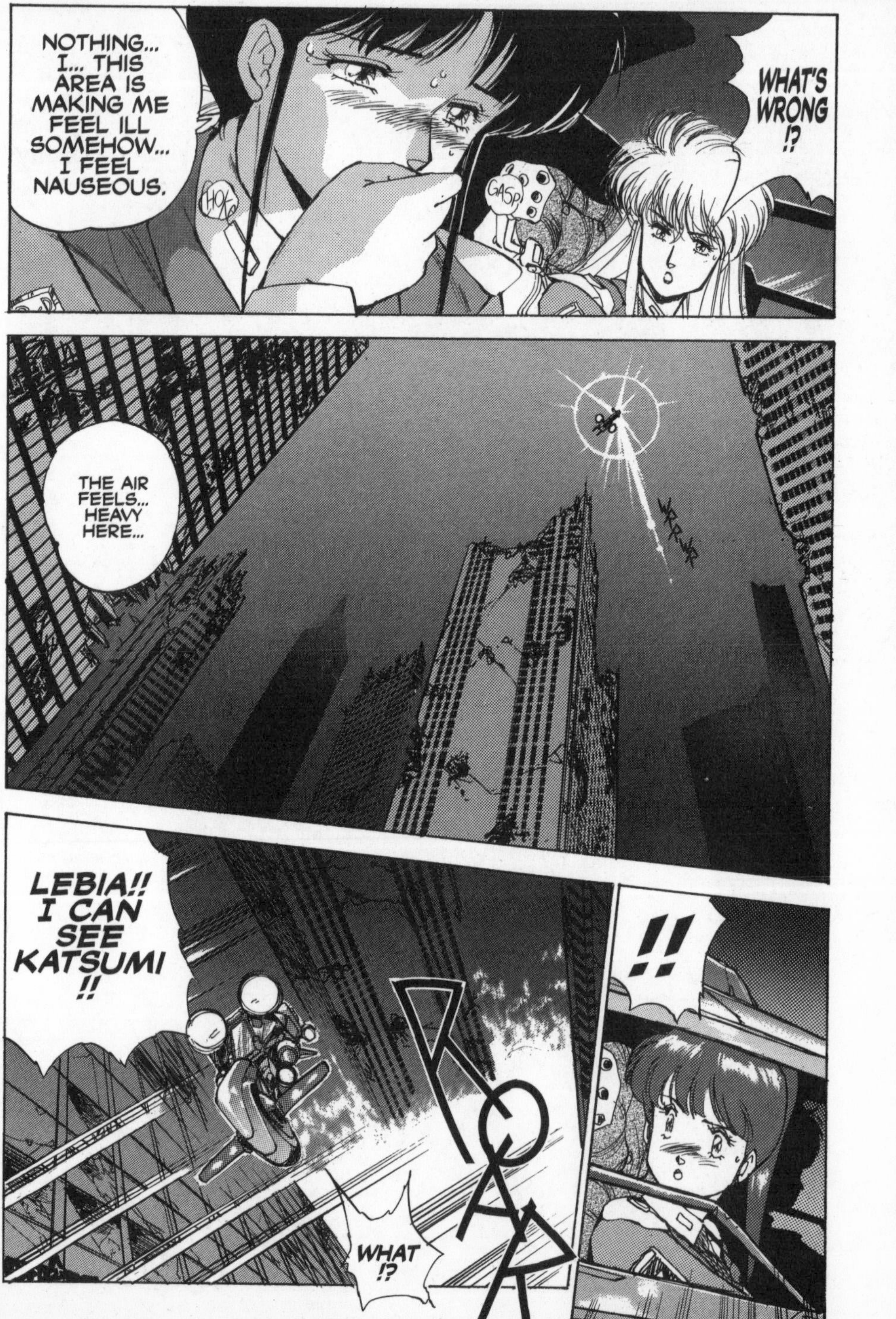
WHAT'S WRONG !?
NOTHING... I... THIS AREA IS MAKING ME FEEL ILL SOMEHOW... I FEEL NAUSEOUS.
GASP
THE AIR FEELS... HEAVY HERE...
!!
LEBIA!! I CAN SEE KATSUMI !!
ROAR
WHAT !?

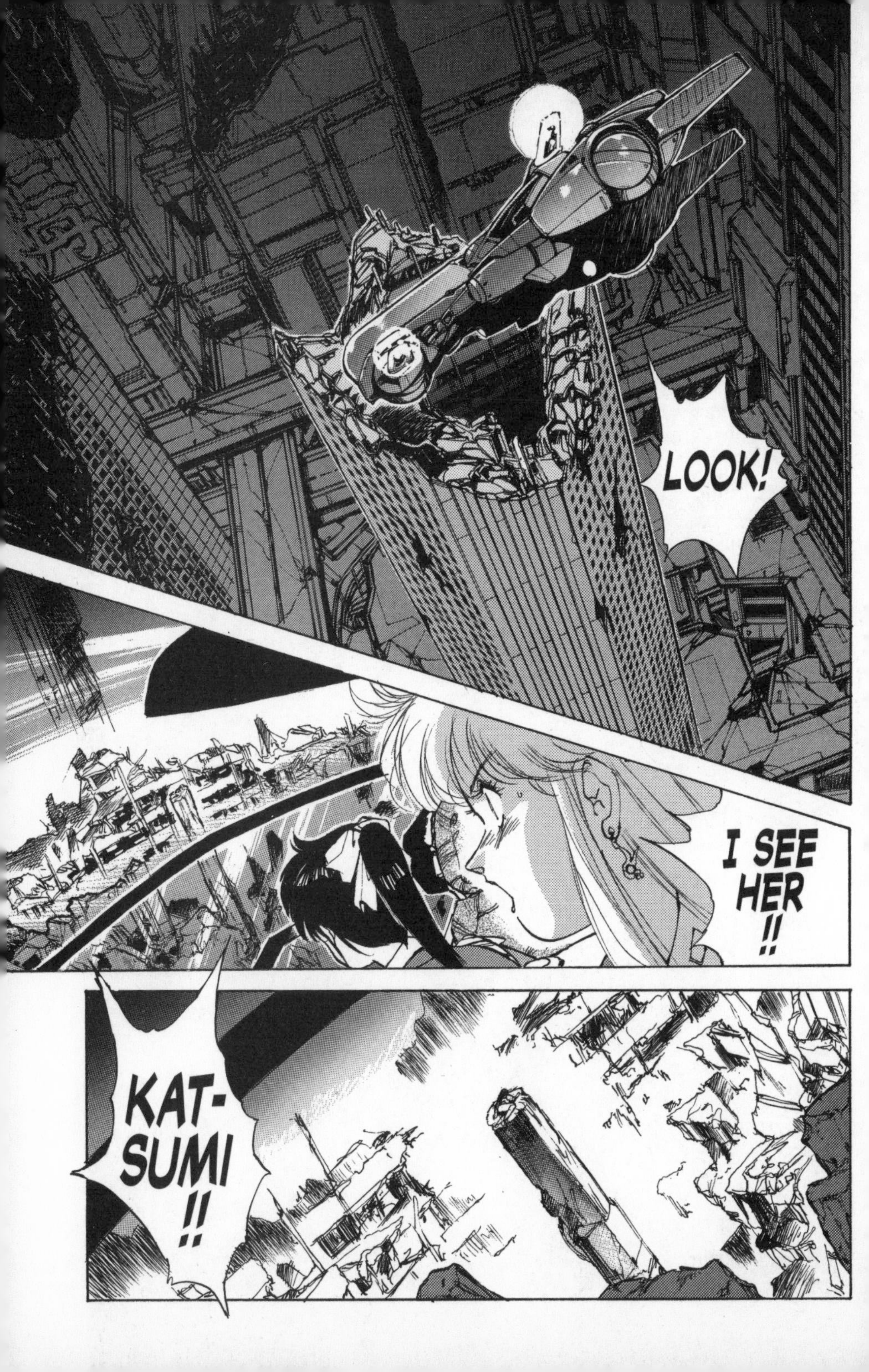
LOOK!
I SEE HER !!
KAT-SUMI !!

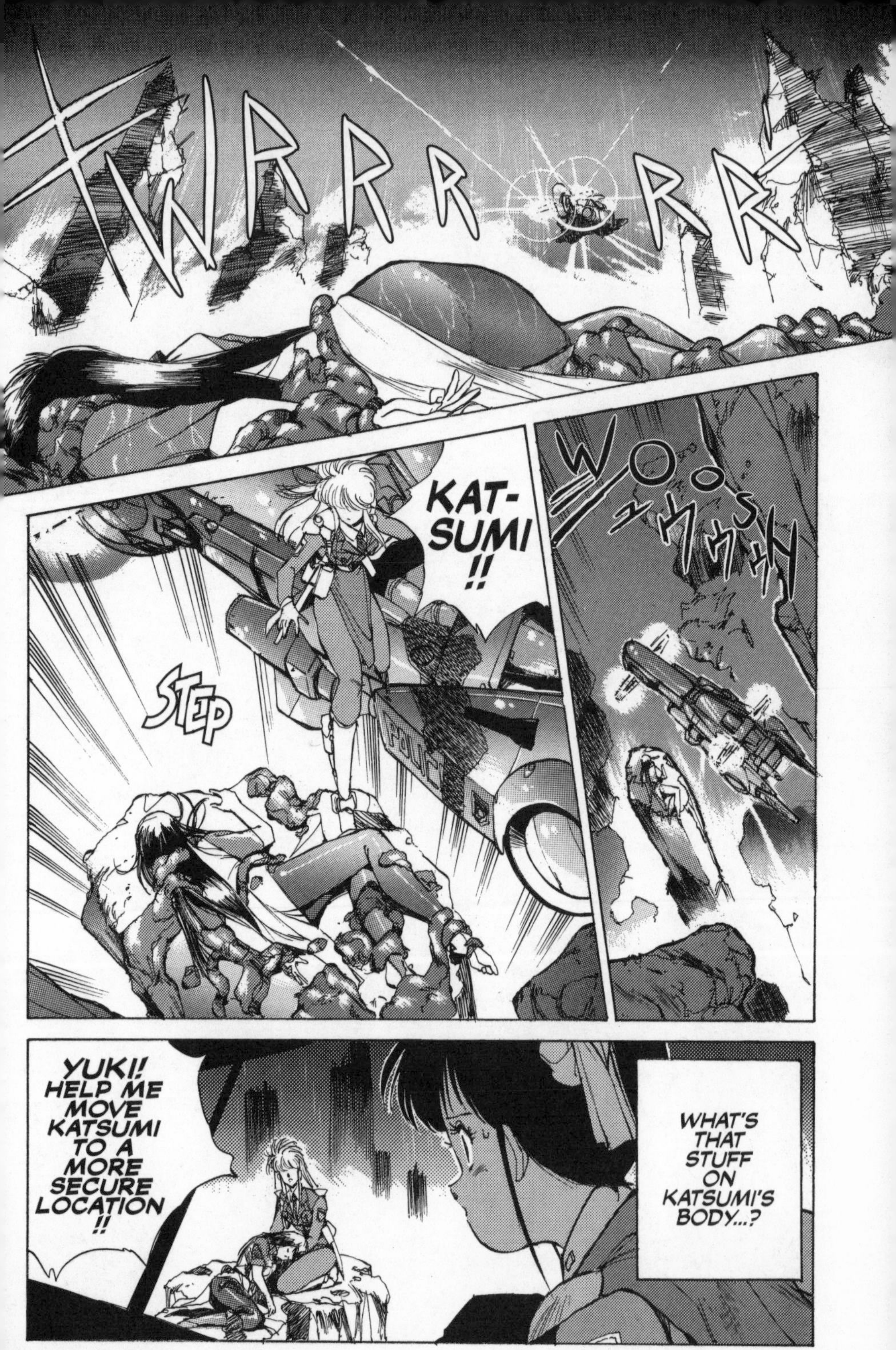
WRRRRR
WOOSH
KAT-SUMI!!
STEP
WHAT'S THAT STUFF ON KATSUMI'S BODY...?
YUKI! HELP ME MOVE KATSUMI TO A MORE SECURE LOCATION!!

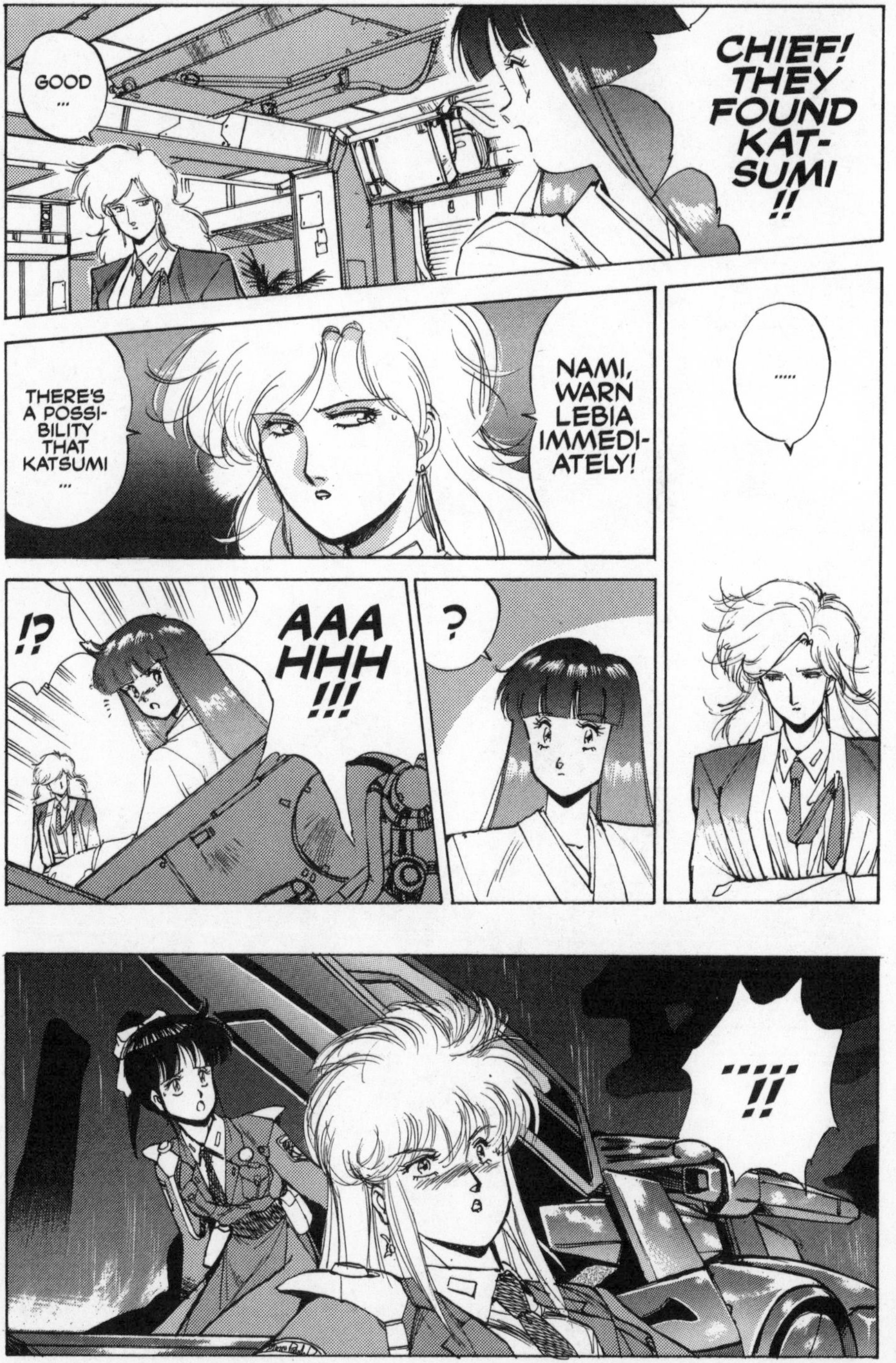

CHIEF! THEY FOUND KAT-SUMI !!
GOOD ...
.....
NAMI, WARN LEBIA IMMEDI-ATELY!
THERE'S A POSSI-BILITY THAT KATSUMI ...
?
AAA HHH !!!
!?
...!!

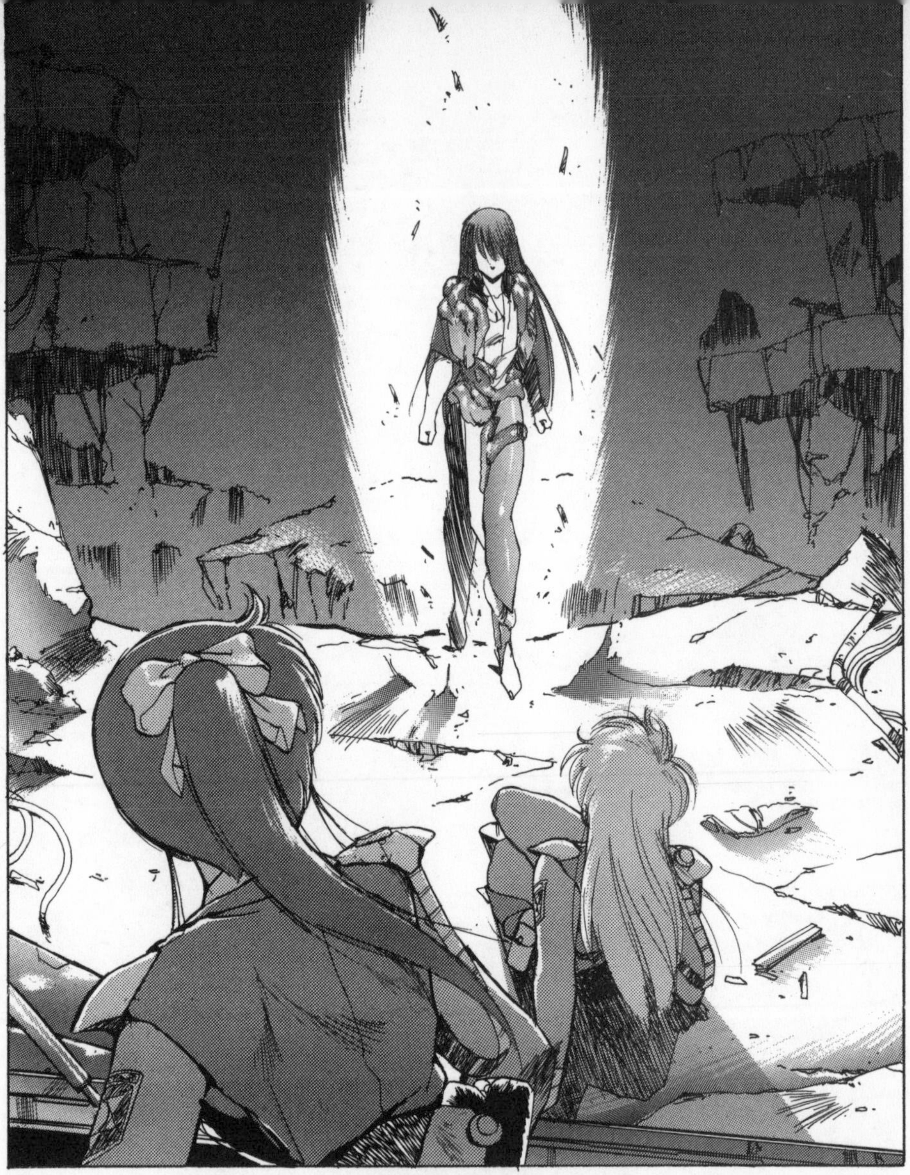
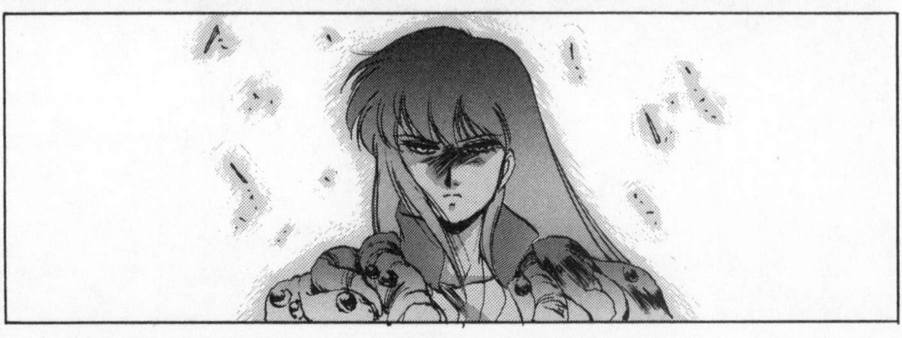

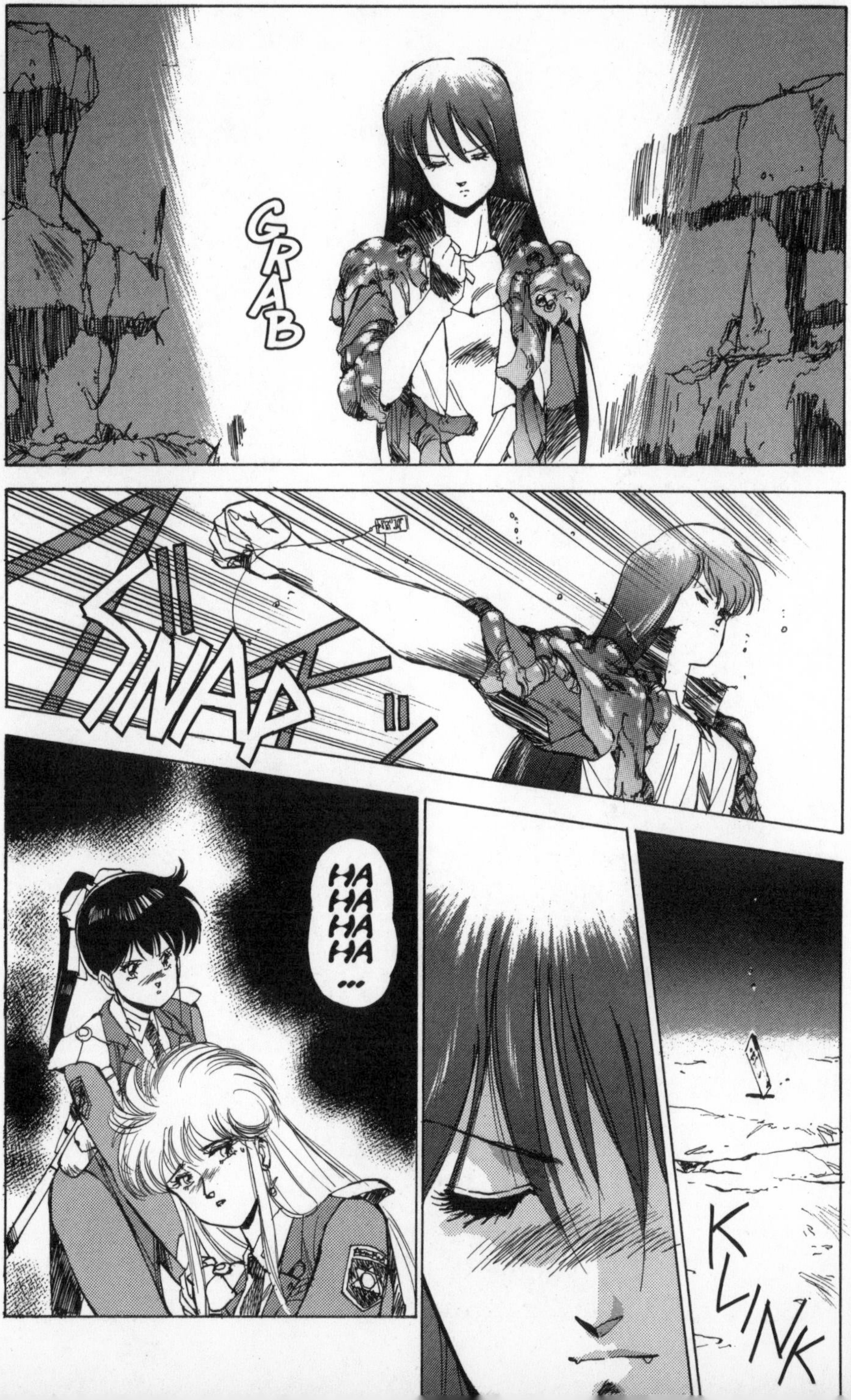
GRAB
SNAP
KLINK
HA HA HA HA ...

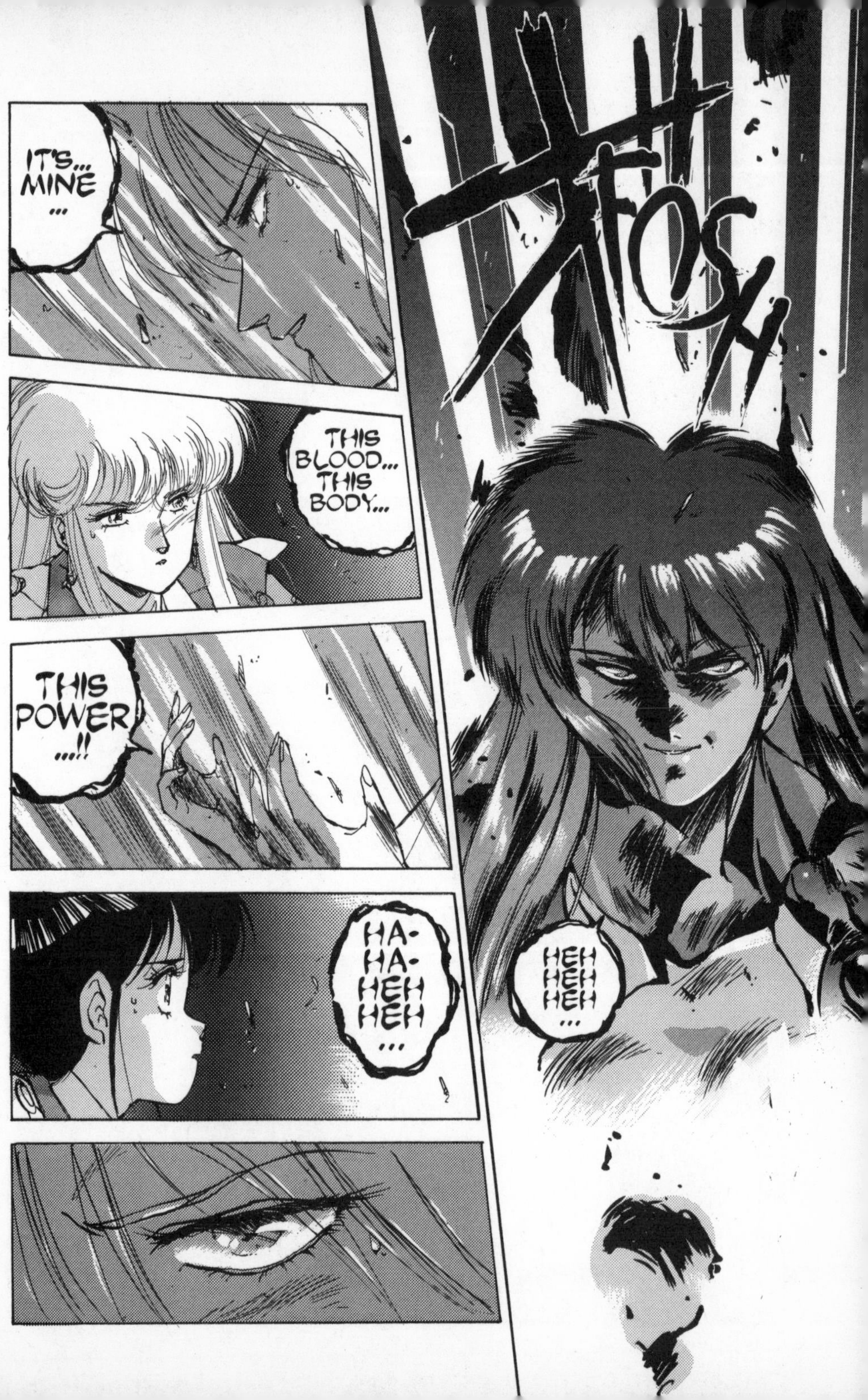
IT'S... MINE ...
THIS BLOOD... THIS BODY...
THIS POWER ...!!
HA-HA-HEH HEH ...
FOSH
HEH HEH HEH ...

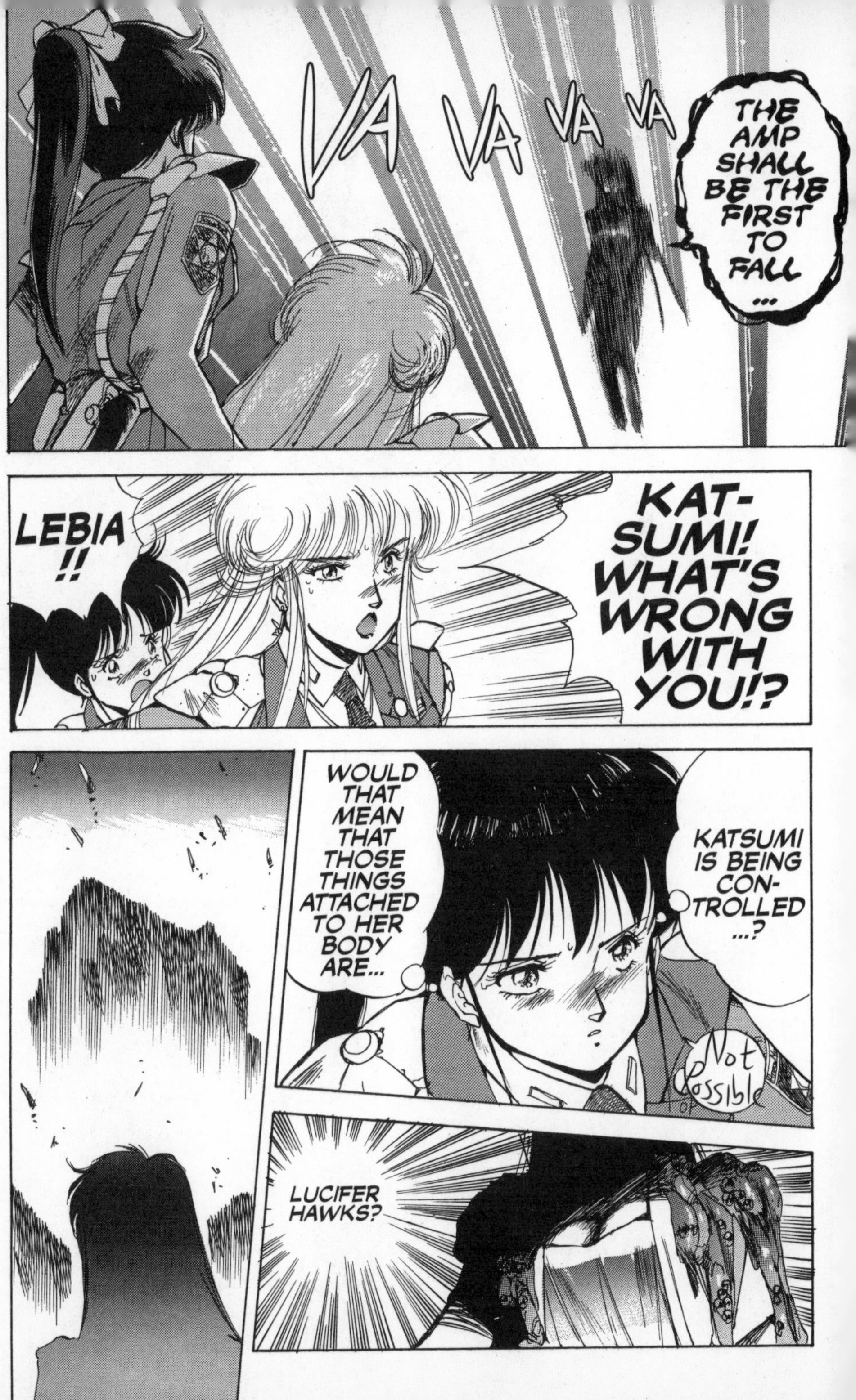
THE AMP SHALL BE THE FIRST TO FALL ...
VA VA VA VA
KAT-SUMI! WHAT'S WRONG WITH YOU!?
LEBIA !!
KATSUMI IS BEING CON-TROLLED ...?
WOULD THAT MEAN THAT THOSE THINGS ATTACHED TO HER BODY ARE...
Not Possible
LUCIFER HAWKS?

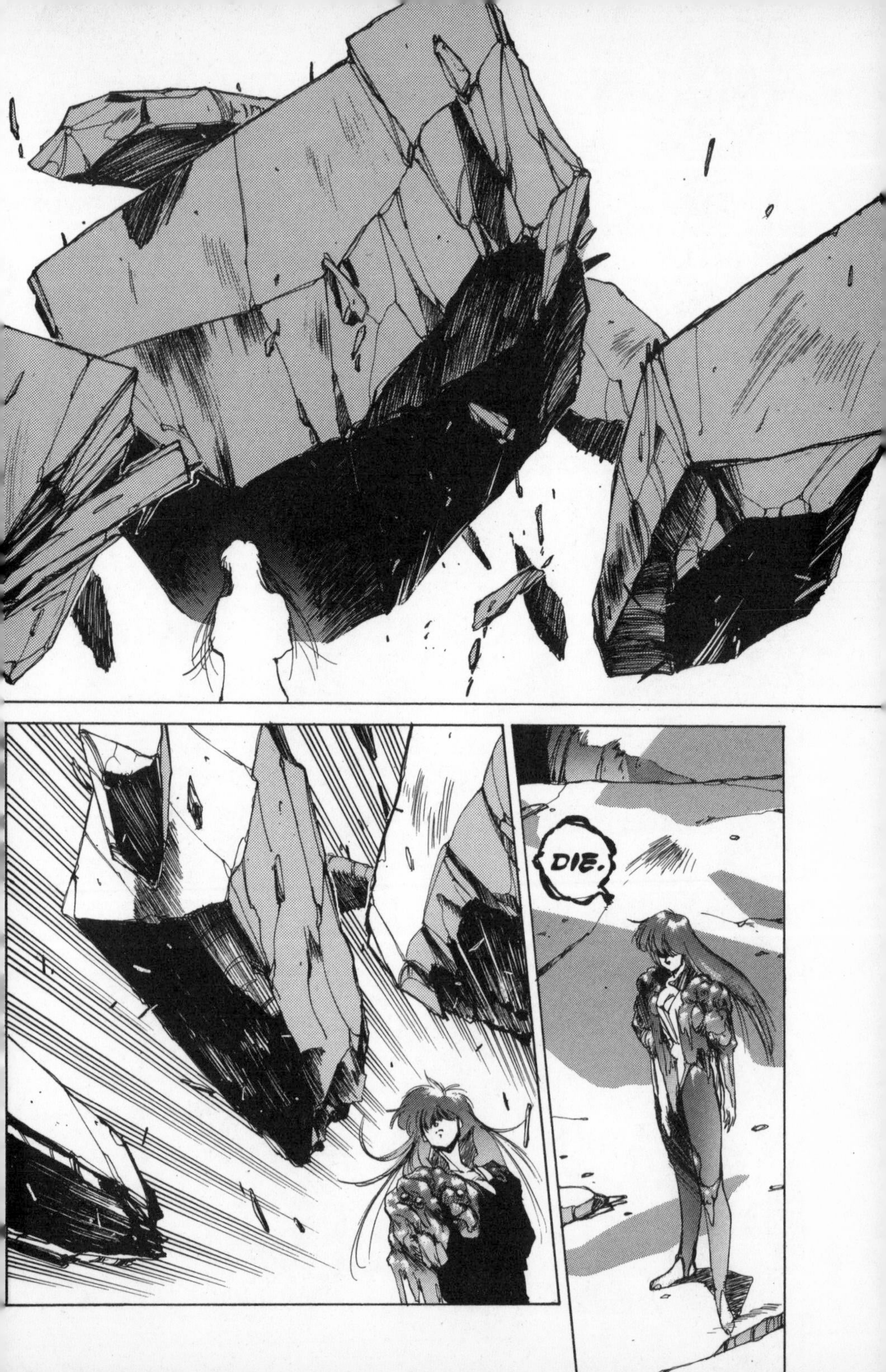
DIE.

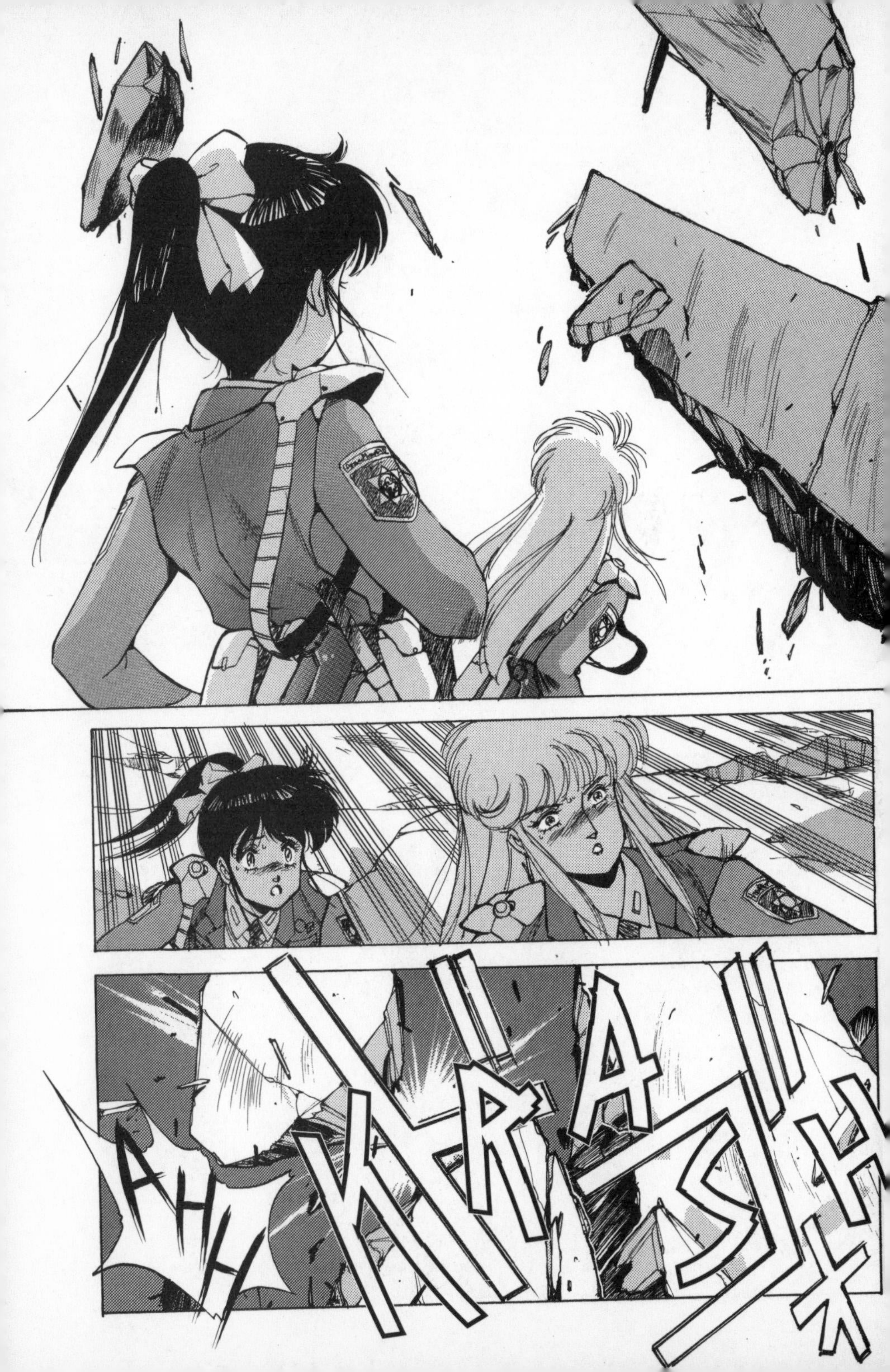
KRASH
AHH

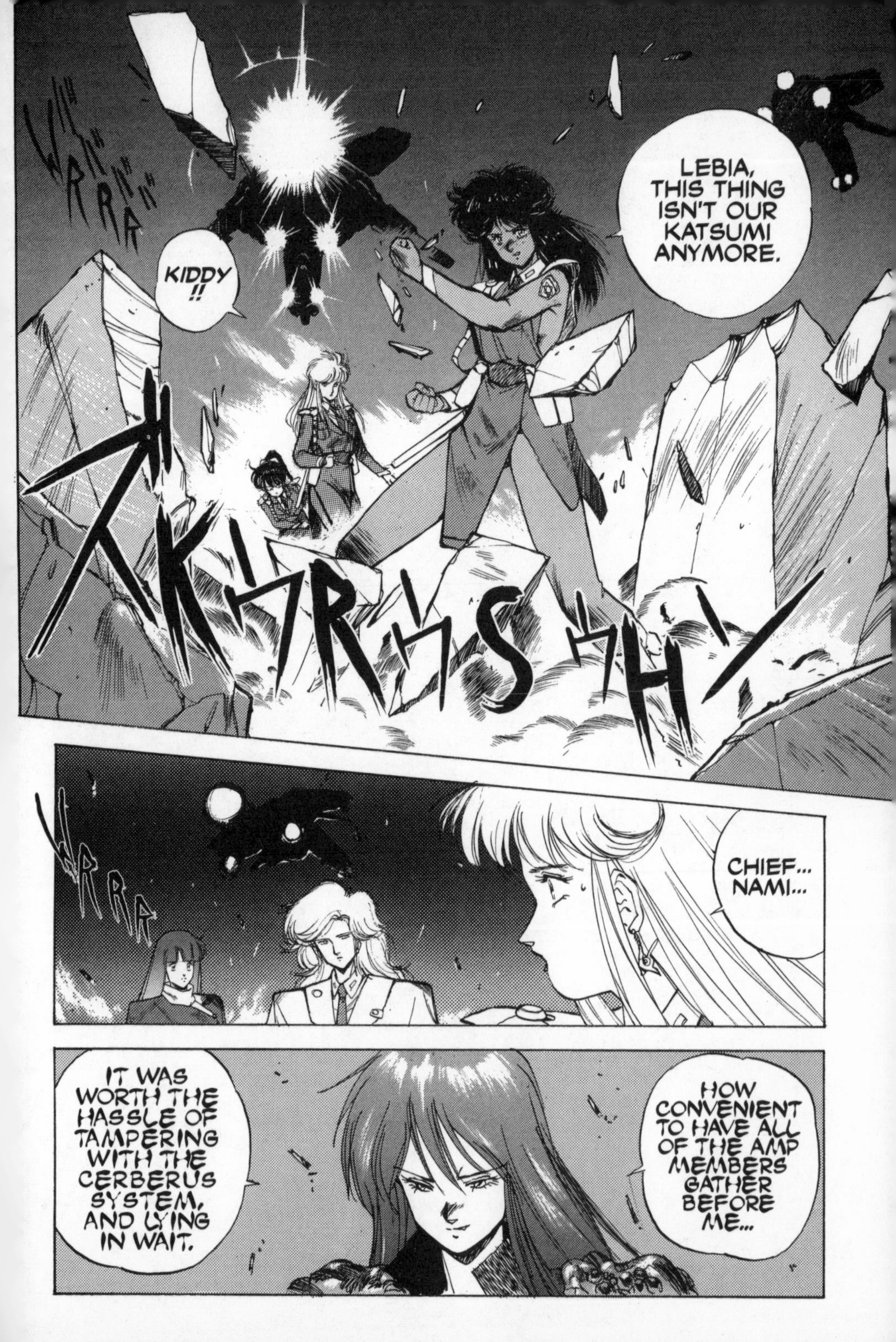
LEBIA, THIS THING ISN'T OUR KATSUMI ANYMORE.
KIDDY!!
CHIEF... NAMI...
HOW CONVENIENT TO HAVE ALL OF THE AMP MEMBERS GATHER BEFORE ME...
IT WAS WORTH THE HASSLE OF TAMPERING WITH THE CERBERUS SYSTEM, AND LYING IN WAIT.

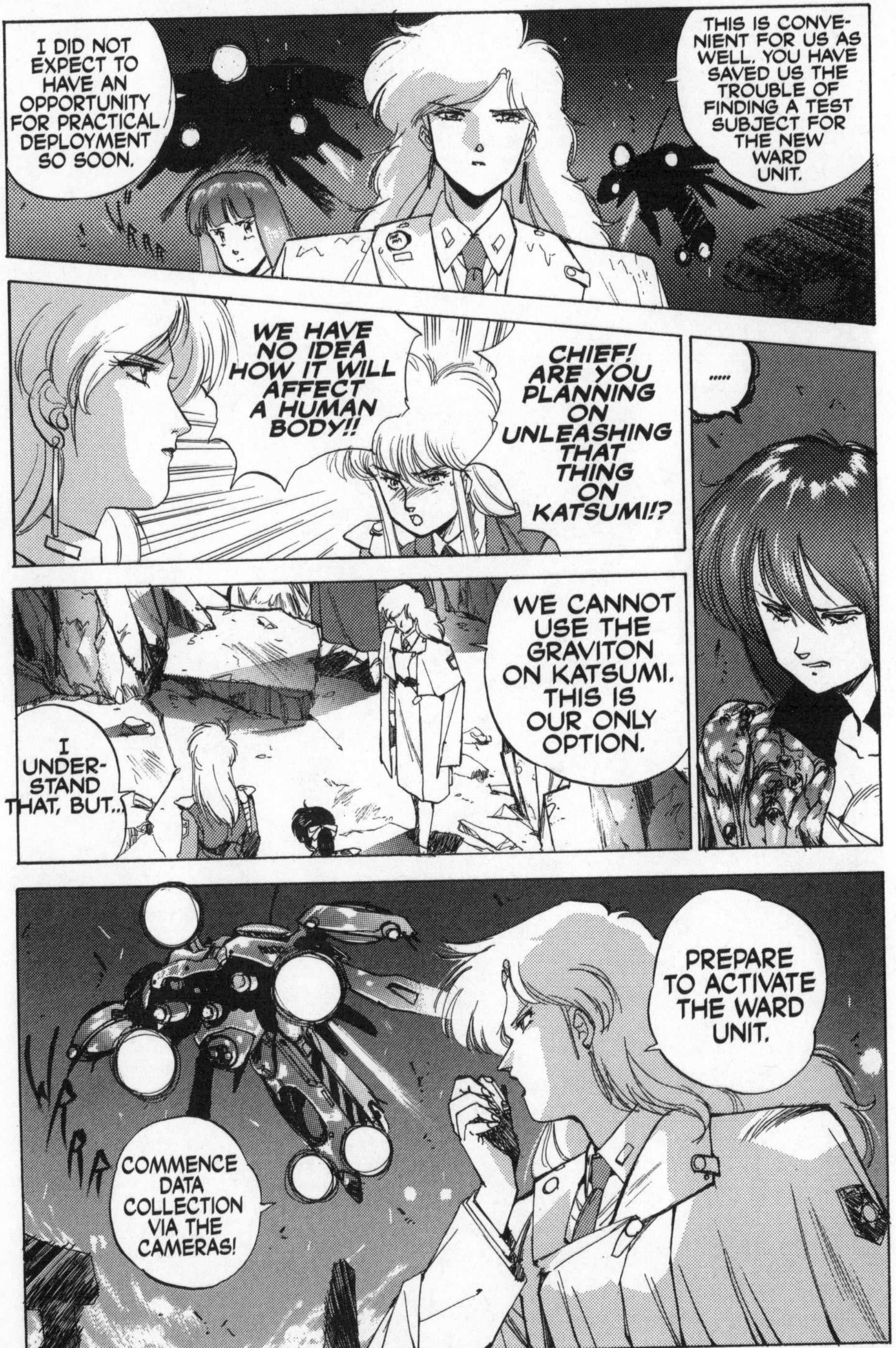
THIS IS CONVENIENT FOR US AS WELL. YOU HAVE SAVED US THE TROUBLE OF FINDING A TEST SUBJECT FOR THE NEW WARD UNIT.
I DID NOT EXPECT TO HAVE AN OPPORTUNITY FOR PRACTICAL DEPLOYMENT SO SOON.
.....
CHIEF! ARE YOU PLANNING ON UNLEASHING THAT THING ON KATSUMI!?
WE HAVE NO IDEA HOW IT WILL AFFECT A HUMAN BODY!!
WE CANNOT USE THE GRAVITON ON KATSUMI. THIS IS OUR ONLY OPTION.
I UNDERSTAND THAT, BUT...
PREPARE TO ACTIVATE THE WARD UNIT.
COMMENCE DATA COLLECTION VIA THE CAMERAS!

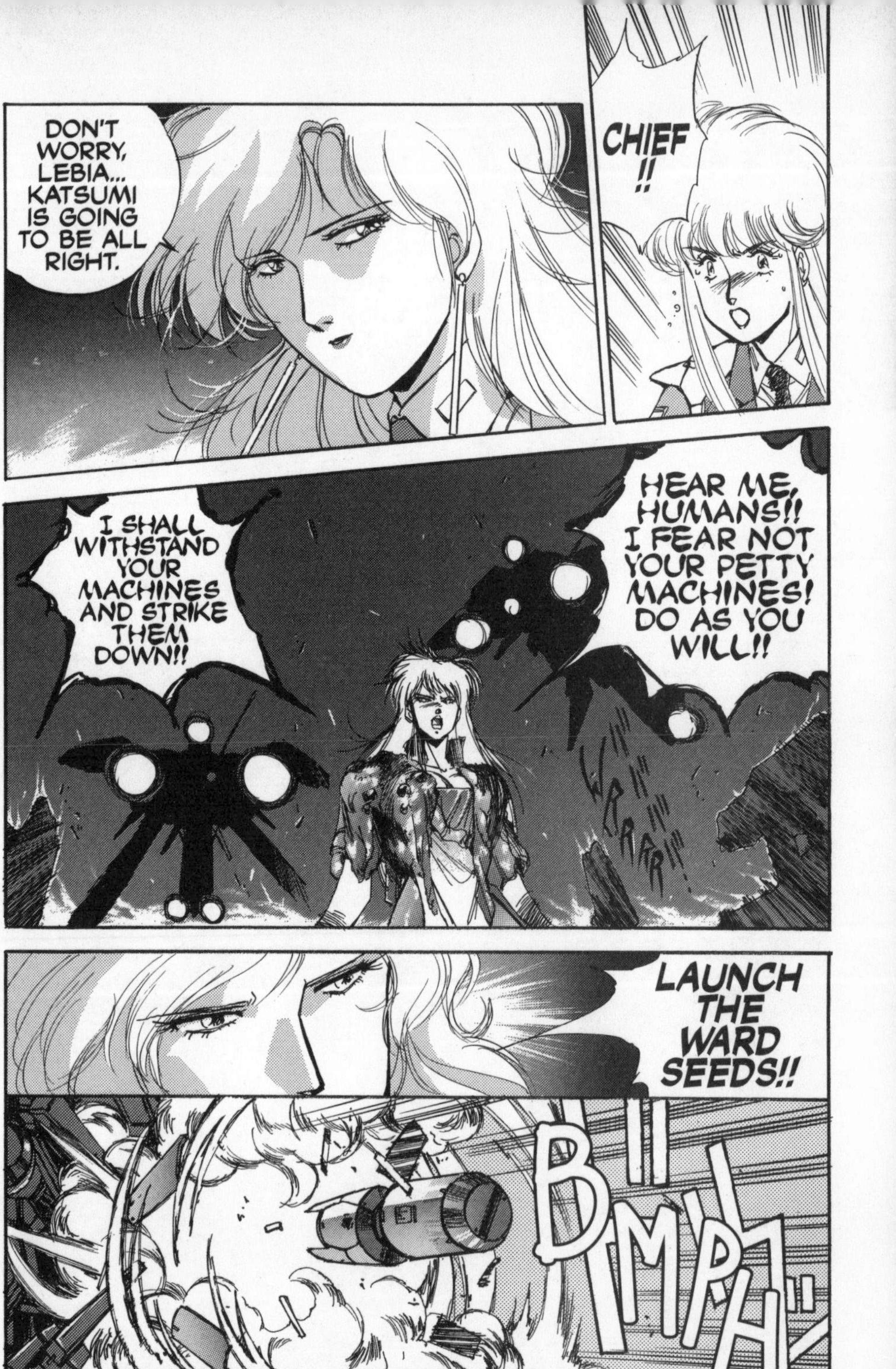
CHIEF !!
DON'T WORRY, LEBIA... KATSUMI IS GOING TO BE ALL RIGHT.
HEAR ME, HUMANS!! I FEAR NOT YOUR PETTY MACHINES! DO AS YOU WILL!!
I SHALL WITHSTAND YOUR MACHINES AND STRIKE THEM DOWN!!
WRRRR
LAUNCH THE WARD SEEDS!!
BMPH

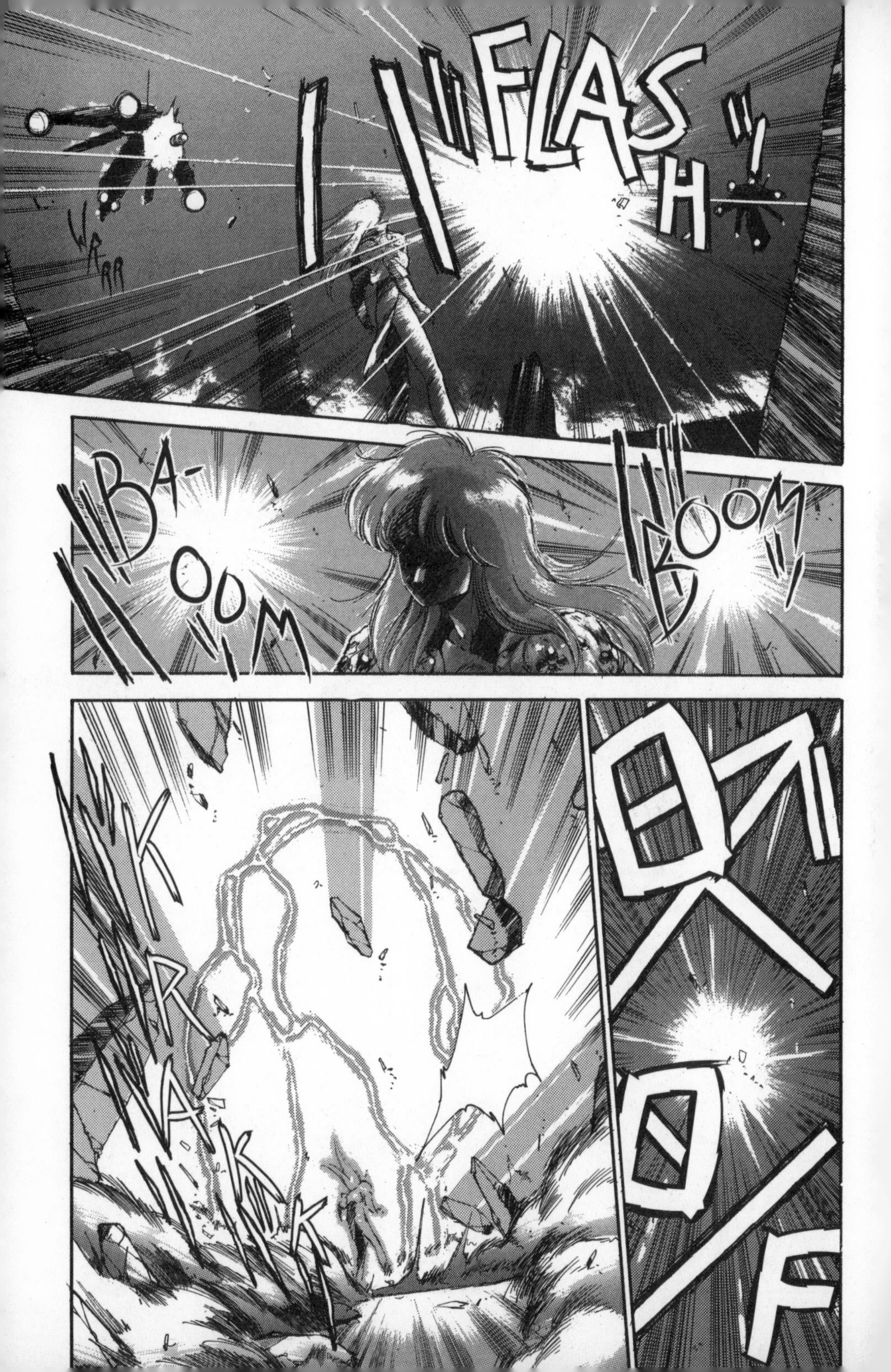
FLASH!
WARRR
BOOM
BA-OOOM
KRAKKK

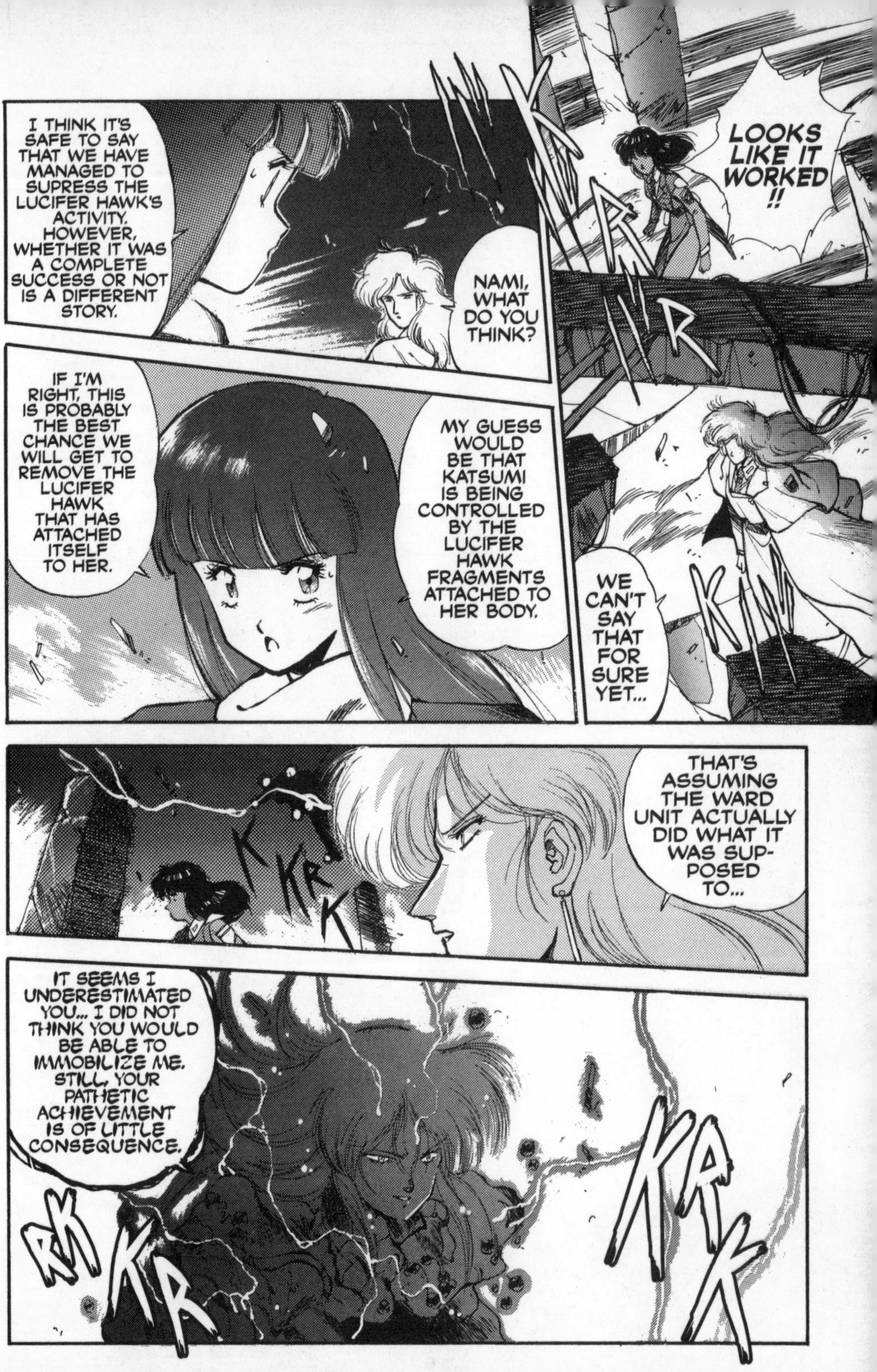

KRRR
LOOKS LIKE IT WORKED!!
I THINK IT'S SAFE TO SAY THAT WE HAVE MANAGED TO SUPRESS THE LUCIFER HAWK'S ACTIVITY. HOWEVER, WHETHER IT WAS A COMPLETE SUCCESS OR NOT IS A DIFFERENT STORY.
NAMI, WHAT DO YOU THINK?
KRK
WE CAN'T SAY THAT FOR SURE YET...
MY GUESS WOULD BE THAT KATSUMI IS BEING CONTROLLED BY THE LUCIFER HAWK FRAGMENTS ATTACHED TO HER BODY.
IF I'M RIGHT, THIS IS PROBABLY THE BEST CHANCE WE WILL GET TO REMOVE THE LUCIFER HAWK THAT HAS ATTACHED ITSELF TO HER.
THAT'S ASSUMING THE WARD UNIT ACTUALLY DID WHAT IT WAS SUP-POSED TO...
KKRK
KRK
IT SEEMS I UNDERESTIMATED YOU... I DID NOT THINK YOU WOULD BE ABLE TO IMMOBILIZE ME. STILL, YOUR PATHETIC ACHIEVEMENT IS OF LITTLE CONSEQUENCE.
RK KR R

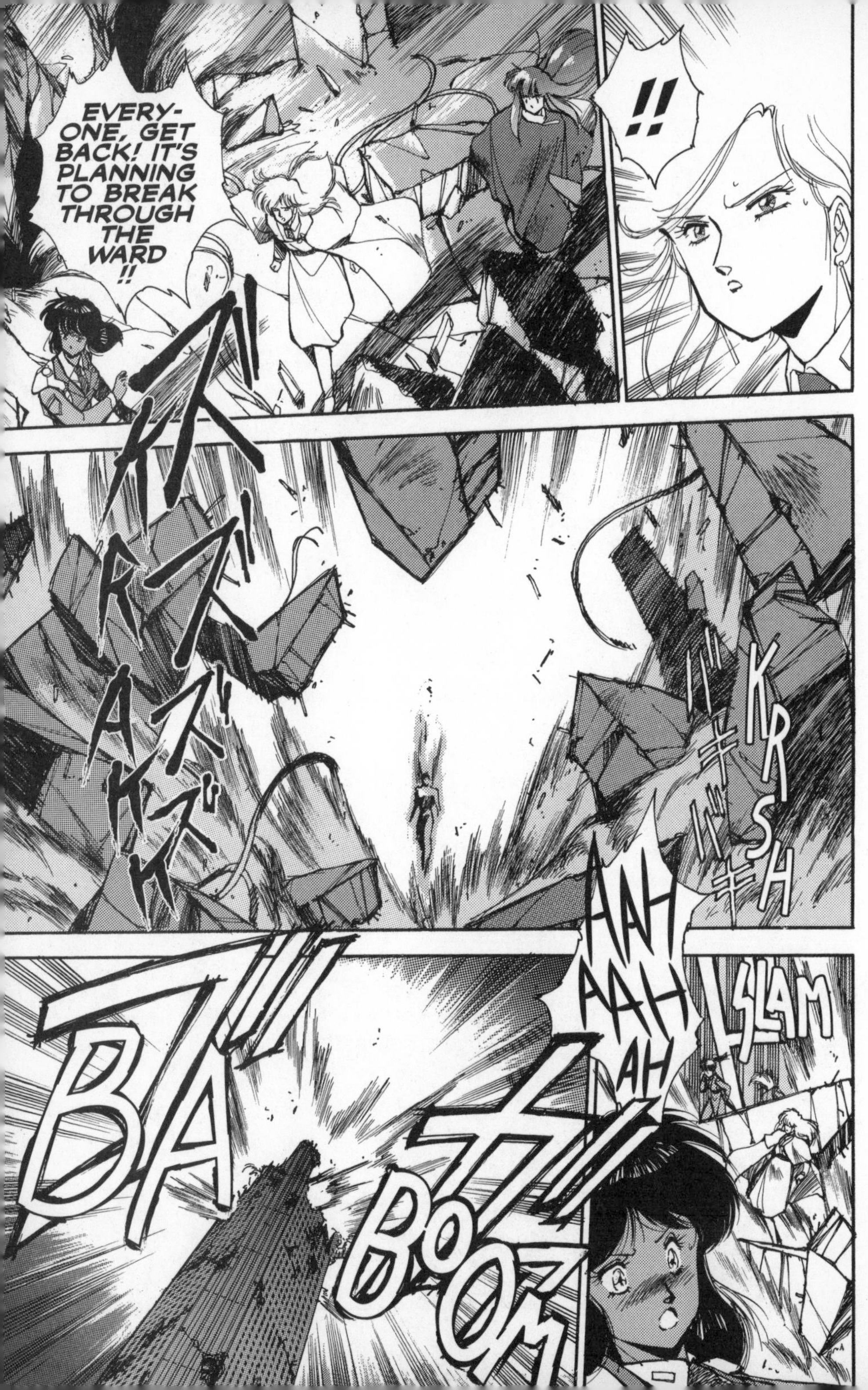
!!
EVERY-ONE, GET BACK! IT'S PLANNING TO BREAK THROUGH THE WARD !!
KRSH
RAHH
AAH AAH AH
SLAM
BOOM
BA

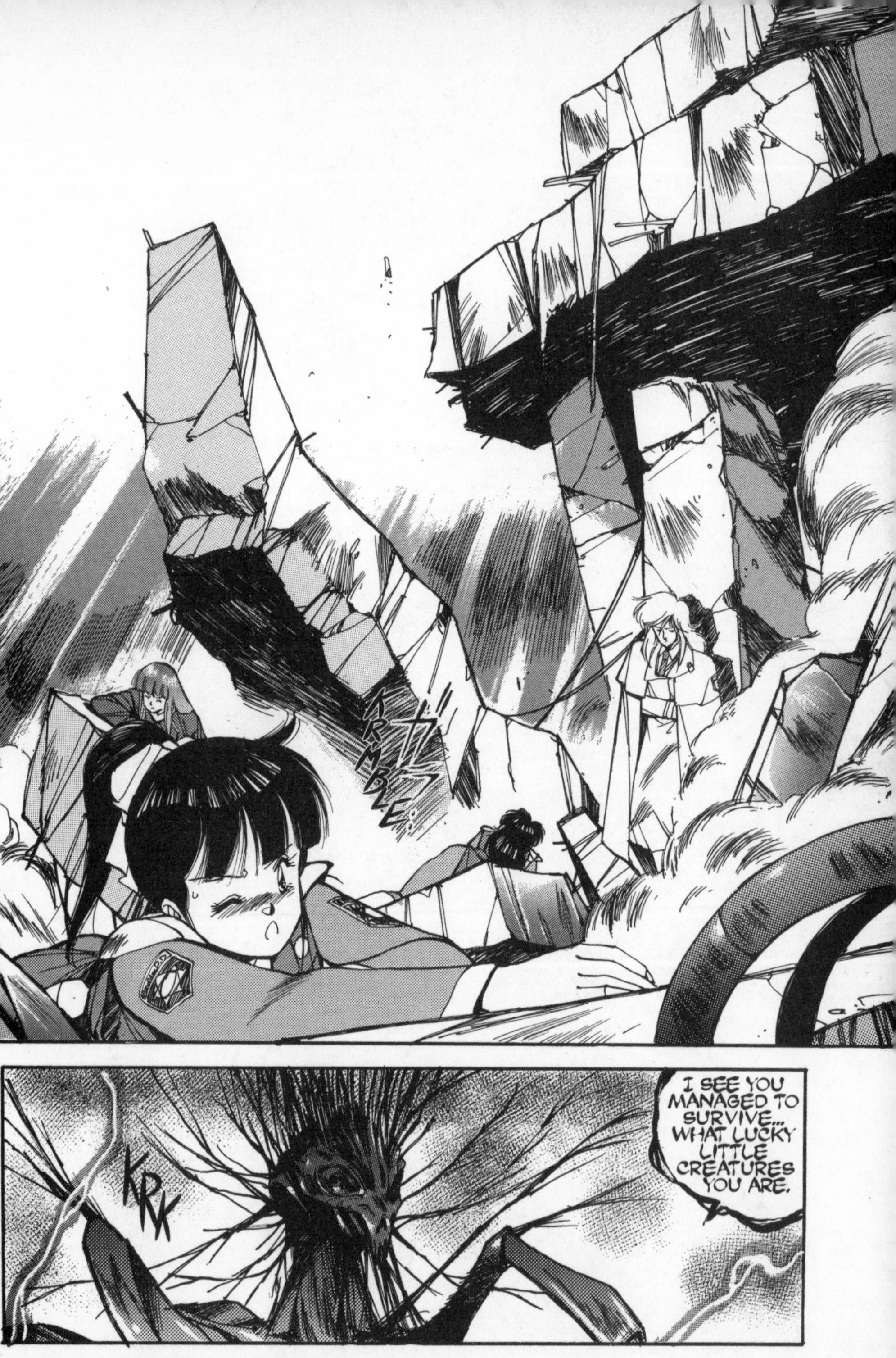
KRRMBLE!
I SEE YOU MANAGED TO SURVIVE... WHAT LUCKY LITTLE CREATURES YOU ARE.
KRK

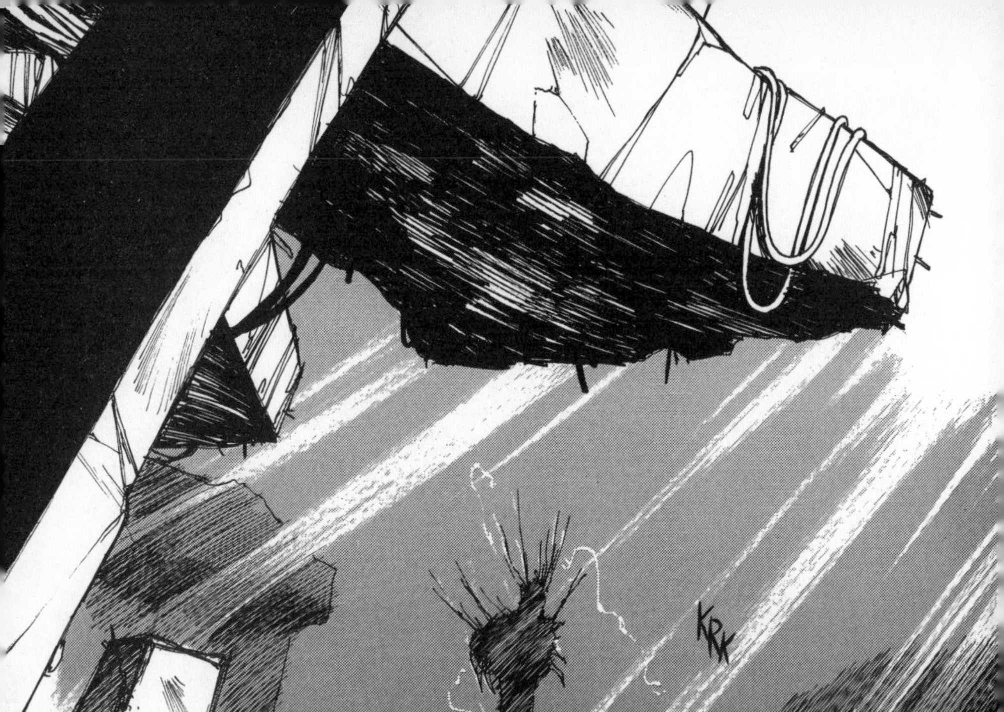
KRNK

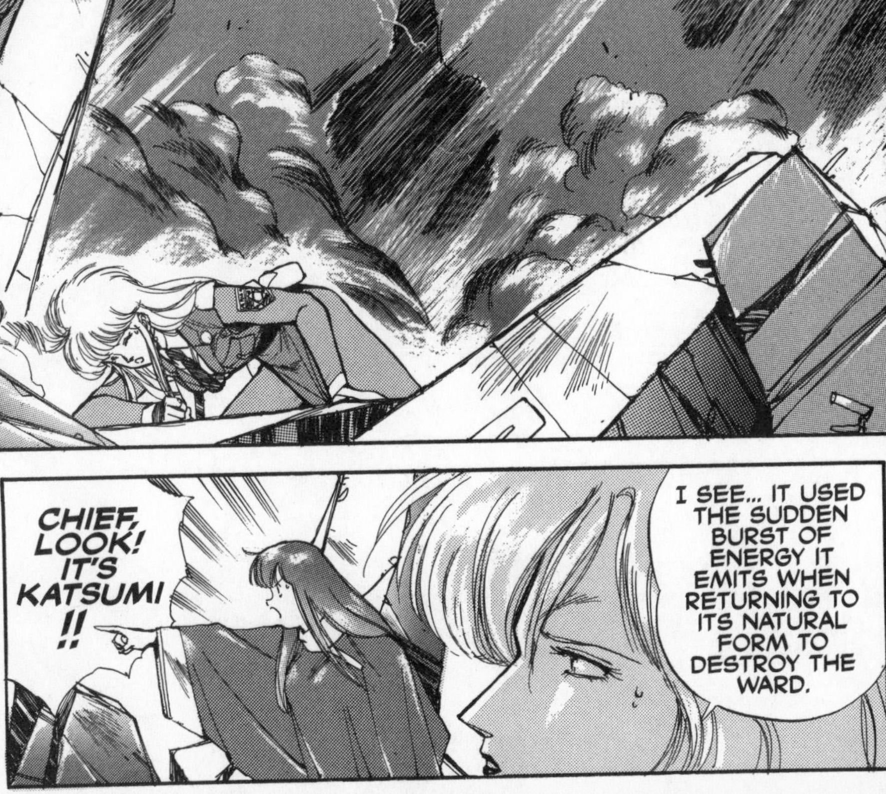
I SEE... IT USED THE SUDDEN BURST OF ENERGY IT EMITS WHEN RETURNING TO ITS NATURAL FORM TO DESTROY THE WARD.
CHIEF, LOOK! IT'S KATSUMI !!

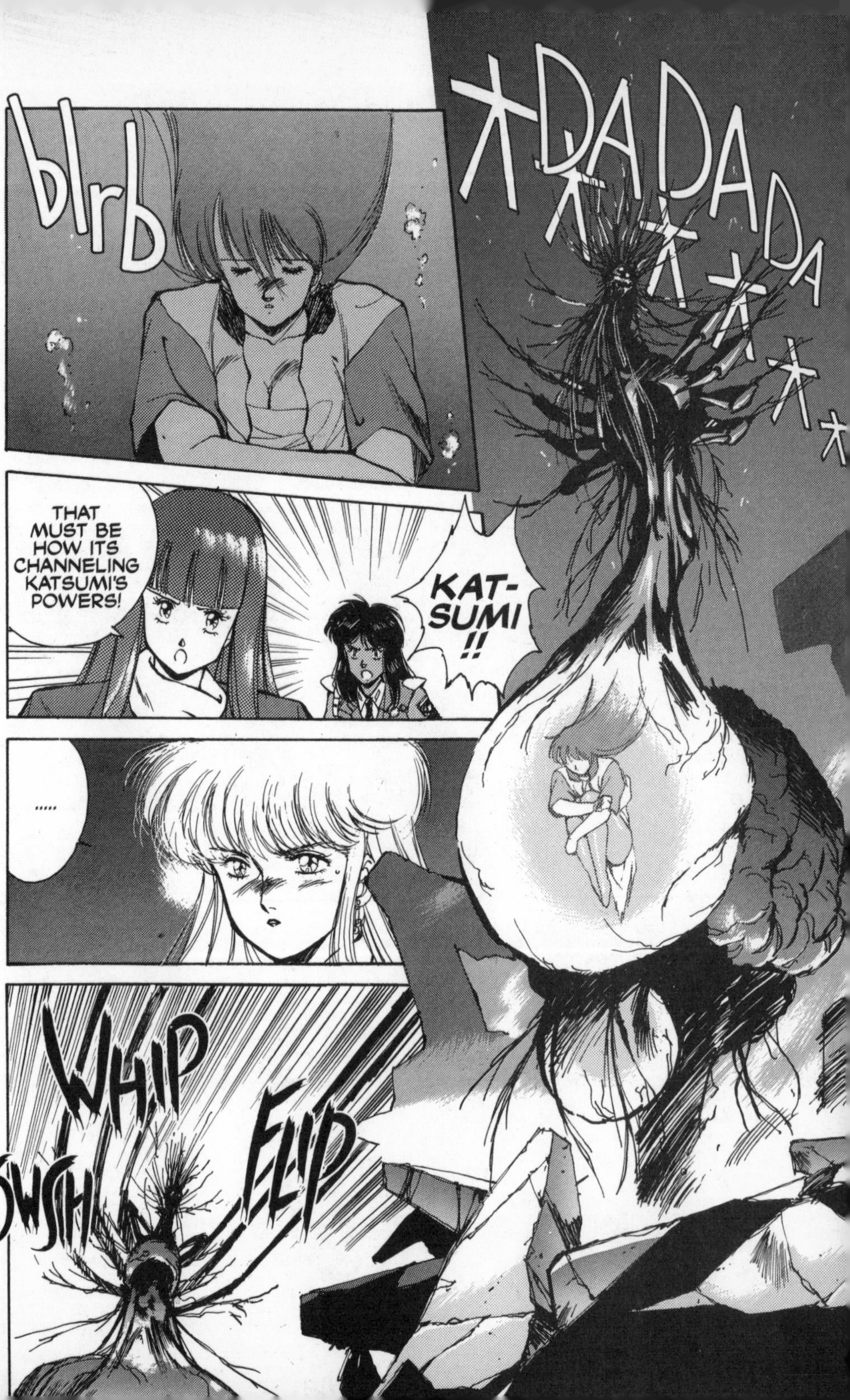
DADADADA
blrb
KAT-SUMI!!
THAT MUST BE HOW ITS CHANNELING KATSUMI'S POWERS!
.....
WHIP
FLIP
SWSH

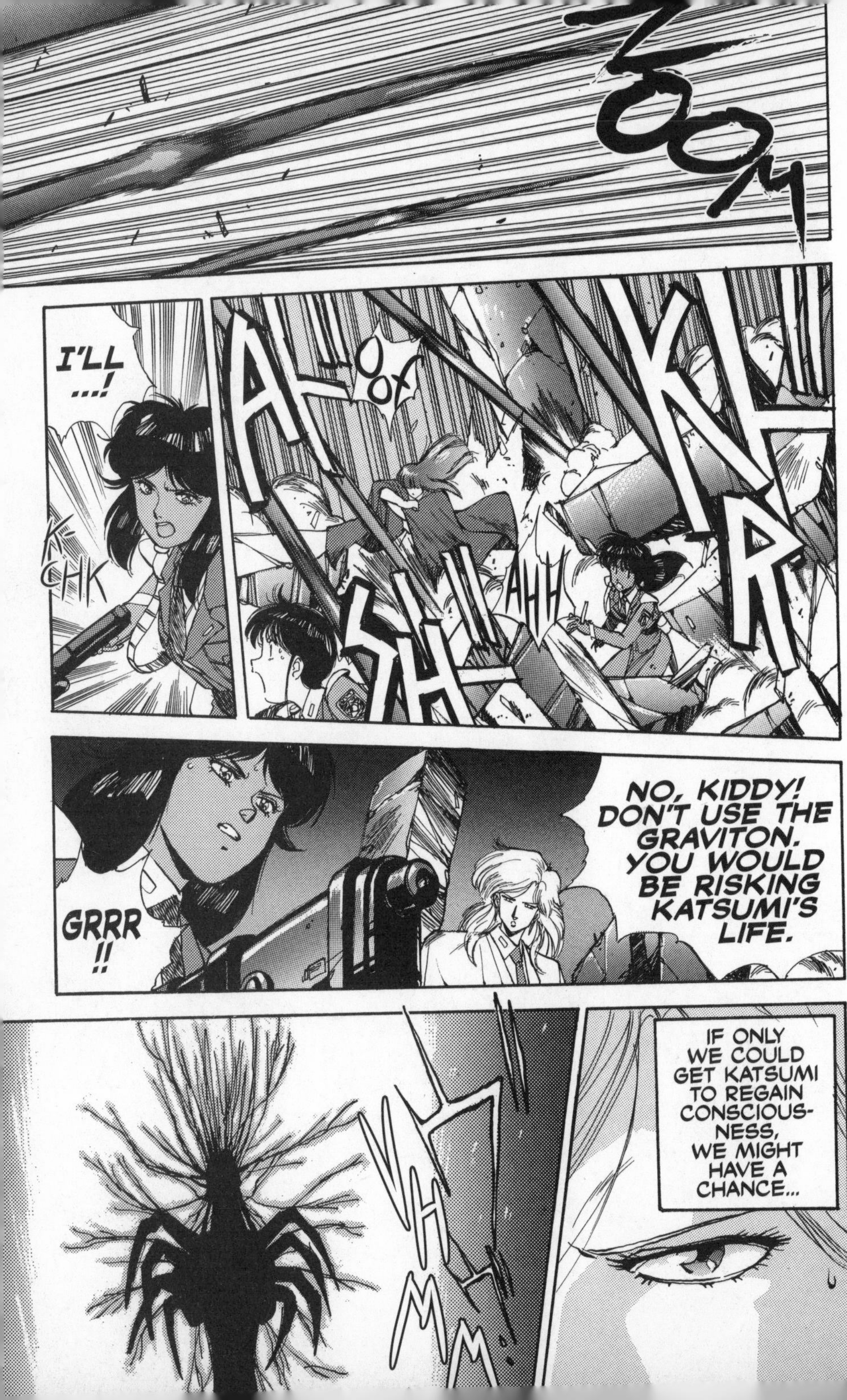
ZOOM
KRR
A—
OOF
SHH
AHH
I'LL ...!
KA-CHK
NO, KIDDY! DON'T USE THE GRAVITON. YOU WOULD BE RISKING KATSUMI'S LIFE.
GRRR !!
IF ONLY WE COULD GET KATSUMI TO REGAIN CONSCIOUS-NESS, WE MIGHT HAVE A CHANCE...
VHMM

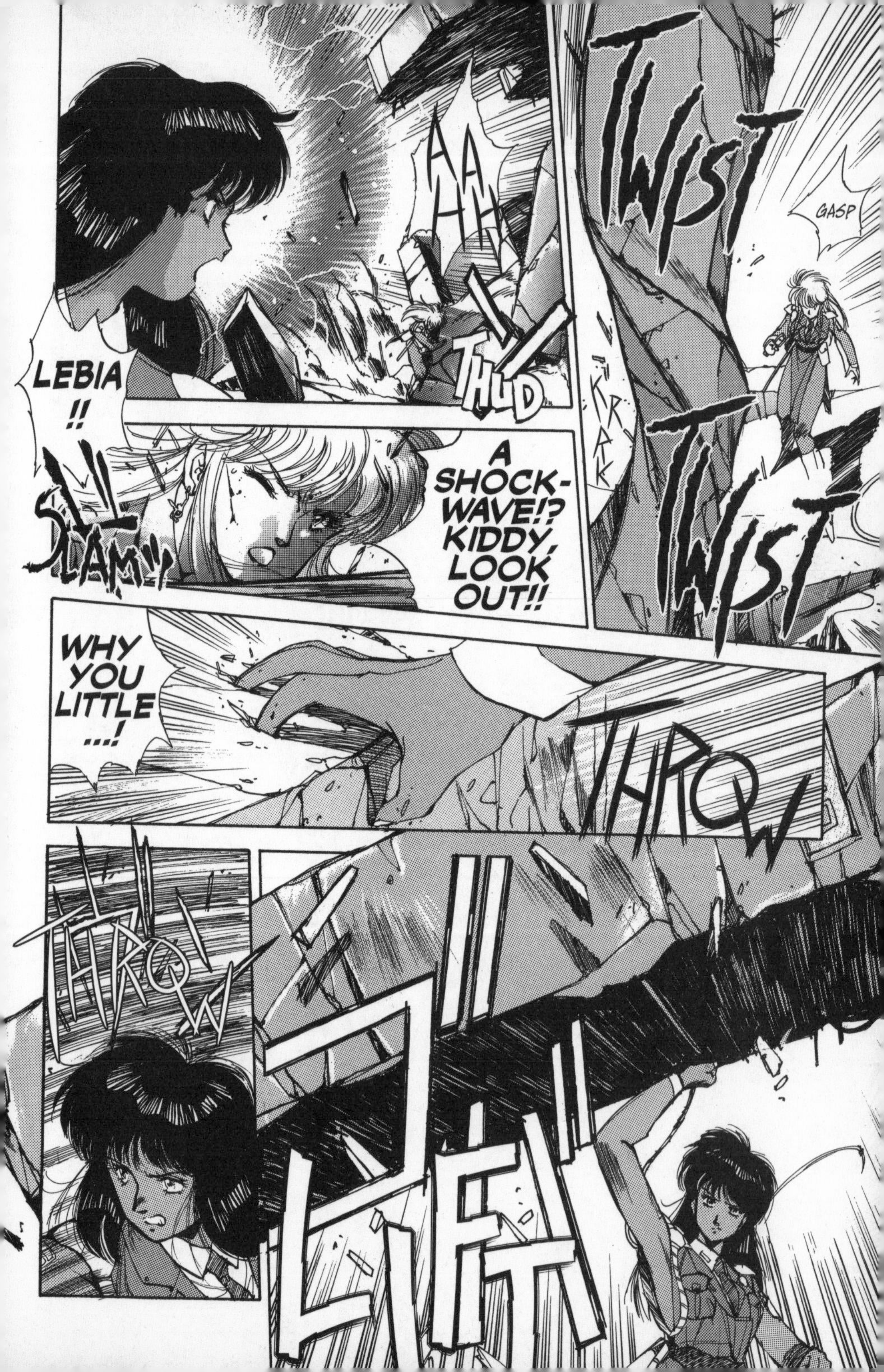
TWIST
GASP
KRAK
TWIST
AAHH
THUD
LEBIA !!
A SHOCK-WAVE!? KIDDY, LOOK OUT!!
SLAM
WHY YOU LITTLE ...!
THROW
LIFT
THROW

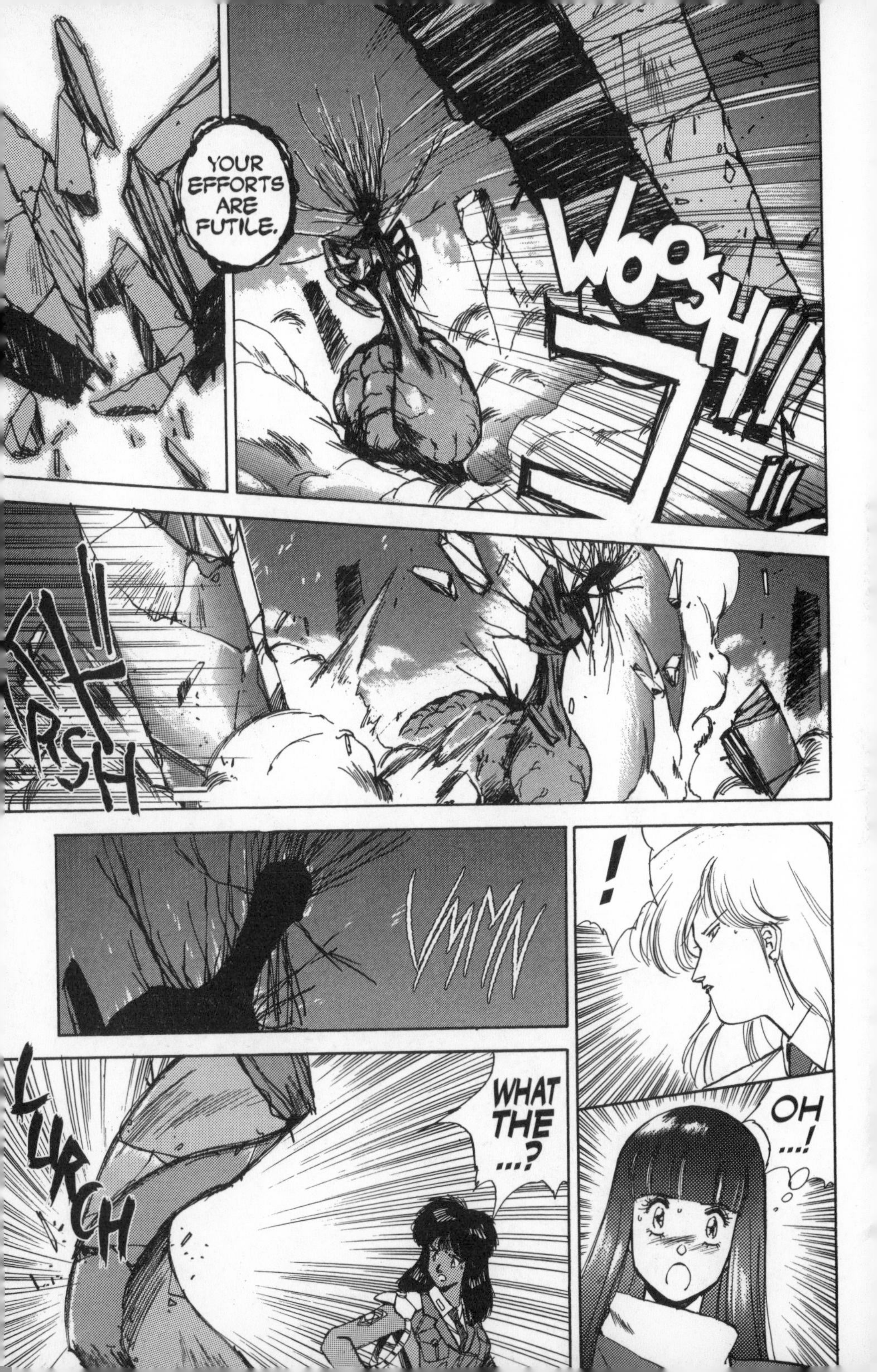

YOUR EFFORTS ARE FUTILE.
WOOSH!!
KRSH!!
!
VMMN
OH ...!
WHAT THE ...?
LURCH

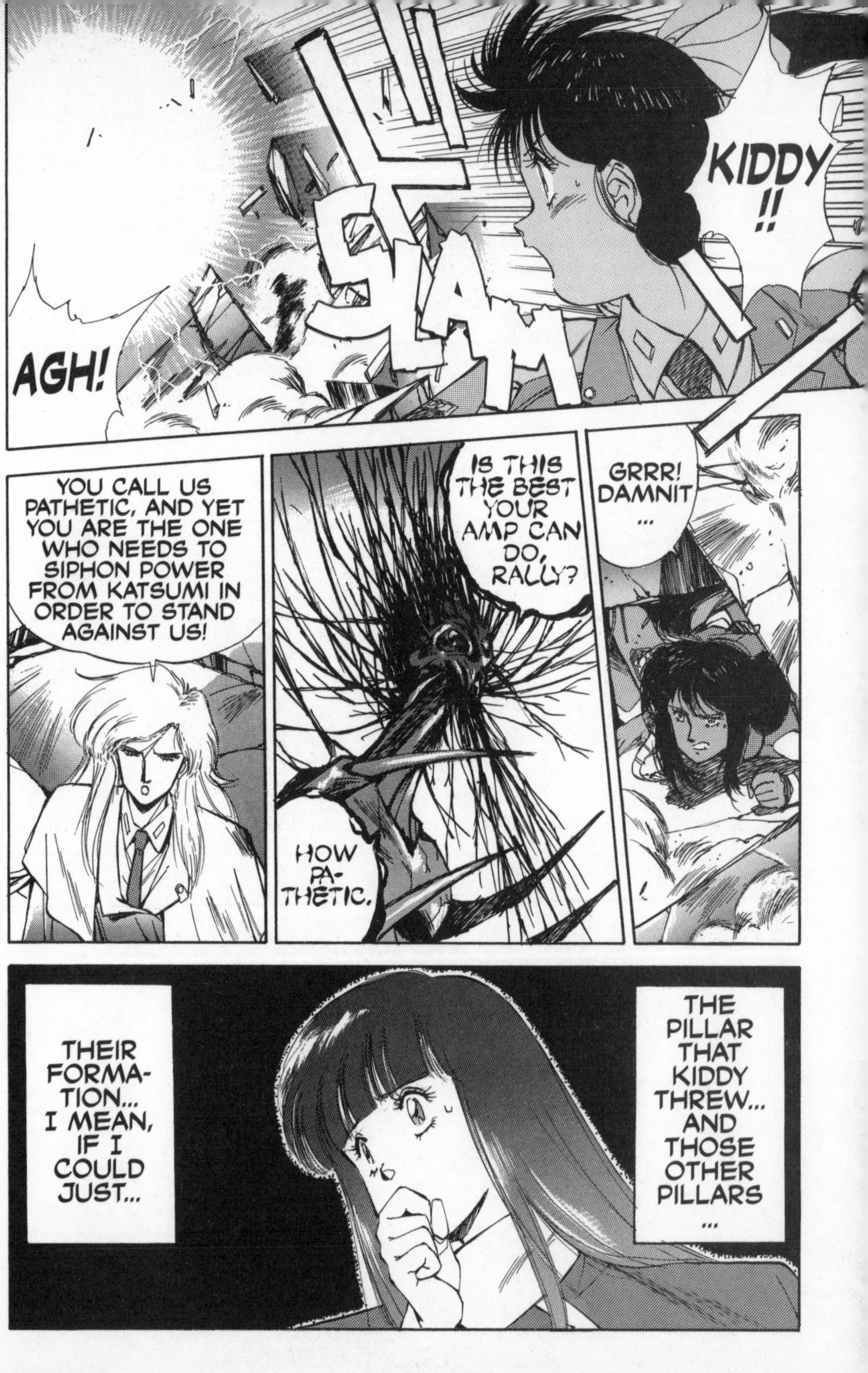
KIDDY !!
SLAM
AGH!
GRRR! DAMNIT ...
IS THIS THE BEST YOUR AMP CAN DO, RALLY?
HOW PA-THETIC.
YOU CALL US PATHETIC, AND YET YOU ARE THE ONE WHO NEEDS TO SIPHON POWER FROM KATSUMI IN ORDER TO STAND AGAINST US!
THE PILLAR THAT KIDDY THREW... AND THOSE OTHER PILLARS ...
THEIR FORMA-TION... I MEAN, IF I COULD JUST...

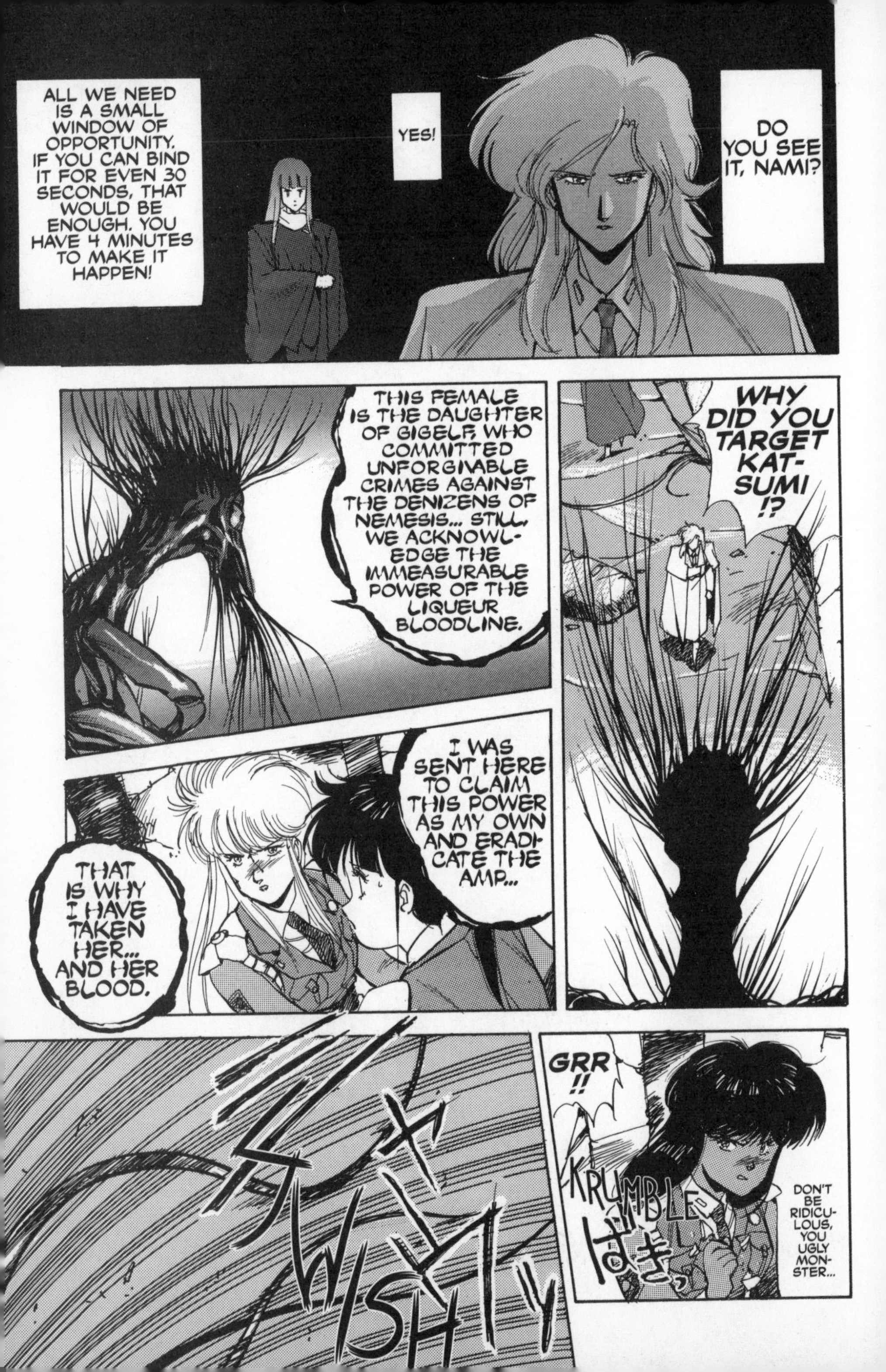
DO YOU SEE IT, NAMI?
YES!
ALL WE NEED IS A SMALL WINDOW OF OPPORTUNITY. IF YOU CAN BIND IT FOR EVEN 30 SECONDS, THAT WOULD BE ENOUGH. YOU HAVE 4 MINUTES TO MAKE IT HAPPEN!
WHY DID YOU TARGET KAT-SUMI!?
THIS FEMALE IS THE DAUGHTER OF GIGELF, WHO COMMITTED UNFORGIVABLE CRIMES AGAINST THE DENIZENS OF NEMESIS... STILL, WE ACKNOWL-EDGE THE IMMEASURABLE POWER OF THE LIQUEUR BLOODLINE.
I WAS SENT HERE TO CLAIM THIS POWER AS MY OWN AND ERADI-CATE THE AMP...
THAT IS WHY I HAVE TAKEN HER... AND HER BLOOD.
GRR!!
KRUMBLE
DON'T BE RIDICU-LOUS, YOU UGLY MON-STER...
SWISH

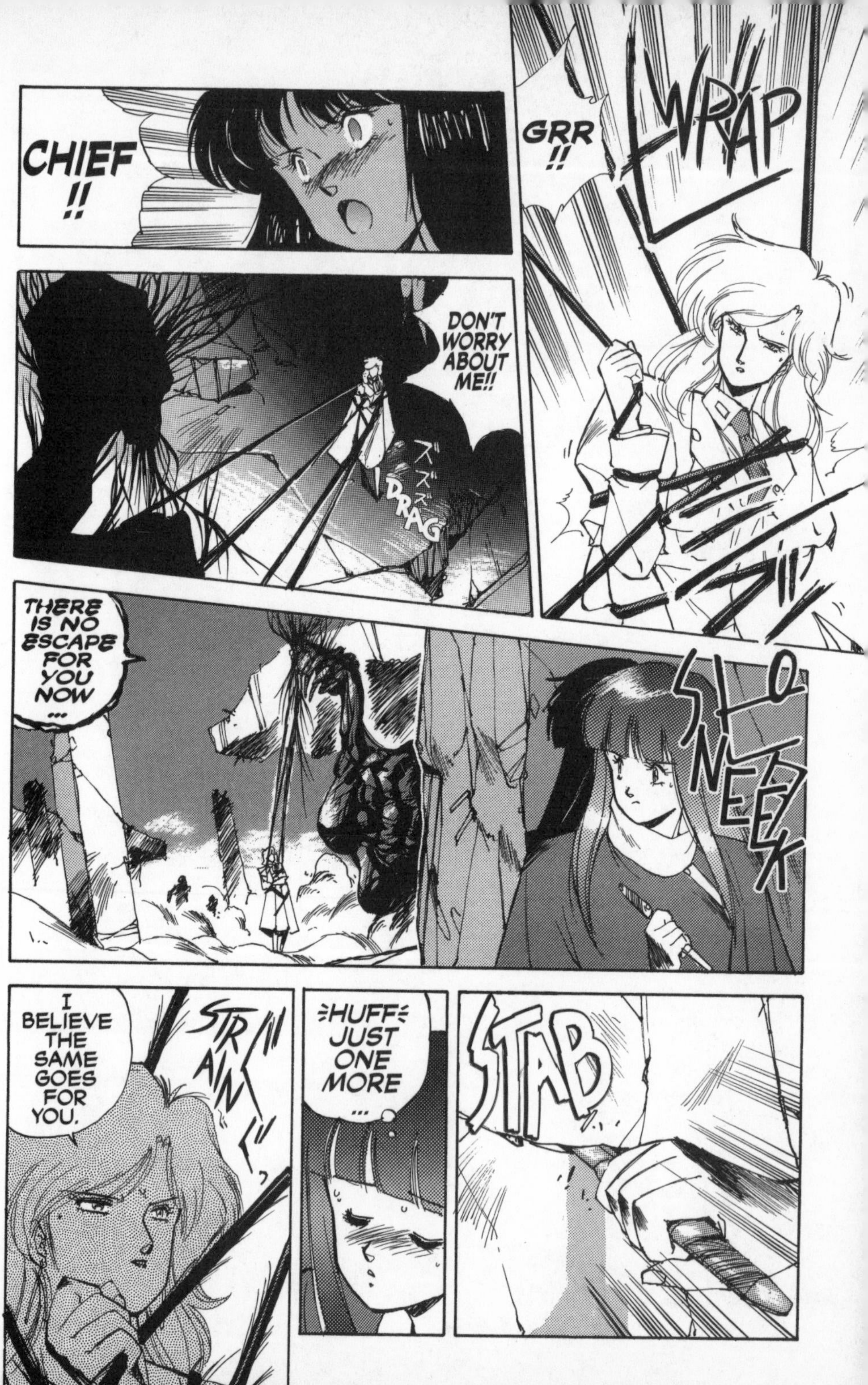
WRAP
GRR!!
CHIEF!!
DON'T WORRY ABOUT ME!!
ズズズ
DRAG
SHNEEK
THERE IS NO ESCAPE FOR YOU NOW...
STAB
HUFF JUST ONE MORE...
I BELIEVE THE SAME GOES FOR YOU.
STRAIN

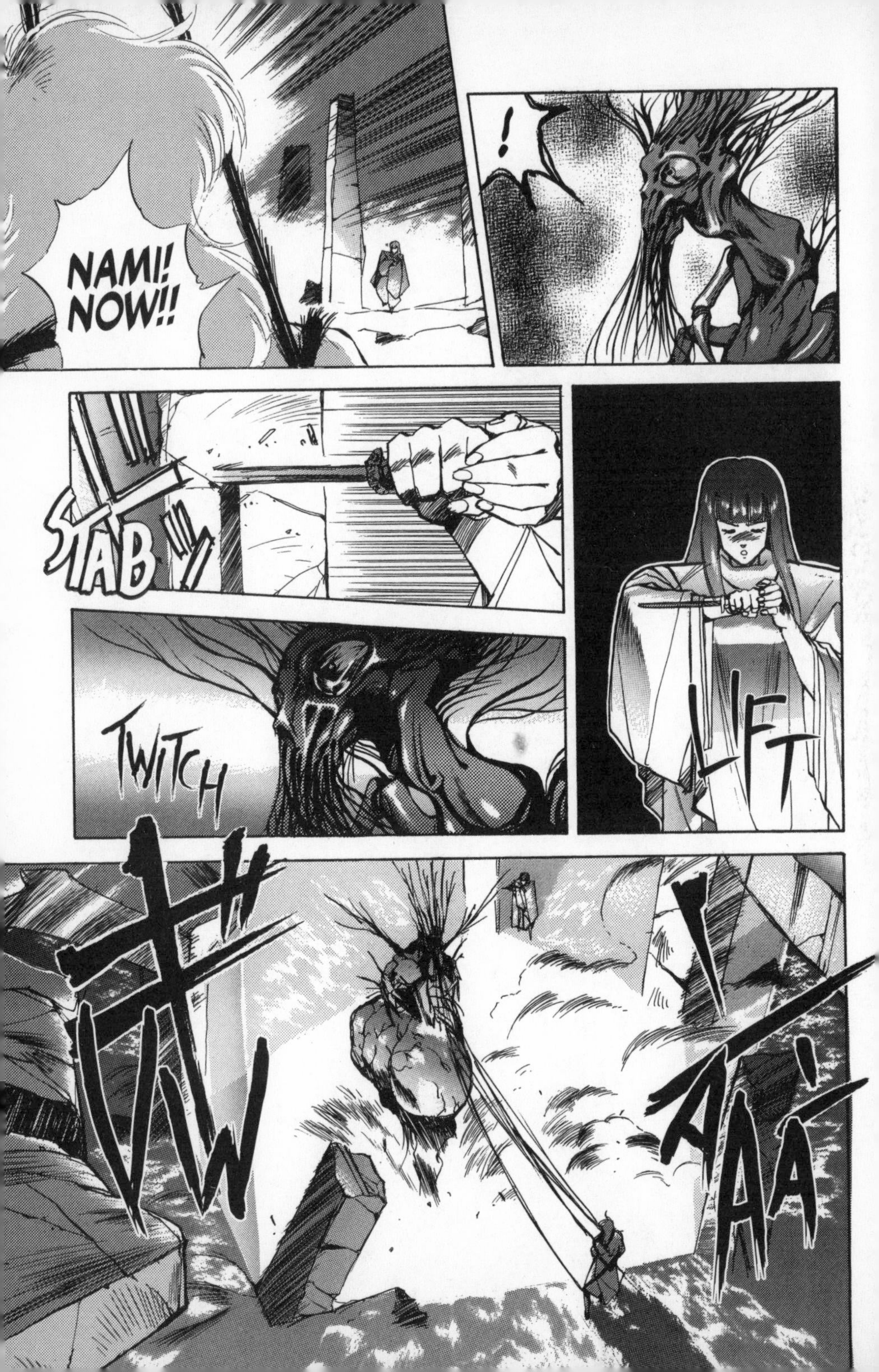
!
NAMI! NOW!!
LIFT
STAB
TWITCH

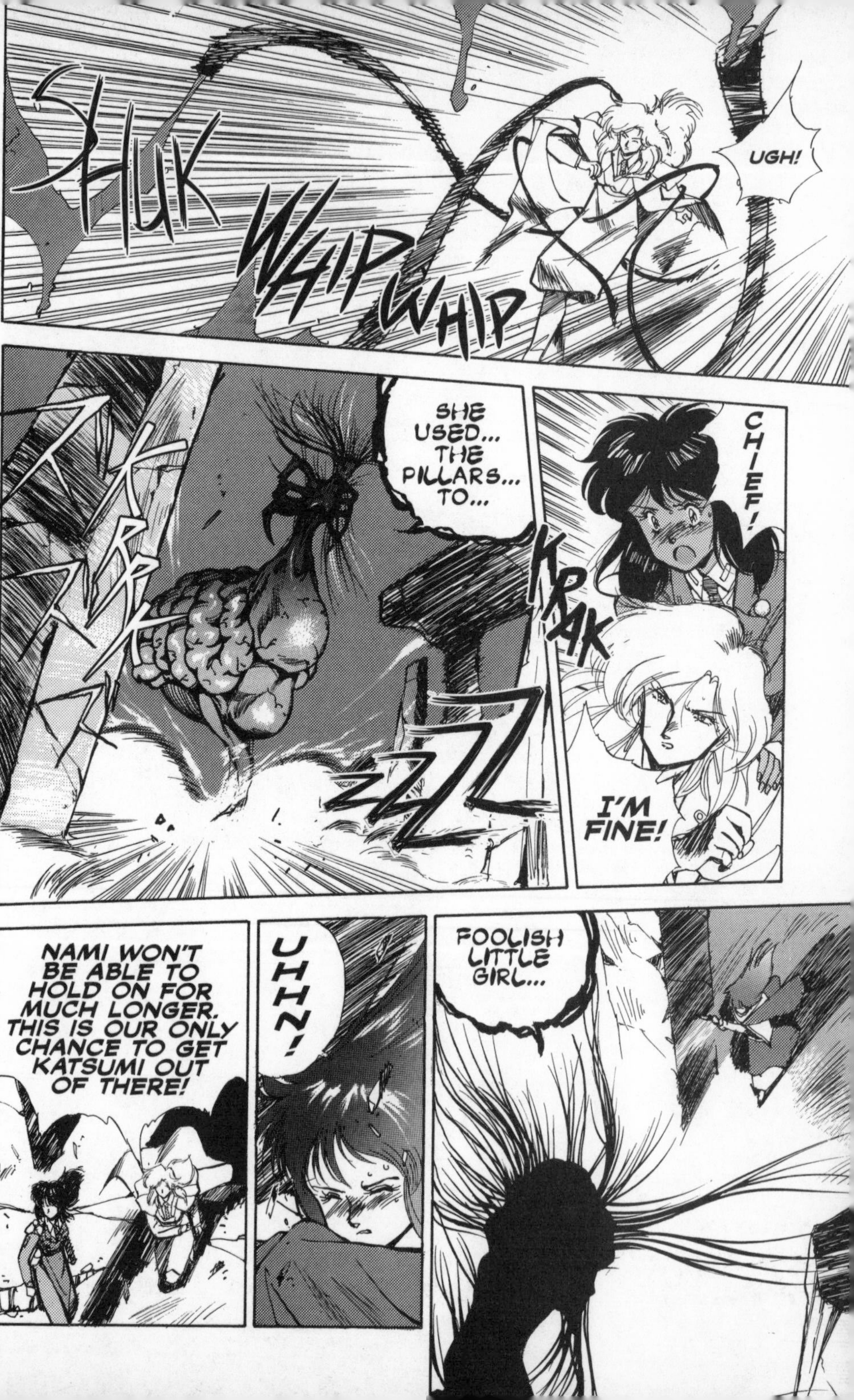
UGH!
SHUK
WHIP
WHIP
CHIEF!
I'M FINE!
SHE USED... THE PILLARS... TO...
KRAK
FOOLISH LITTLE GIRL...
UHHN!
NAMI WON'T BE ABLE TO HOLD ON FOR MUCH LONGER. THIS IS OUR ONLY CHANCE TO GET KATSUMI OUT OF THERE!

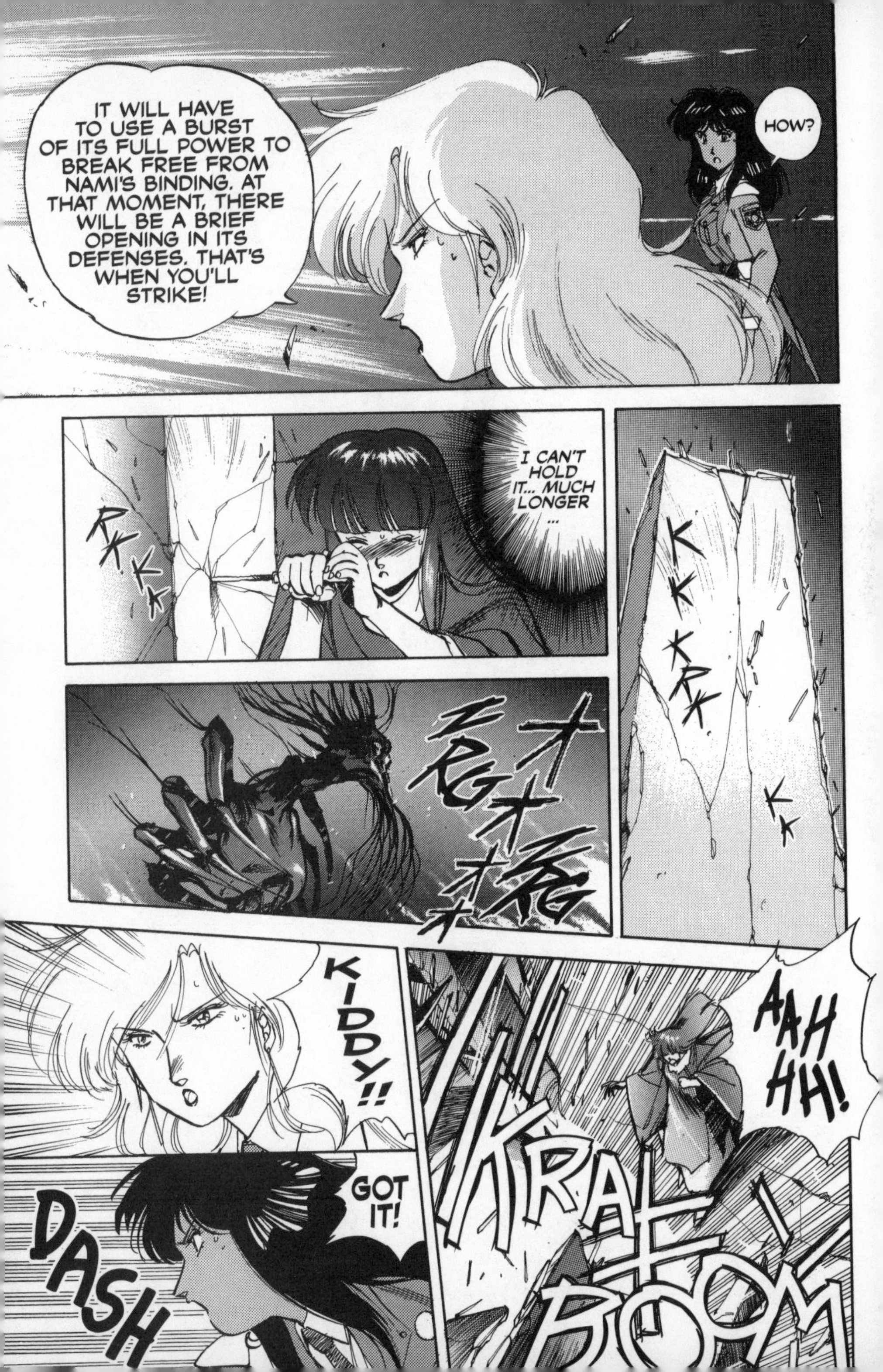
HOW?
IT WILL HAVE TO USE A BURST OF ITS FULL POWER TO BREAK FREE FROM NAMI'S BINDING. AT THAT MOMENT, THERE WILL BE A BRIEF OPENING IN ITS DEFENSES. THAT'S WHEN YOU'LL STRIKE!
KKKKRK
KK
I CAN'T HOLD IT... MUCH LONGER ...
RKKKK
ZRG
ZRG
AAHHH!
KRAK BOOM
KIDDY!!
GOT IT!
DASH

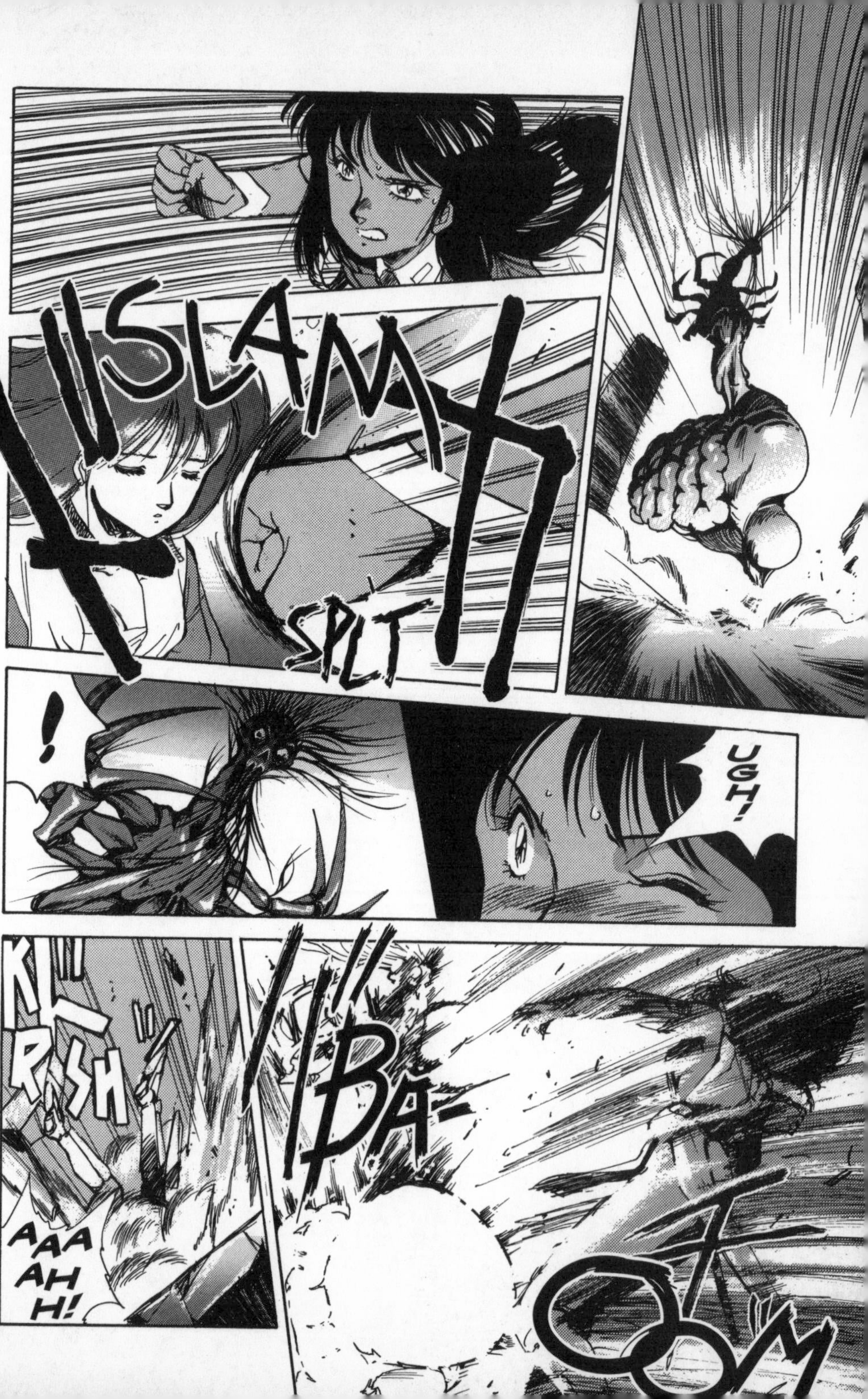
SLAM
SPLT
UGH!
!
BA-
OOM
KLRASH
AAAAHH!

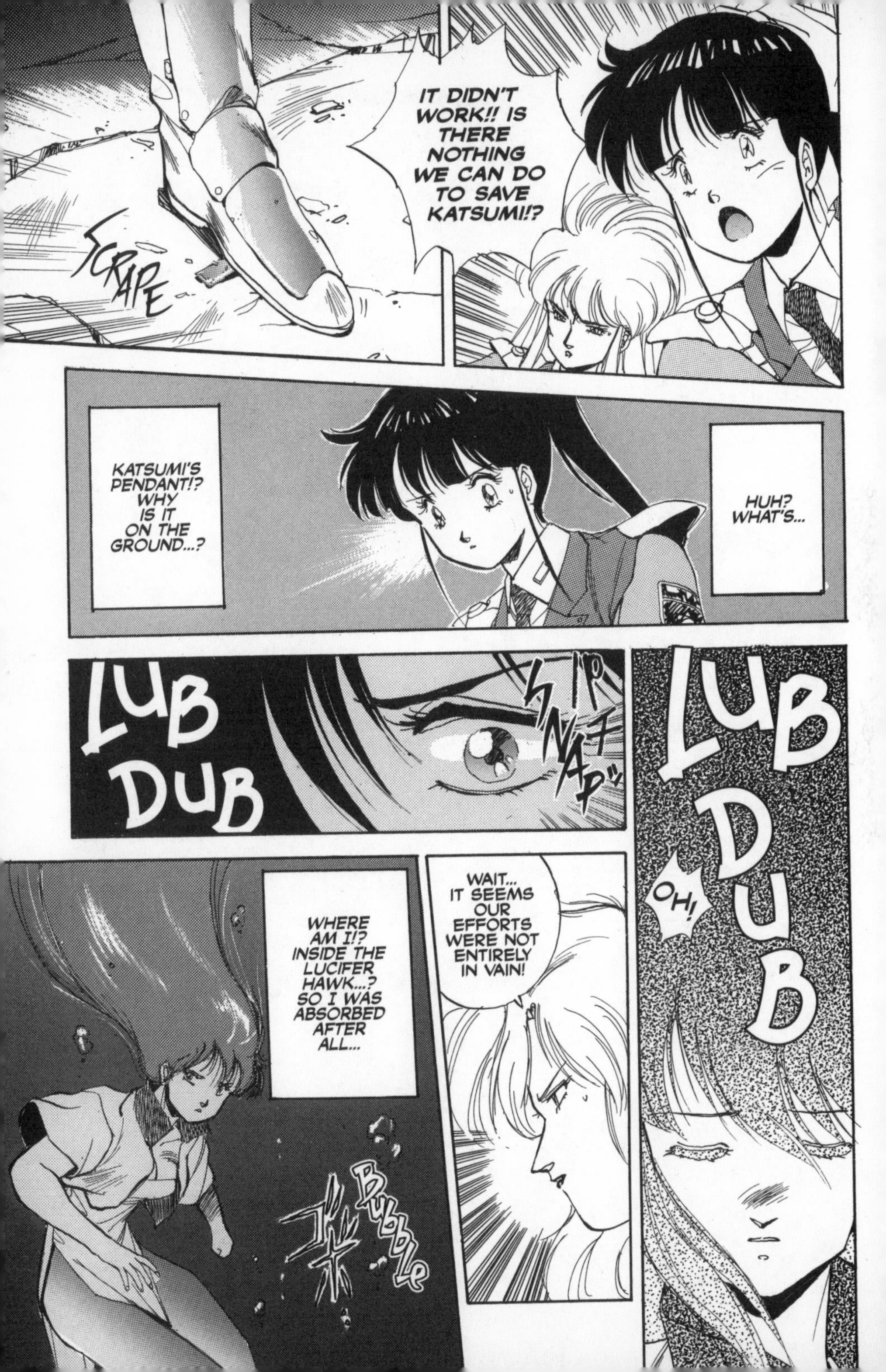
IT DIDN'T WORK!! IS THERE NOTHING WE CAN DO TO SAVE KATSUMI!?
SCRAPE
HUH? WHAT'S...
KATSUMI'S PENDANT!? WHY IS IT ON THE GROUND...?
LUB DUB
OH!
LUB DUB
SNAP
WAIT... IT SEEMS OUR EFFORTS WERE NOT ENTIRELY IN VAIN!
WHERE AM I!? INSIDE THE LUCIFER HAWK...? SO I WAS ABSORBED AFTER ALL...
BUBBLE

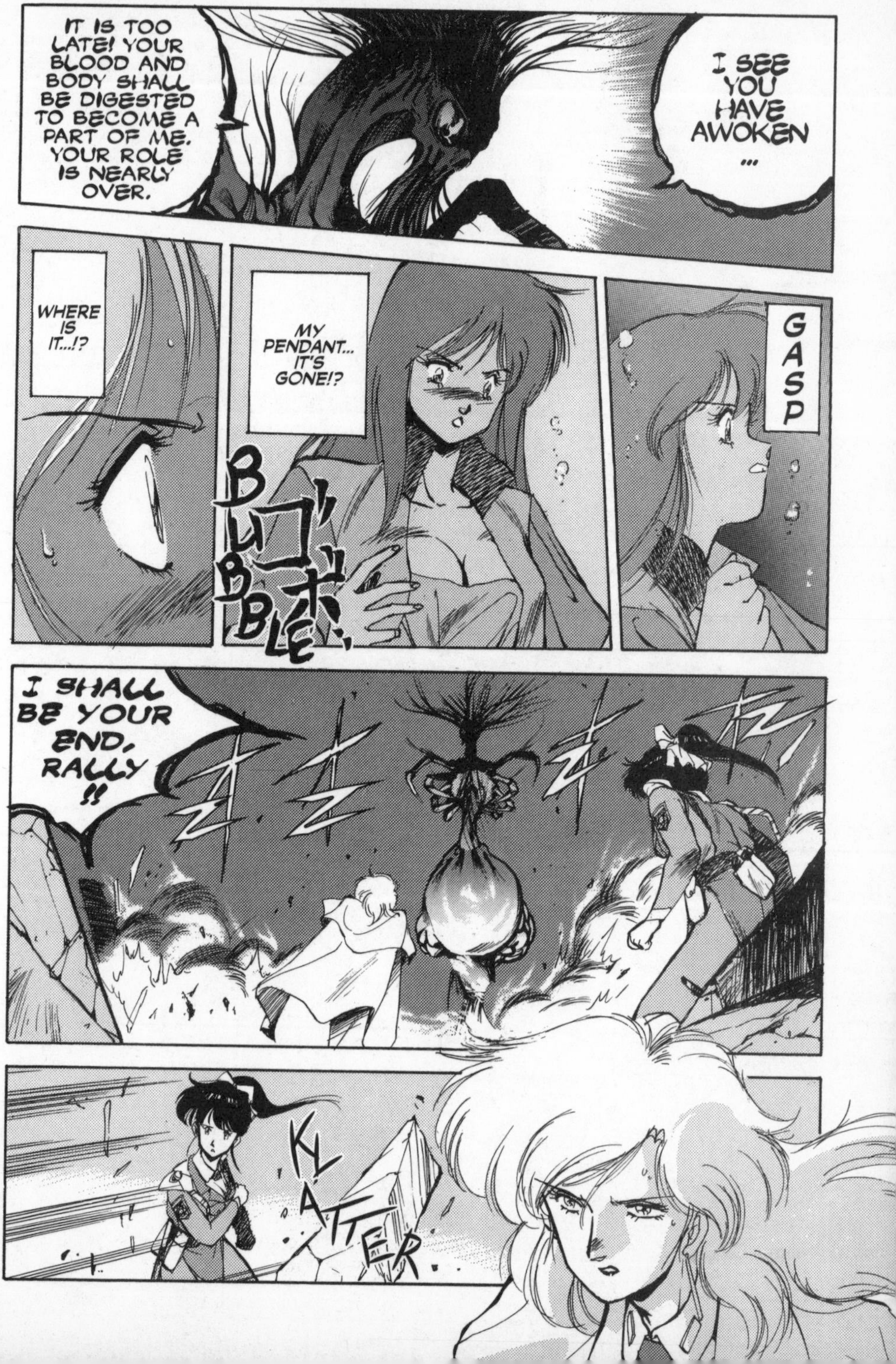
I SEE YOU HAVE AWOKEN ...
IT IS TOO LATE! YOUR BLOOD AND BODY SHALL BE DIGESTED TO BECOME A PART OF ME. YOUR ROLE IS NEARLY OVER.
GASP
MY PENDANT... IT'S GONE!?
BLUBBLE
WHERE IS IT...!?
I SHALL BE YOUR END, RALLY !!
KLATTER

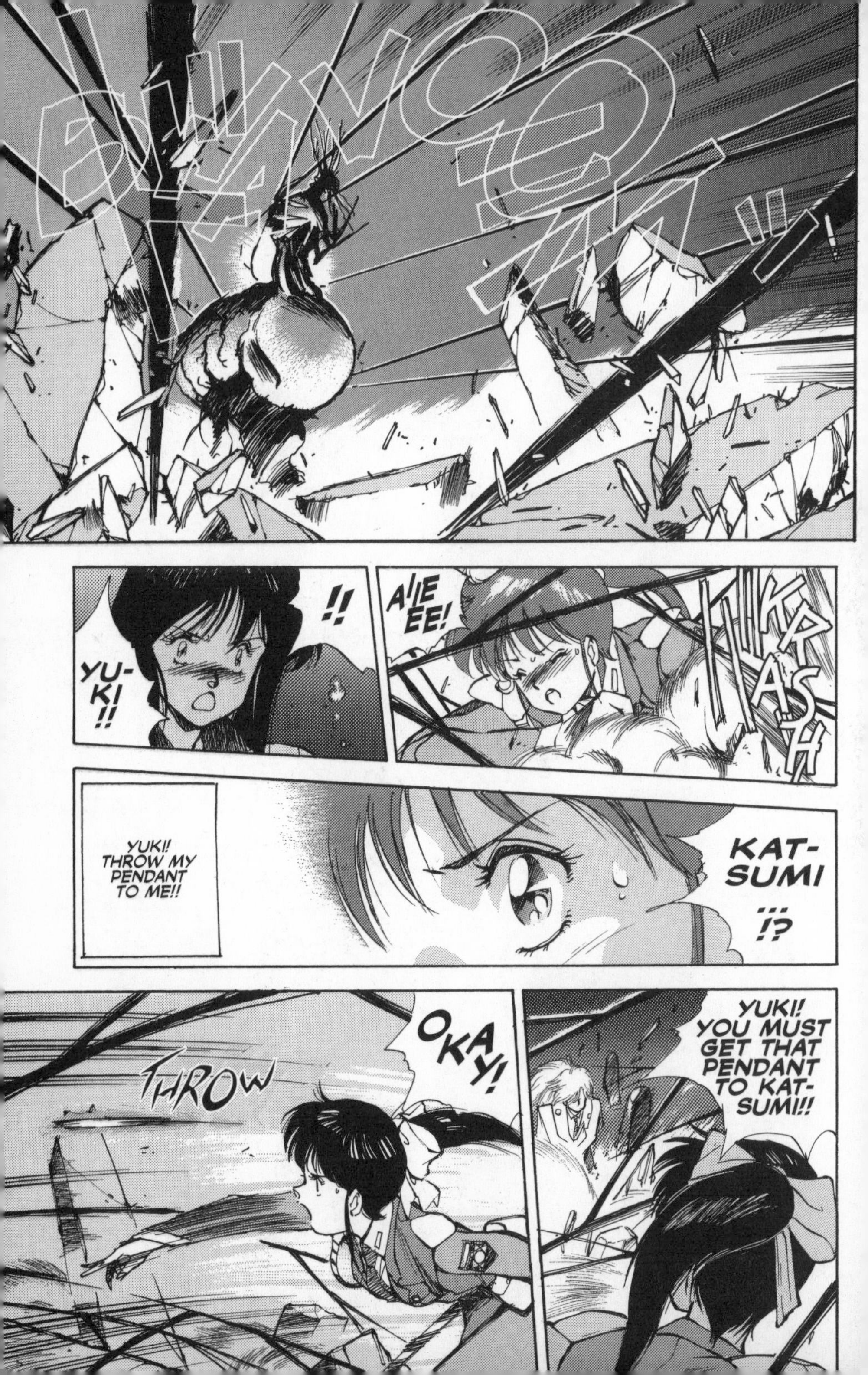
AIIE EE!
KRASH
!!
YUKI!!
KATSUMI ...!?
YUKI! THROW MY PENDANT TO ME!!
YUKI! YOU MUST GET THAT PENDANT TO KATSUMI!!
OKAY!
THROW

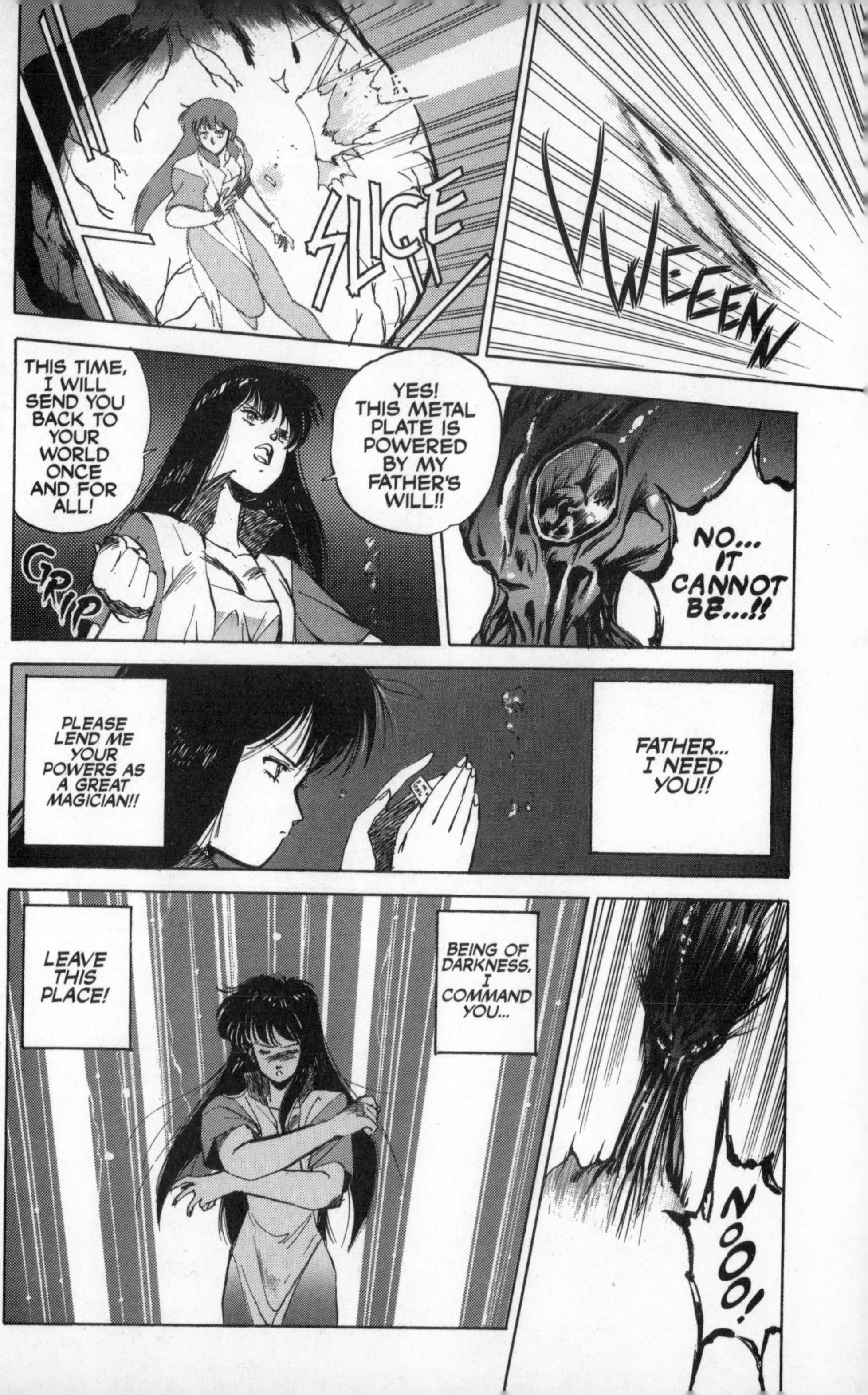
VWEEENN
SLICE
NO... IT CANNOT BE...!!
YES! THIS METAL PLATE IS POWERED BY MY FATHER'S WILL!!
THIS TIME, I WILL SEND YOU BACK TO YOUR WORLD ONCE AND FOR ALL!
GRIP
FATHER... I NEED YOU!!
PLEASE LEND ME YOUR POWERS AS A GREAT MAGICIAN!!
NOOO!
BEING OF DARKNESS, I COMMAND YOU...
LEAVE THIS PLACE!

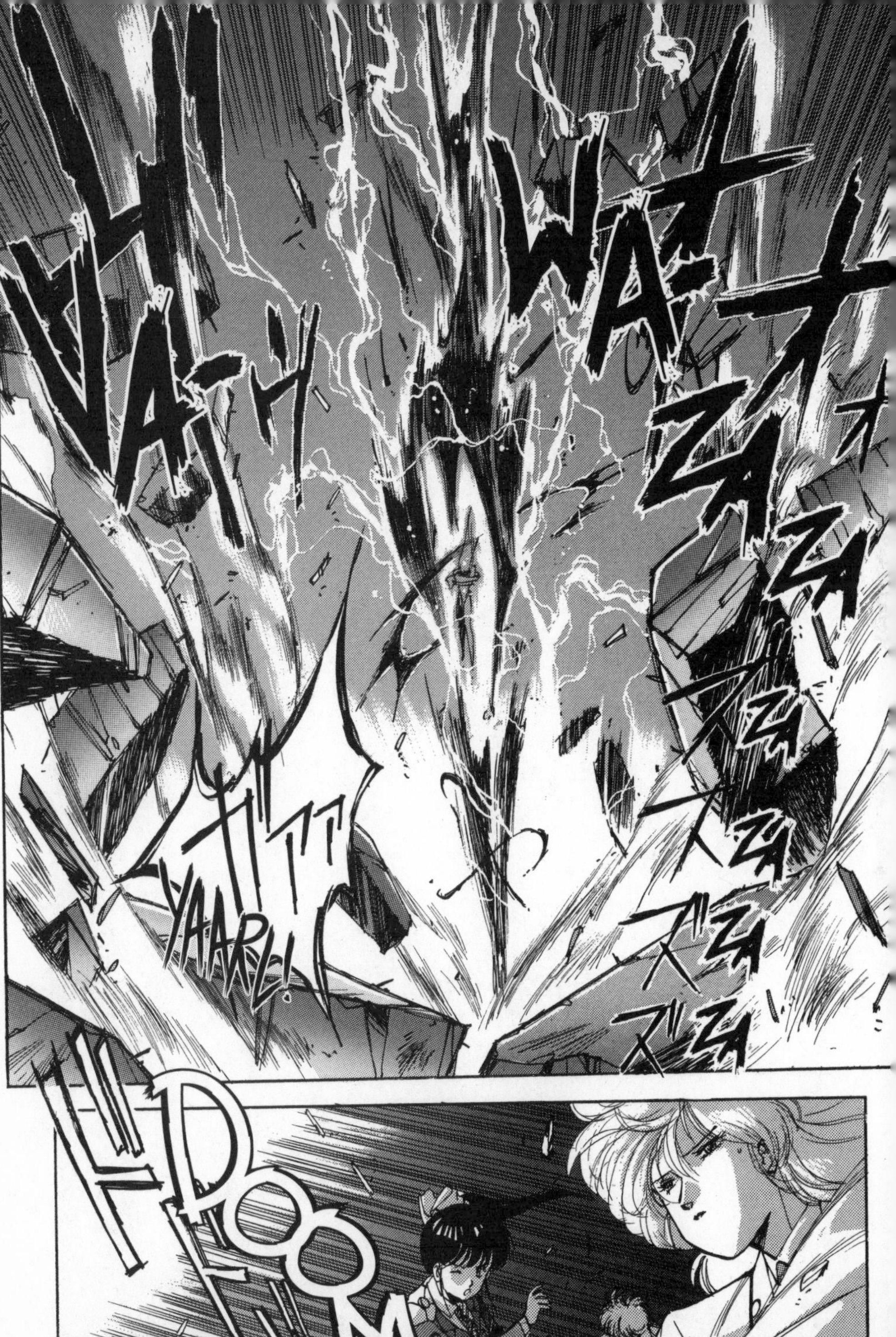
ZA
ZA
ZA
ZA
ZA
ZA
ZA
WA
VA
YAARL!
FDOOM

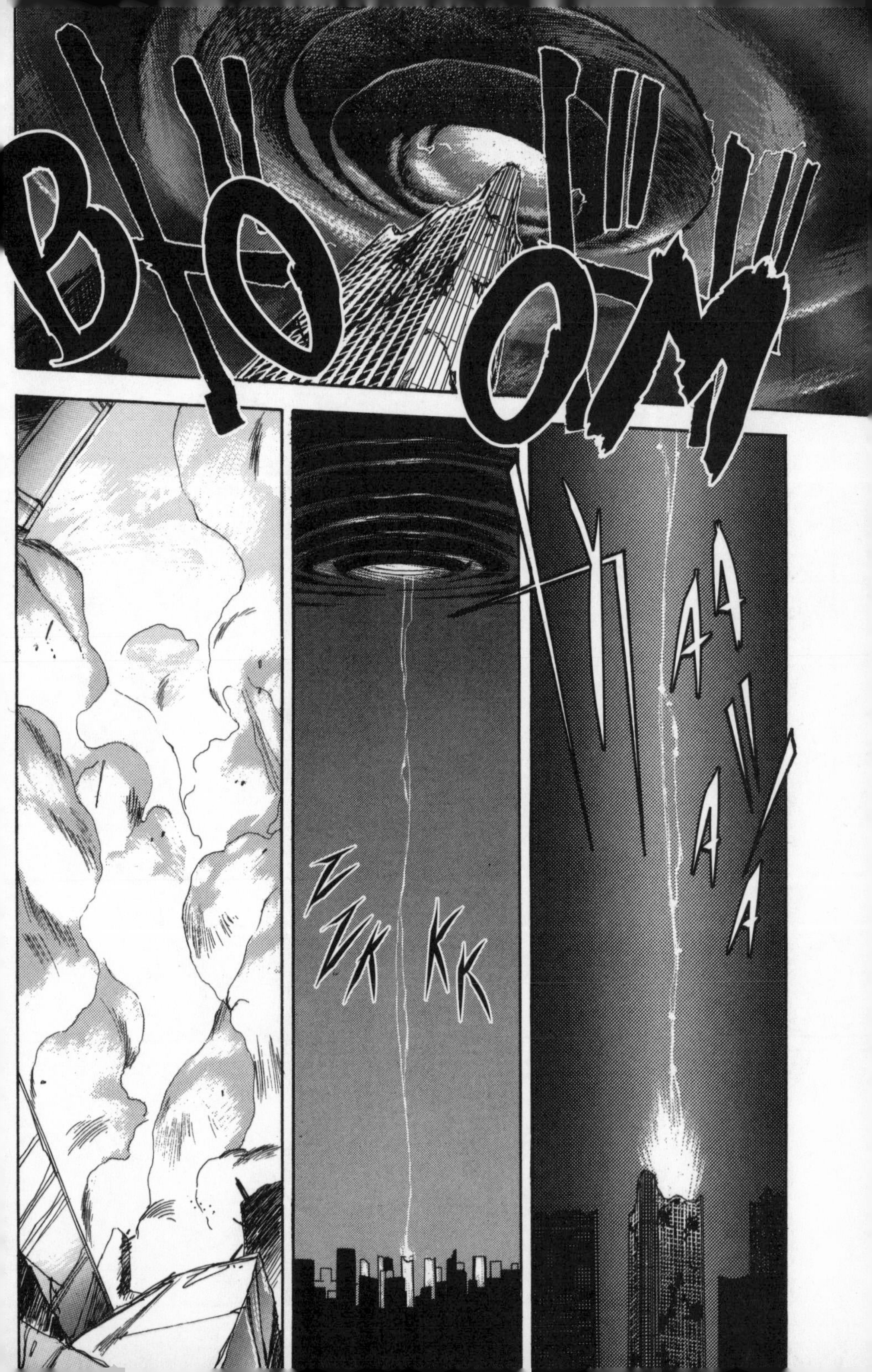
BOOOM
YAAAAA
ZZKKK

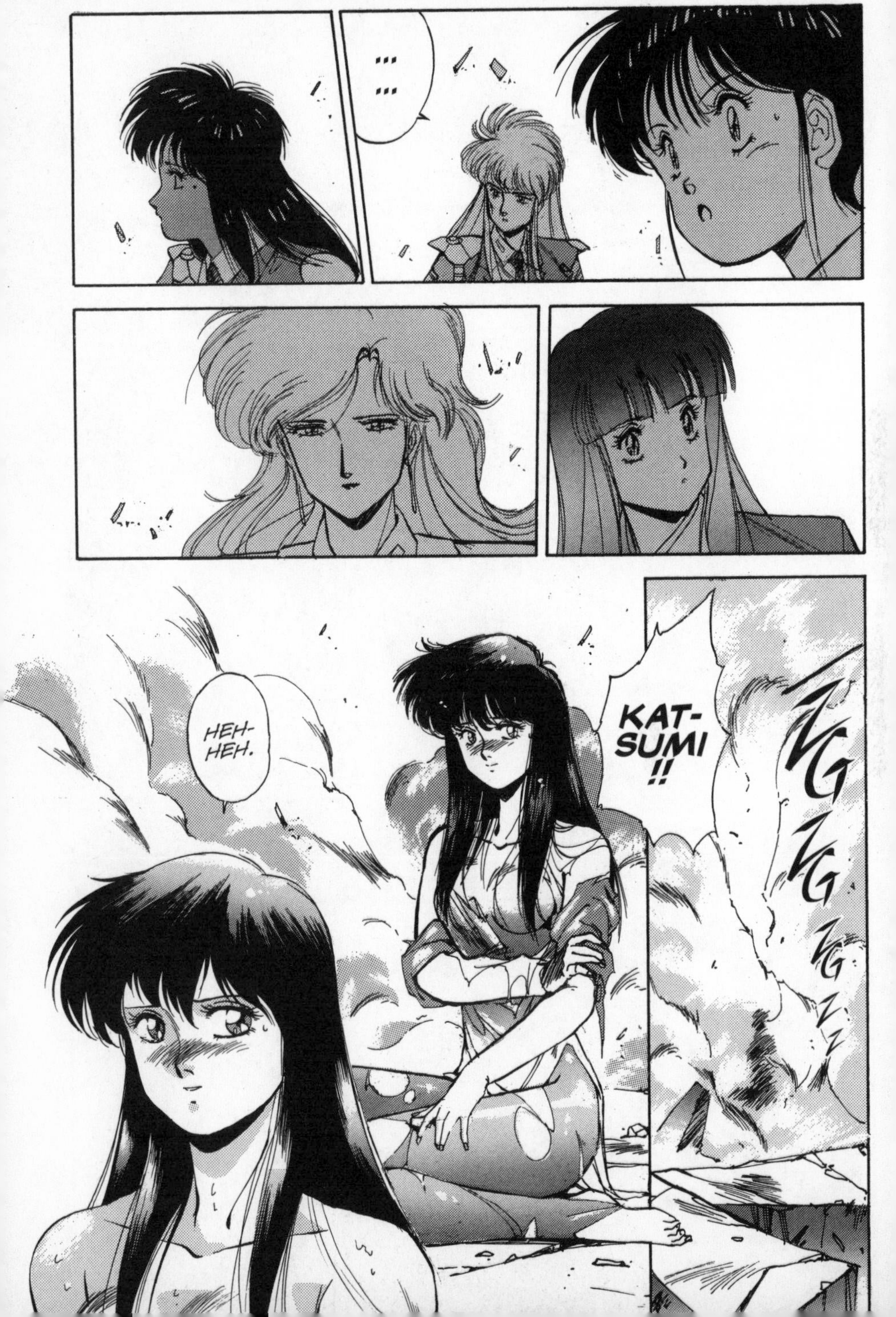
... ...
NGNGNGNGN
KAT-SUMI!!
HEH-HEH.

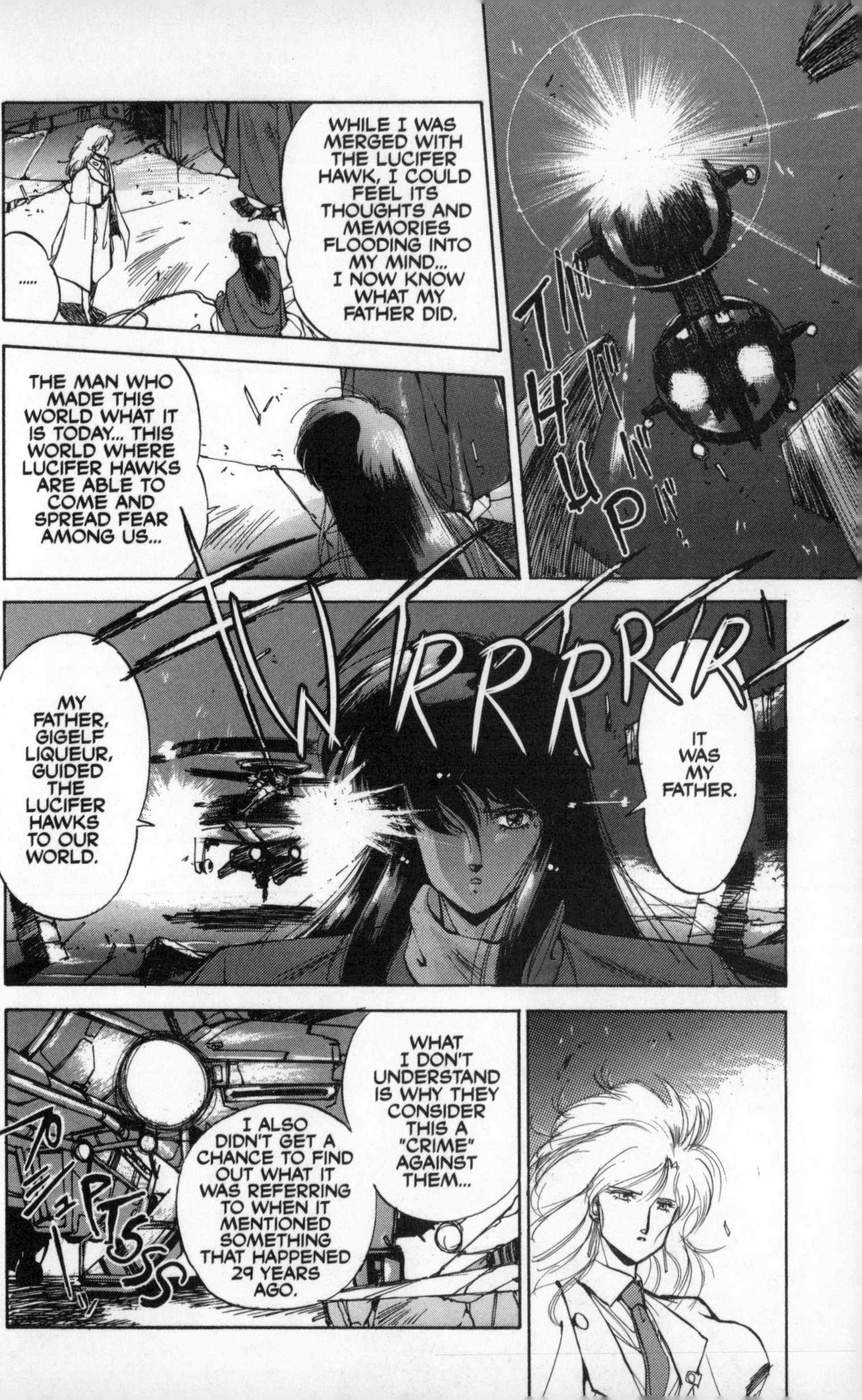
THHUP
WHILE I WAS MERGED WITH THE LUCIFER HAWK, I COULD FEEL ITS THOUGHTS AND MEMORIES FLOODING INTO MY MIND... I NOW KNOW WHAT MY FATHER DID.
.....
THE MAN WHO MADE THIS WORLD WHAT IT IS TODAY... THIS WORLD WHERE LUCIFER HAWKS ARE ABLE TO COME AND SPREAD FEAR AMONG US...
TWRRRRR
IT WAS MY FATHER.
MY FATHER, GIGELF LIQUEUR, GUIDED THE LUCIFER HAWKS TO OUR WORLD.
WHAT I DON'T UNDERSTAND IS WHY THEY CONSIDER THIS A "CRIME" AGAINST THEM...
I ALSO DIDN'T GET A CHANCE TO FIND OUT WHAT IT WAS REFERRING TO WHEN IT MENTIONED SOMETHING THAT HAPPENED 29 YEARS AGO.
PTSSS

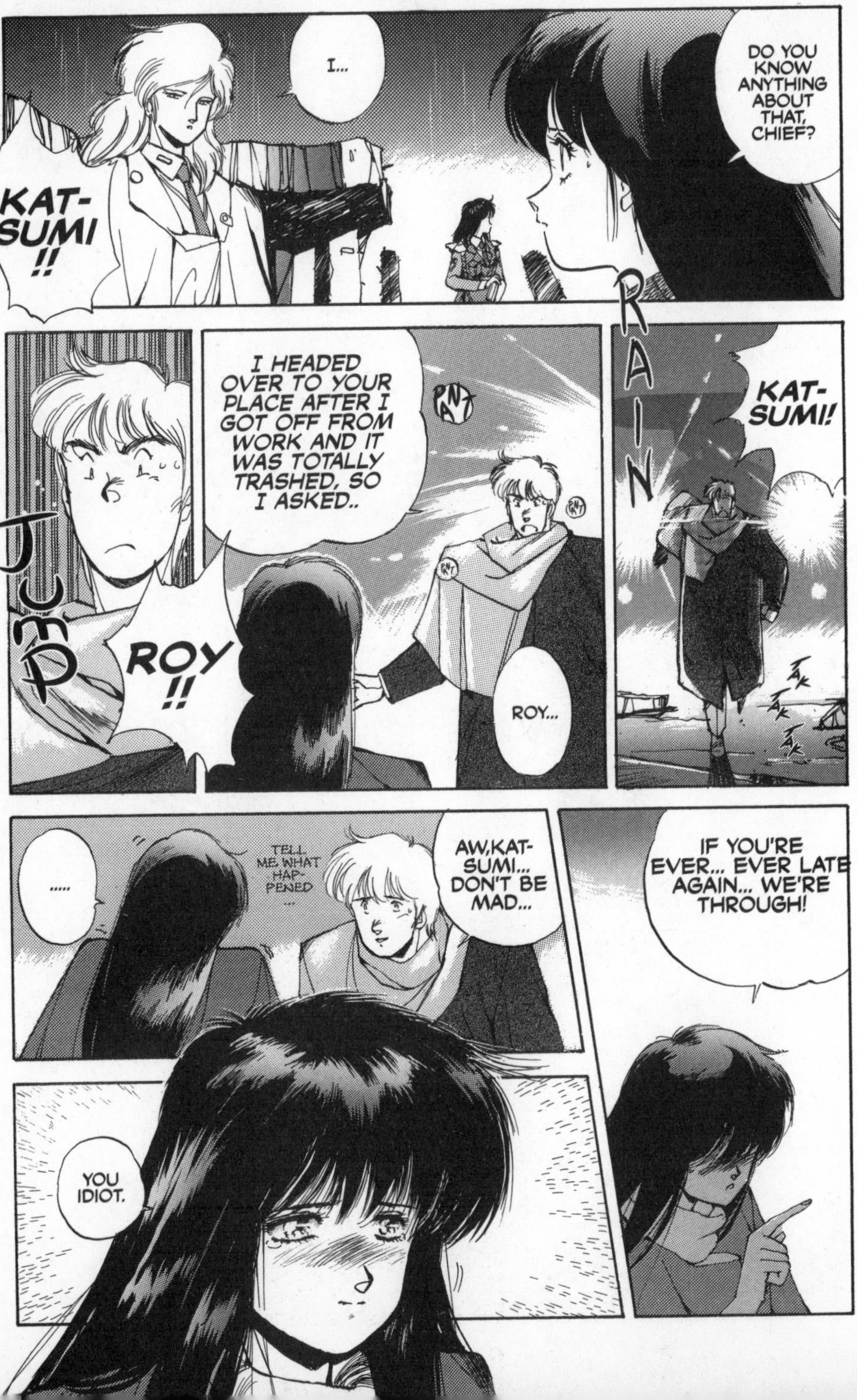
DO YOU KNOW ANYTHING ABOUT THAT, CHIEF?
I...
KAT-SUMI!!
RAIN
KAT-SUMI!
TAK TAK TAK TAK
I HEADED OVER TO YOUR PLACE AFTER I GOT OFF FROM WORK AND IT WAS TOTALLY TRASHED, SO I ASKED..
ROY...
ROY!!
JUMP
IF YOU'RE EVER... EVER LATE AGAIN... WE'RE THROUGH!
AW, KAT-SUMI... DON'T BE MAD...
TELL ME WHAT HAP-PENED ...
.....
YOU IDIOT.

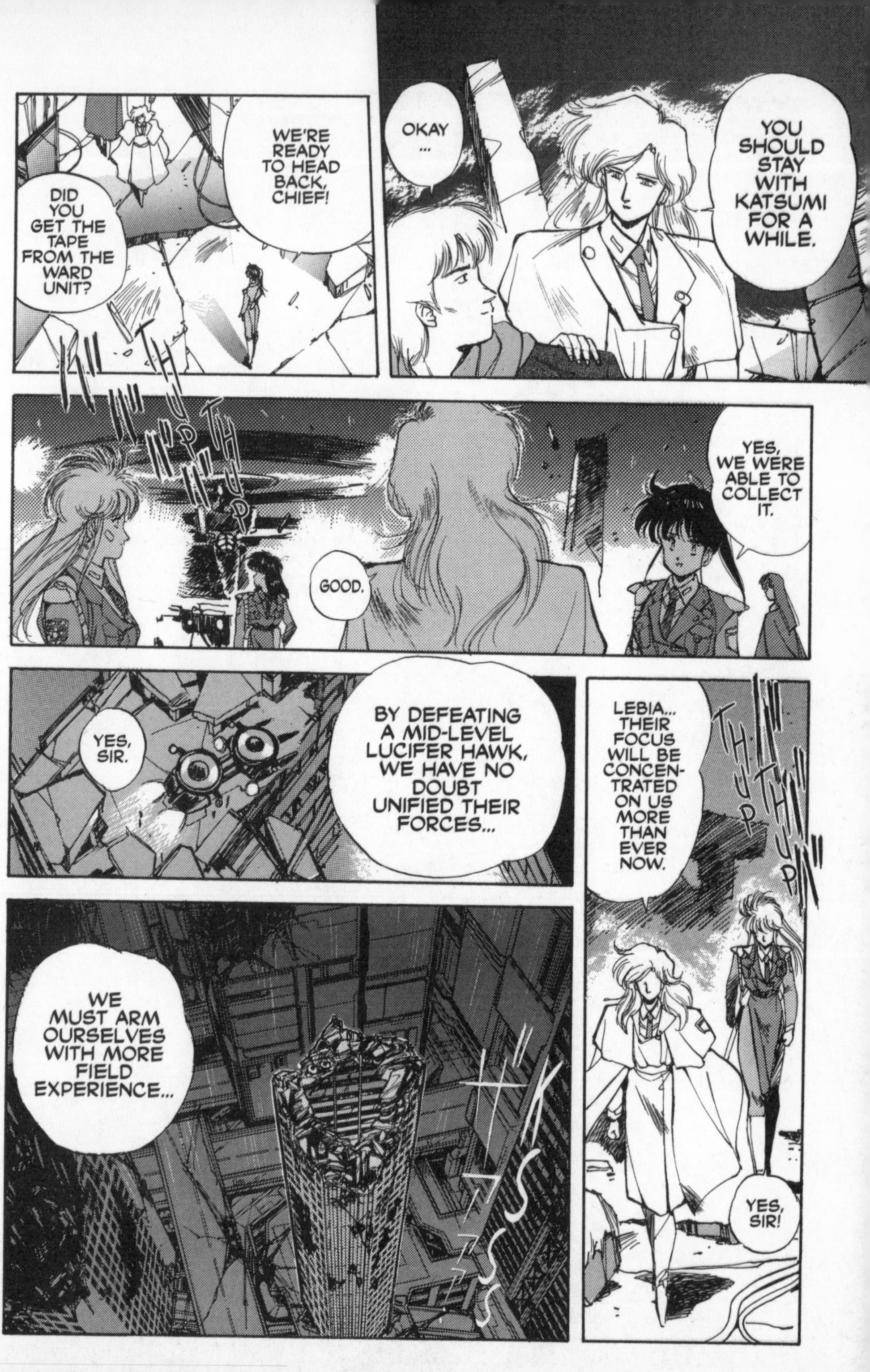
YOU SHOULD STAY WITH KATSUMI FOR A WHILE.
OKAY ...
WE'RE READY TO HEAD BACK, CHIEF!
DID YOU GET THE TAPE FROM THE WARD UNIT?
THUP THUP
YES, WE WERE ABLE TO COLLECT IT.
GOOD.
LEBIA... THEIR FOCUS WILL BE CONCEN-TRATED ON US MORE THAN EVER NOW.
THUP THUP
YES, SIR!
BY DEFEATING A MID-LEVEL LUCIFER HAWK, WE HAVE NO DOUBT UNIFIED THEIR FORCES...
YES, SIR.
WE MUST ARM OURSELVES WITH MORE FIELD EXPERIENCE...

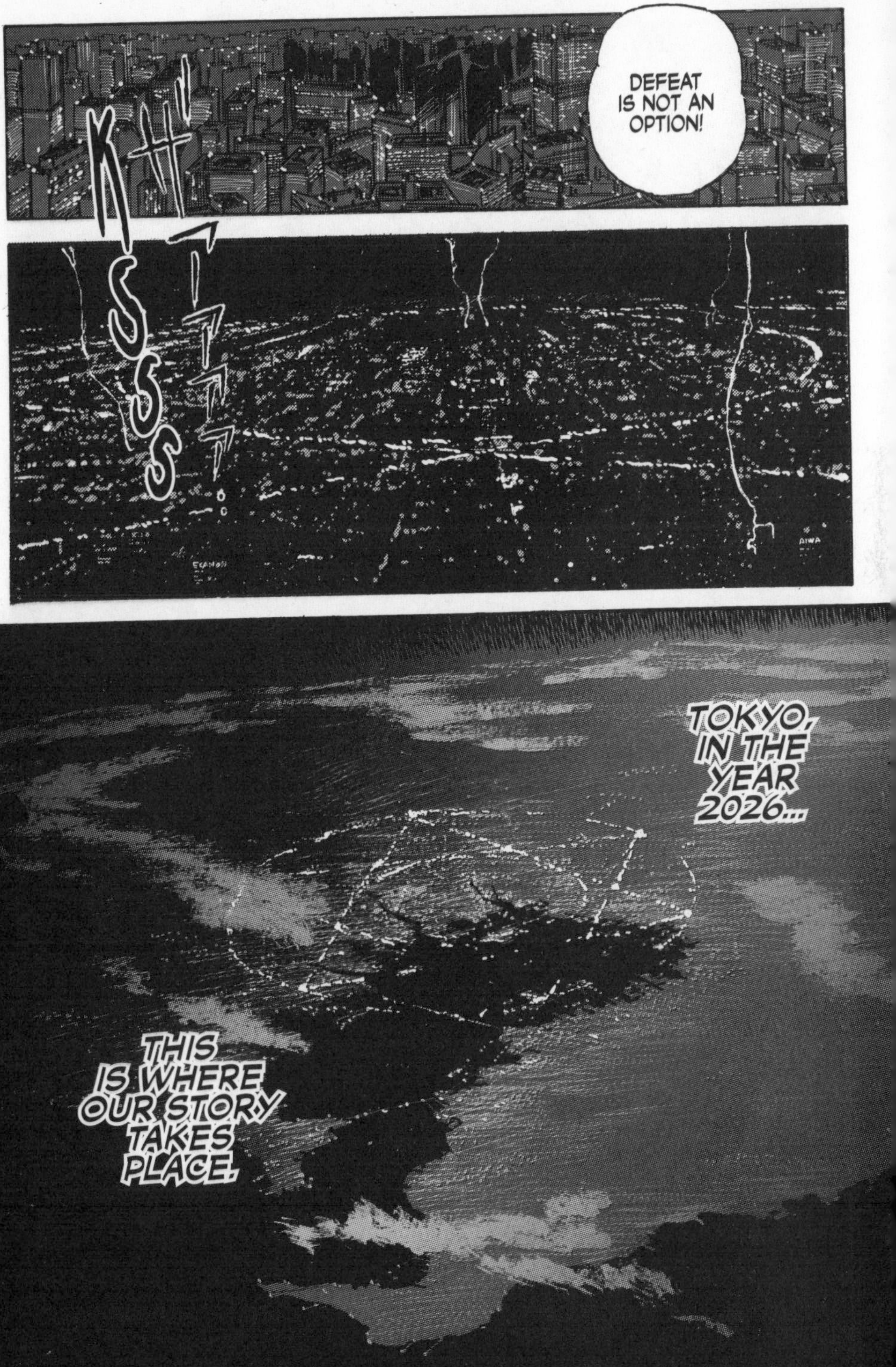
DEFEAT IS NOT AN OPTION!
KSSS
TOKYO, IN THE YEAR 2026...
THIS IS WHERE OUR STORY TAKES PLACE.

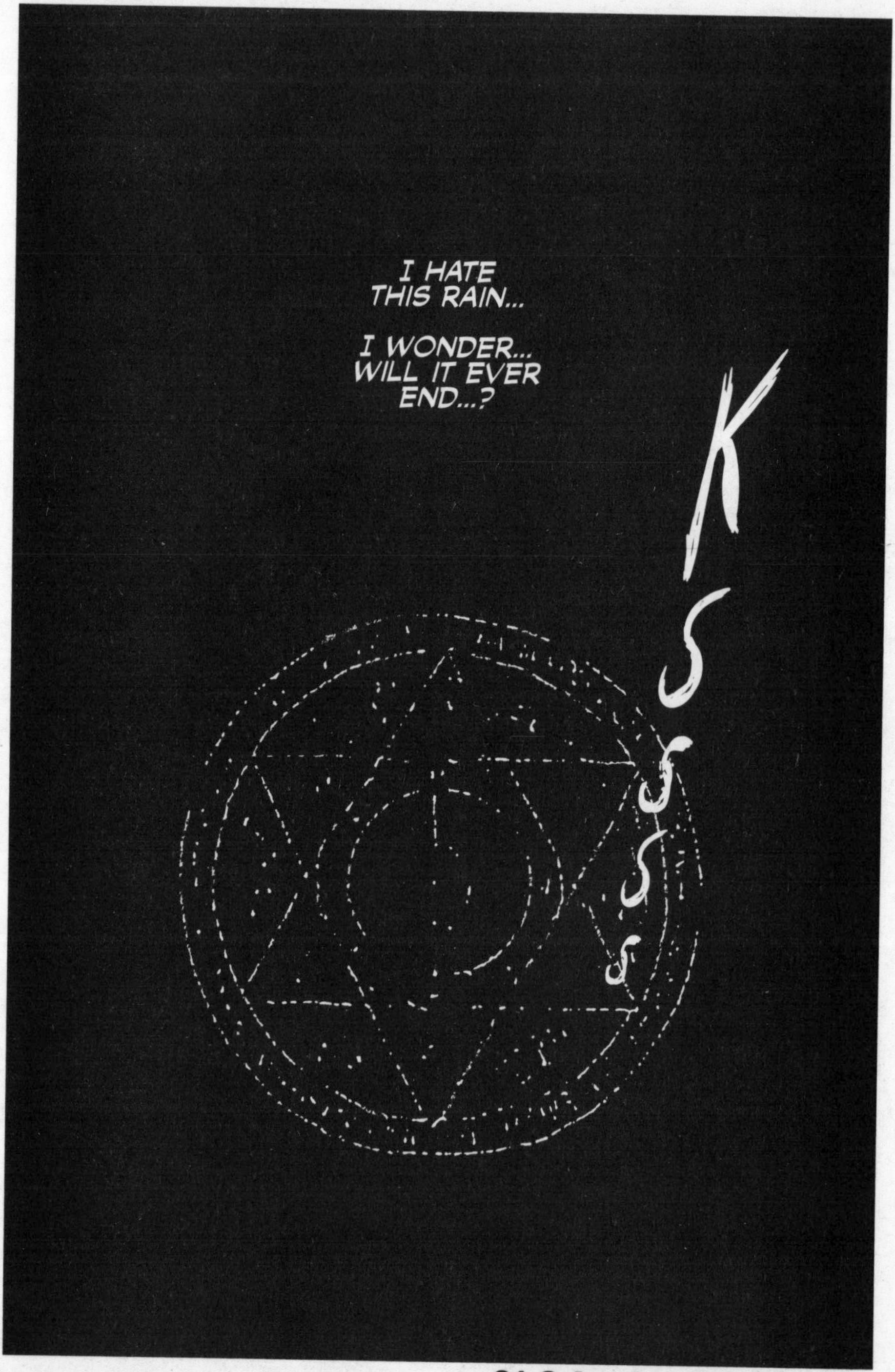
I HATE THIS RAIN...
I WONDER... WILL IT EVER END...?
KSSSSS

01: Cyber Psychic City -Fin-

02:

Nami Yamigumo

闇雲那魅

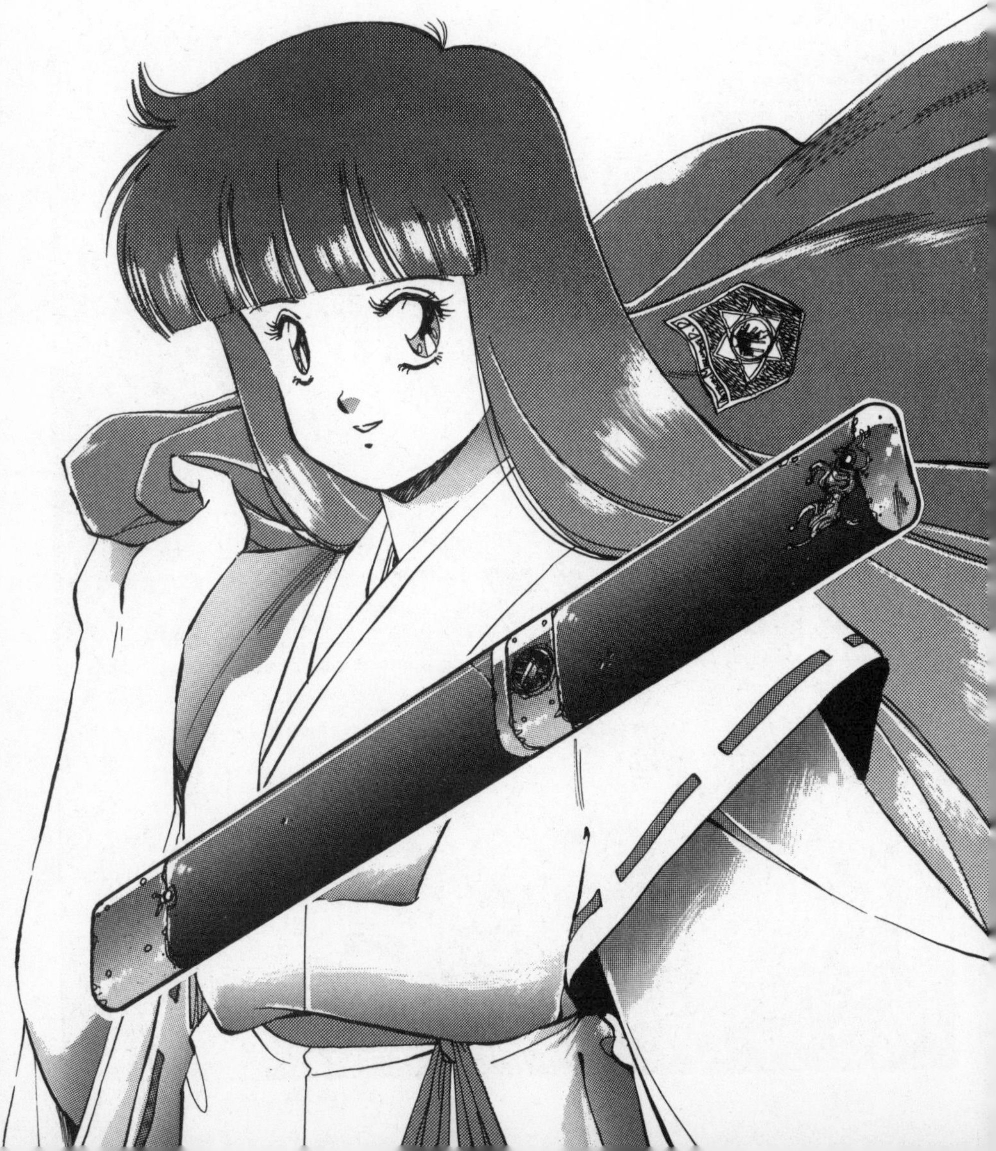

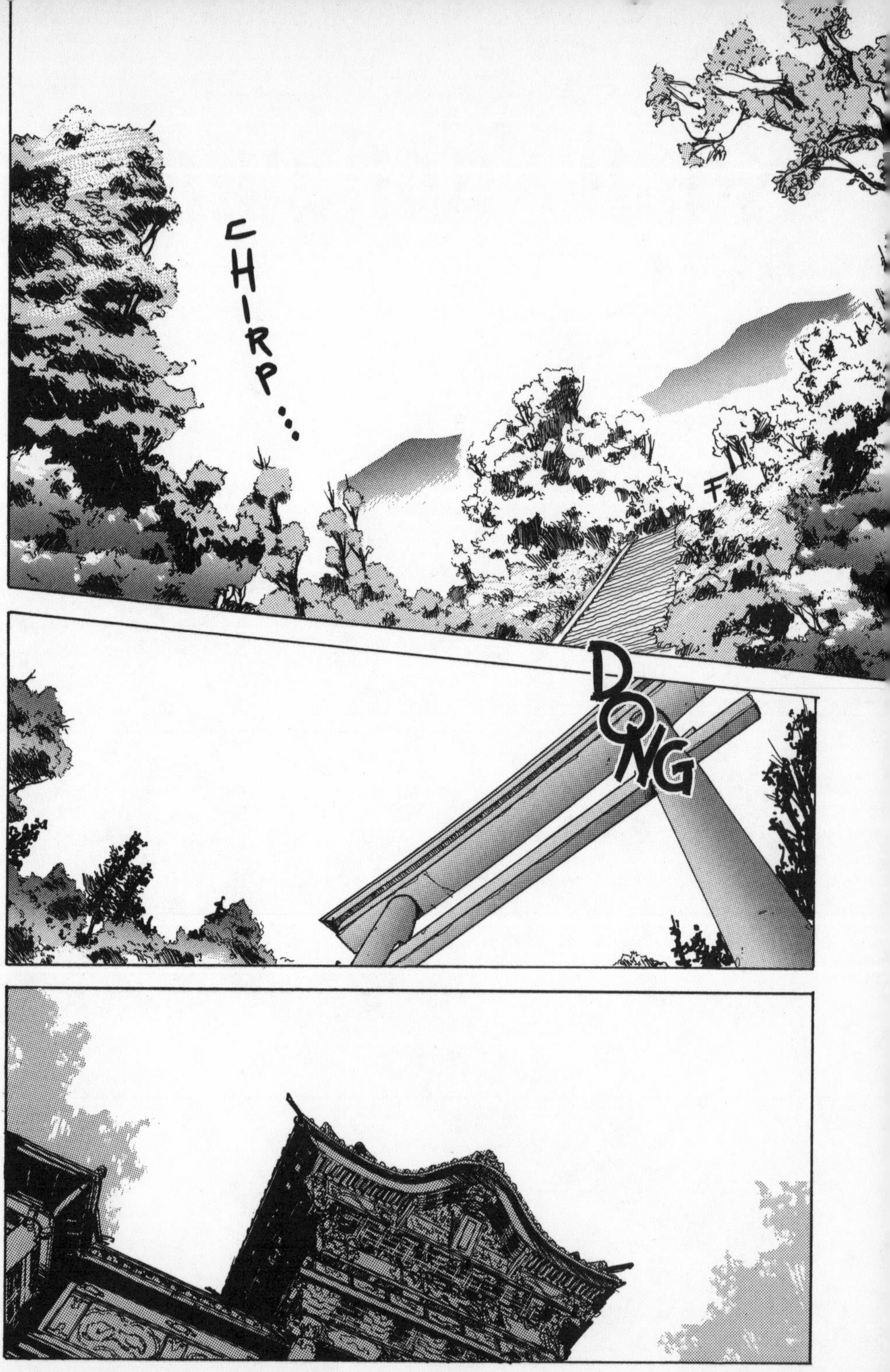
CHIRP...
DONG

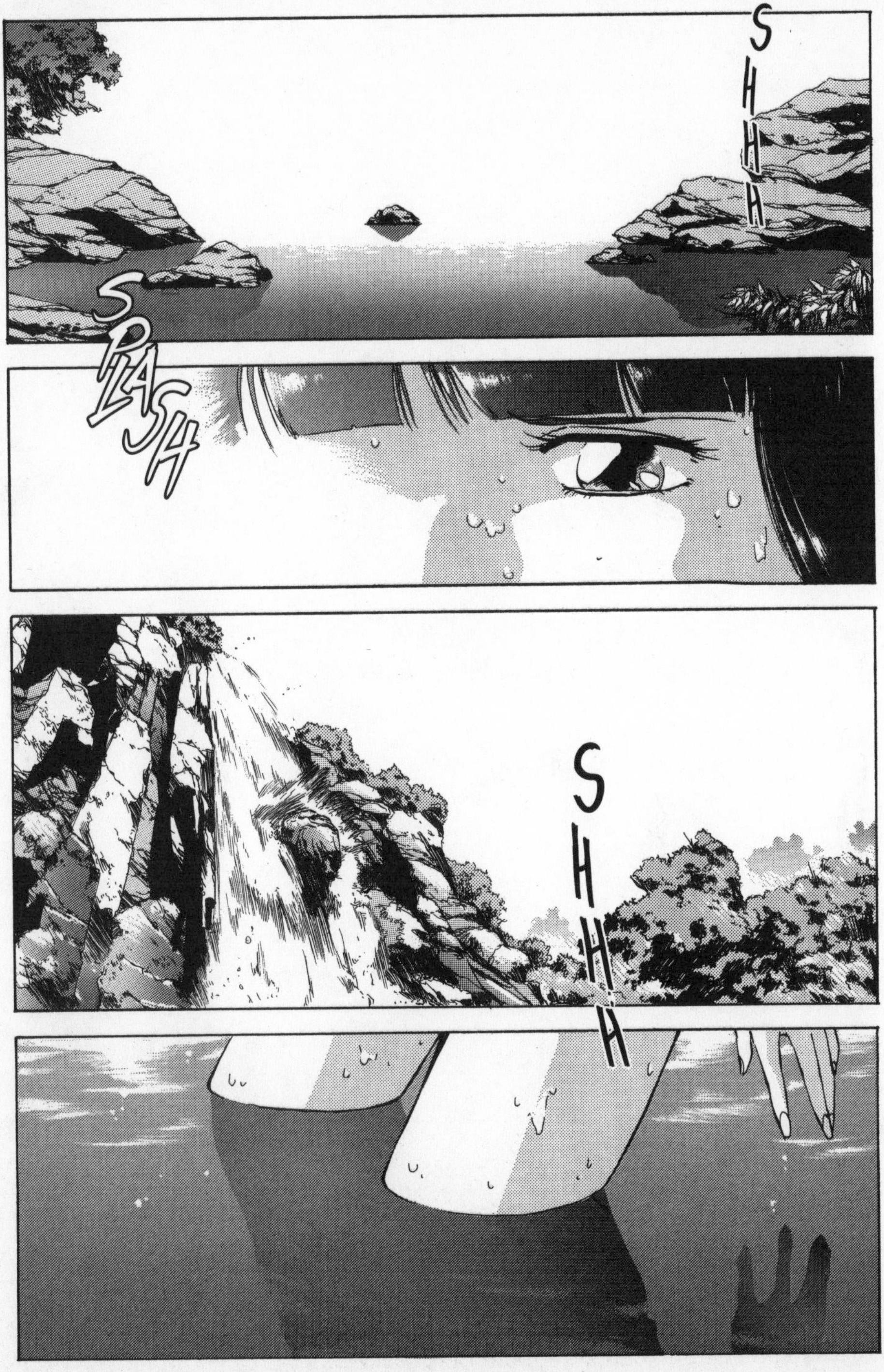

SHHH
SPLASH
SHHHH

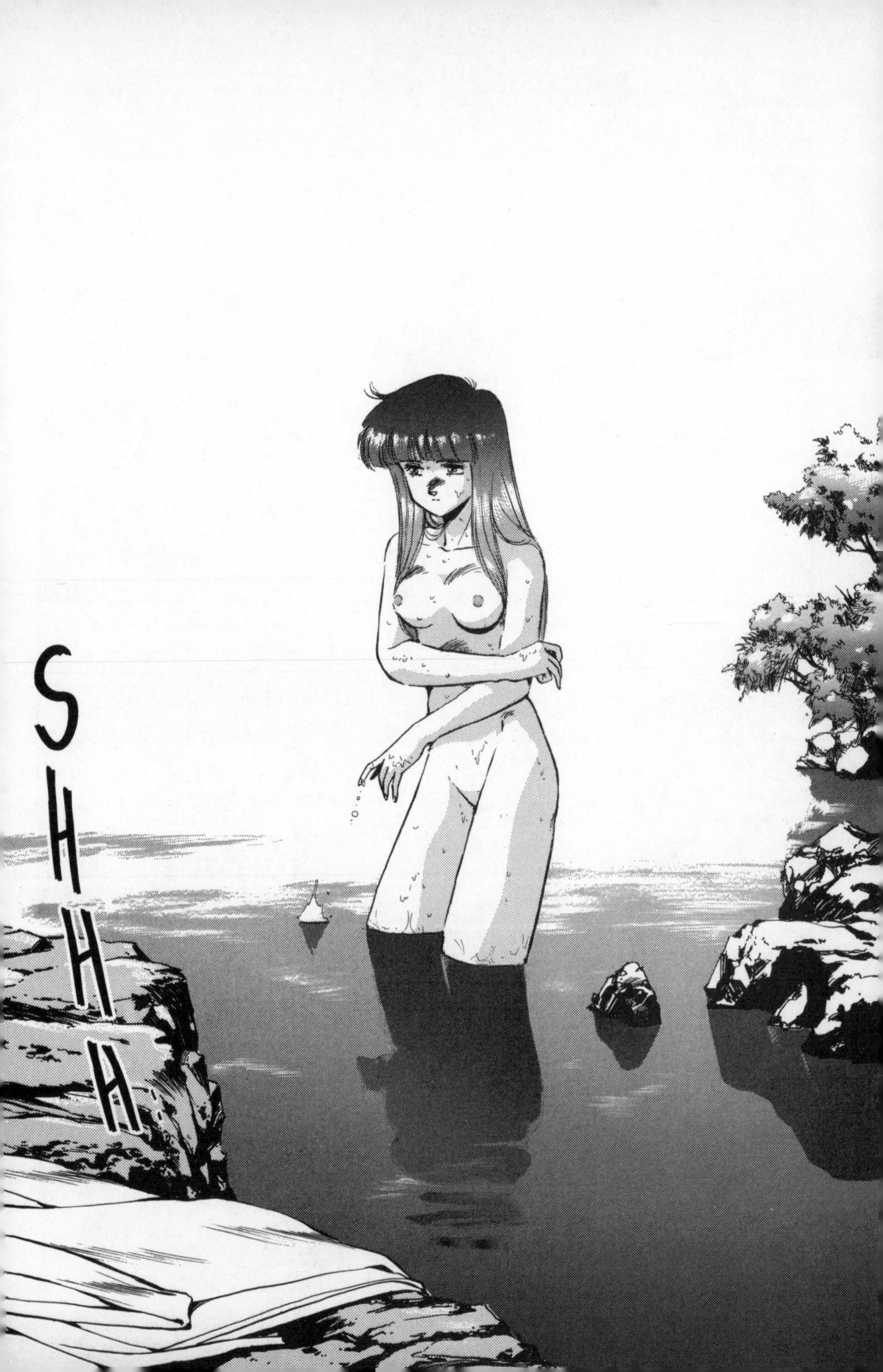
SHHH...

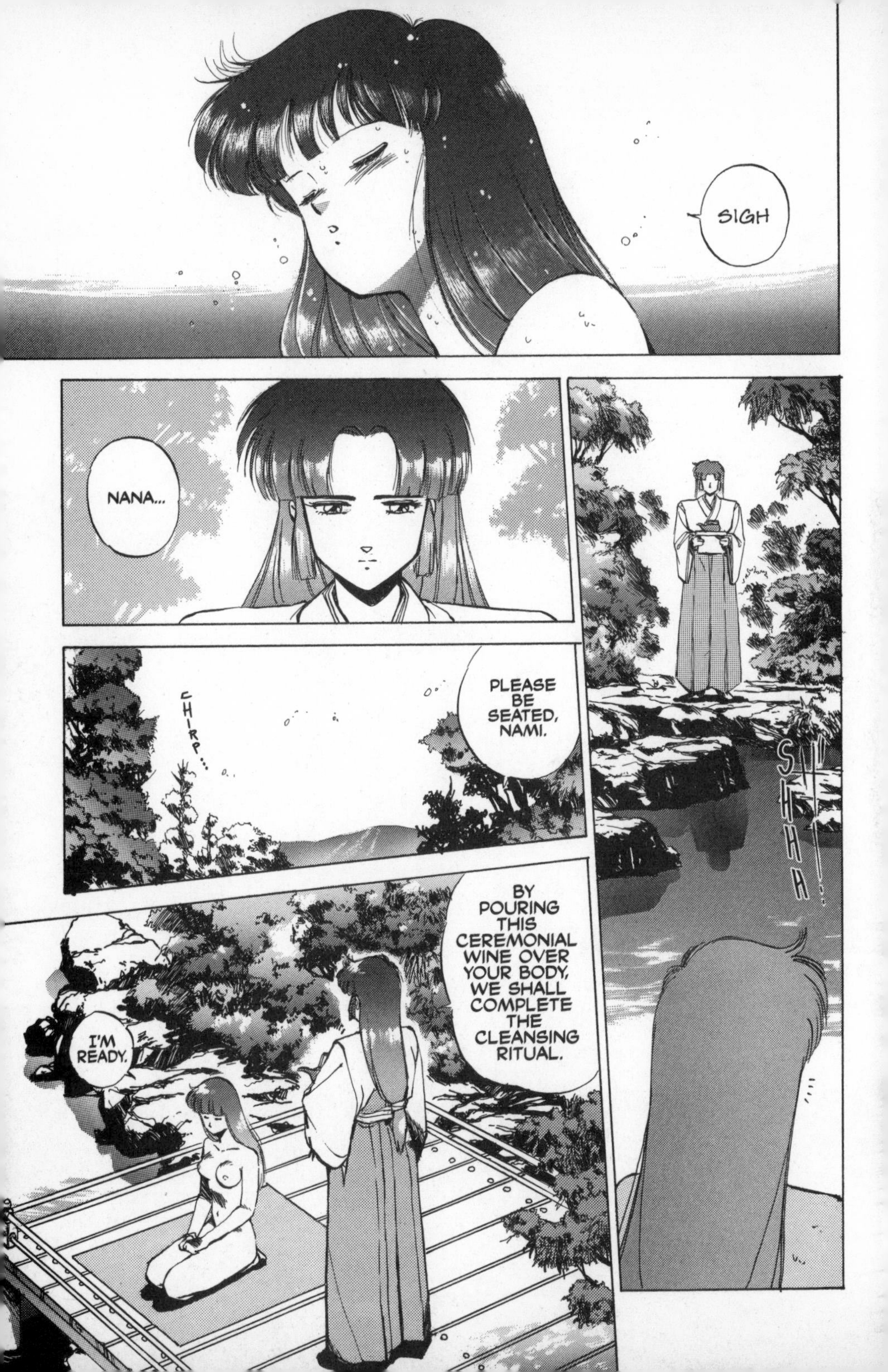
SIGH
SHHHA!!
NANA...
PLEASE BE SEATED, NAMI.
CHIRP...
BY POURING THIS CEREMONIAL WINE OVER YOUR BODY, WE SHALL COMPLETE THE CLEANSING RITUAL.
I'M READY.

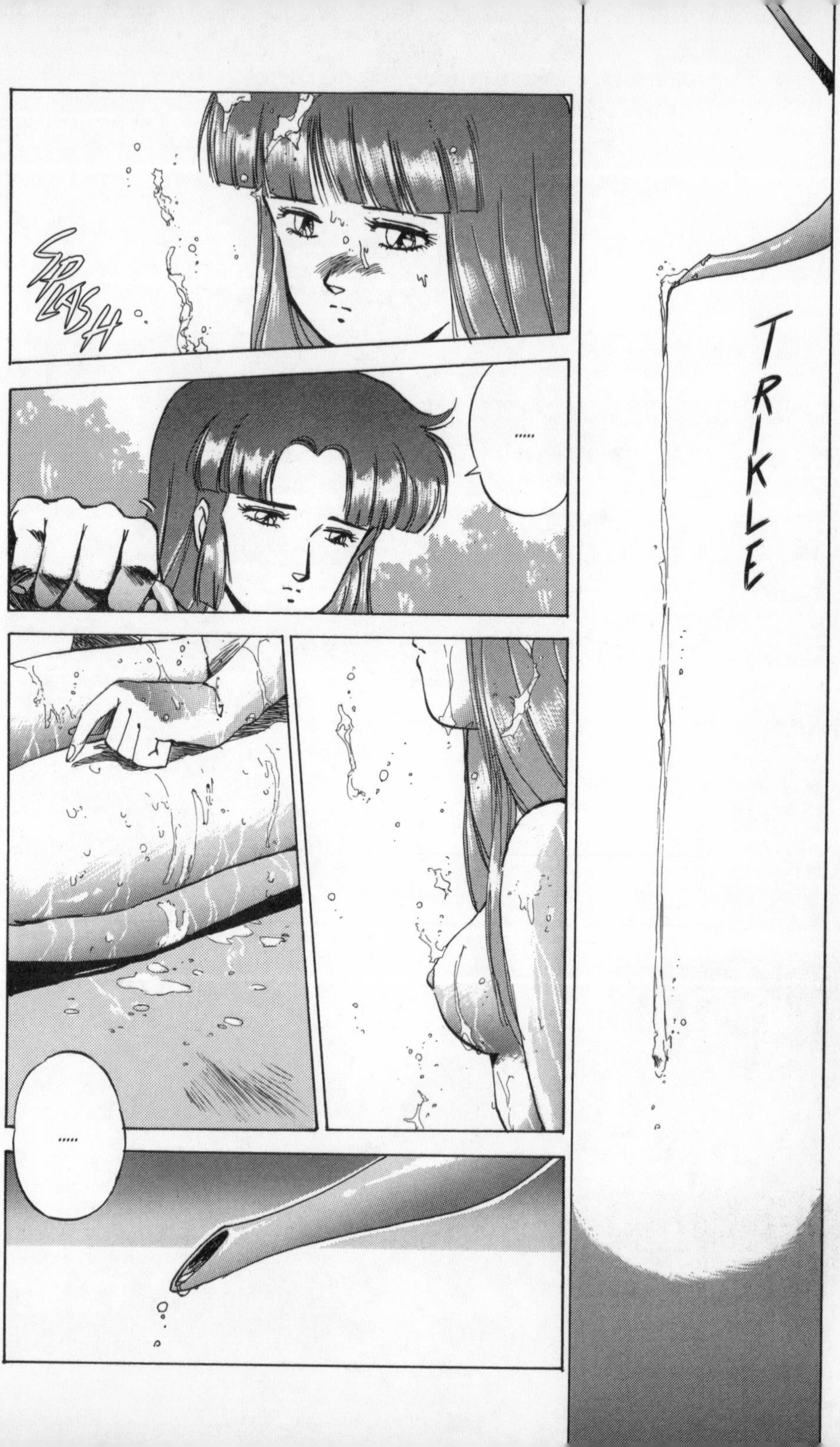
TRIKLE
SPLASH
.....
.....

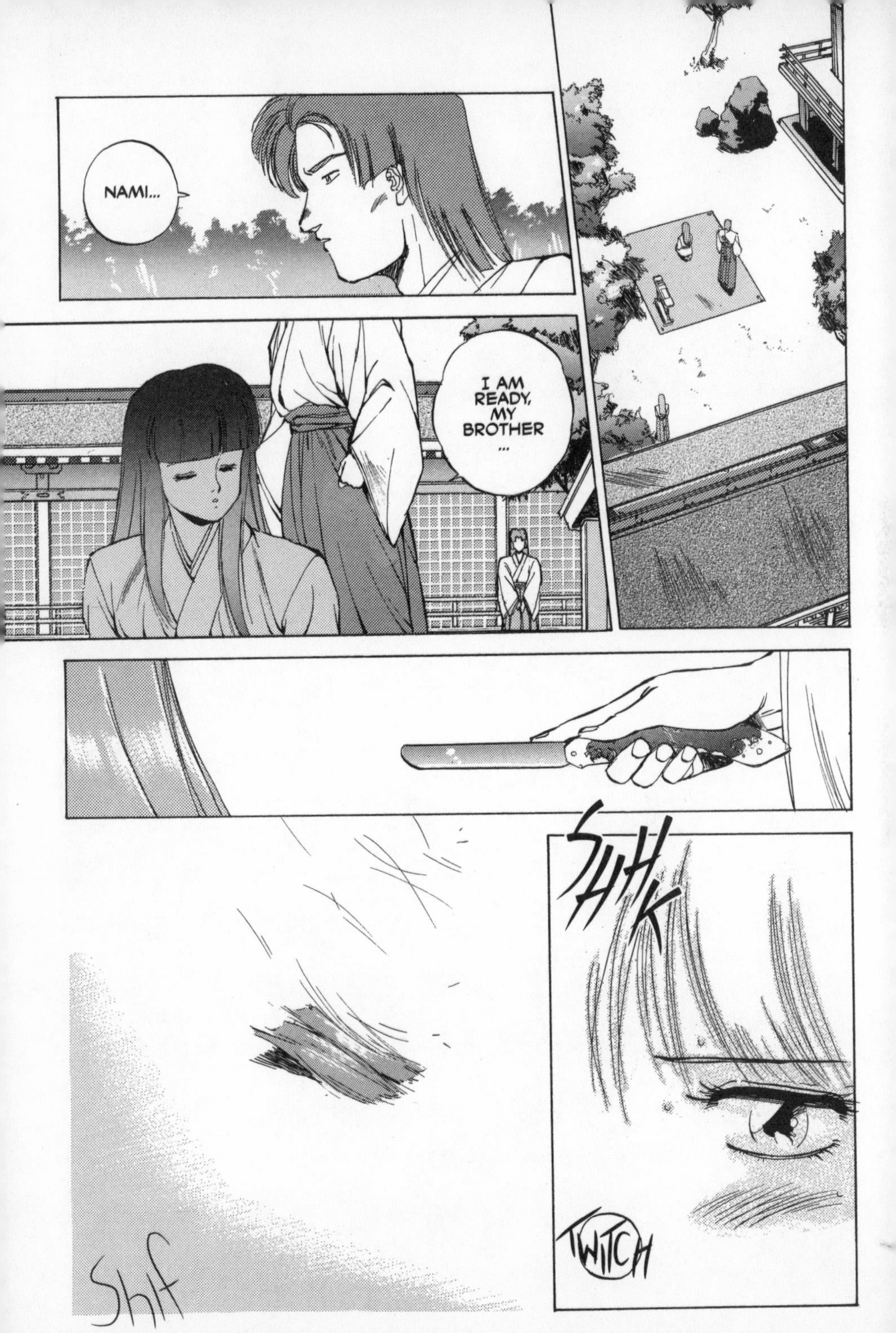
NAMI...
I AM READY, MY BROTHER ...
SHHK
TWITCH
Shif

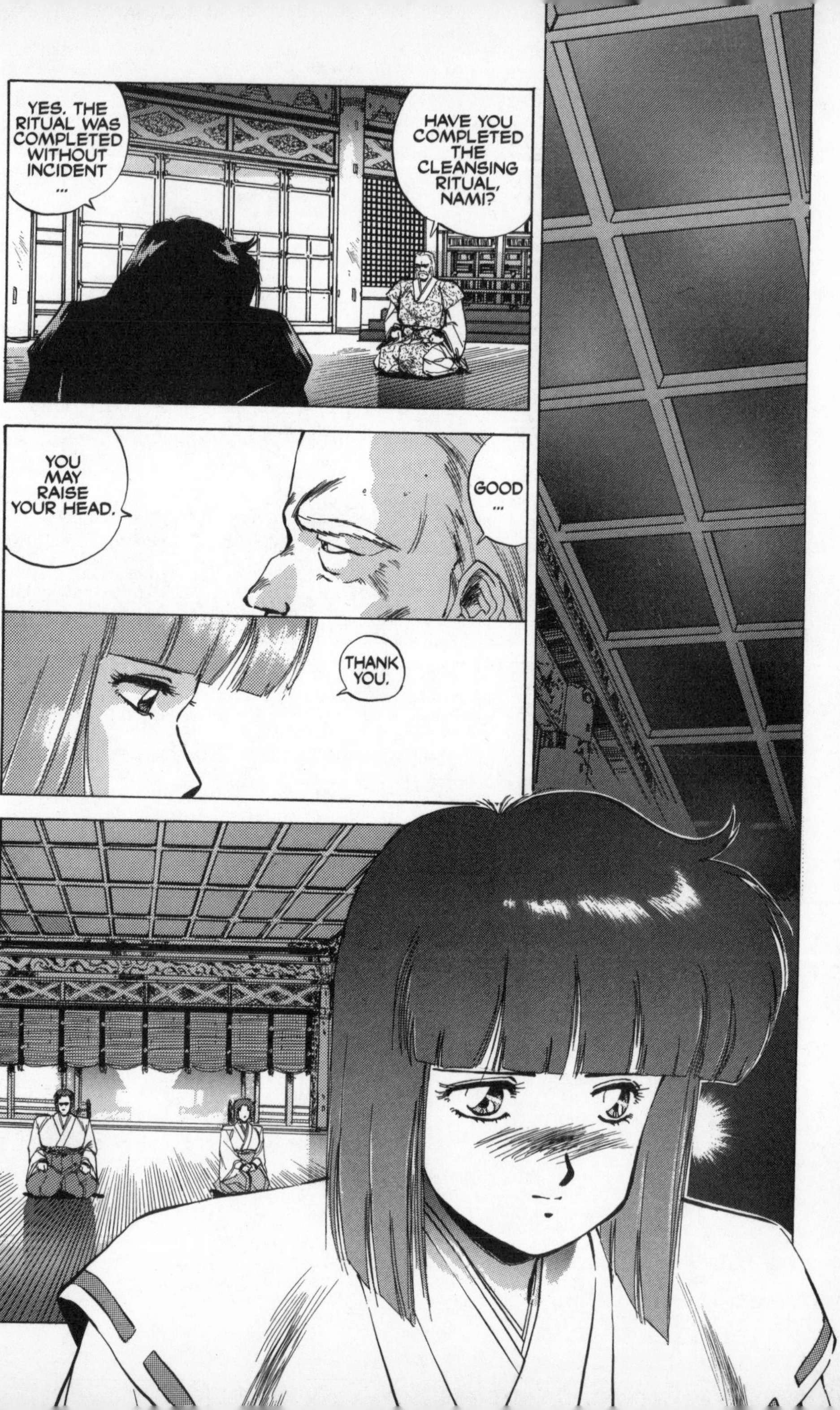
HAVE YOU COMPLETED THE CLEANSING RITUAL, NAMI?
YES. THE RITUAL WAS COMPLETED WITHOUT INCIDENT ...
GOOD ...
YOU MAY RAISE YOUR HEAD.
THANK YOU.

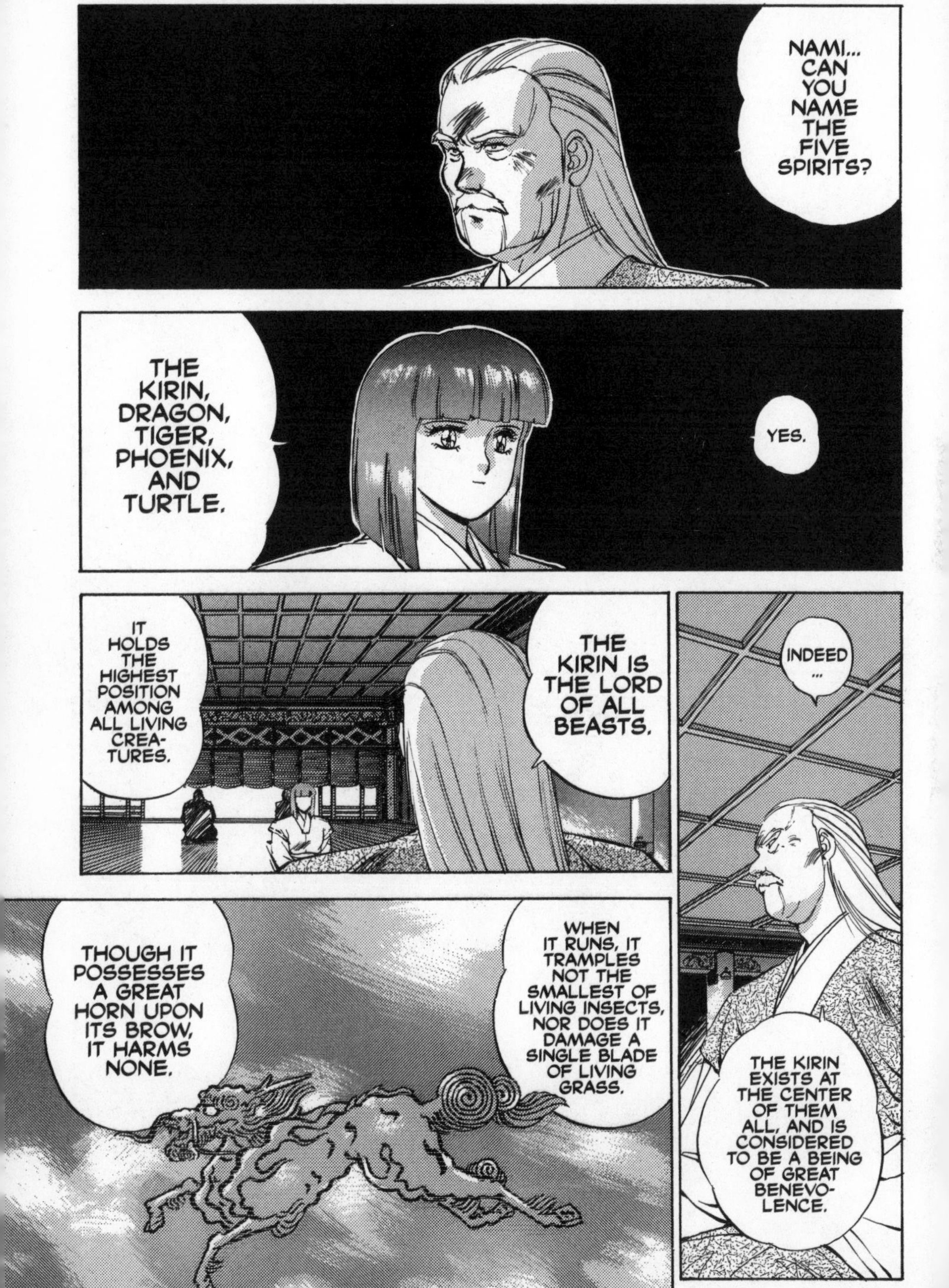

NAMI... CAN YOU NAME THE FIVE SPIRITS?
YES.
THE KIRIN, DRAGON, TIGER, PHOENIX, AND TURTLE.
INDEED...
THE KIRIN EXISTS AT THE CENTER OF THEM ALL, AND IS CONSIDERED TO BE A BEING OF GREAT BENEVO-LENCE.
THE KIRIN IS THE LORD OF ALL BEASTS.
IT HOLDS THE HIGHEST POSITION AMONG ALL LIVING CREA-TURES.
WHEN IT RUNS, IT TRAMPLES NOT THE SMALLEST OF LIVING INSECTS, NOR DOES IT DAMAGE A SINGLE BLADE OF LIVING GRASS.
THOUGH IT POSSESSES A GREAT HORN UPON ITS BROW, IT HARMS NONE.

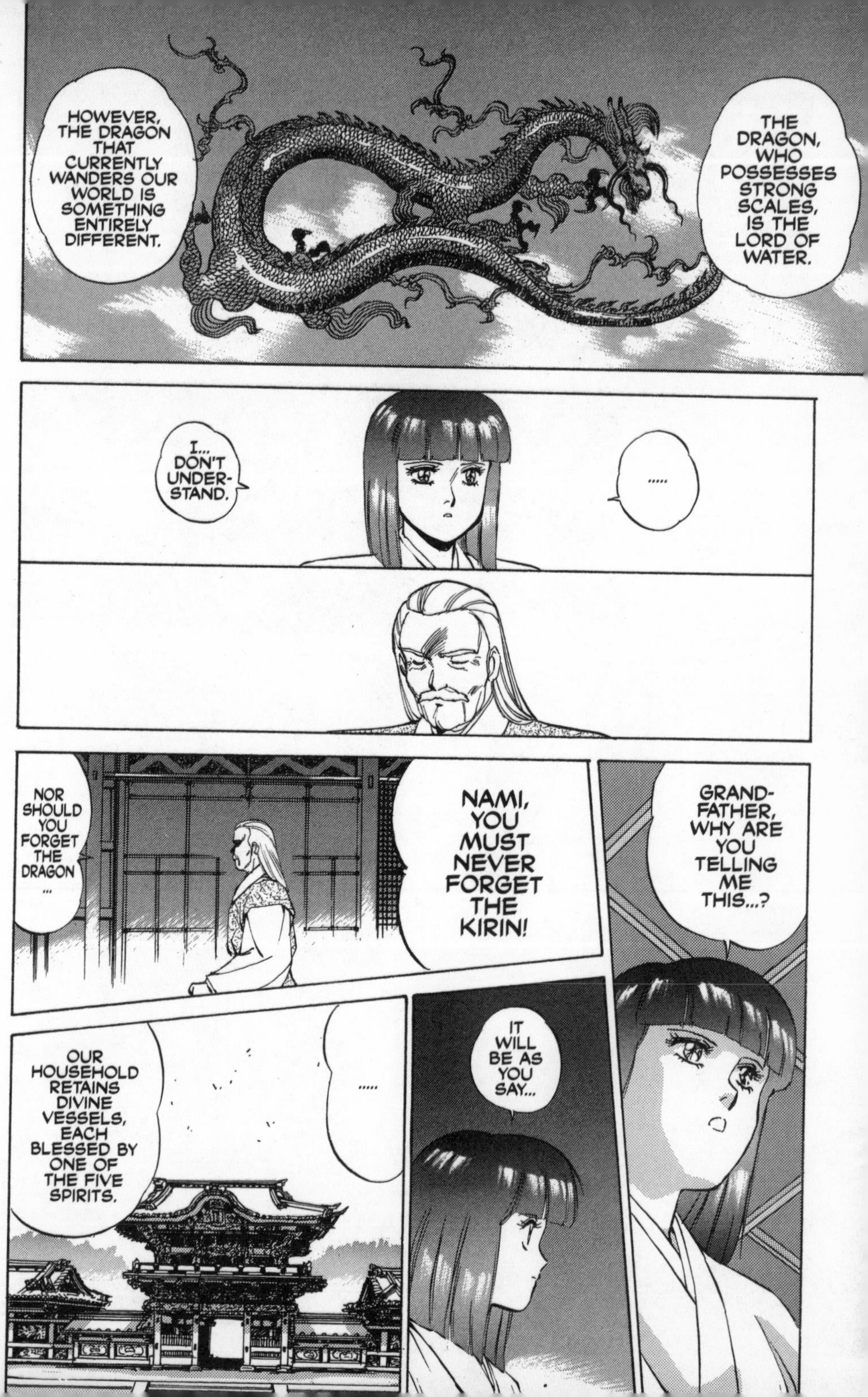
THE DRAGON, WHO POSSESSES STRONG SCALES, IS THE LORD OF WATER.
HOWEVER, THE DRAGON THAT CURRENTLY WANDERS OUR WORLD IS SOMETHING ENTIRELY DIFFERENT.
.....
I... DON'T UNDER-STAND.
GRAND-FATHER, WHY ARE YOU TELLING ME THIS...?
NAMI, YOU MUST NEVER FORGET THE KIRIN!
NOR SHOULD YOU FORGET THE DRAGON ...
IT WILL BE AS YOU SAY...
.....
OUR HOUSEHOLD RETAINS DIVINE VESSELS, EACH BLESSED BY ONE OF THE FIVE SPIRITS.

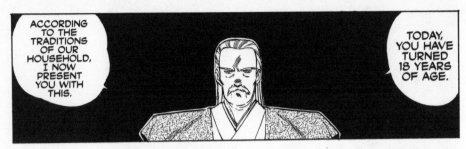

TODAY, YOU HAVE TURNED 18 YEARS OF AGE.
ACCORDING TO THE TRADITIONS OF OUR HOUSEHOLD, I NOW PRESENT YOU WITH THIS.
IT IS A BLESSED BLADE THAT HAS BEEN PASSED DOWN FROM GENERATION TO GENER-ATION.
THIS BLADE IDENTIFIES YOU AS THE CHOSEN HEIR OF THE YAMIGUMO HOUSEHOLD.
WIELD IT WITH CARE.
I SHALL.
SHK
CHOK

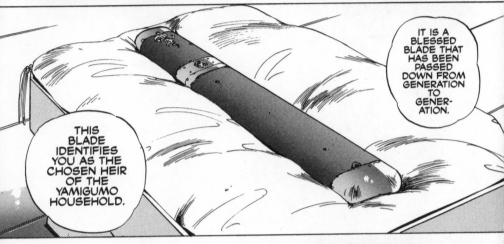

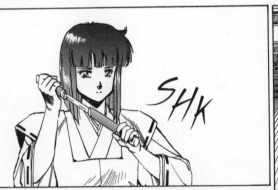

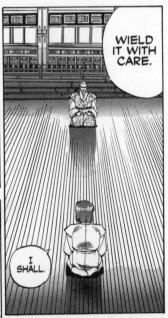

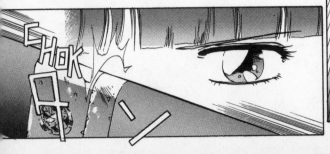

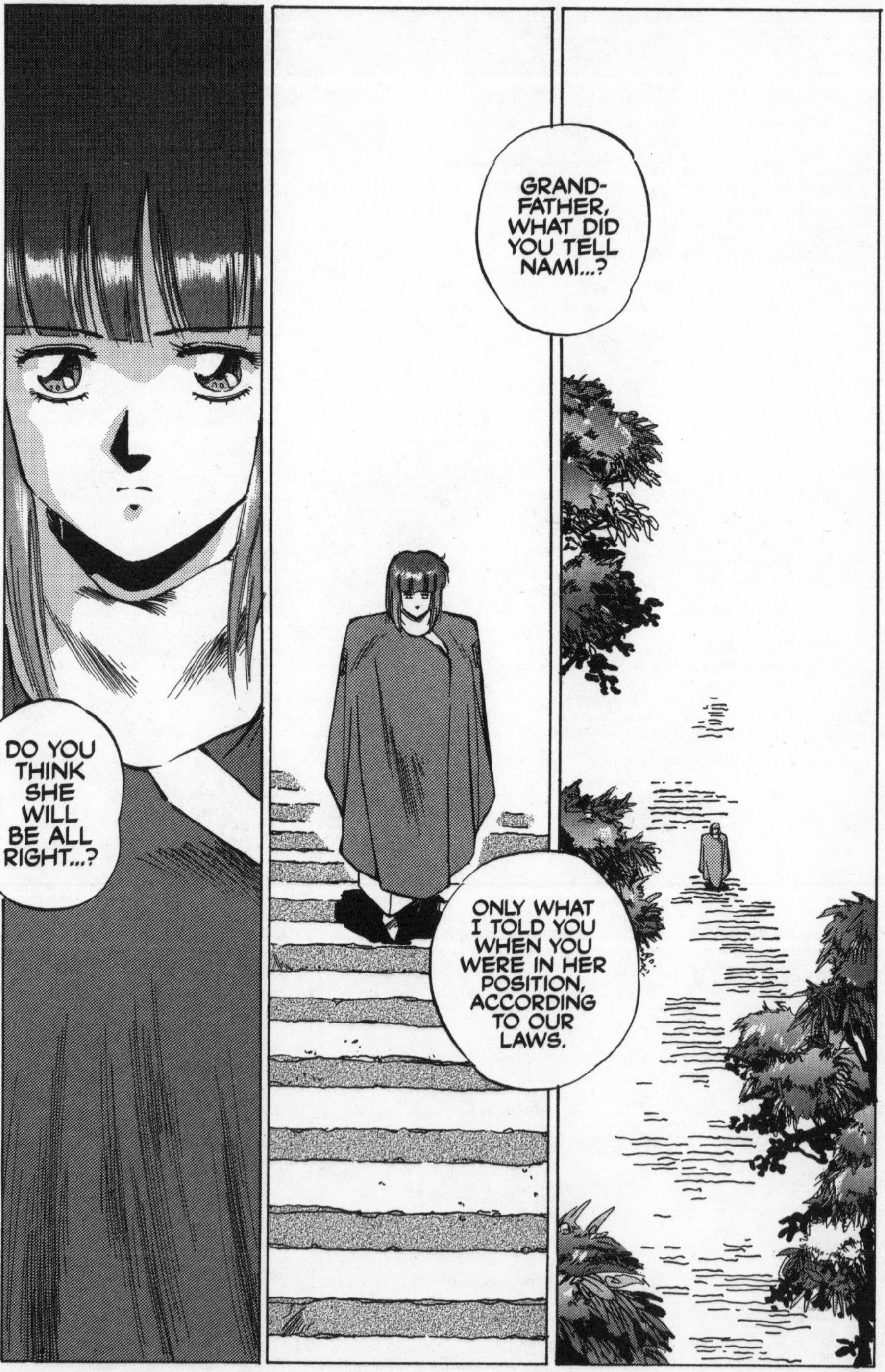
GRAND-FATHER, WHAT DID YOU TELL NAMI...?
ONLY WHAT I TOLD YOU WHEN YOU WERE IN HER POSITION, ACCORDING TO OUR LAWS.
DO YOU THINK SHE WILL BE ALL RIGHT...?

I DO NOT KNOW. EVEN YOU TWO WERE UNABLE TO SUFFER THE TRIALS OF OUR HOUSEHOLD, AND FORFEITED YOUR RIGHT TO BE THE CHOSEN HEIR...
IF SHE CANNOT SURVIVE THIS TRIAL, SHE WILL HAVE BEEN PROVEN UNWORTHY, AND WOULD THEREFORE BE USELESS TO US!
THE YAMIGUMO HOUSEHOLD HAS SECRETLY SAFEGUARDED THIS WORLD SINCE THE DAYS OF OLD, AND WE ARE THE ABSOLUTE AUTHORITY ON ALL RELIGIOUS MATTERS.
THE CHOSEN HEIR OF THE YAMIGUMO HOUSEHOLD MUST POSSESSES SIGNIFICANTLY GREATER ENDURANCE, INTELLIGENCE, AND SPIRITUALITY THAN THE AVERAGE PERSON.
FOR NAMI, THIS TRIAL IS SIMPLY THE FIRST STEP IN HER LONG JOURNEY TOWARDS TAKING OVER THE YAMIGUMO HOUSEHOLD ...
THE BLADE SHE NOW CARRIES WITH HER WILL ONLY REVEAL ITS TRUE POWER TO ONE THAT IT DEEMS WORTHY.
IT IS NOT FOR ME TO KNOW WHETHER SHE WILL BE ABLE TO DRAW OUT THE BLADE'S FULL POTENTIAL.
GRAND-FATHER, WHAT WILL NAMI'S TRIAL CONSIST OF...?
WELL...

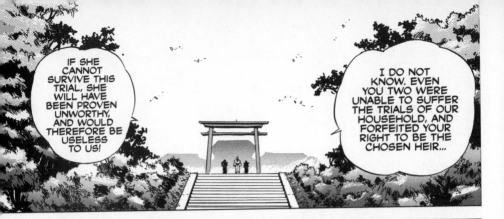

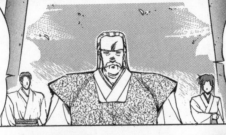

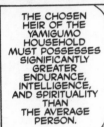

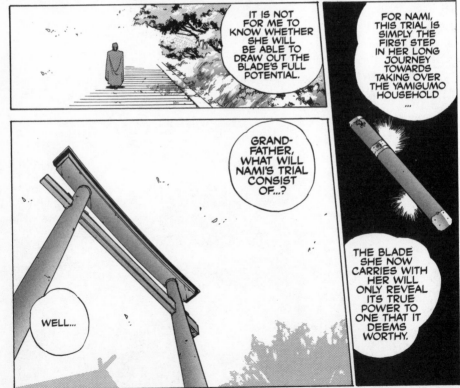

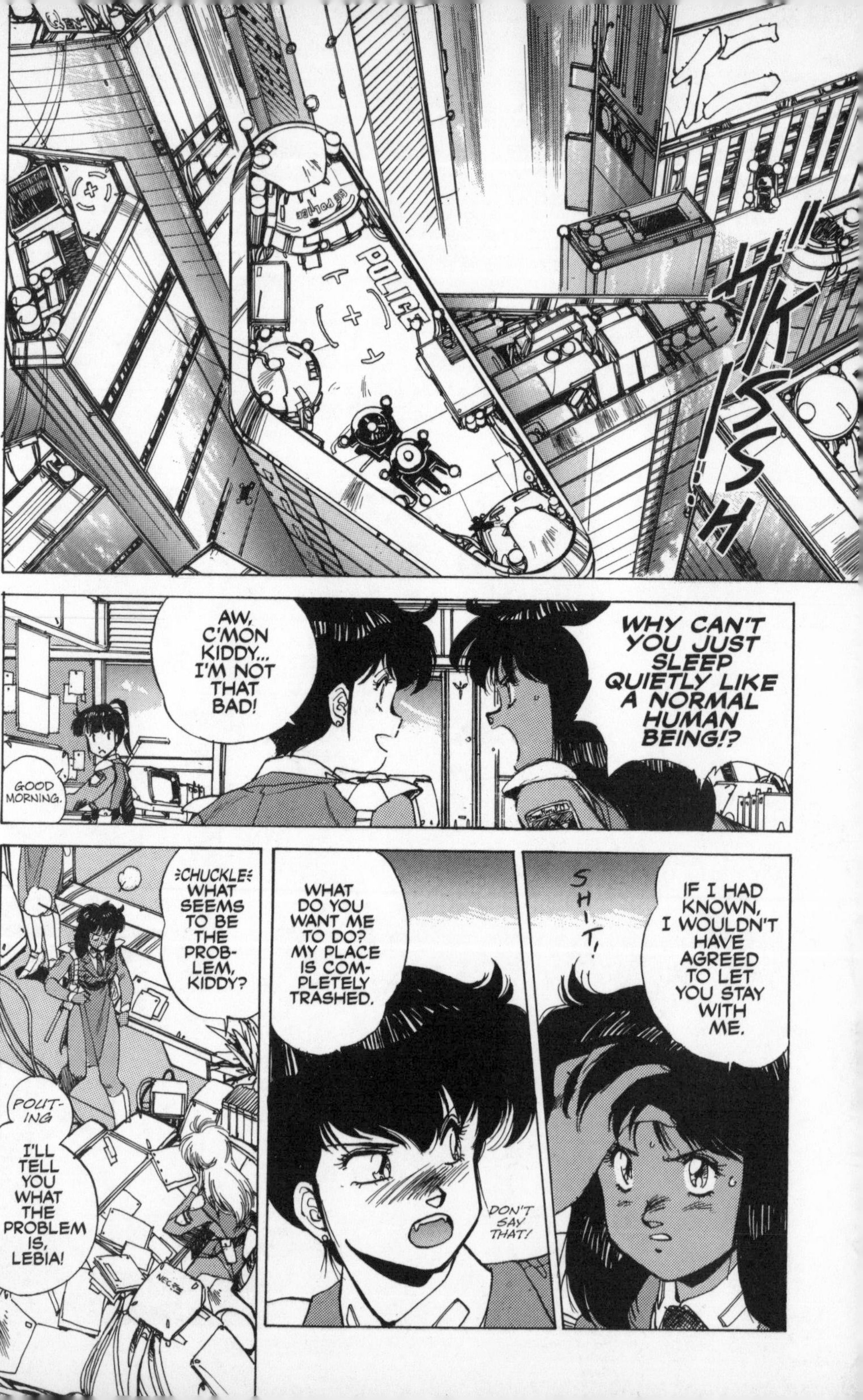
HKISSH!!
WHY CAN'T YOU JUST SLEEP QUIETLY LIKE A NORMAL HUMAN BEING!?
AW, C'MON KIDDY... I'M NOT THAT BAD!
GOOD MORNING.
IF I HAD KNOWN, I WOULDN'T HAVE AGREED TO LET YOU STAY WITH ME.
SHIT!
WHAT DO YOU WANT ME TO DO? MY PLACE IS COMPLETELY TRASHED.
DON'T SAY THAT!
CHUCKLE WHAT SEEMS TO BE THE PROBLEM, KIDDY?
POUTING
I'LL TELL YOU WHAT THE PROBLEM IS, LEBIA!

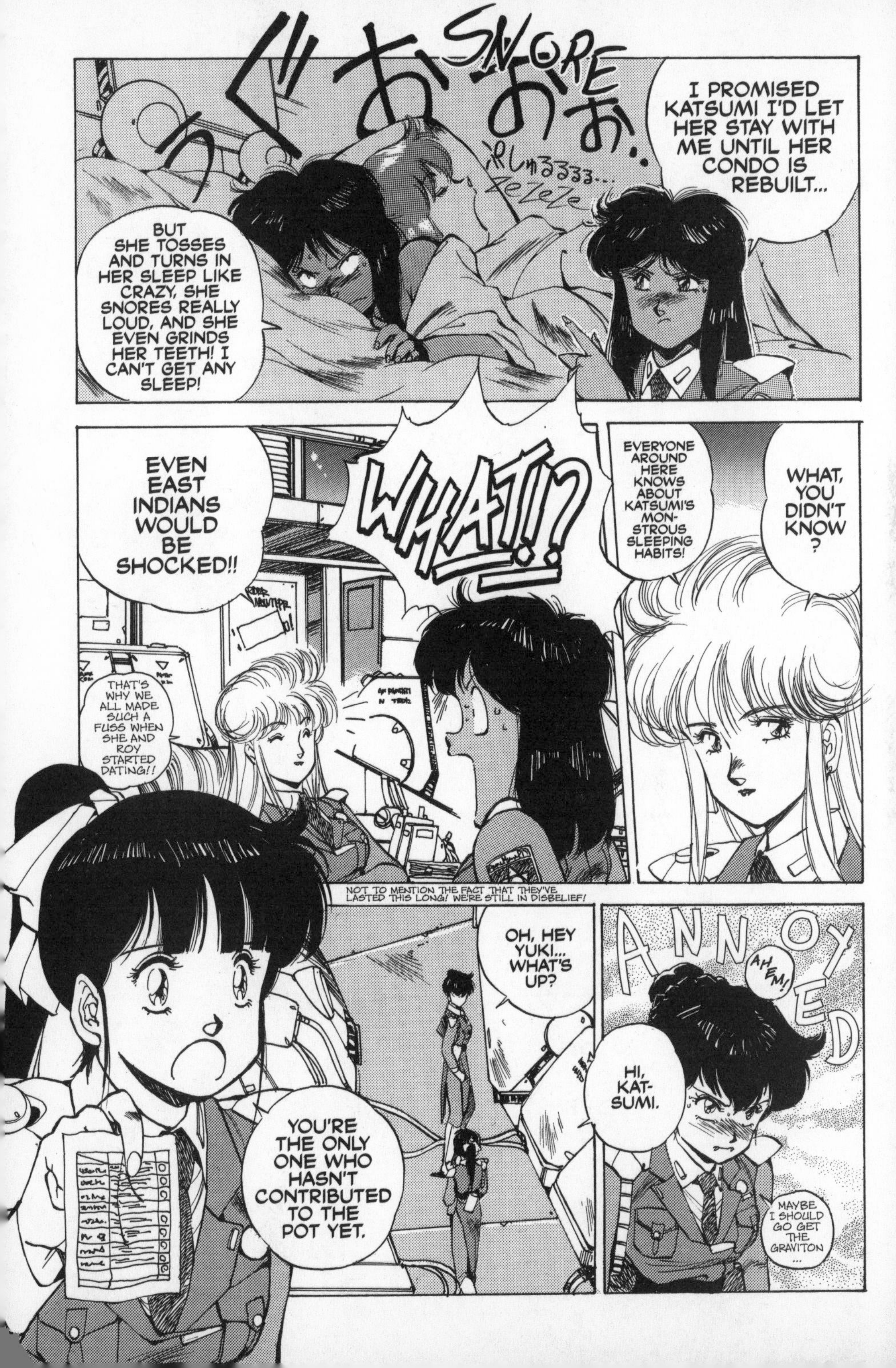
I PROMISED KATSUMI I'D LET HER STAY WITH ME UNTIL HER CONDO IS REBUILT...
ぐおおおお..
SNORE
ぷしゅるるるるる...
ZeZeZe
BUT SHE TOSSES AND TURNS IN HER SLEEP LIKE CRAZY, SHE SNORES REALLY LOUD, AND SHE EVEN GRINDS HER TEETH! I CAN'T GET ANY SLEEP!
WHAT, YOU DIDN'T KNOW?
EVERYONE AROUND HERE KNOWS ABOUT KATSUMI'S MON-STROUS SLEEPING HABITS!
WHAT!?
EVEN EAST INDIANS WOULD BE SHOCKED!!
THAT'S WHY WE ALL MADE SUCH A FUSS WHEN SHE AND ROY STARTED DATING!!
NOT TO MENTION THE FACT THAT THEY'VE LASTED THIS LONG! WE'RE STILL IN DISBELIEF!
ANNOYED
AHEM!
HI, KAT-SUMI.
MAYBE I SHOULD GO GET THE GRAVITON ...
OH, HEY YUKI... WHAT'S UP?
YOU'RE THE ONLY ONE WHO HASN'T CONTRIBUTED TO THE POT YET.

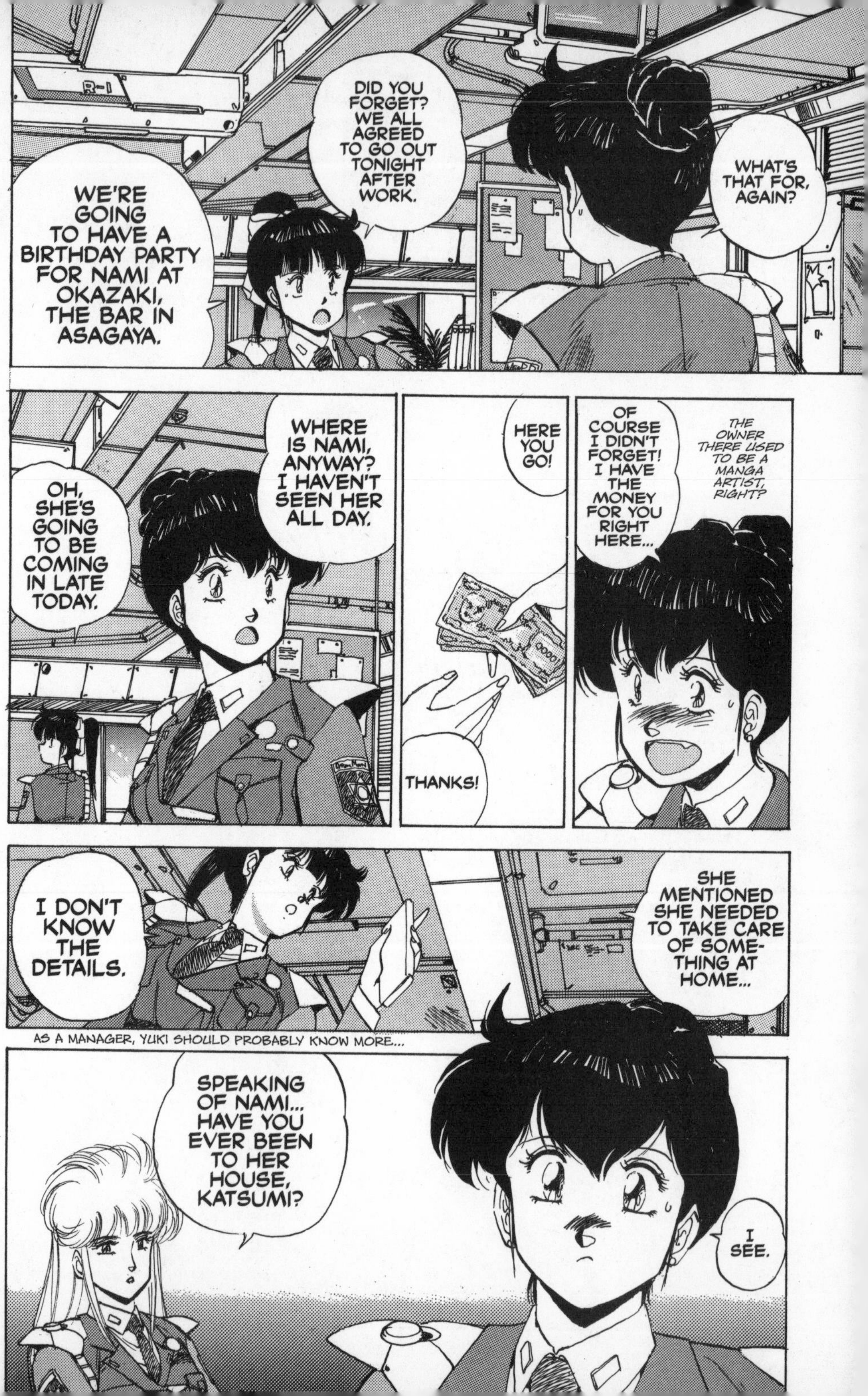
WHAT'S THAT FOR, AGAIN?
DID YOU FORGET? WE ALL AGREED TO GO OUT TONIGHT AFTER WORK.
WE'RE GOING TO HAVE A BIRTHDAY PARTY FOR NAMI AT OKAZAKI, THE BAR IN ASAGAYA.
THE OWNER THERE USED TO BE A MANGA ARTIST, RIGHT?
OF COURSE I DIDN'T FORGET! I HAVE THE MONEY FOR YOU RIGHT HERE...
HERE YOU GO!
THANKS!
WHERE IS NAMI, ANYWAY? I HAVEN'T SEEN HER ALL DAY.
OH, SHE'S GOING TO BE COMING IN LATE TODAY.
SHE MENTIONED SHE NEEDED TO TAKE CARE OF SOME-THING AT HOME...
I DON'T KNOW THE DETAILS.
AS A MANAGER, YUKI SHOULD PROBABLY KNOW MORE...
I SEE.
SPEAKING OF NAMI... HAVE YOU EVER BEEN TO HER HOUSE, KATSUMI?

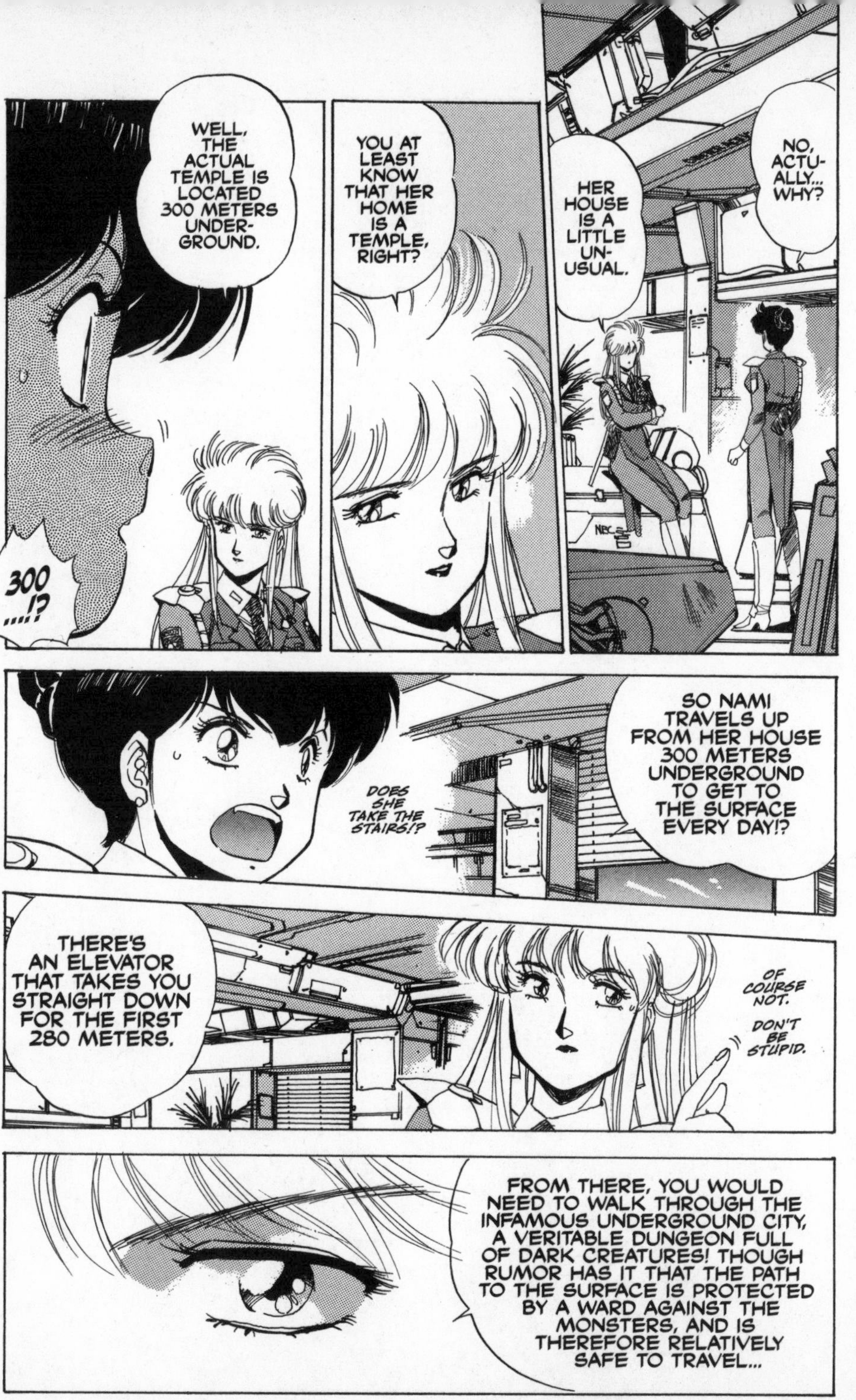
NO, ACTU-ALLY... WHY?
HER HOUSE IS A LITTLE UN-USUAL.
YOU AT LEAST KNOW THAT HER HOME IS A TEMPLE, RIGHT?
WELL, THE ACTUAL TEMPLE IS LOCATED 300 METERS UNDER-GROUND.
300 ...!?
SO NAMI TRAVELS UP FROM HER HOUSE 300 METERS UNDERGROUND TO GET TO THE SURFACE EVERY DAY!?
DOES SHE TAKE THE STAIRS!?
OF COURSE NOT.
DON'T BE STUPID.
THERE'S AN ELEVATOR THAT TAKES YOU STRAIGHT DOWN FOR THE FIRST 280 METERS.
FROM THERE, YOU WOULD NEED TO WALK THROUGH THE INFAMOUS UNDERGROUND CITY, A VERITABLE DUNGEON FULL OF DARK CREATURES! THOUGH RUMOR HAS IT THAT THE PATH TO THE SURFACE IS PROTECTED BY A WARD AGAINST THE MONSTERS, AND IS THEREFORE RELATIVELY SAFE TO TRAVEL...

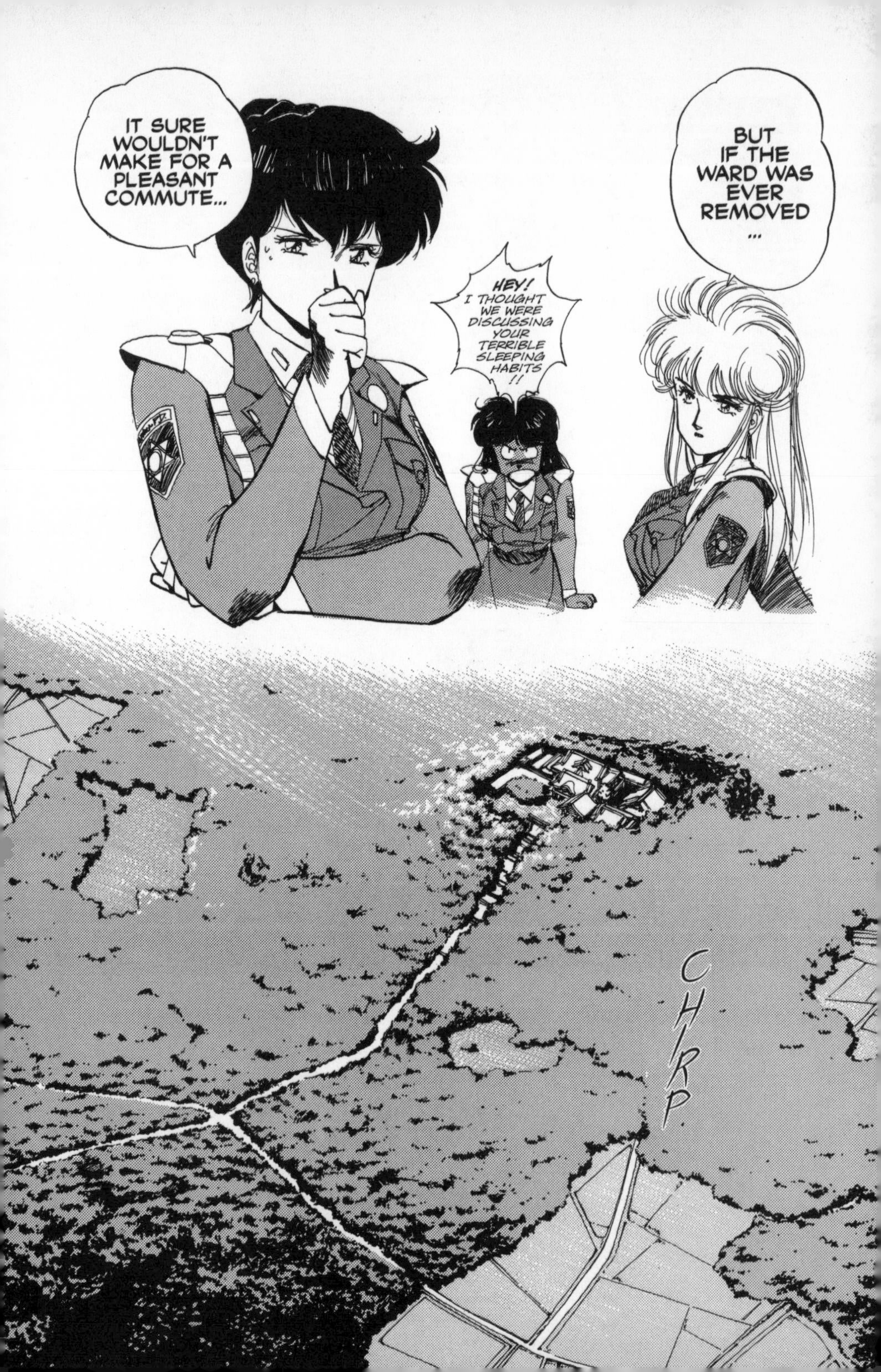
BUT IF THE WARD WAS EVER REMOVED ...
IT SURE WOULDN'T MAKE FOR A PLEASANT COMMUTE...
HEY! I THOUGHT WE WERE DISCUSSING YOUR TERRIBLE SLEEPING HABITS !!
CHIRP

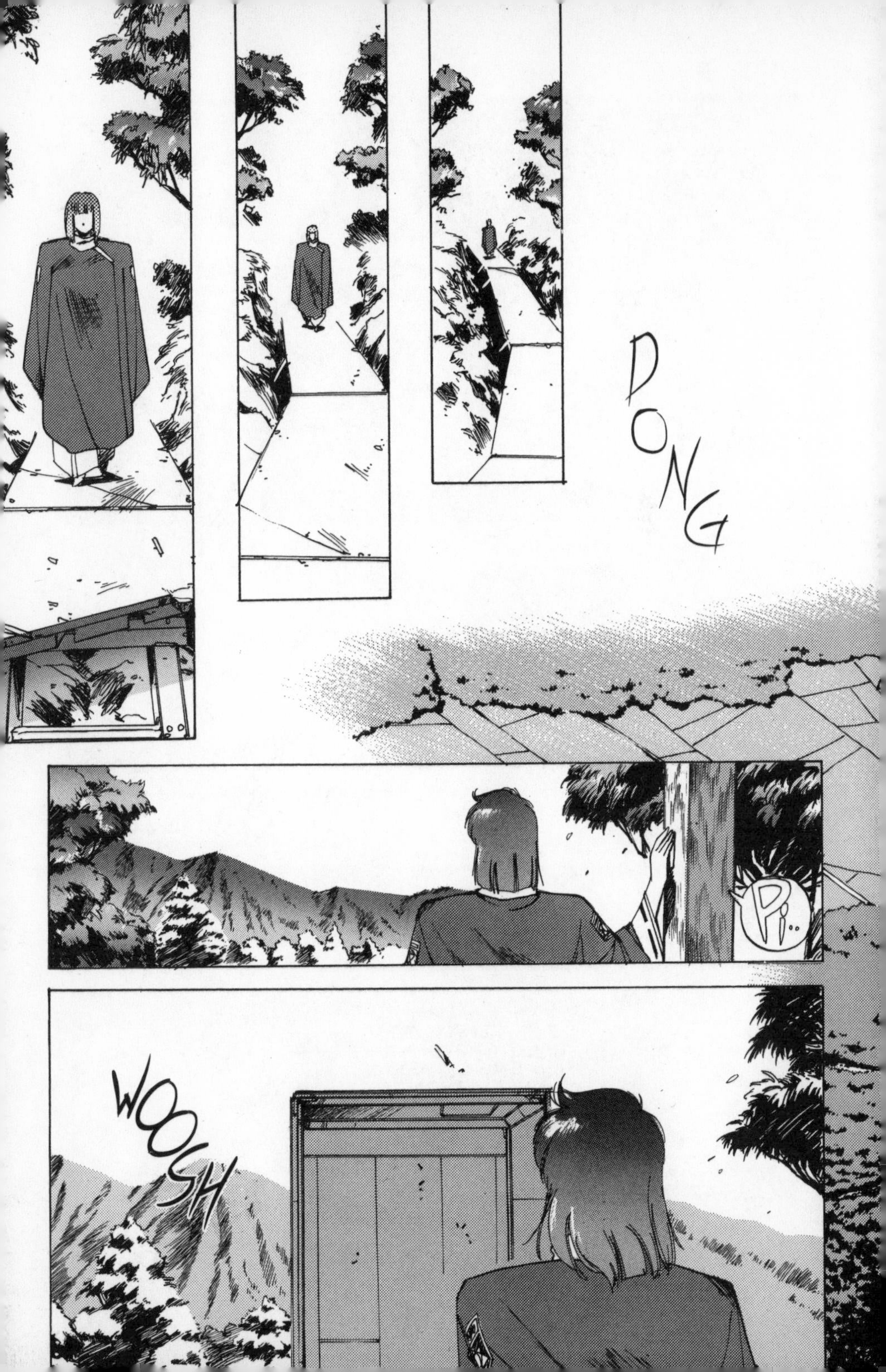
DONG
Pi..
WOOSH

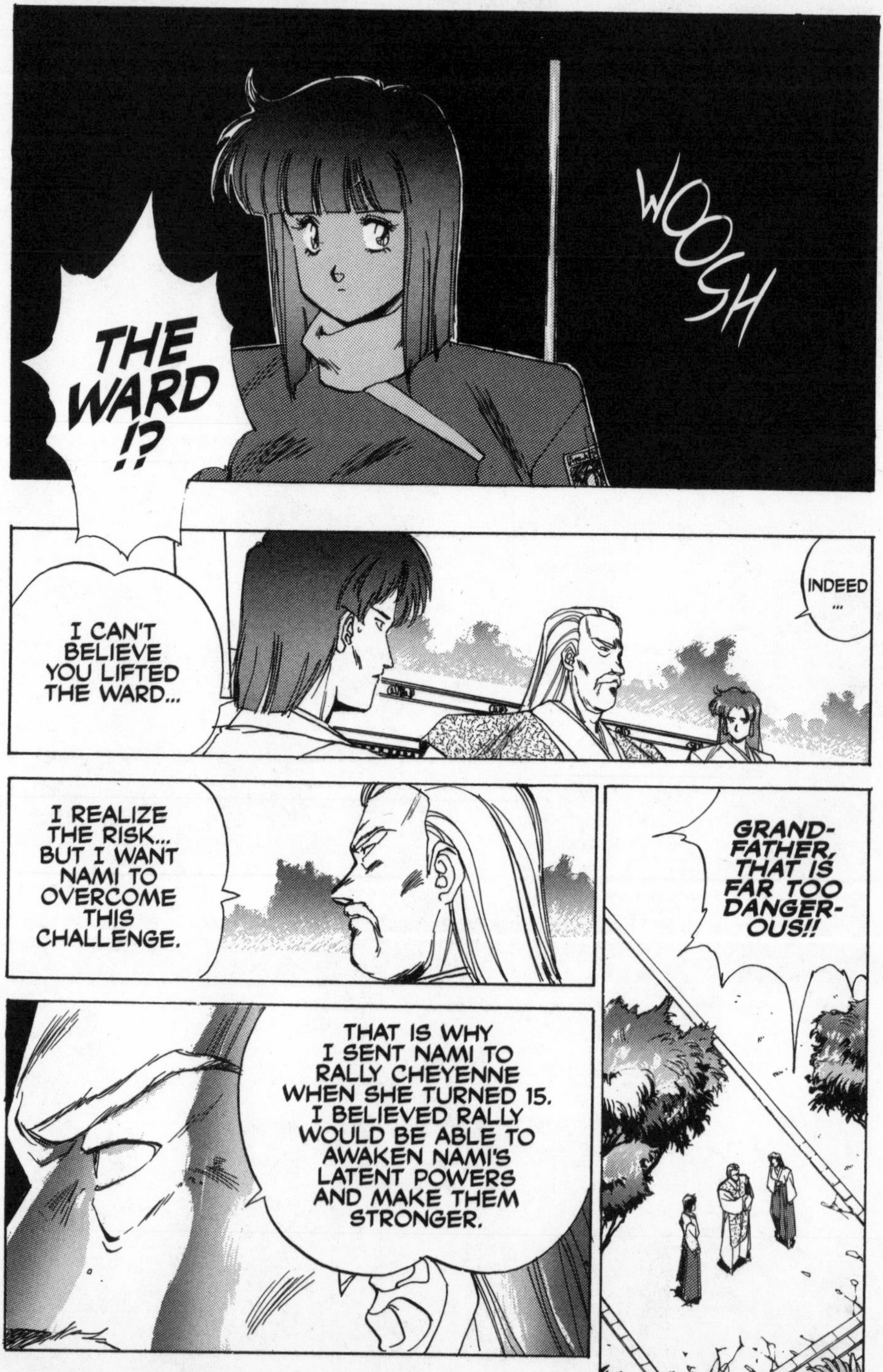
WOOSH
THE WARD !?
INDEED...
I CAN'T BELIEVE YOU LIFTED THE WARD...
GRAND-FATHER, THAT IS FAR TOO DANGER-OUS!!
I REALIZE THE RISK... BUT I WANT NAMI TO OVERCOME THIS CHALLENGE.
THAT IS WHY I SENT NAMI TO RALLY CHEYENNE WHEN SHE TURNED 15. I BELIEVED RALLY WOULD BE ABLE TO AWAKEN NAMI'S LATENT POWERS AND MAKE THEM STRONGER.

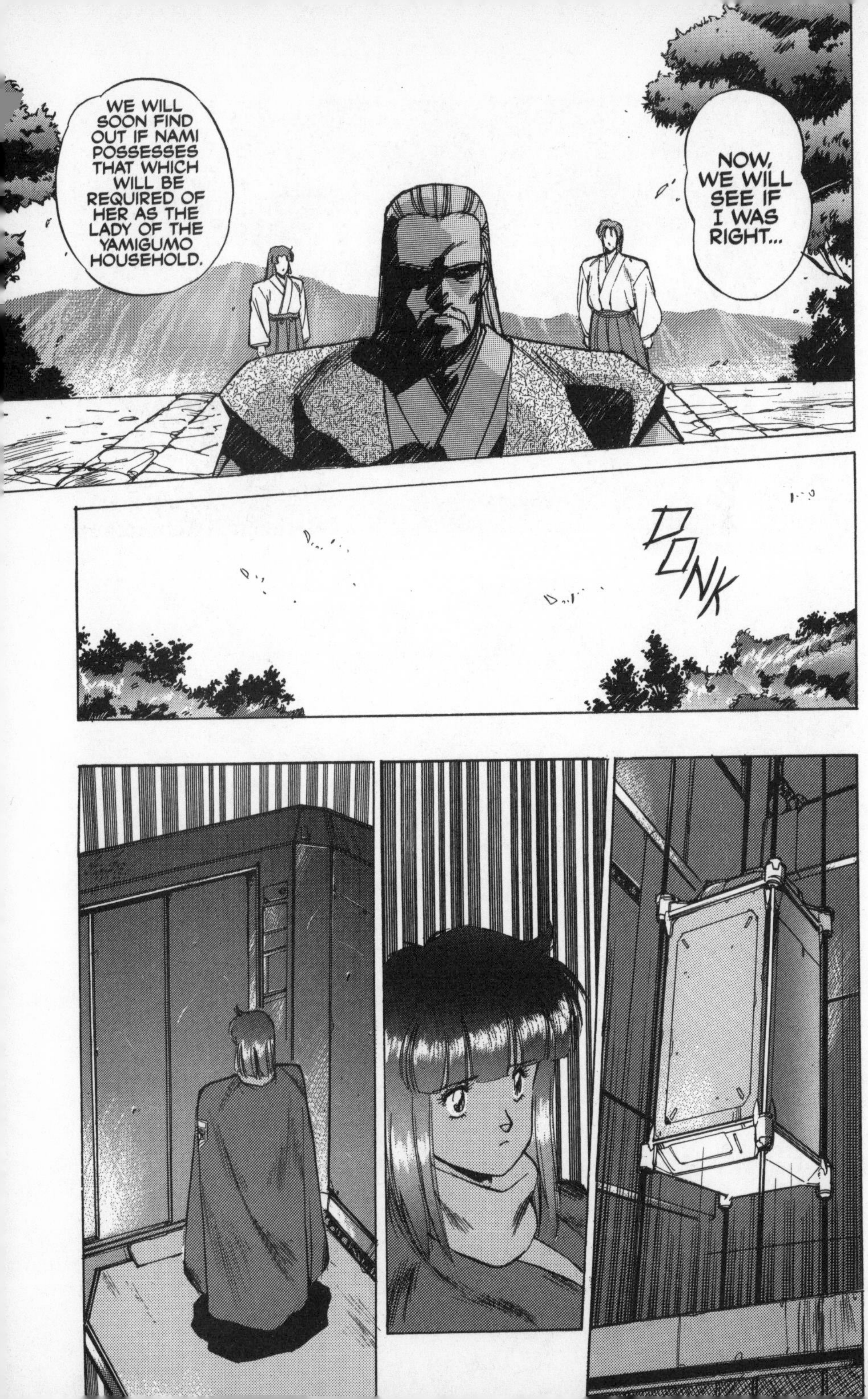
NOW, WE WILL SEE IF I WAS RIGHT...
WE WILL SOON FIND OUT IF NAMI POSSESSES THAT WHICH WILL BE REQUIRED OF HER AS THE LADY OF THE YAMIGUMO HOUSEHOLD.
DONK

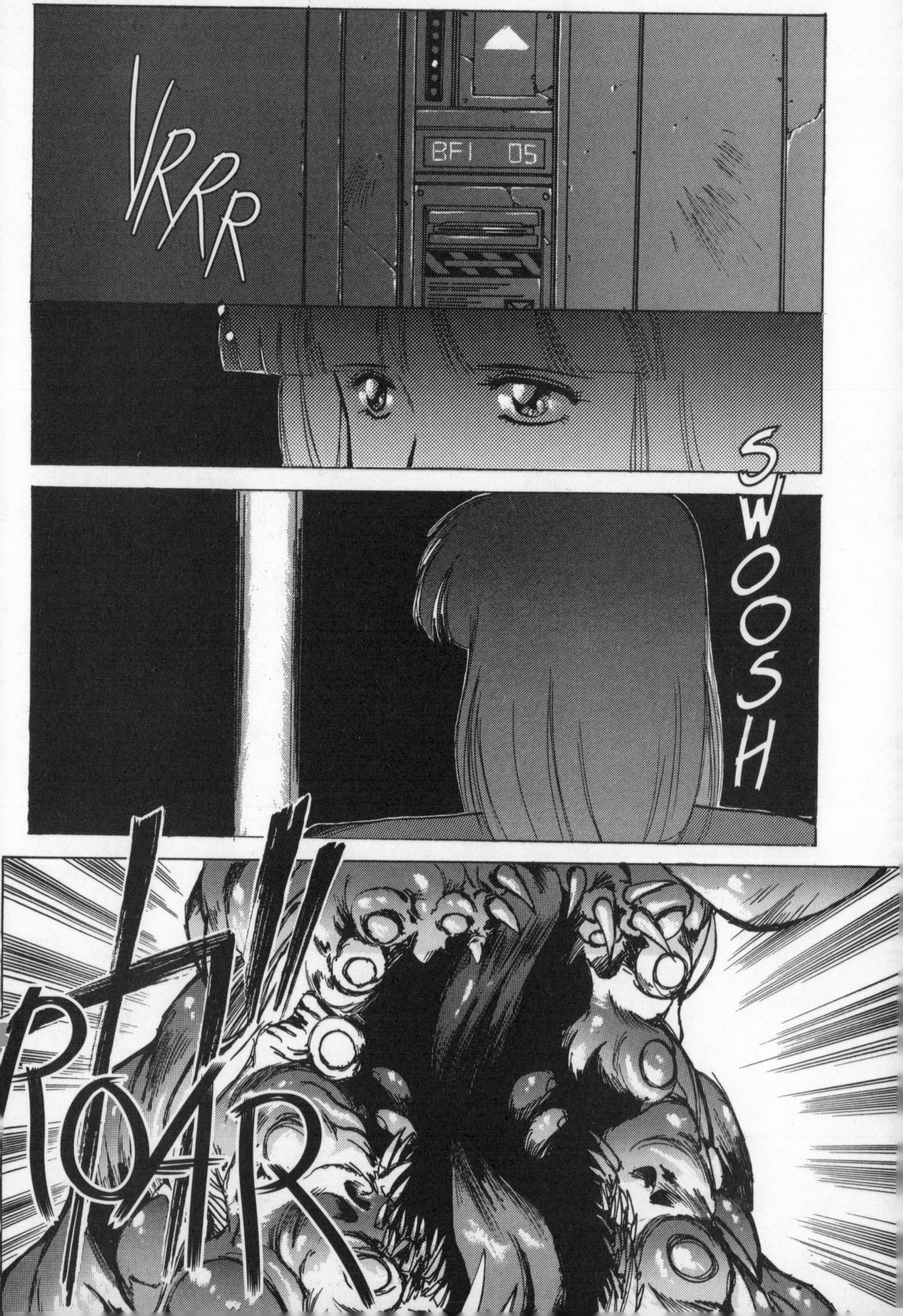
BF1 05
VRRR
SWOOSH
ROAR

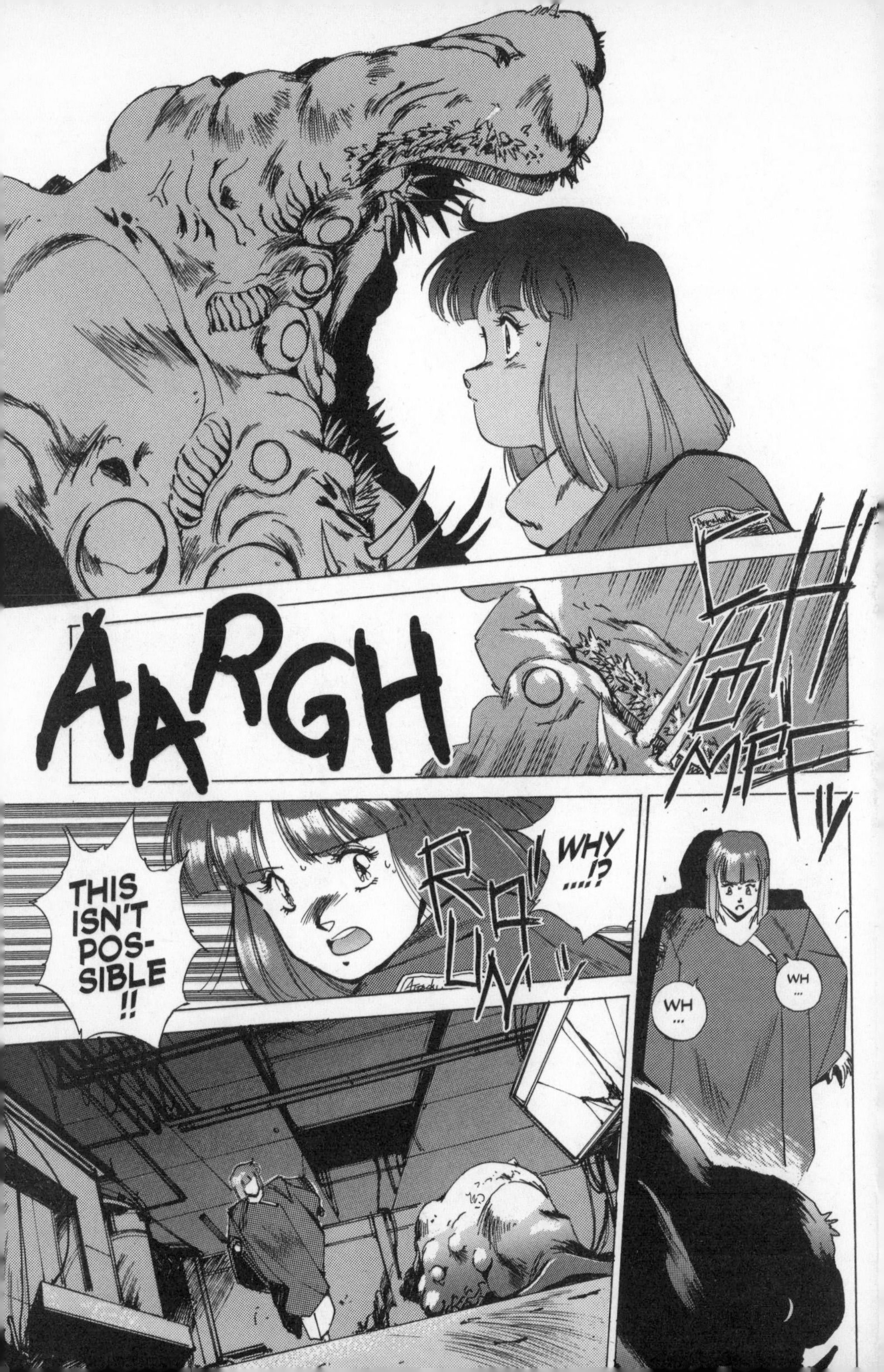
AARGH
WH ...
WH ...
WHY ....!?
THIS ISN'T POS-SIBLE !!

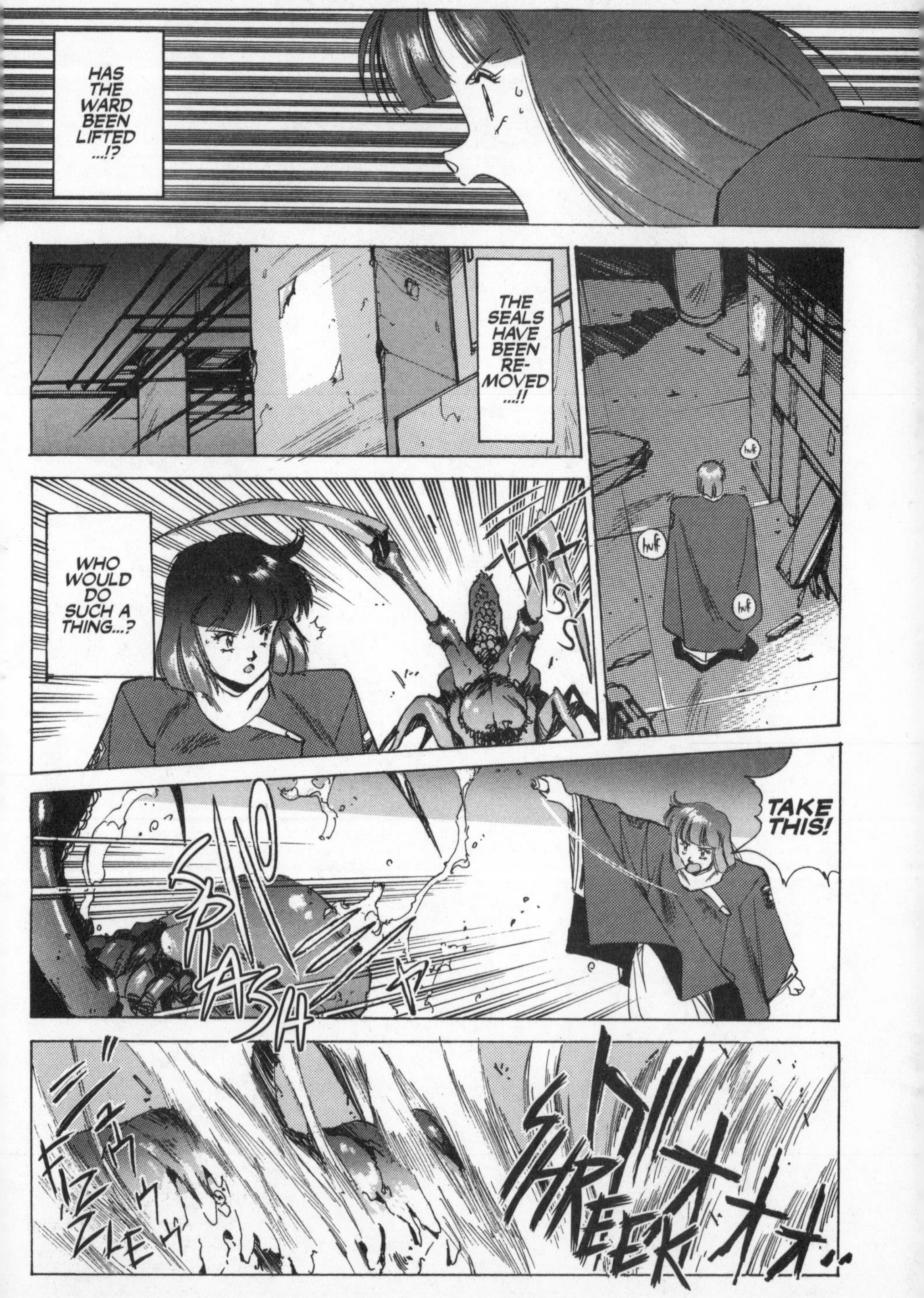
HAS THE WARD BEEN LIFTED ...!?
huff
huff
huff
THE SEALS HAVE BEEN RE-MOVED ...!!
WHO WOULD DO SUCH A THING...?
HISS
TAKE THIS!
SPLASH
SHREEK
FIZZLE

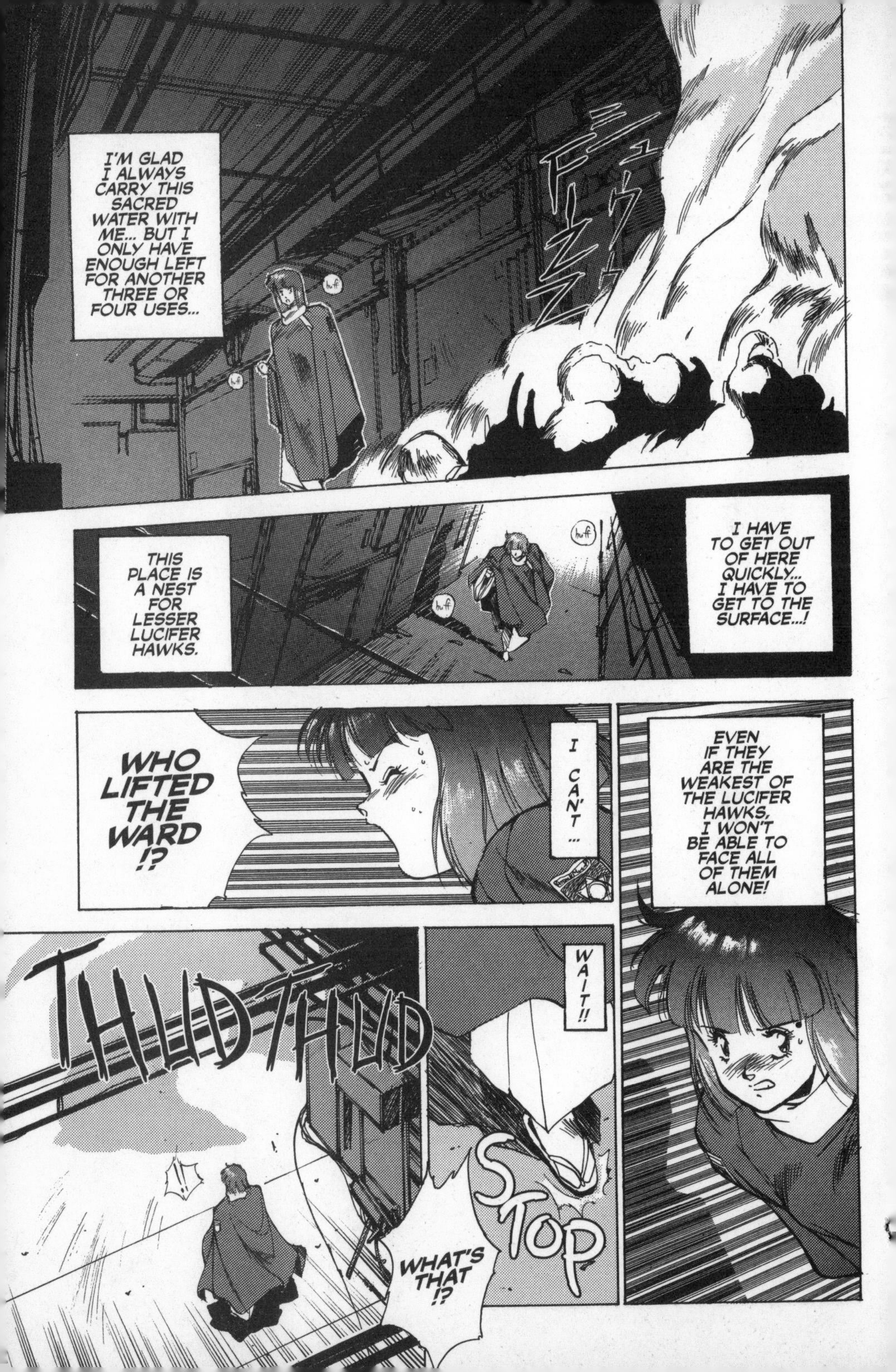
I'M GLAD I ALWAYS CARRY THIS SACRED WATER WITH ME... BUT I ONLY HAVE ENOUGH LEFT FOR ANOTHER THREE OR FOUR USES...
シュウウウ
FIZZZ
huff
huff
I HAVE TO GET OUT OF HERE QUICKLY... I HAVE TO GET TO THE SURFACE...!
huff
huff
THIS PLACE IS A NEST FOR LESSER LUCIFER HAWKS.
EVEN IF THEY ARE THE WEAKEST OF THE LUCIFER HAWKS, I WON'T BE ABLE TO FACE ALL OF THEM ALONE!
I CAN'T ...
WHO LIFTED THE WARD !?
WAIT!!
STOP
THUD THUD
!!
WHAT'S THAT !?

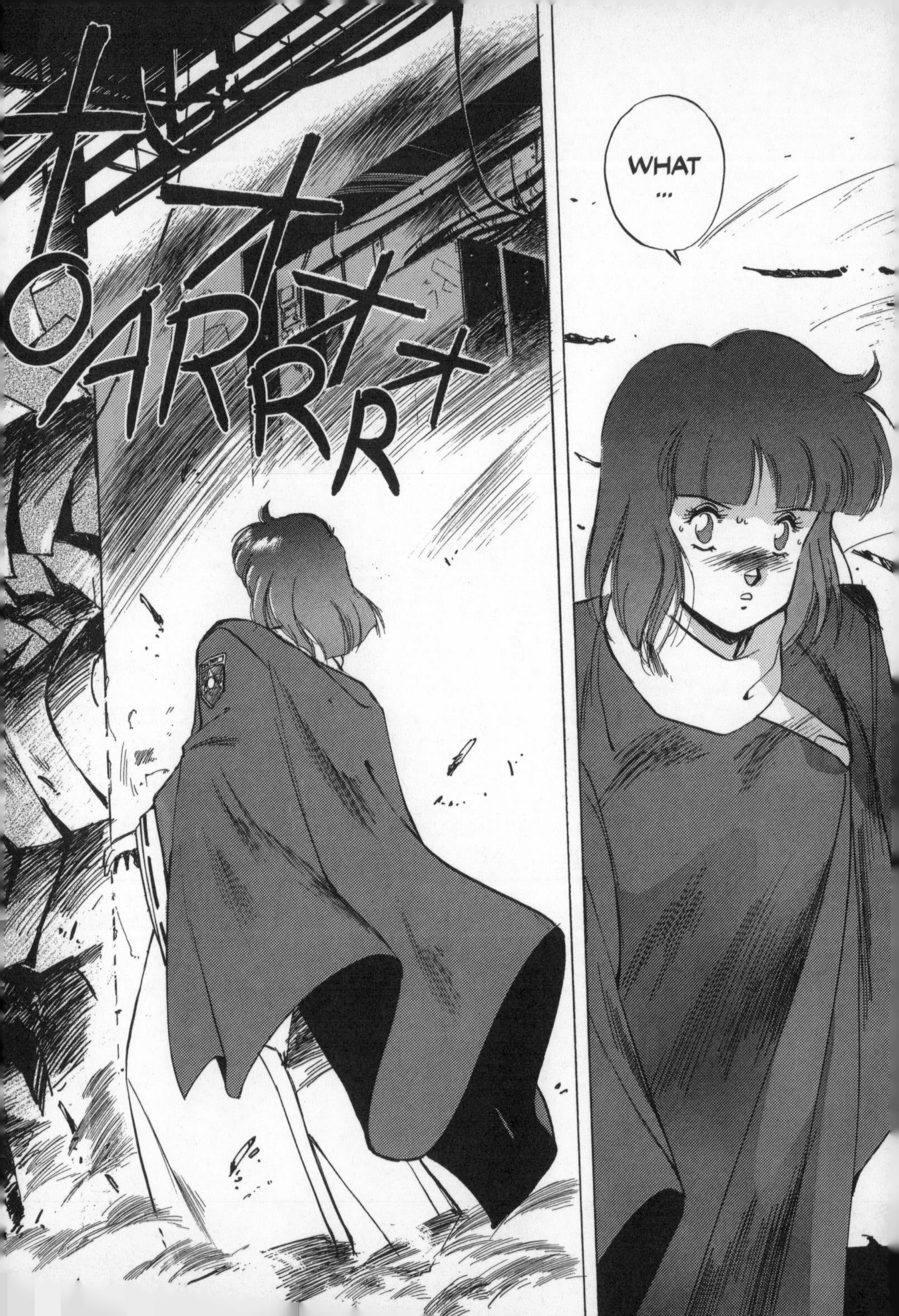
WHAT ...
OARRR

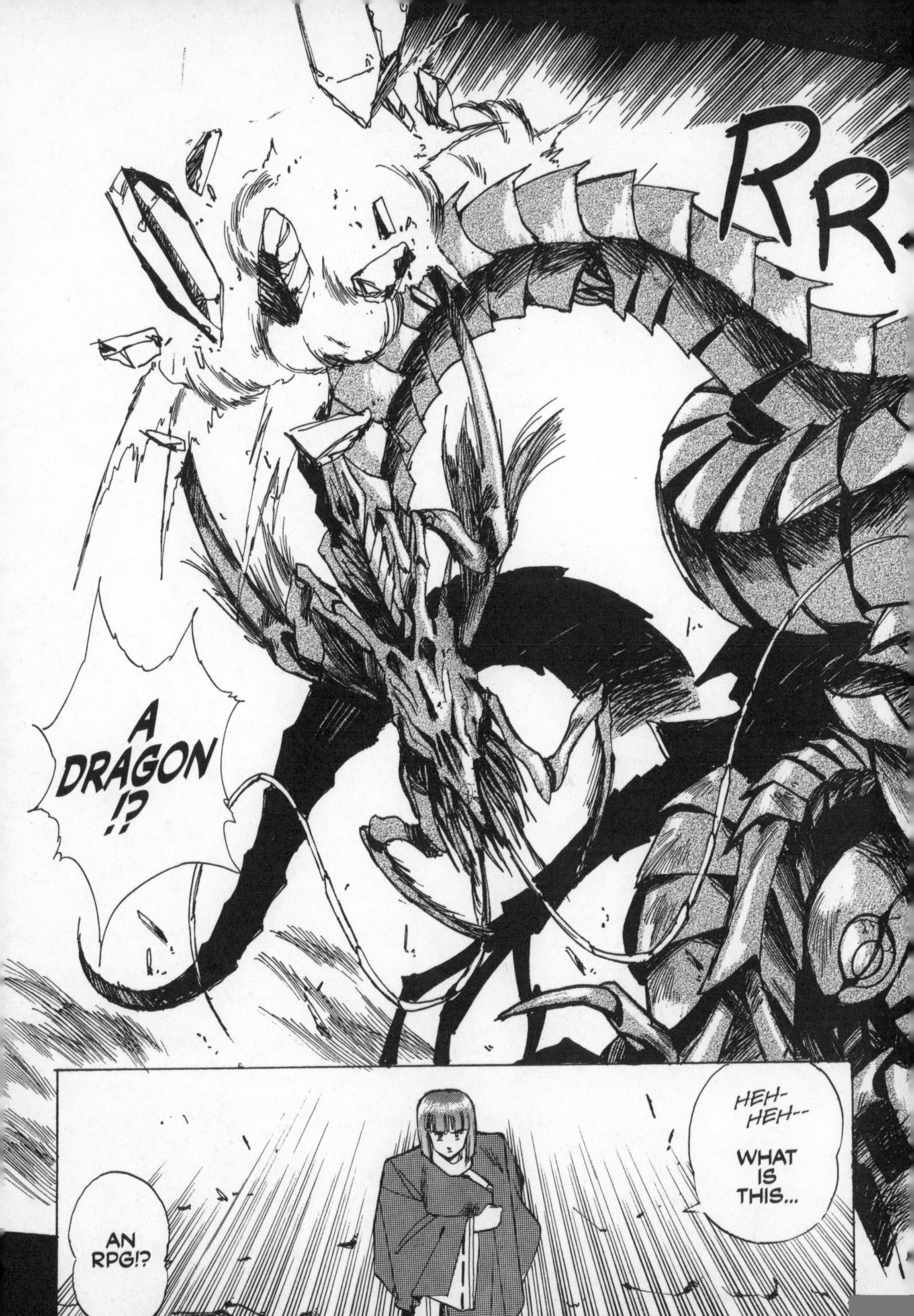
RR-
A DRAGON!?
HEH-HEH-- WHAT IS THIS...
AN RPG!?

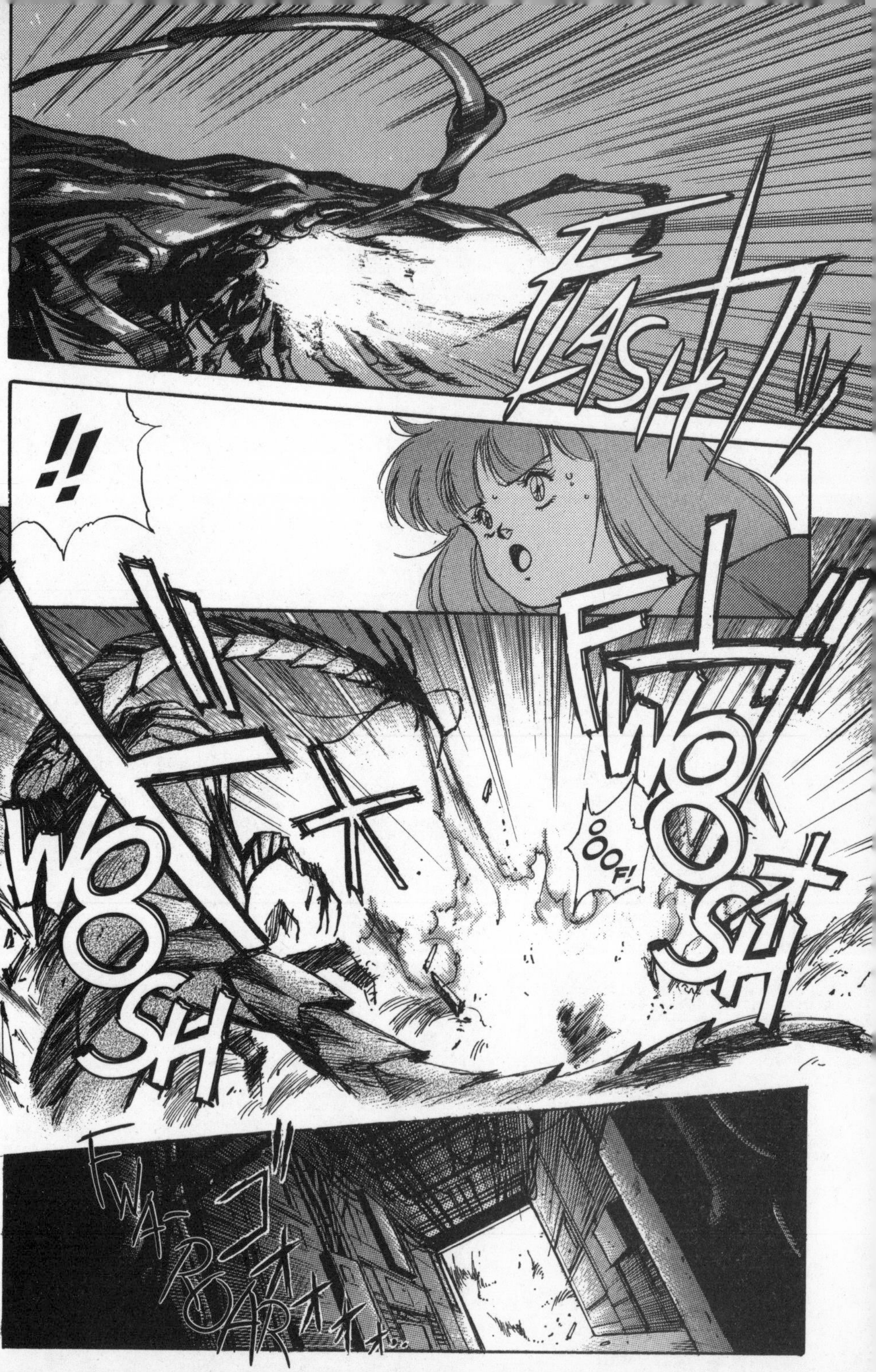
FLASH
!!
FWOOSH
OOOF!
WOOSH
FWA-ROAR

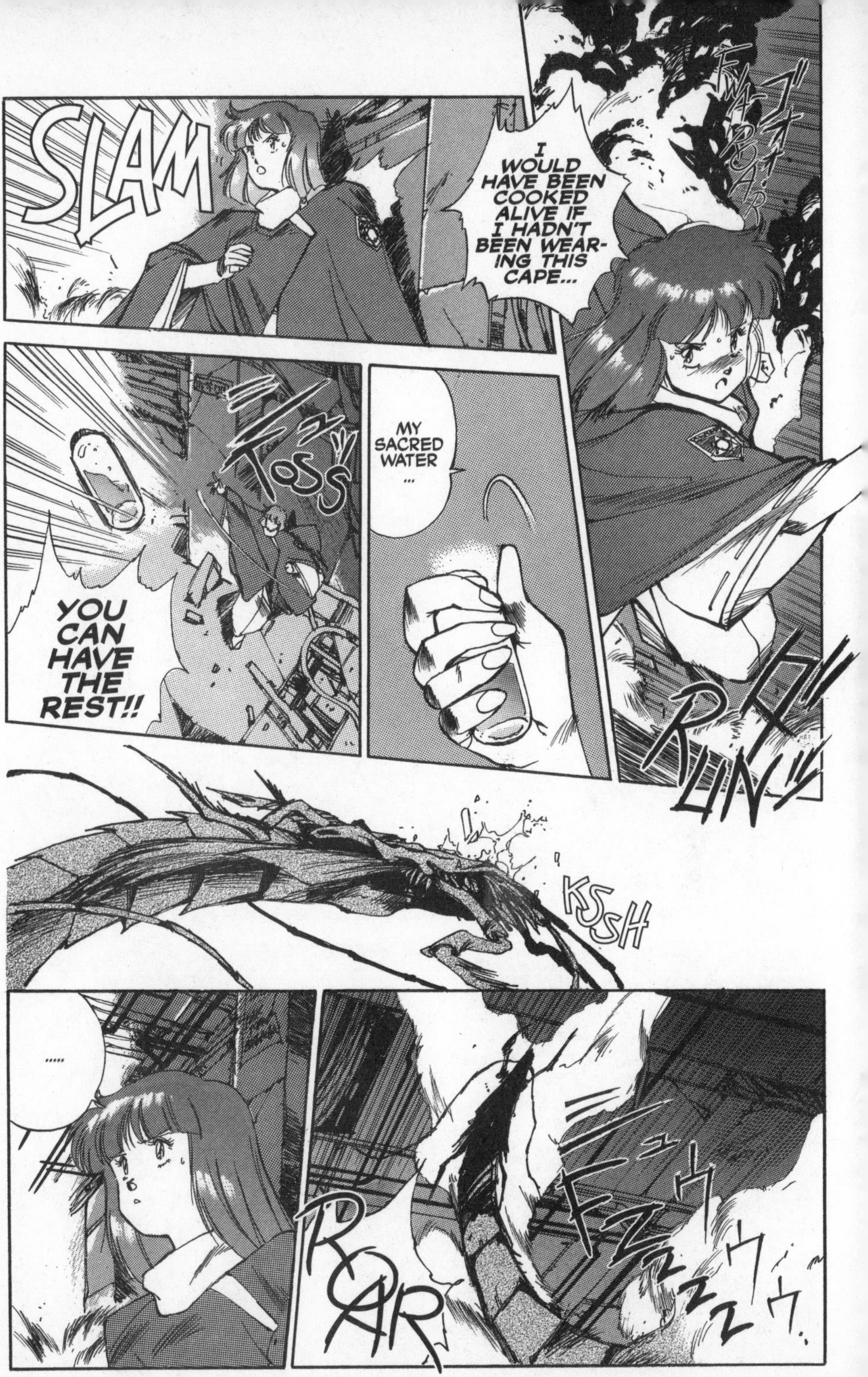

FWA-ROAR
I WOULD HAVE BEEN COOKED ALIVE IF I HADN'T BEEN WEAR-ING THIS CAPE...
SLAM
MY SACRED WATER ...
TOSS
YOU CAN HAVE THE REST!!
KSSH
FZZZZ
ROAR
......

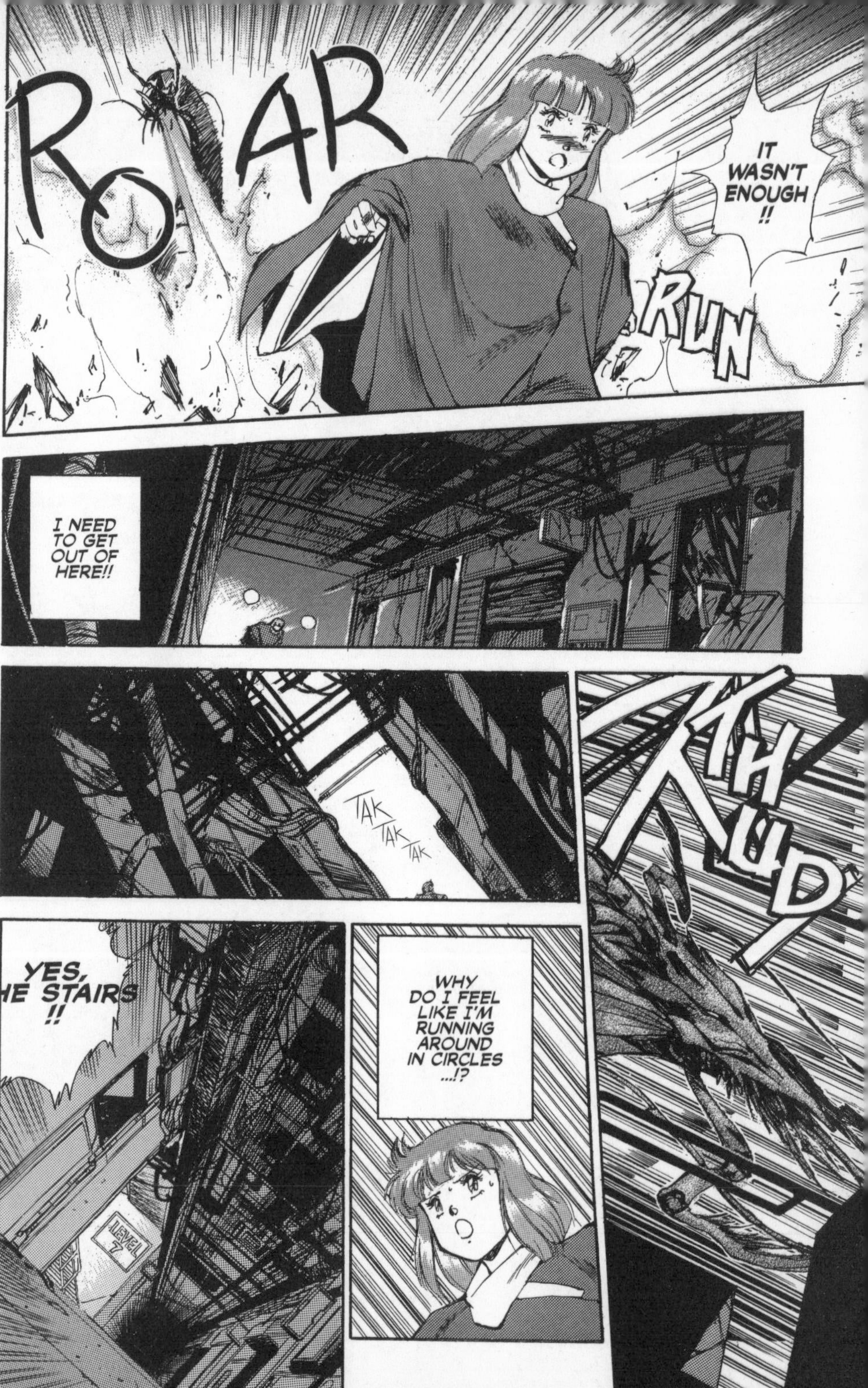

ROAR
IT WASN'T ENOUGH !!
RUN
I NEED TO GET OUT OF HERE!!
KTHUD!
TAK TAK TAK
WHY DO I FEEL LIKE I'M RUNNING AROUND IN CIRCLES ...!?
YES, THE STAIRS !!
LEVEL 7

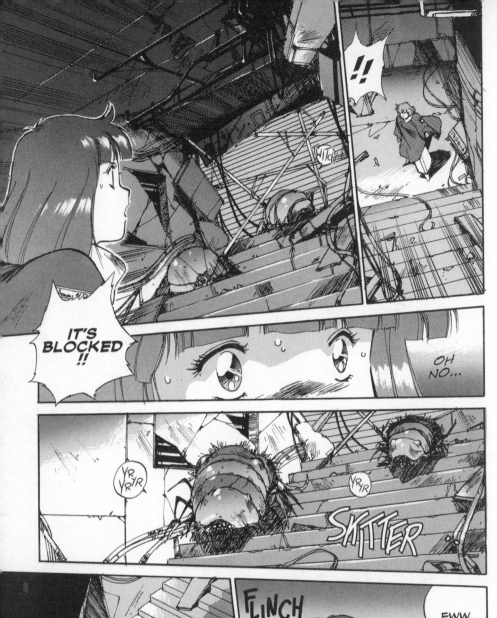

IT'S BLOCKED!!

OH NO...

SKITTER

FLINCH

EWW... BUGS...

IT SEEMS NAMI CAN'T STAND INSECTS...

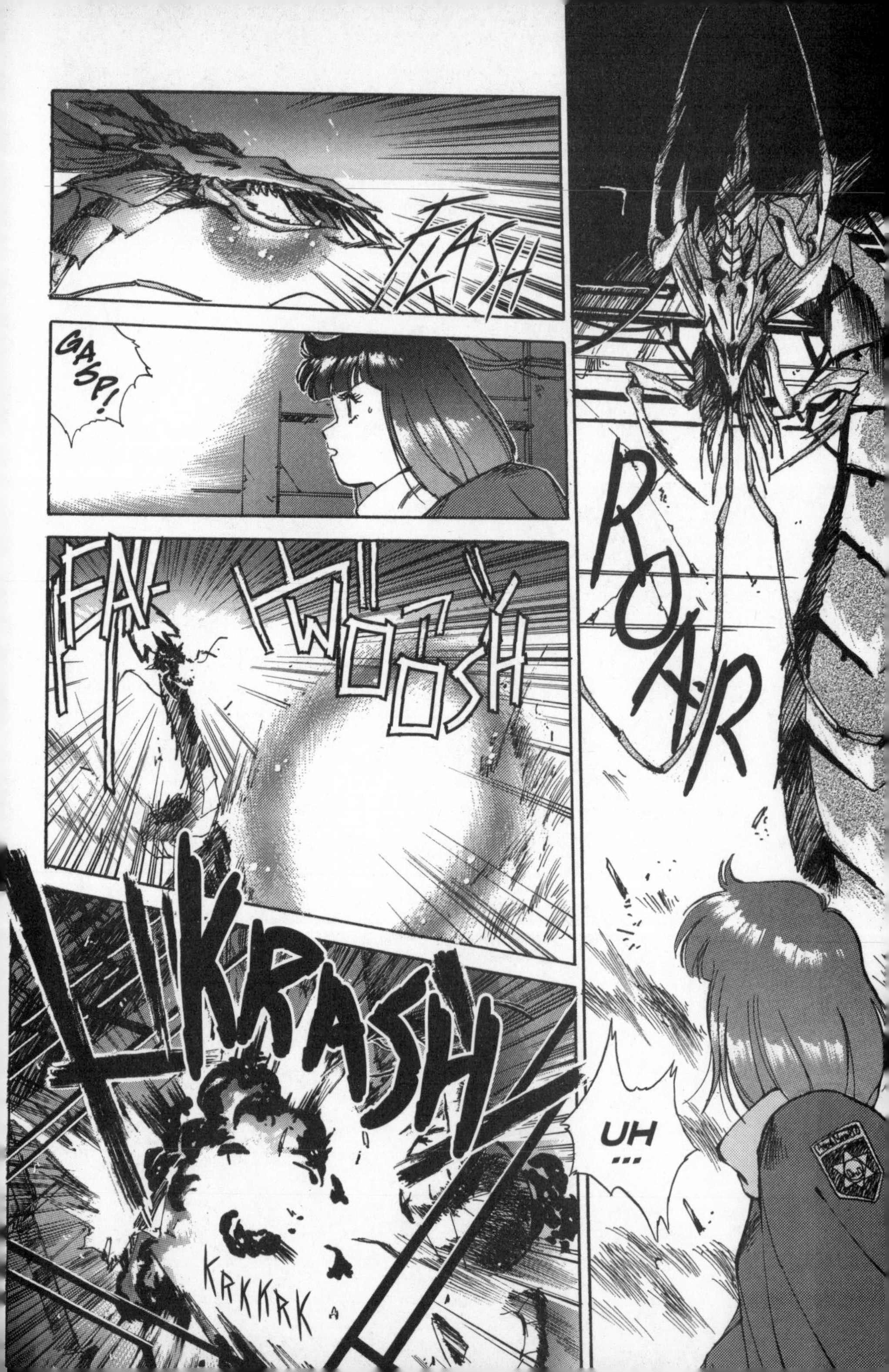
ROAR
UH...
FLASH
GASP!
FWOOSH
FA-
KRASH
KRKKRK

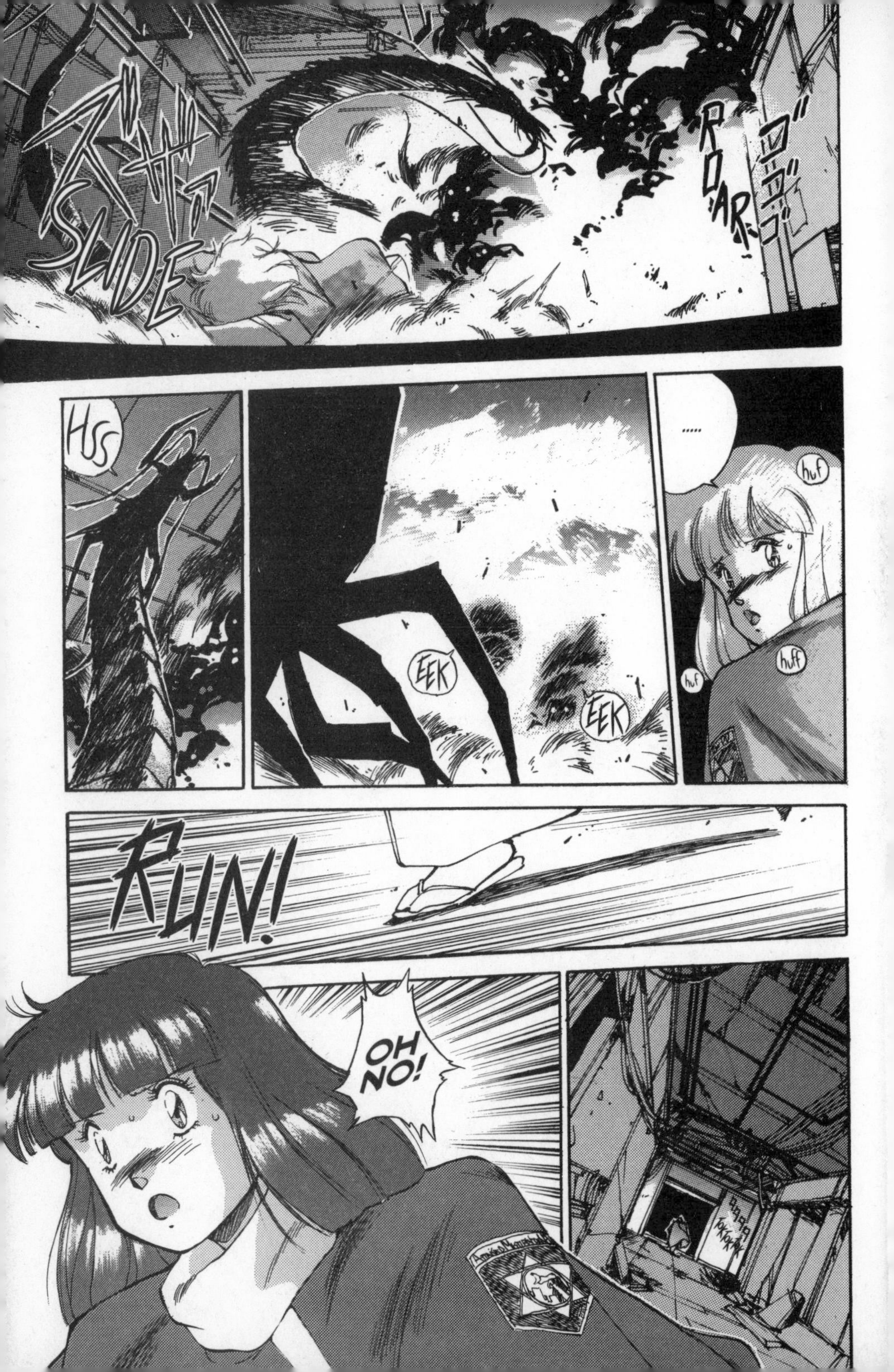
ROAR!
SLIDE
.....
huf
huff
huf
EEK
EEK
HSS
RUN!
OH NO!

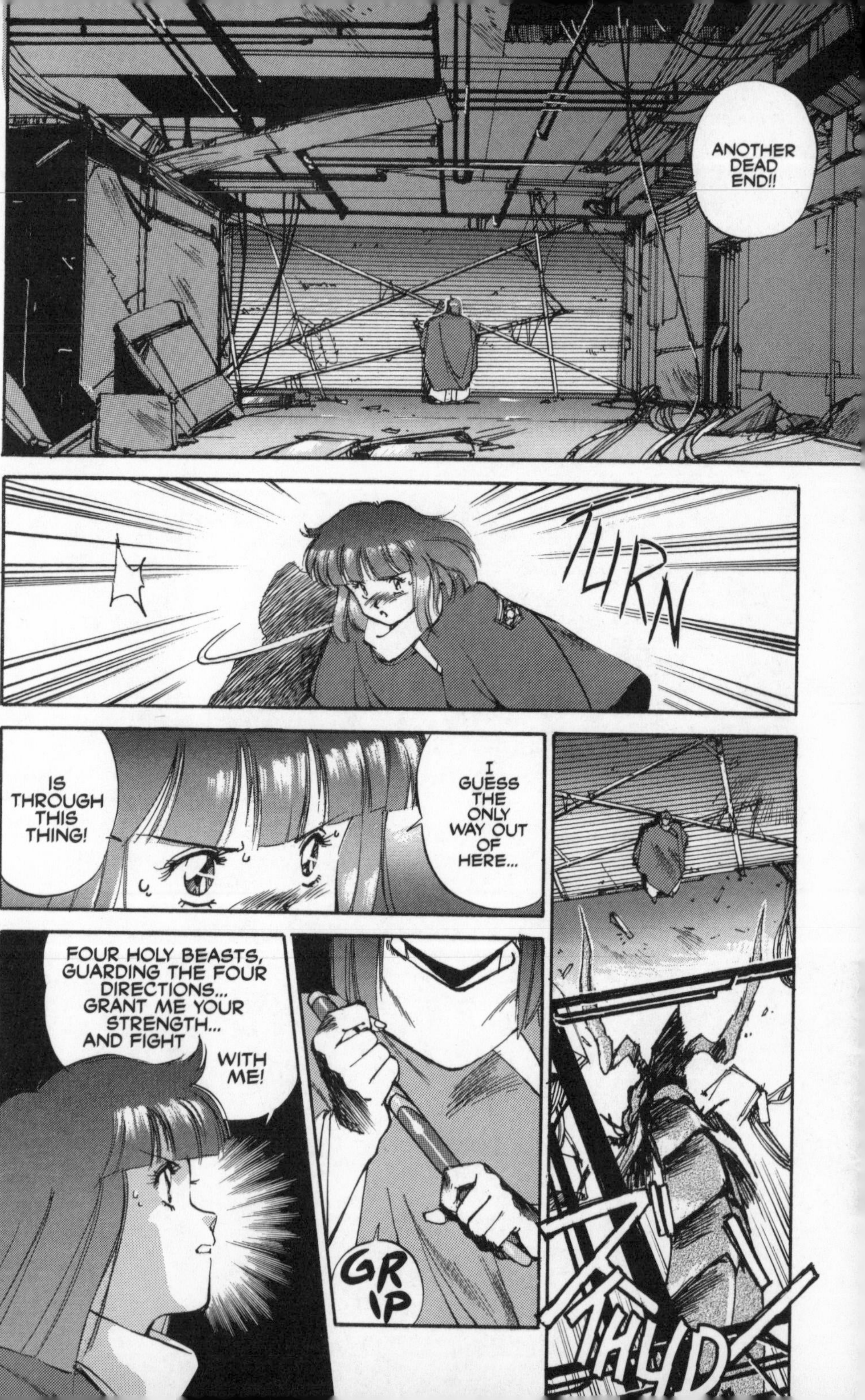
ANOTHER DEAD END!!
TURN
I GUESS THE ONLY WAY OUT OF HERE...
IS THROUGH THIS THING!
THUD
GRIP
FOUR HOLY BEASTS, GUARDING THE FOUR DIRECTIONS... GRANT ME YOUR STRENGTH... AND FIGHT
WITH ME!

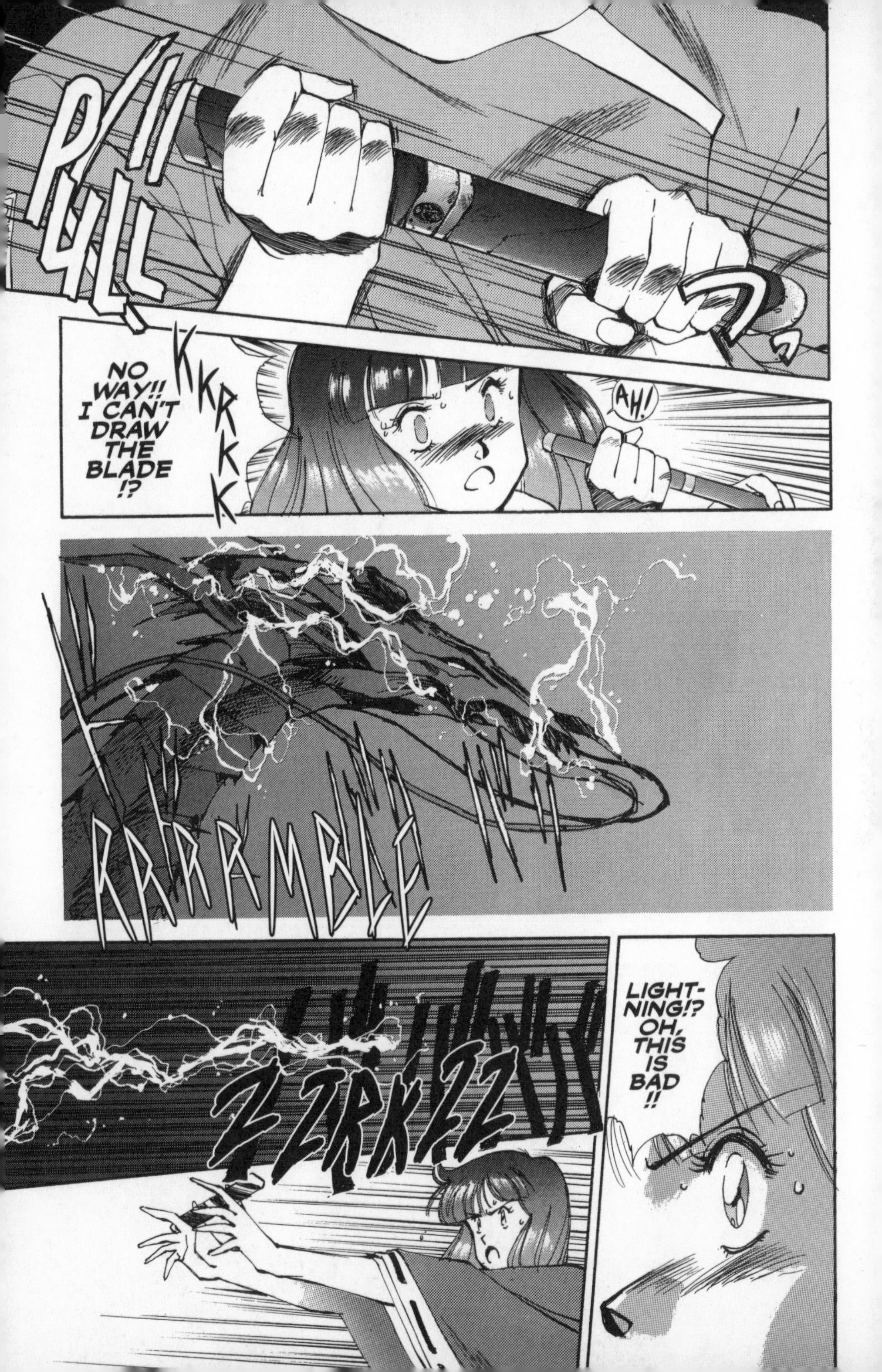
PULL
AH!
KKRKKK
NO WAY!! I CAN'T DRAW THE BLADE !?
RRRRAMBLE
LIGHT-NING!? OH, THIS IS BAD !!
ZZRKZZ

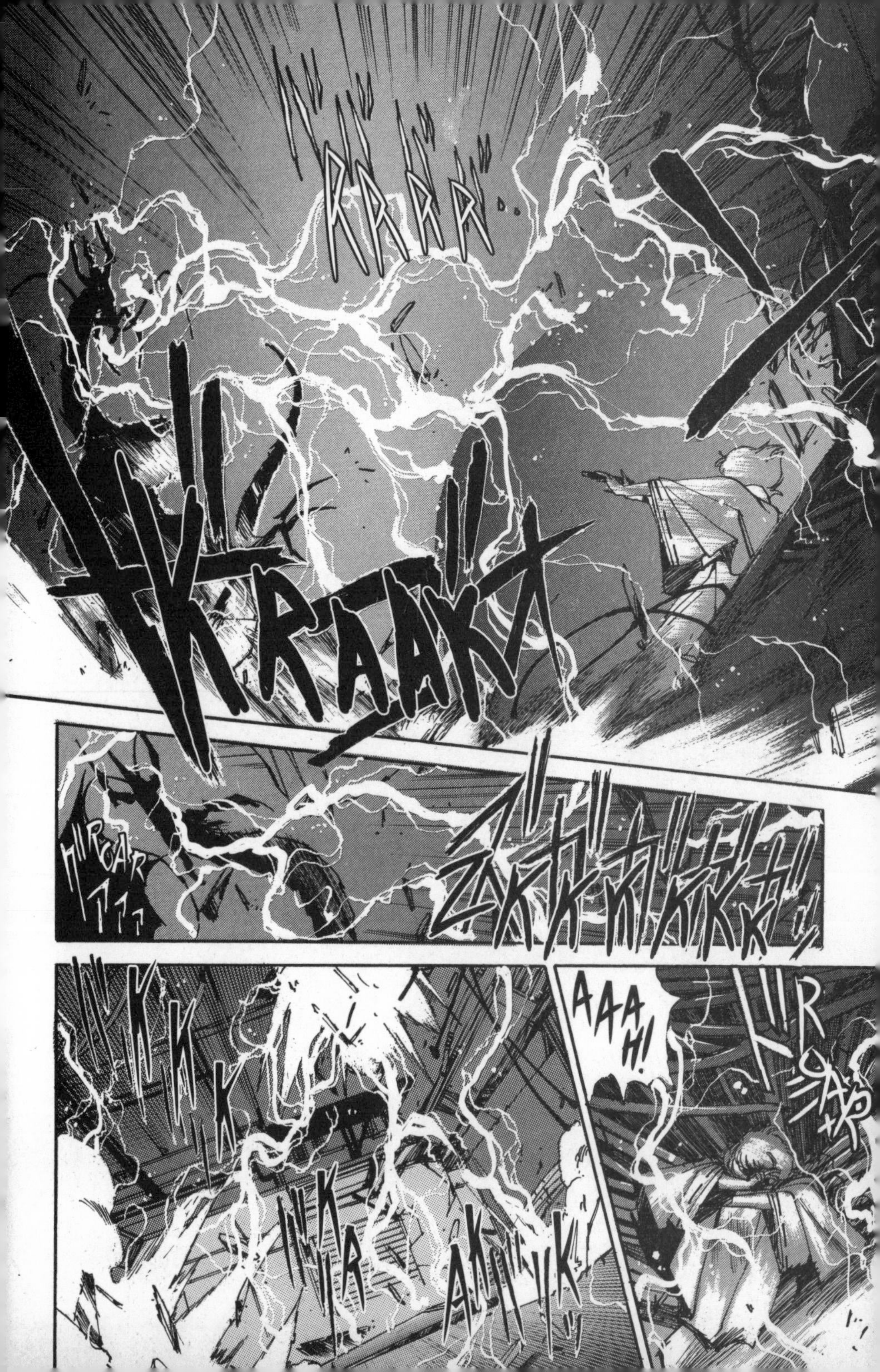
RRRRR
KRAAK
AAAH!

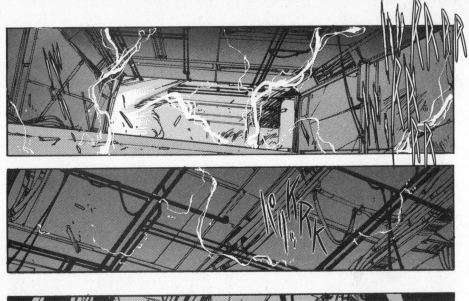

KRRRR
RRR
KRRR

I'M SO STUPID... I DIDN'T EVEN THINK ABOUT HOW THE ELECTRICITY WOULD AFFECT MY SURROUND-INGS...

.....

OR
...

I WONDER IF THE DRAGON DIED...

EVERY-THING'S... GOING DARK...

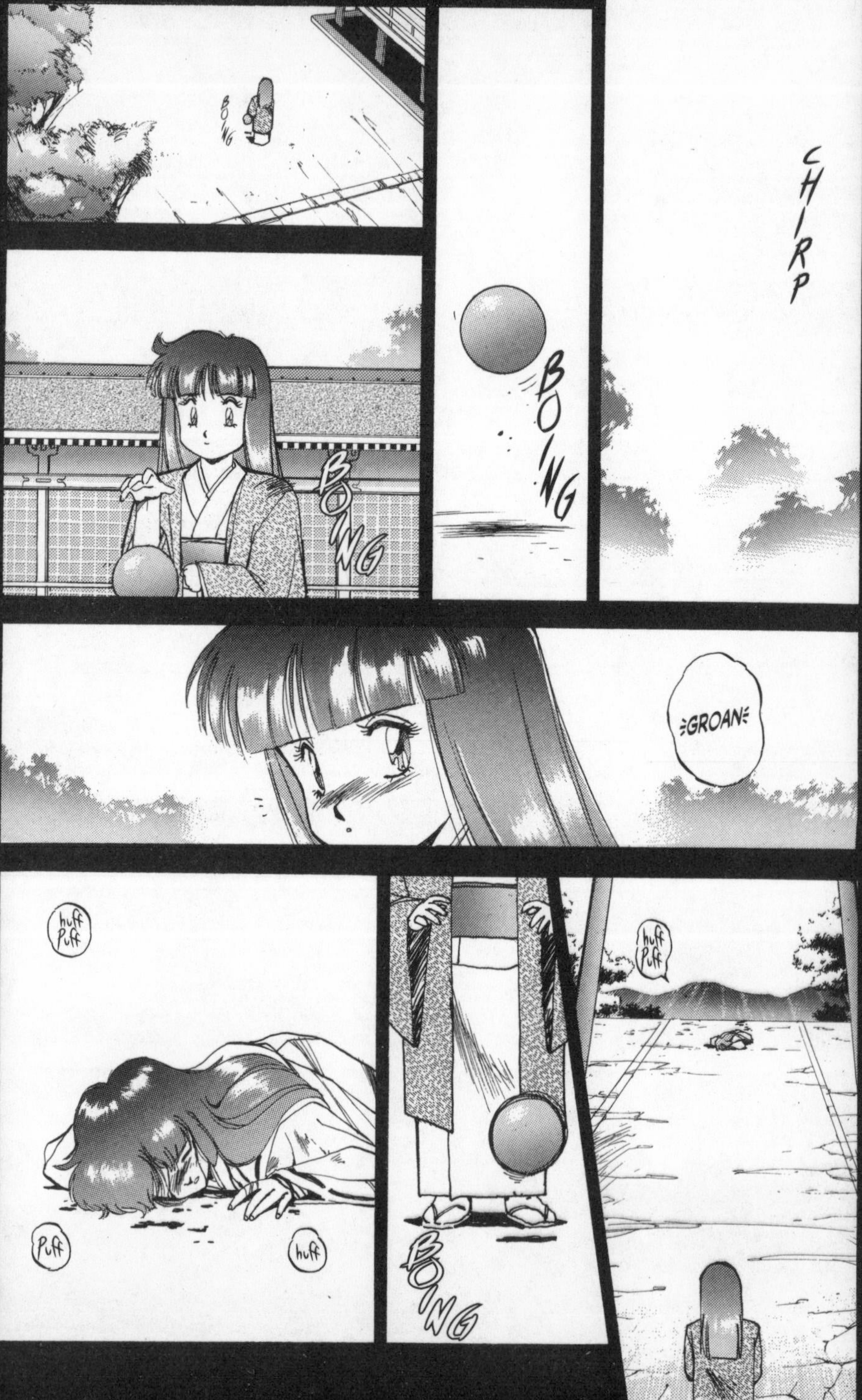
CHIRP
BOING
BOING
BOING
GROAN
huff puff
BOING
huff puff
puff
huff

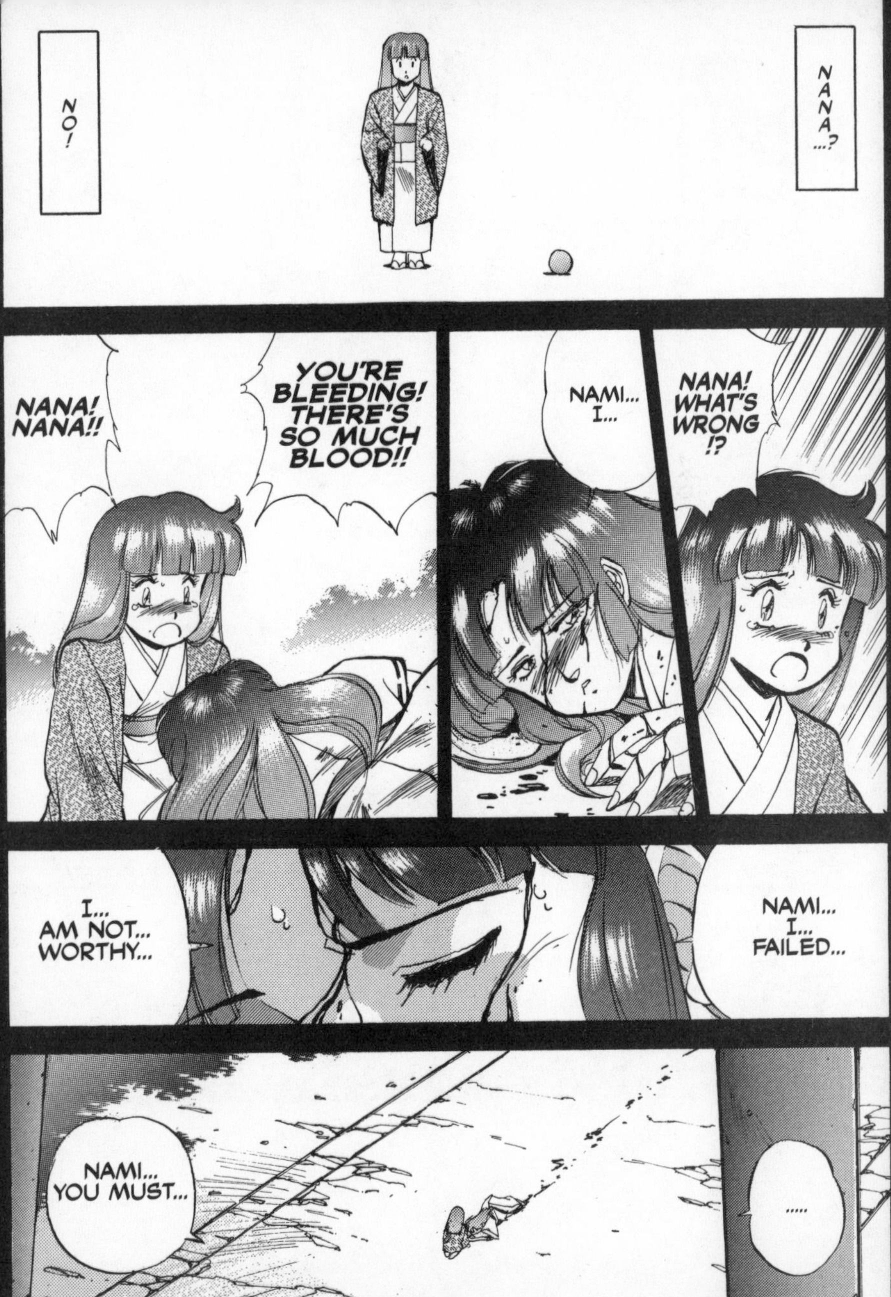
NANA...?
NO!
NANA! WHAT'S WRONG!?
NAMI... I...
YOU'RE BLEEDING! THERE'S SO MUCH BLOOD!!
NANA! NANA!!
NAMI... I... FAILED...
I... AM NOT... WORTHY...
.....
NAMI... YOU MUST...

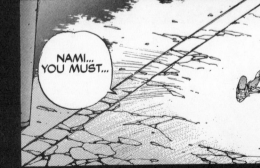

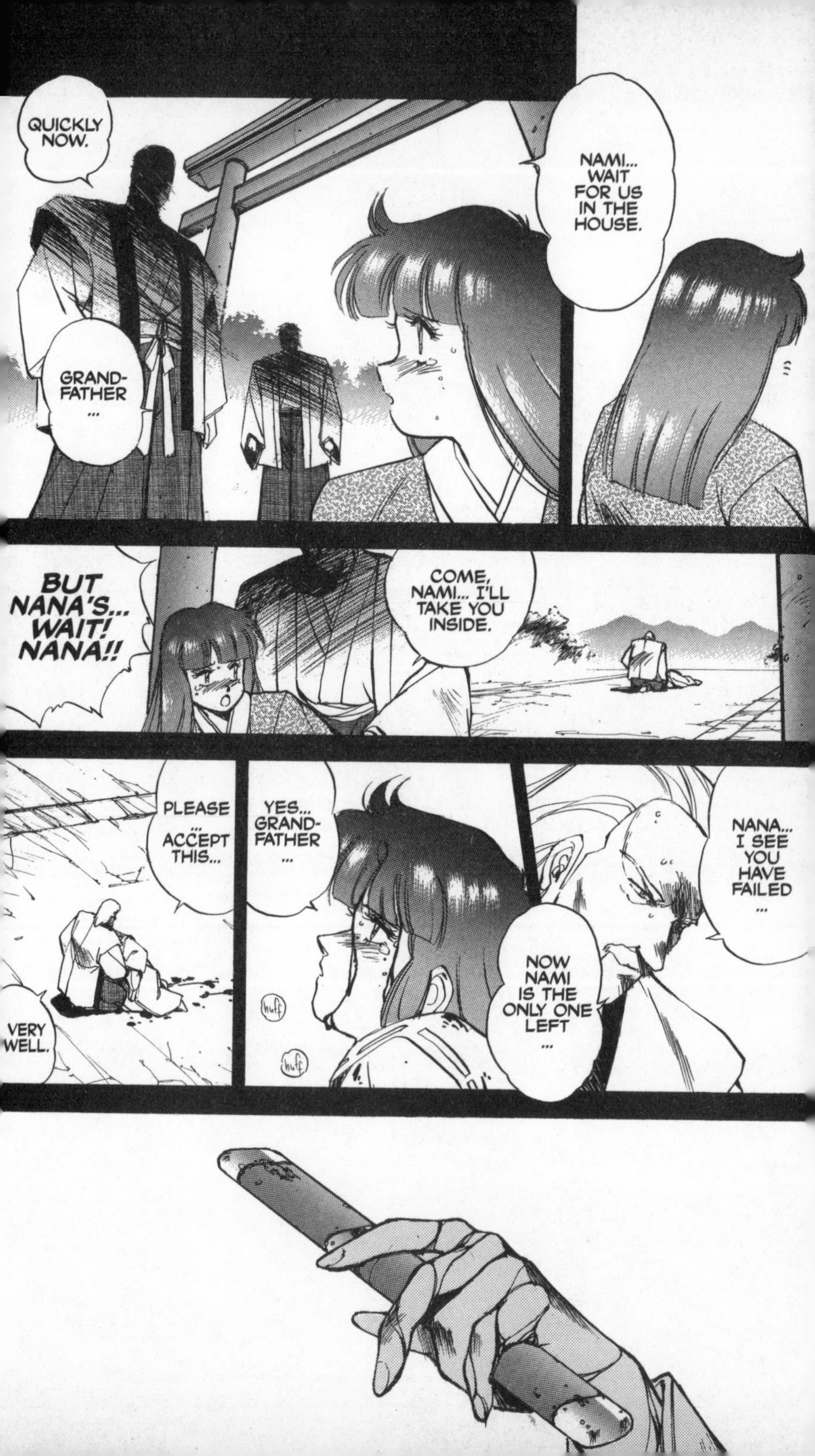
NAMI... WAIT FOR US IN THE HOUSE.
QUICKLY NOW.
GRANDFATHER ...
COME, NAMI... I'LL TAKE YOU INSIDE.
BUT NANA'S... WAIT! NANA!!
NANA... I SEE YOU HAVE FAILED ...
NOW NAMI IS THE ONLY ONE LEFT ...
YES... GRANDFATHER ...
huff
huff
PLEASE ... ACCEPT THIS...
VERY WELL.

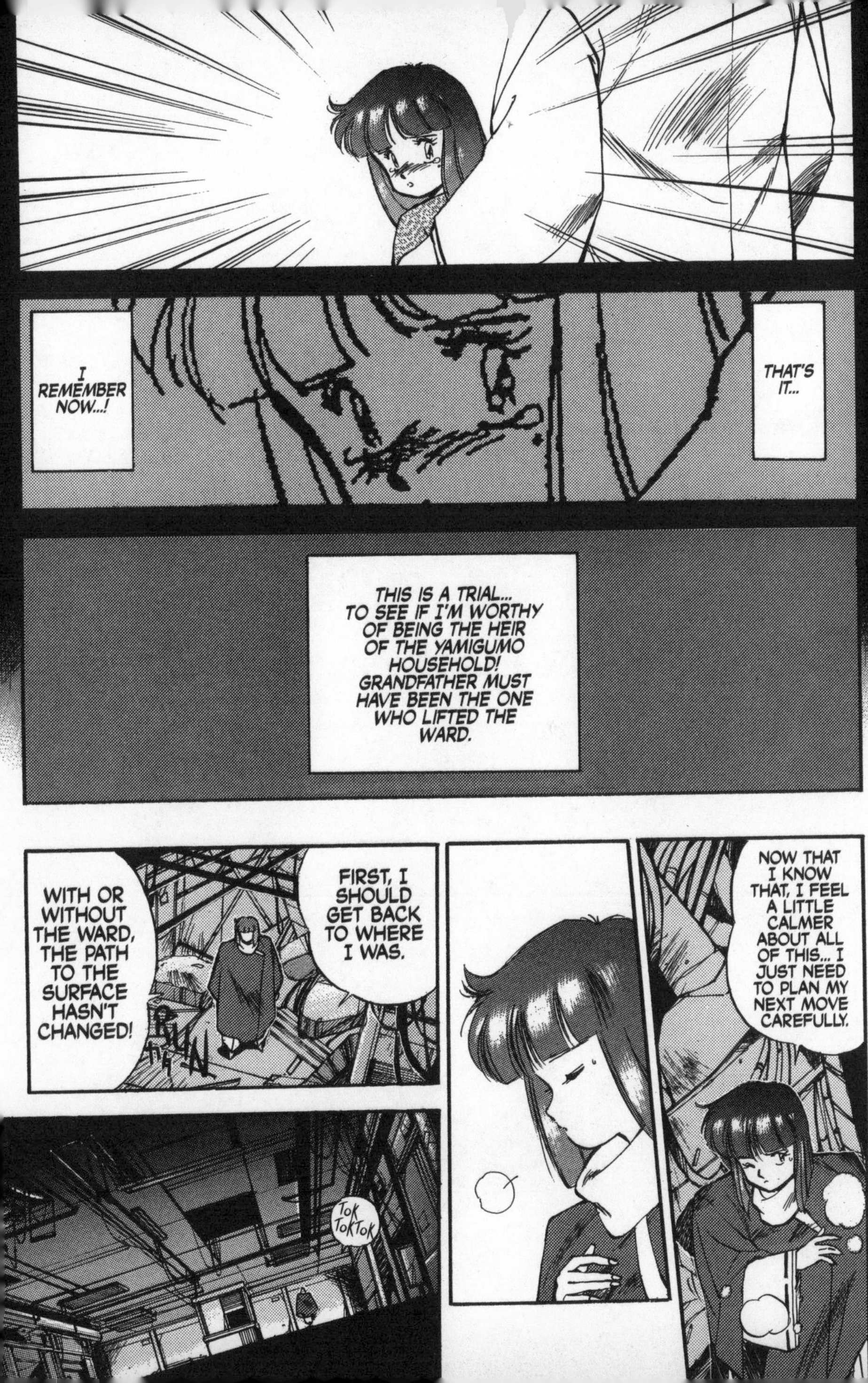

THAT'S IT...
I REMEMBER NOW...!
THIS IS A TRIAL... TO SEE IF I'M WORTHY OF BEING THE HEIR OF THE YAMIGUMO HOUSEHOLD! GRANDFATHER MUST HAVE BEEN THE ONE WHO LIFTED THE WARD.
NOW THAT I KNOW THAT, I FEEL A LITTLE CALMER ABOUT ALL OF THIS... I JUST NEED TO PLAN MY NEXT MOVE CAREFULLY.
FIRST, I SHOULD GET BACK TO WHERE I WAS.
WITH OR WITHOUT THE WARD, THE PATH TO THE SURFACE HASN'T CHANGED!
TOK TOKTOK

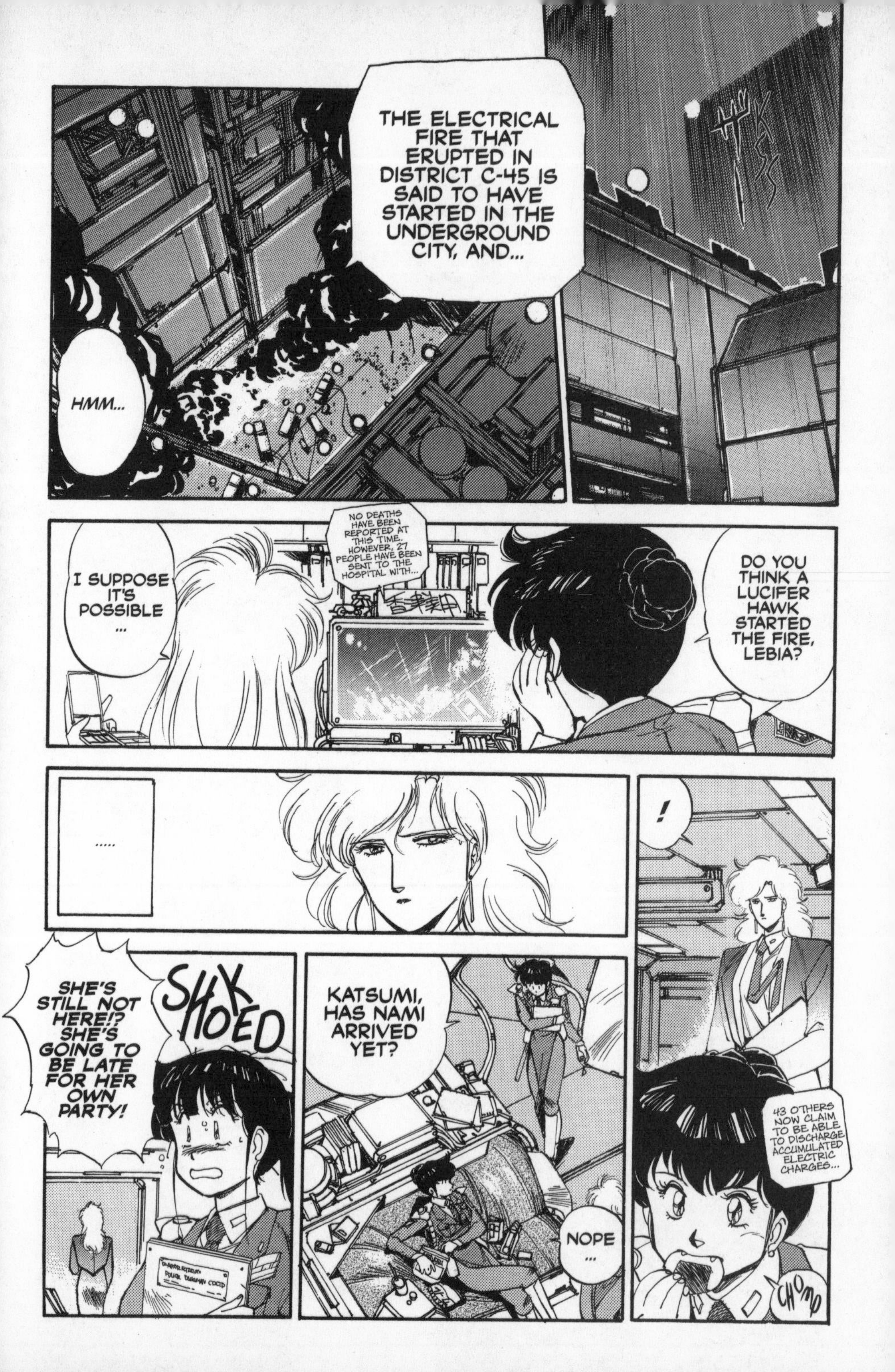
THE ELECTRICAL FIRE THAT ERUPTED IN DISTRICT C-45 IS SAID TO HAVE STARTED IN THE UNDERGROUND CITY, AND...
HMM...
DO YOU THINK A LUCIFER HAWK STARTED THE FIRE, LEBIA?
NO DEATHS HAVE BEEN REPORTED AT THIS TIME. HOWEVER, 27 PEOPLE HAVE BEEN SENT TO THE HOSPITAL WITH...
I SUPPOSE IT'S POSSIBLE ...
!
43 OTHERS NOW CLAIM TO BE ABLE TO DISCHARGE ACCUMULATED ELECTRIC CHARGES...
CHOMP
.....
KATSUMI, HAS NAMI ARRIVED YET?
NOPE ...
SHE'S STILL NOT HERE!? SHE'S GOING TO BE LATE FOR HER OWN PARTY!
SHOCKED

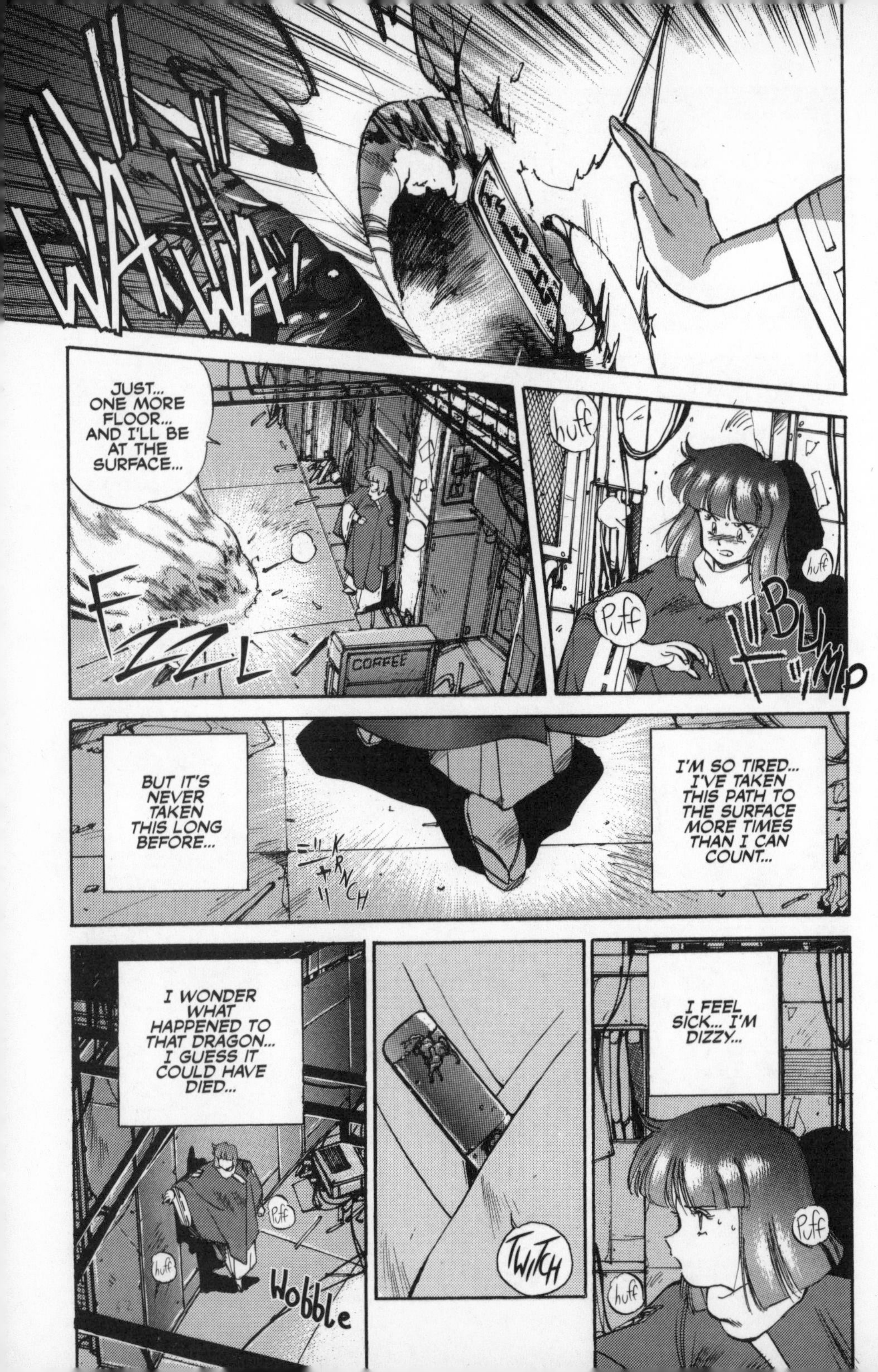
WAWA!
huff
Puff
huff
BUMP
JUST... ONE MORE FLOOR... AND I'LL BE AT THE SURFACE...
FZZZL
COFFEE
I'M SO TIRED... I'VE TAKEN THIS PATH TO THE SURFACE MORE TIMES THAN I CAN COUNT...
BUT IT'S NEVER TAKEN THIS LONG BEFORE...
KRNCH
I FEEL SICK... I'M DIZZY...
Puff
huff
TWITCH
I WONDER WHAT HAPPENED TO THAT DRAGON... I GUESS IT COULD HAVE DIED...
Puff
huff
Wobble

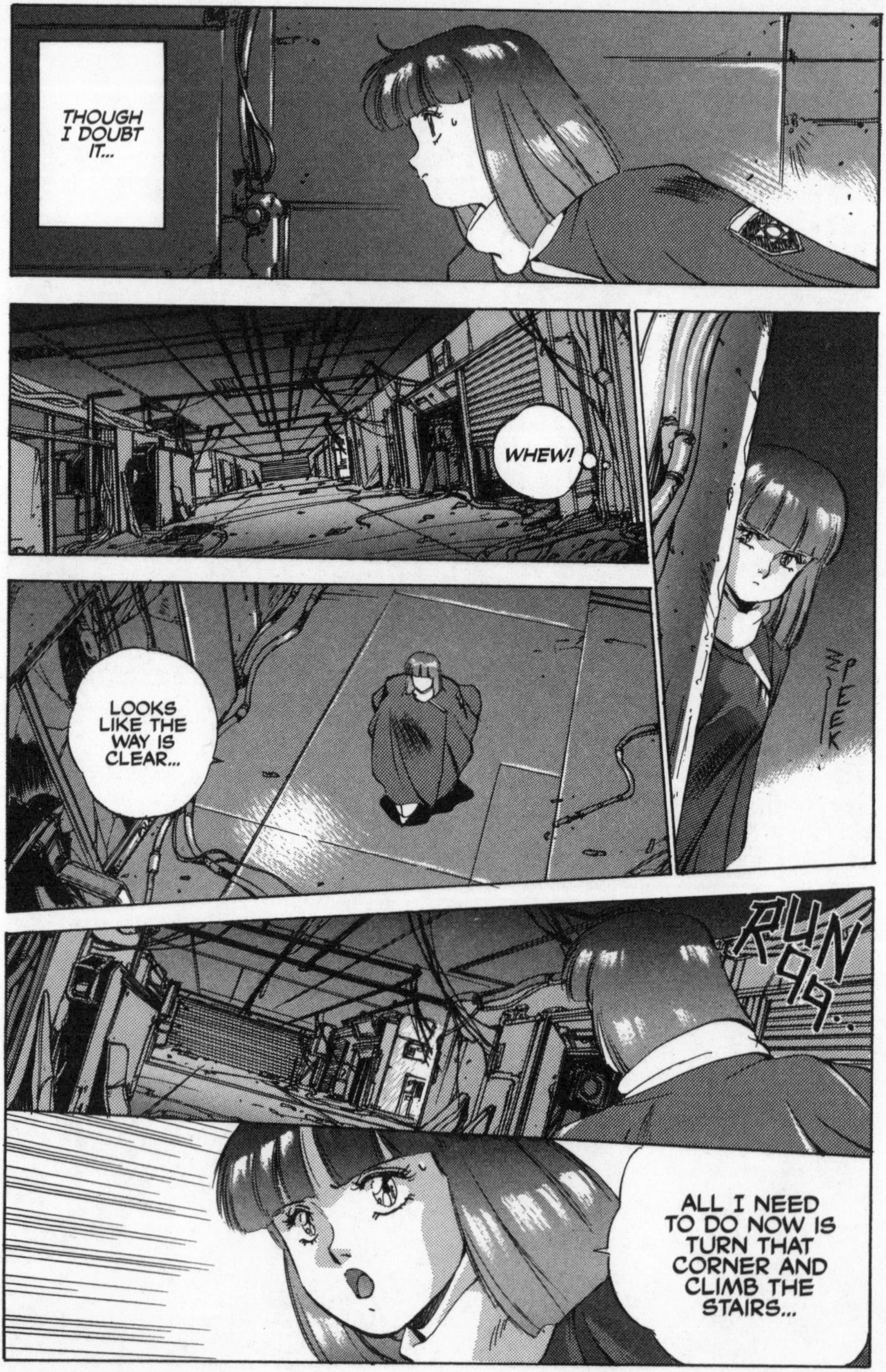
THOUGH I DOUBT IT...
PEEK
WHEW!
LOOKS LIKE THE WAY IS CLEAR...
RUN
ALL I NEED TO DO NOW IS TURN THAT CORNER AND CLIMB THE STAIRS...

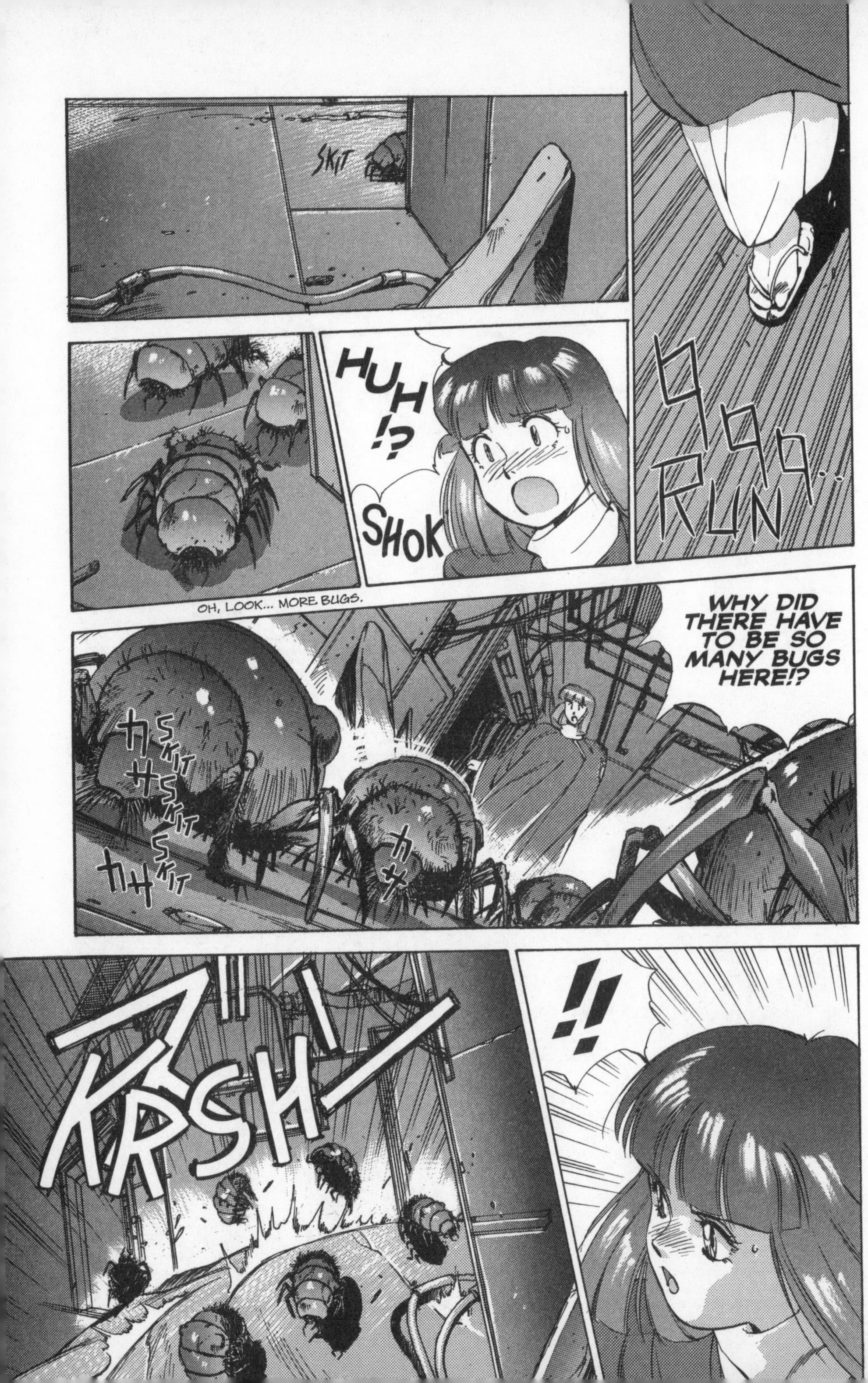
RUN...
SKIT
HUH!?
SHOK
OH, LOOK... MORE BUGS.
WHY DID THERE HAVE TO BE SO MANY BUGS HERE!?
SKIT
SKIT
SKIT
SKIT
!!
KRSH

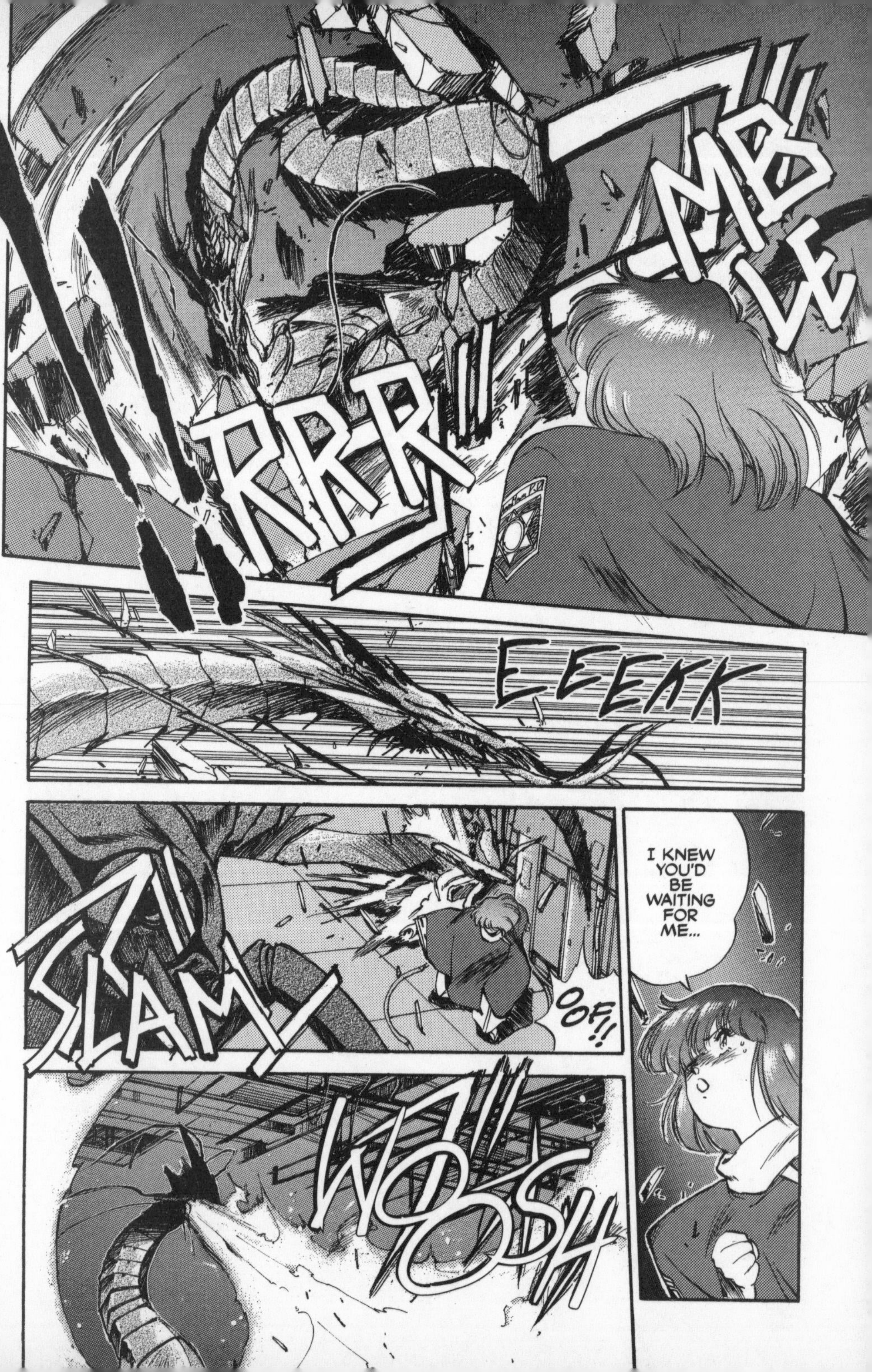
MBLE
RR-R
EEEKK
I KNEW YOU'D BE WAITING FOR ME...
OOF!!
SLAM!
WOOSH

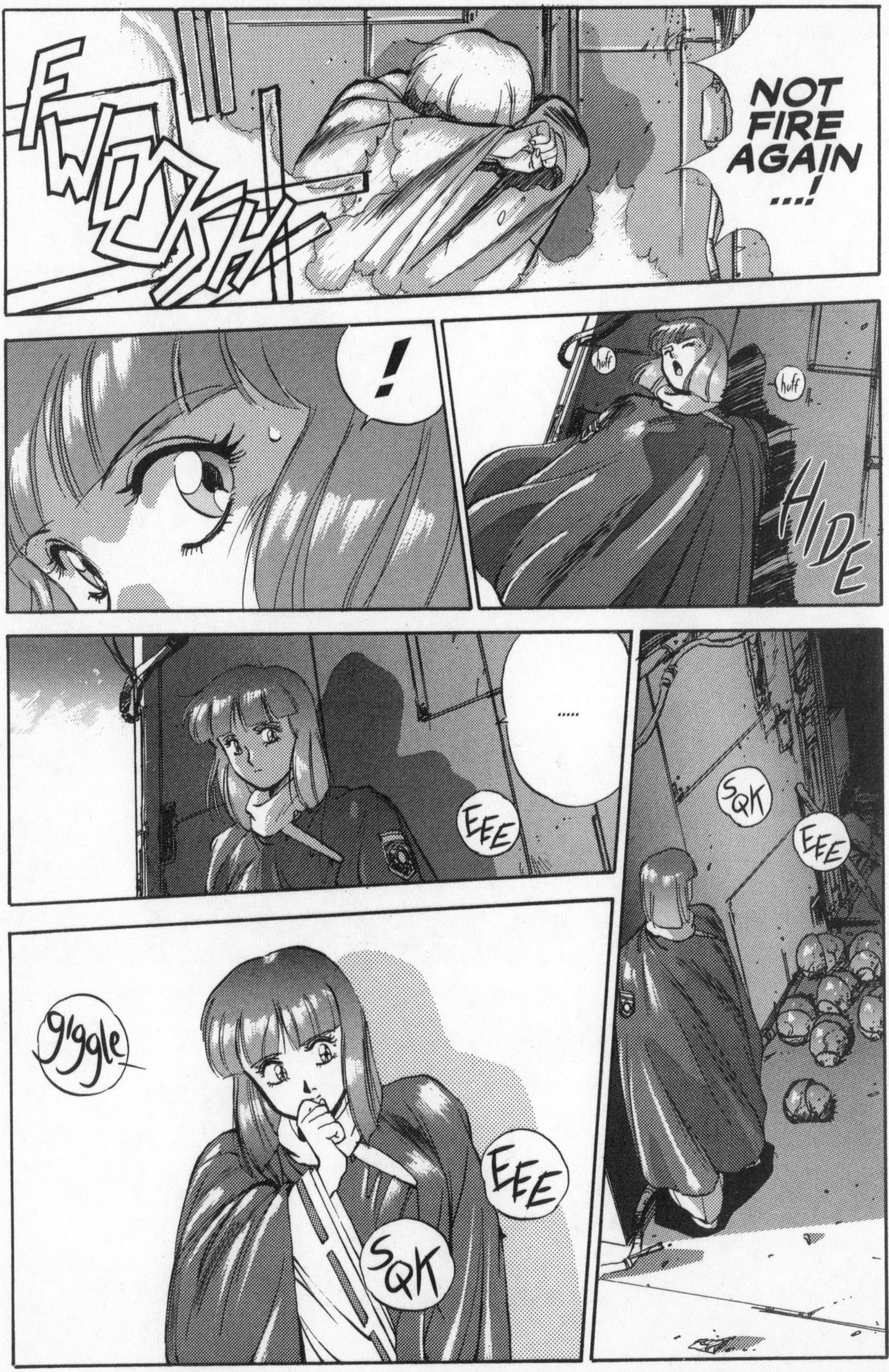
NOT FIRE AGAIN ....!
FWOOSH
huff
huff
HIDE
!
SQK
EEE
.....
EEE
giggle
EEE
SQK

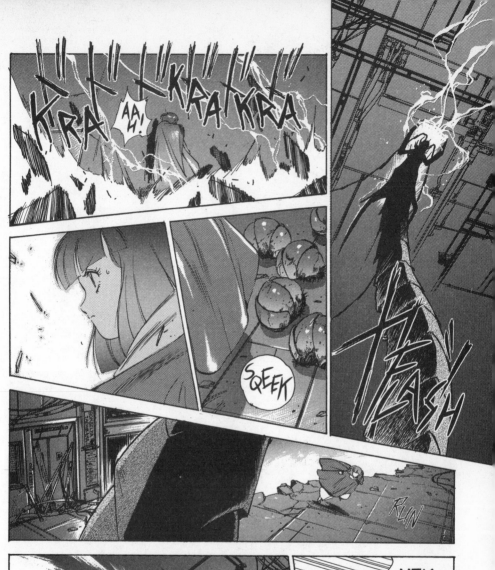

KRA KRA KRAKRA

AA!

SQEEK

FLASH

RUN

WOOSH

HEY, OVER HERE! COME ON!!

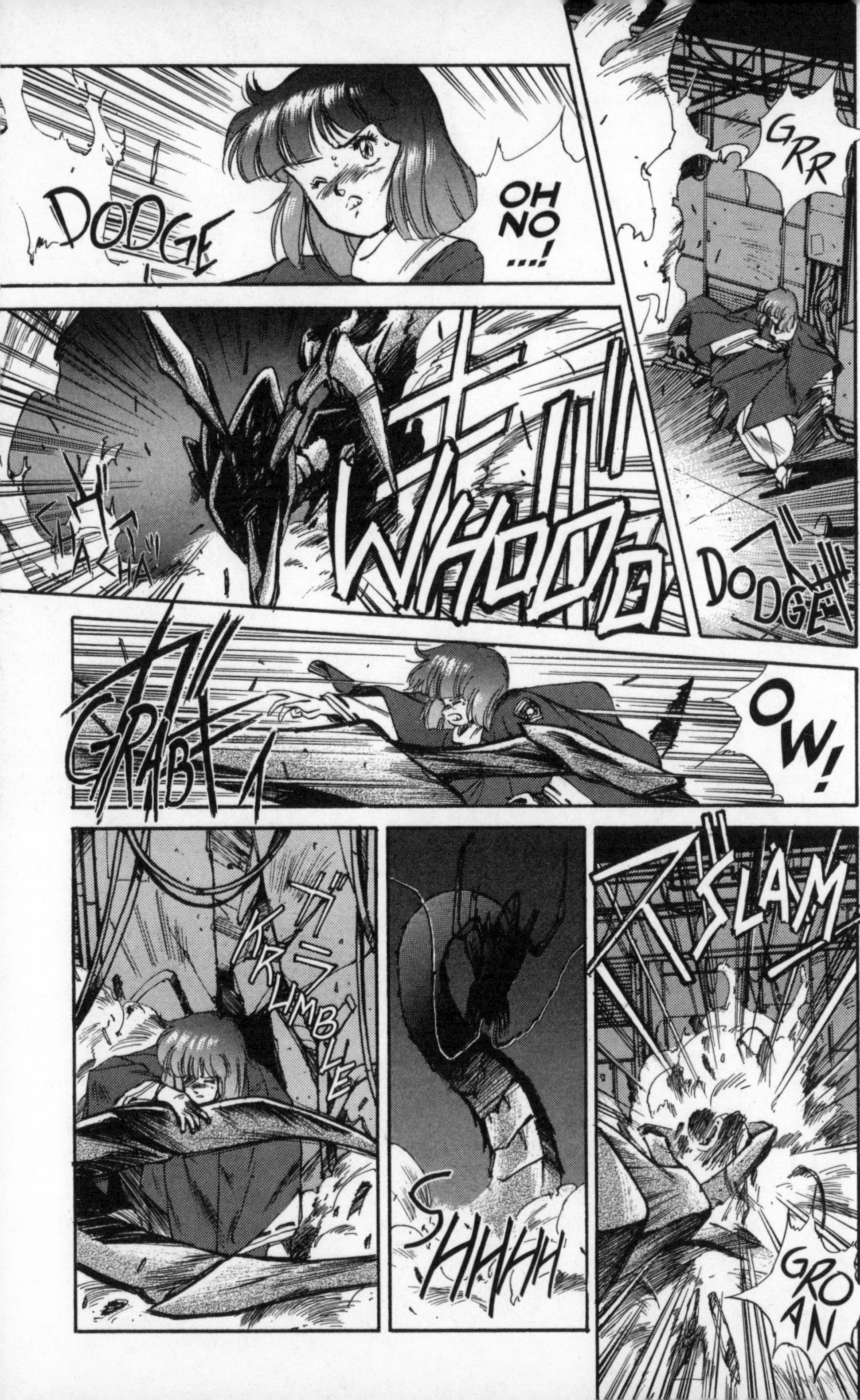
GRR
DODGE
OH NO ....!
DODGE
WHOOS
CHA CHA!
OW!
GRAB
SLAM
GROAN
SHHHH
KRUMBLE

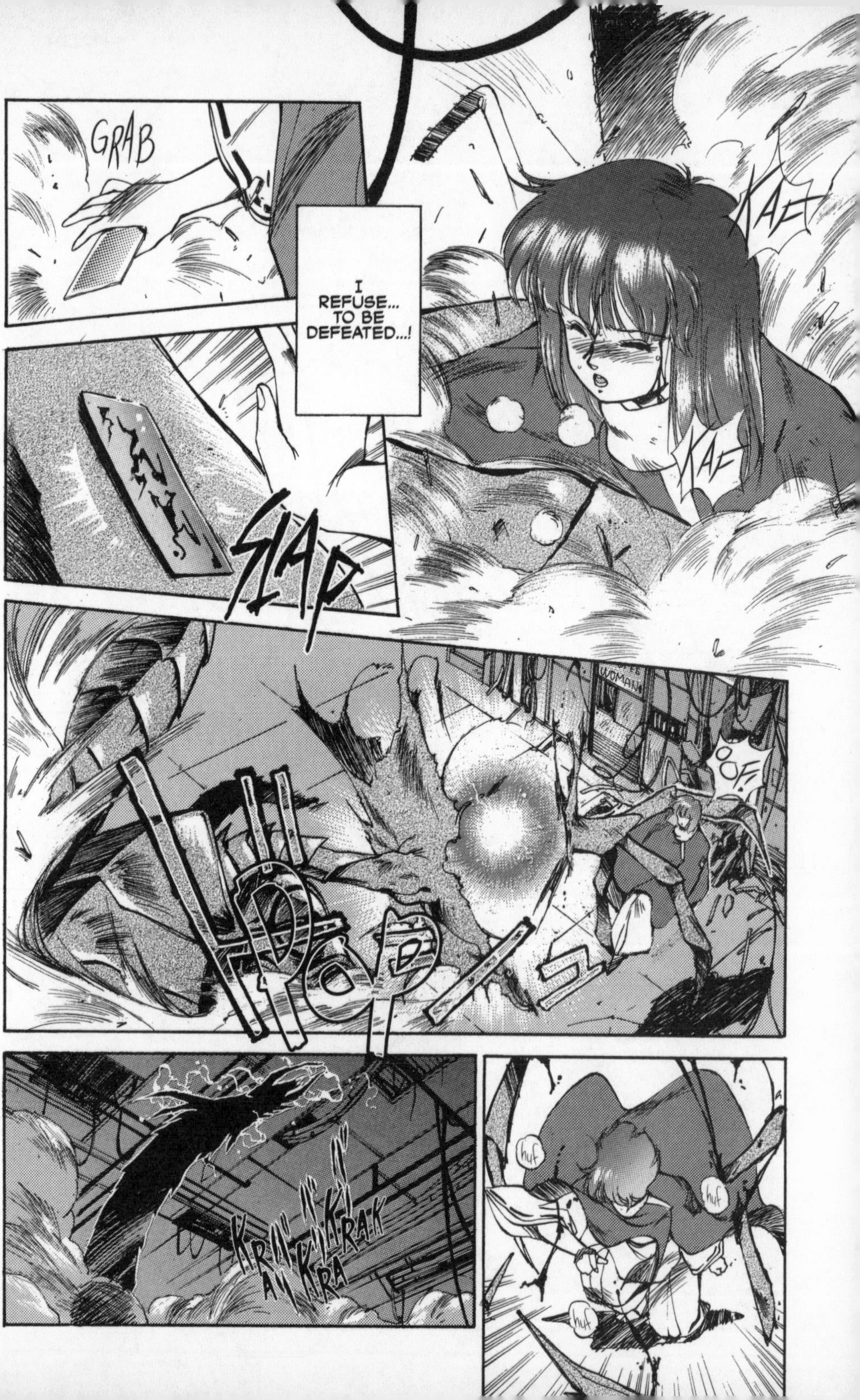
KAF
KAF
I REFUSE... TO BE DEFEATED...!
GRAB
SLAP
WOMAN
OOF!
huf
huf
huf
KRAK

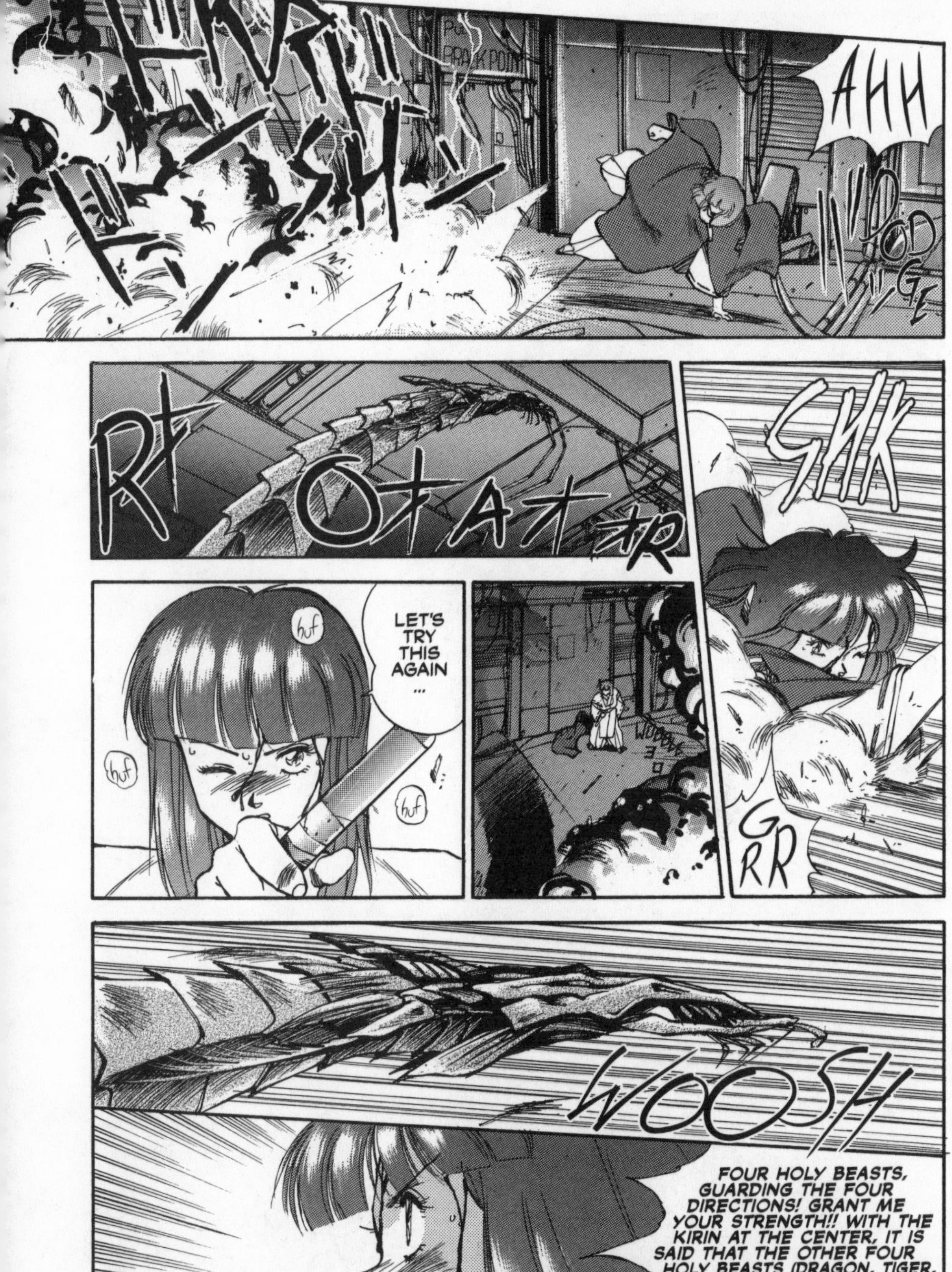
AHH
DODGE
KRASH
SNK
GRR
ROAR
LET'S TRY THIS AGAIN ...
huf
huf
huf
WOOSH
FOUR HOLY BEASTS, GUARDING THE FOUR DIRECTIONS! GRANT ME YOUR STRENGTH!! WITH THE KIRIN AT THE CENTER, IT IS SAID THAT THE OTHER FOUR HOLY BEASTS (DRAGON, TIGER, PHOENIX, TURTLE) EACH STANDS AT ONE OF THE FOUR COMPASS POINTS.

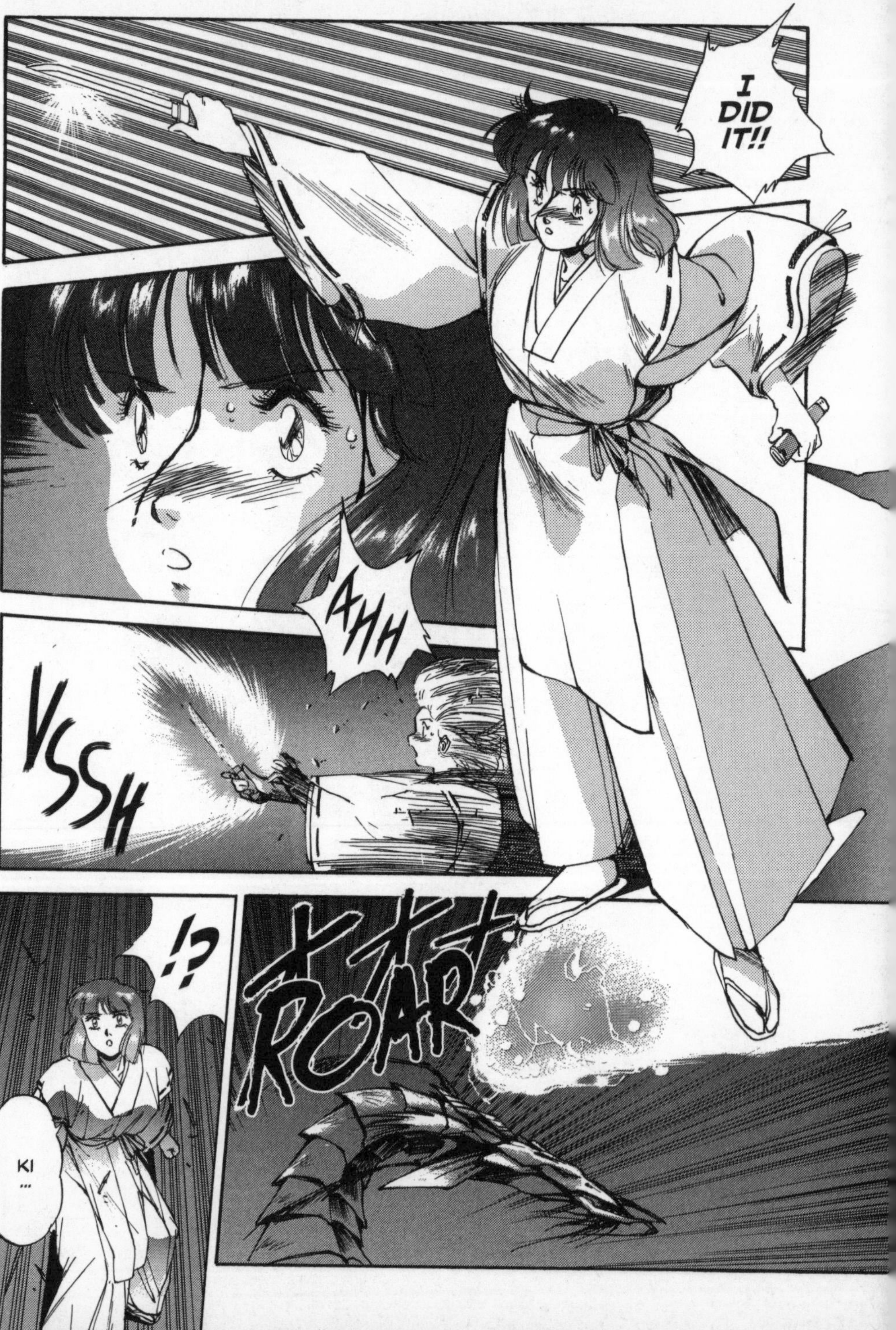
I DID IT!!
AHH
VSSH
ROAR
!?
KI ...

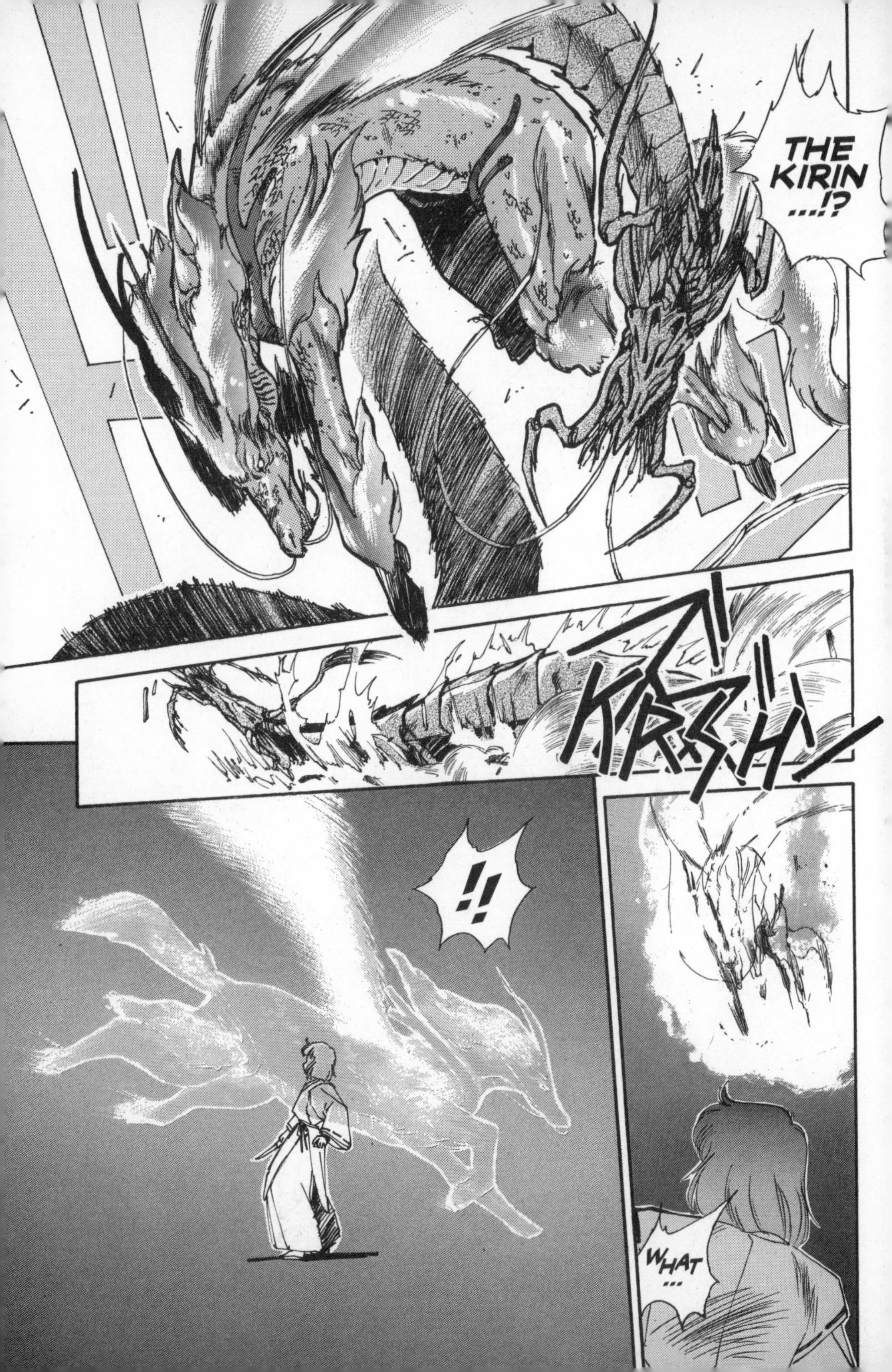
THE KIRIN ...!?
KRSH!
WHAT ...
!!

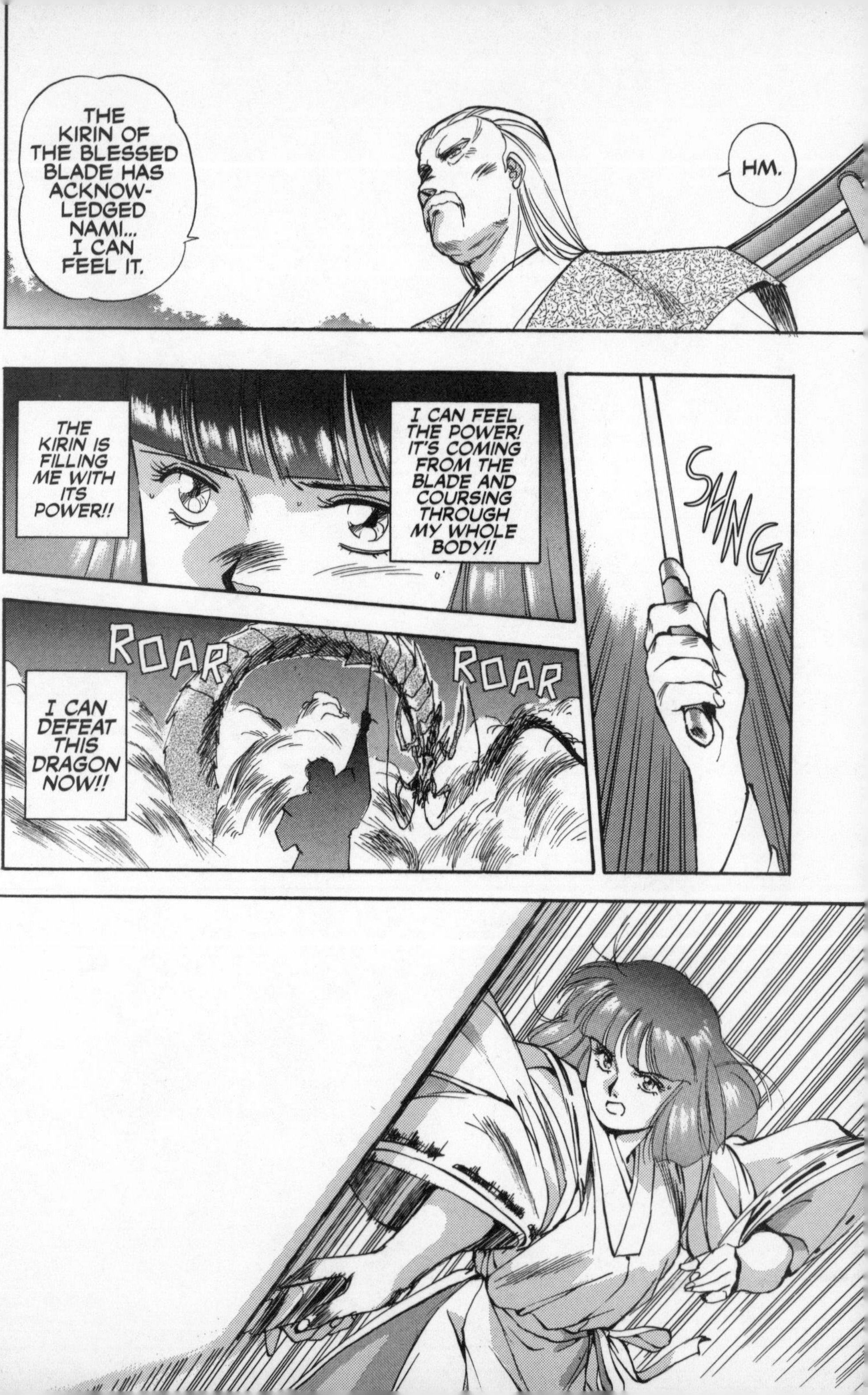
HM.
THE KIRIN OF THE BLESSED BLADE HAS ACKNOW-LEDGED NAMI... I CAN FEEL IT.
SHNG
I CAN FEEL THE POWER! IT'S COMING FROM THE BLADE AND COURSING THROUGH MY WHOLE BODY!!
THE KIRIN IS FILLING ME WITH ITS POWER!!
ROAR
ROAR
I CAN DEFEAT THIS DRAGON NOW!!

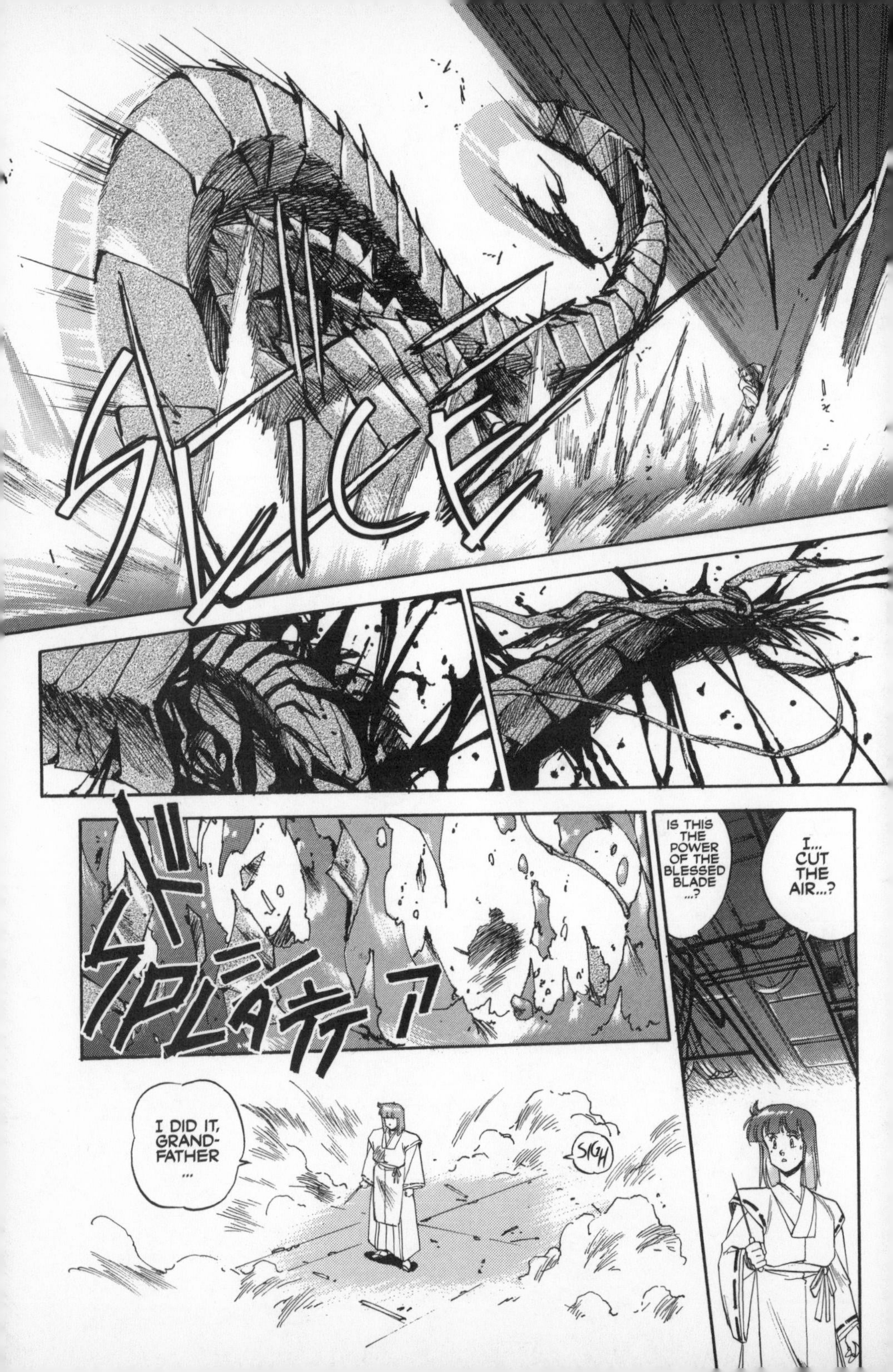
SLICE
I... CUT THE AIR...?
IS THIS THE POWER OF THE BLESSED BLADE ...?
SPLATTER
SIGH
I DID IT, GRANDFATHER ...

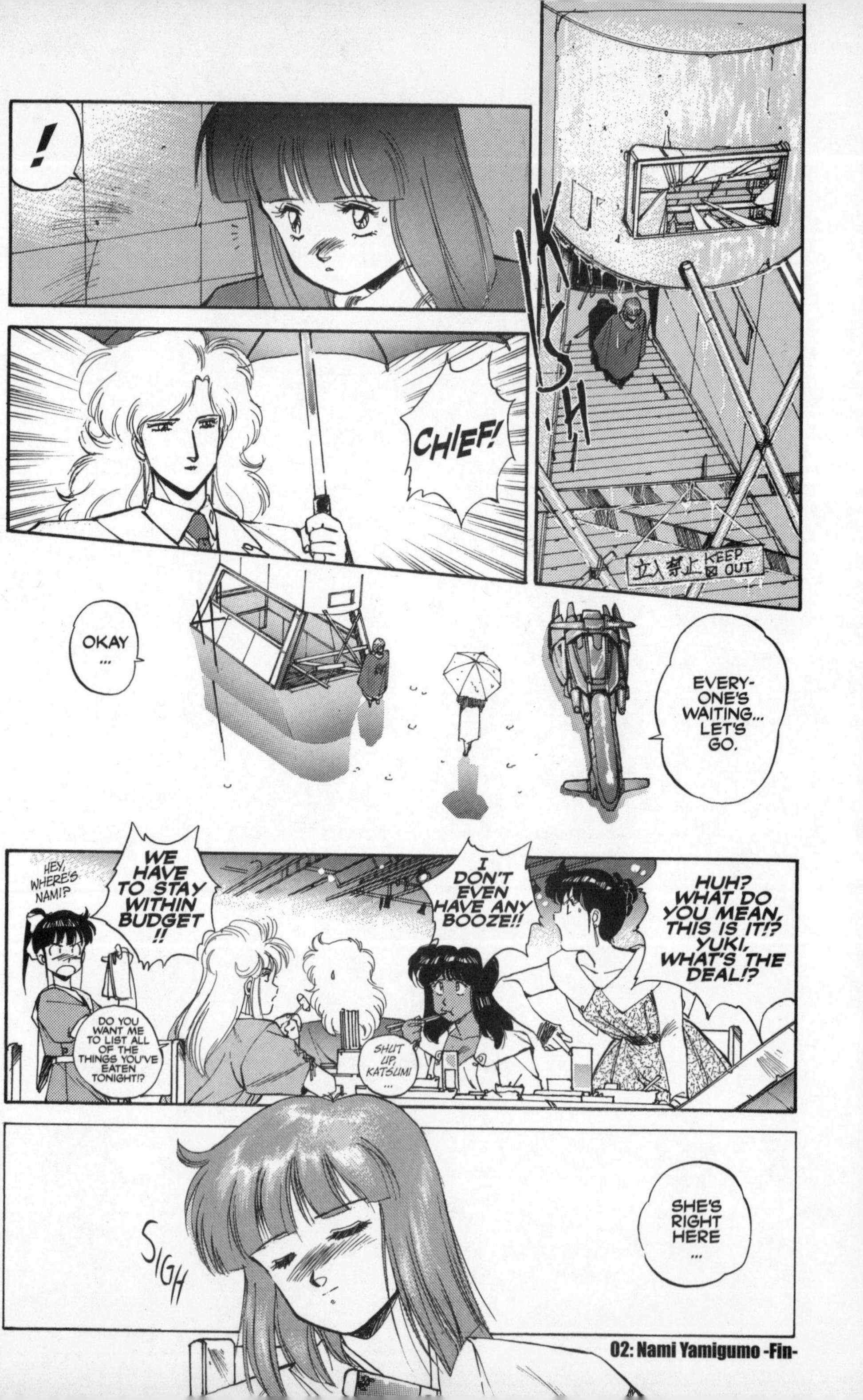
KSH
!
CHIEF!
EVERY-ONE'S WAITING... LET'S GO.
OKAY ...
HUH? WHAT DO YOU MEAN, THIS IS IT!? YUKI, WHAT'S THE DEAL!?
I DON'T EVEN HAVE ANY BOOZE!!
SHUT UP, KATSUMI ...
WE HAVE TO STAY WITHIN BUDGET !!
DO YOU WANT ME TO LIST ALL OF THE THINGS YOU'VE EATEN TONIGHT!?
HEY, WHERE'S NAMI!?
SHE'S RIGHT HERE ...
SIGH

02: Nami Yamigumo -Fin-

03:
Kiddy Phenil (Part 1)
キディ・フェニル（前編）

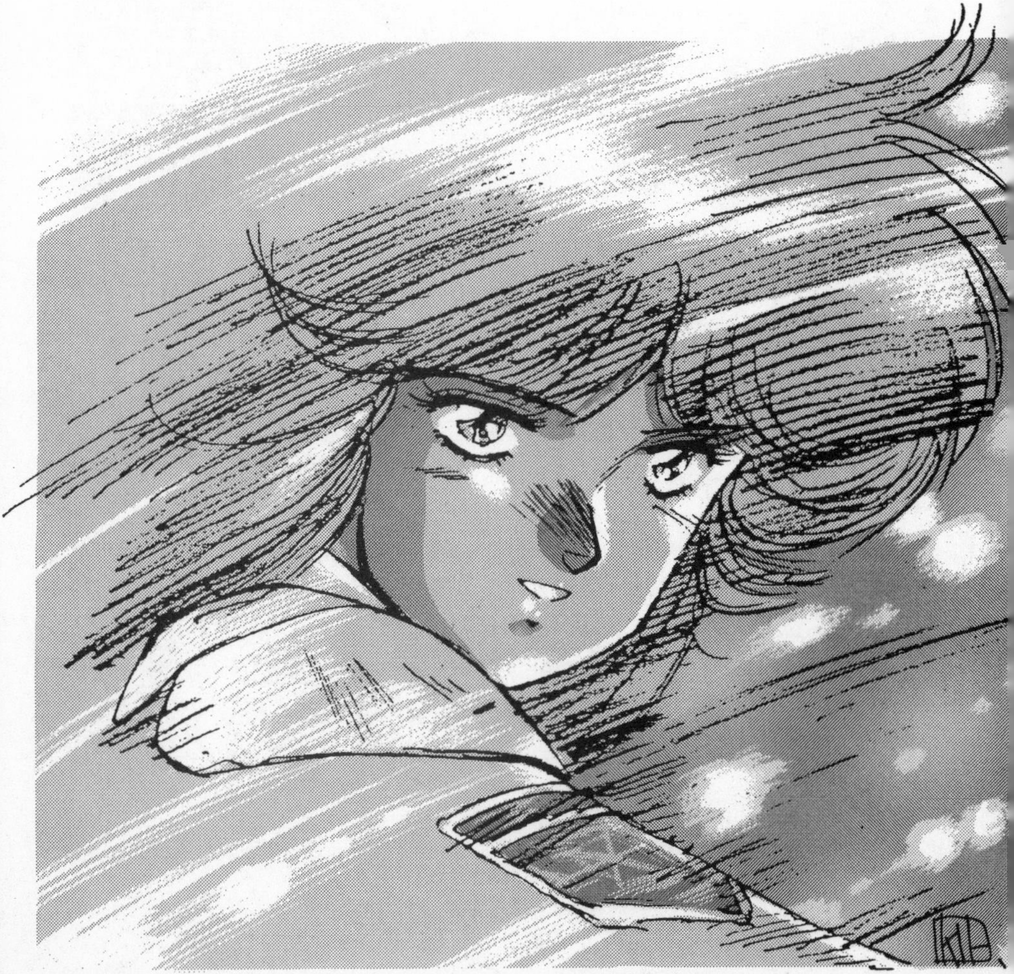

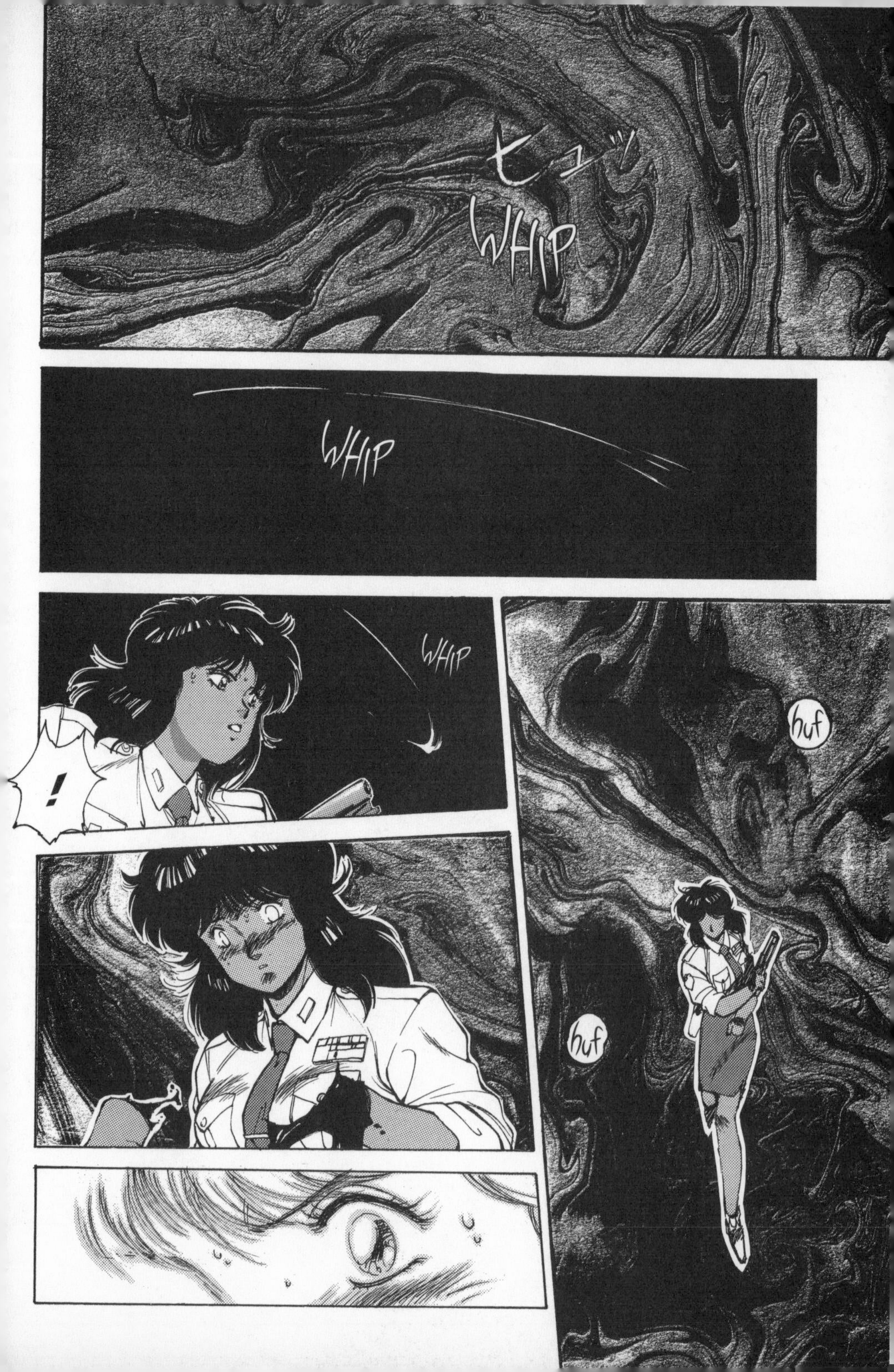
ヒュッ
WHIP
WHIP
huf
huf
WHIP
!

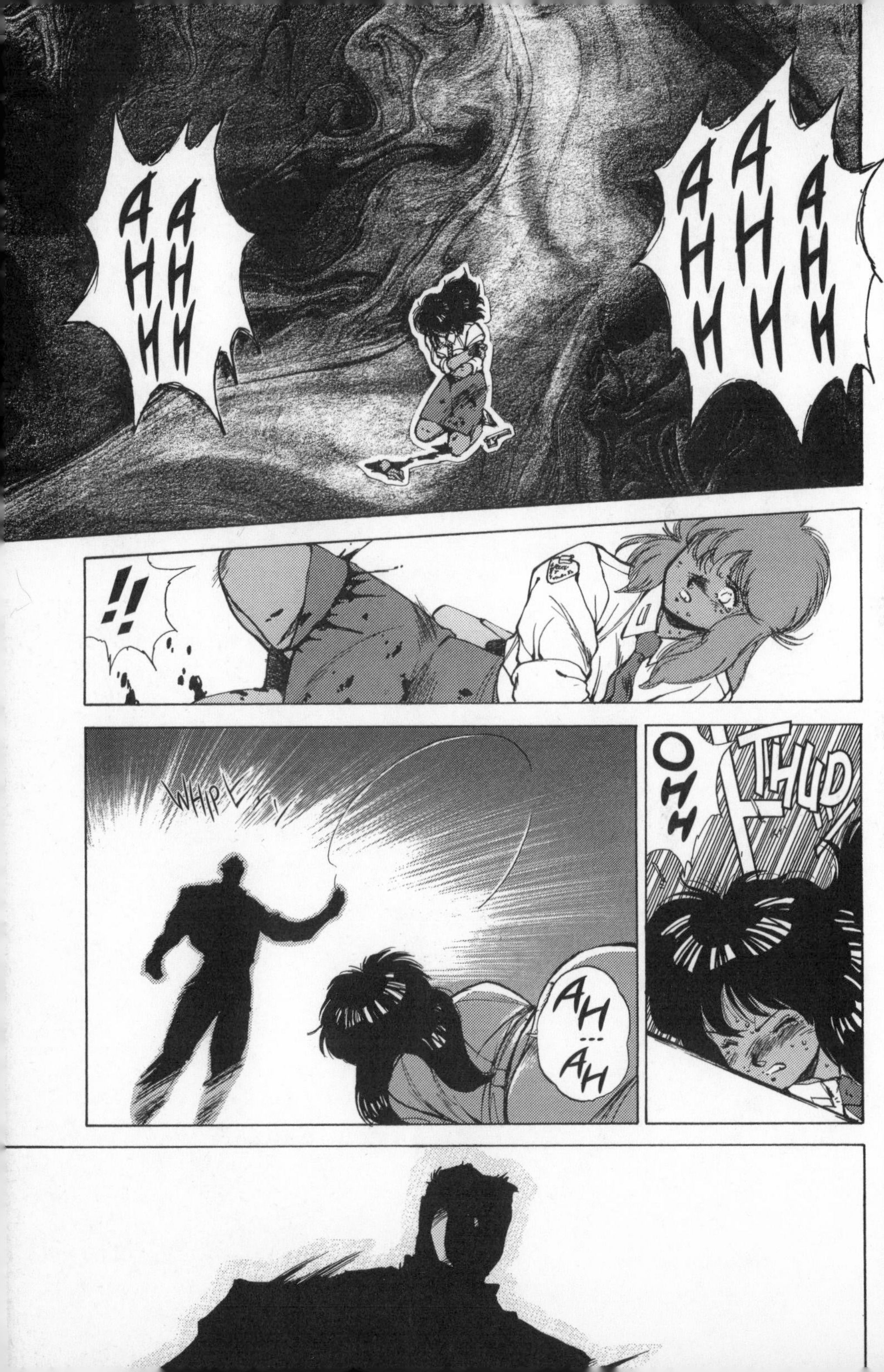
AAAHHHHHHHHH
AAHHHHHH
!!
OHH
THUD!
WHIP
AH... AH

AHAH
AHAH

OOOHH...
OHHH...

WHAT THE HELL, KIDDY!?

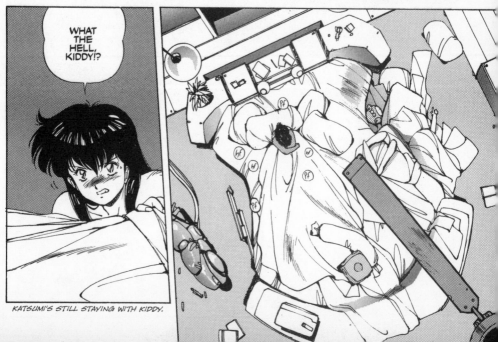

KATSUMI'S STILL STAYING WITH KIDDY.

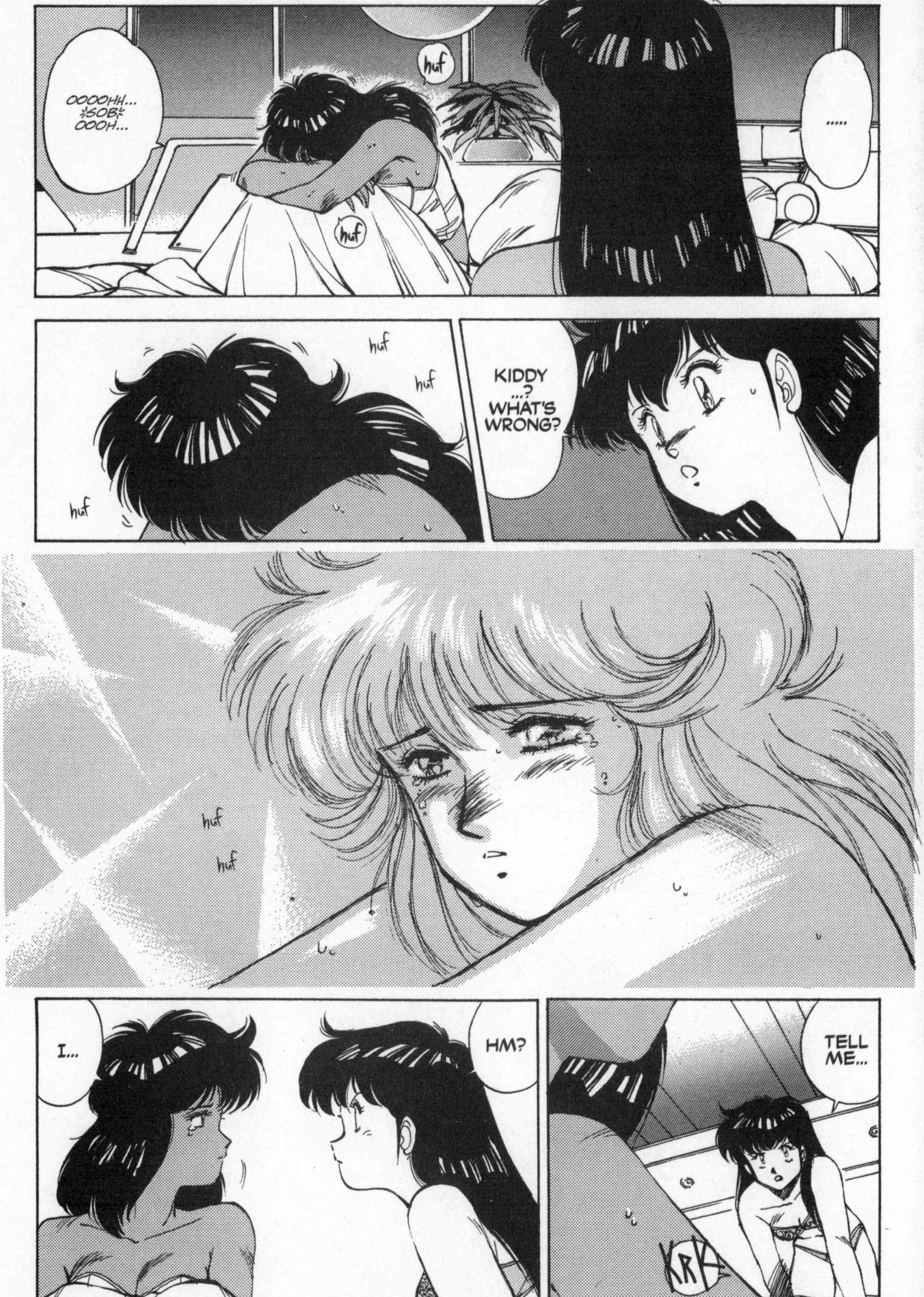
.....
huf
OOOOHH... *SOB* OOOH...
huf
KIDDY ...? WHAT'S WRONG?
huf
huf
huf
huf
huf
TELL ME...
KRK
HM?
I...

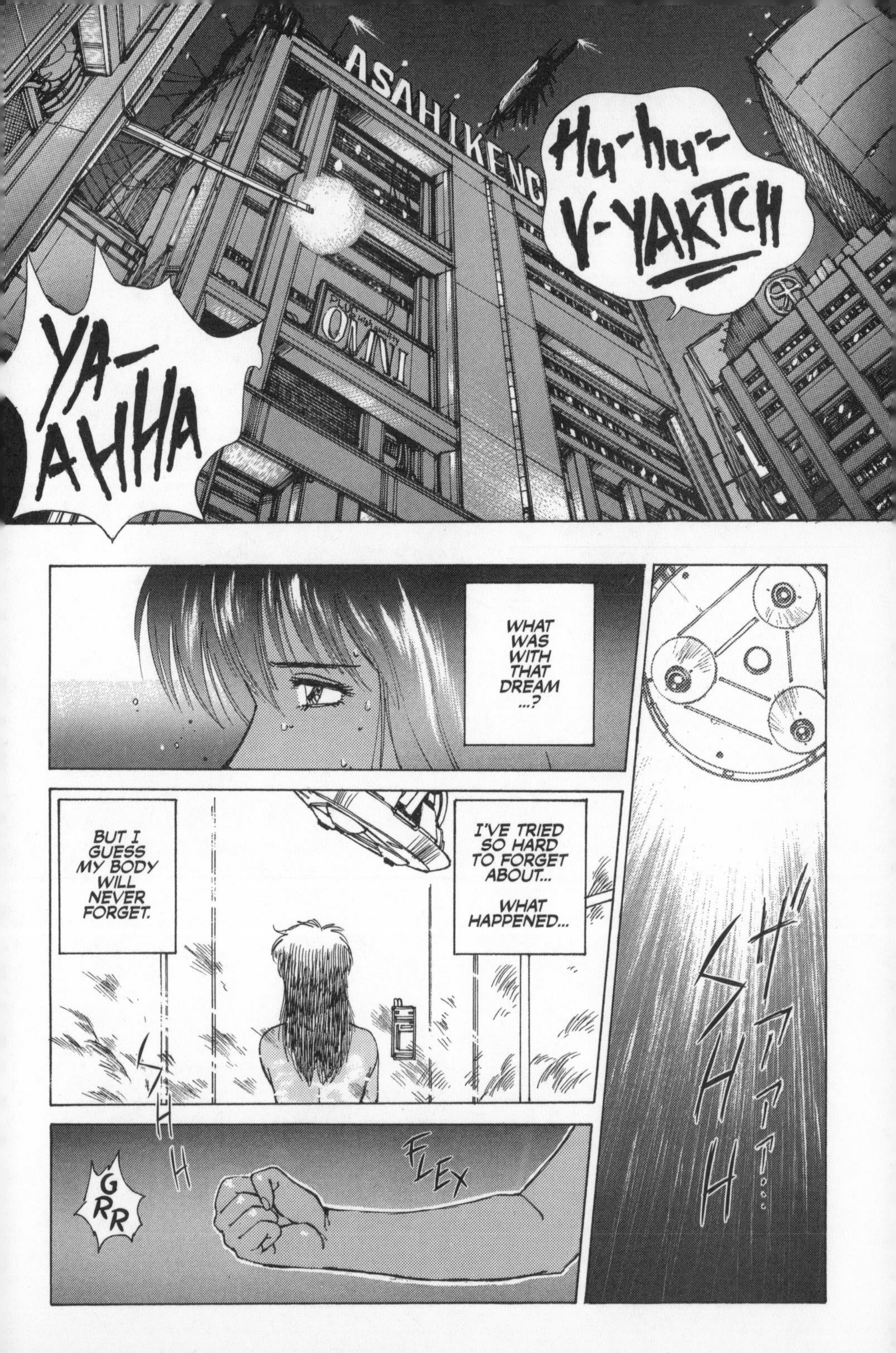
ASAHIKENG
OMNI
Hu-hu- V-YAKTCH
YA-AHHA
SHHH
WHAT WAS WITH THAT DREAM ...?
I'VE TRIED SO HARD TO FORGET ABOUT... WHAT HAPPENED...
BUT I GUESS MY BODY WILL NEVER FORGET.
SHHH
FLEX
GRR

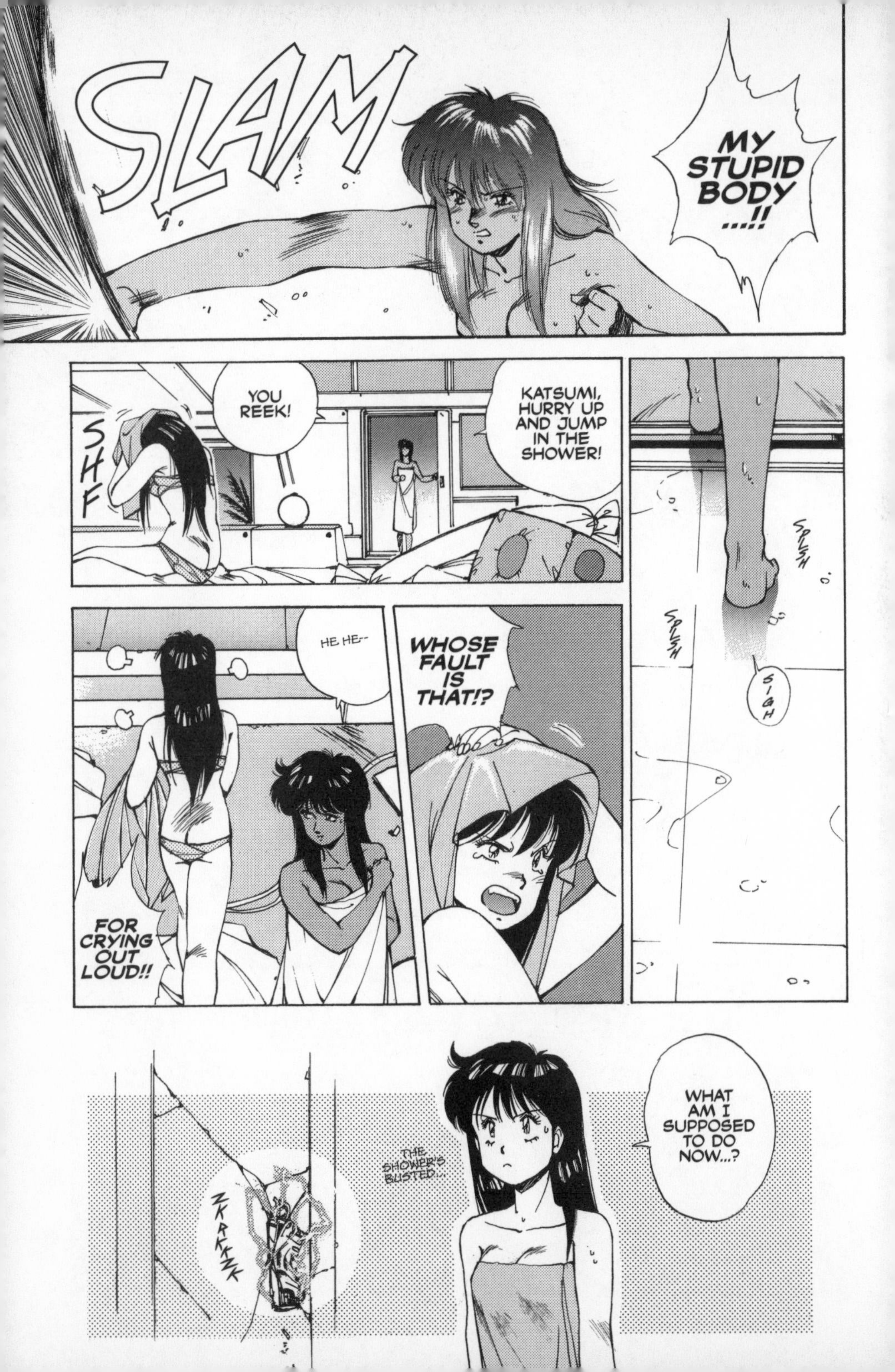
MY STUPID BODY ...!!
SLAM
SPLSH
SPLSH
SIGH
KATSUMI, HURRY UP AND JUMP IN THE SHOWER!
YOU REEK!
SHF
WHOSE FAULT IS THAT!?
HE HE--
FOR CRYING OUT LOUD!!
WHAT AM I SUPPOSED TO DO NOW...?
THE SHOWER'S BUSTED...
ZKRKKZK

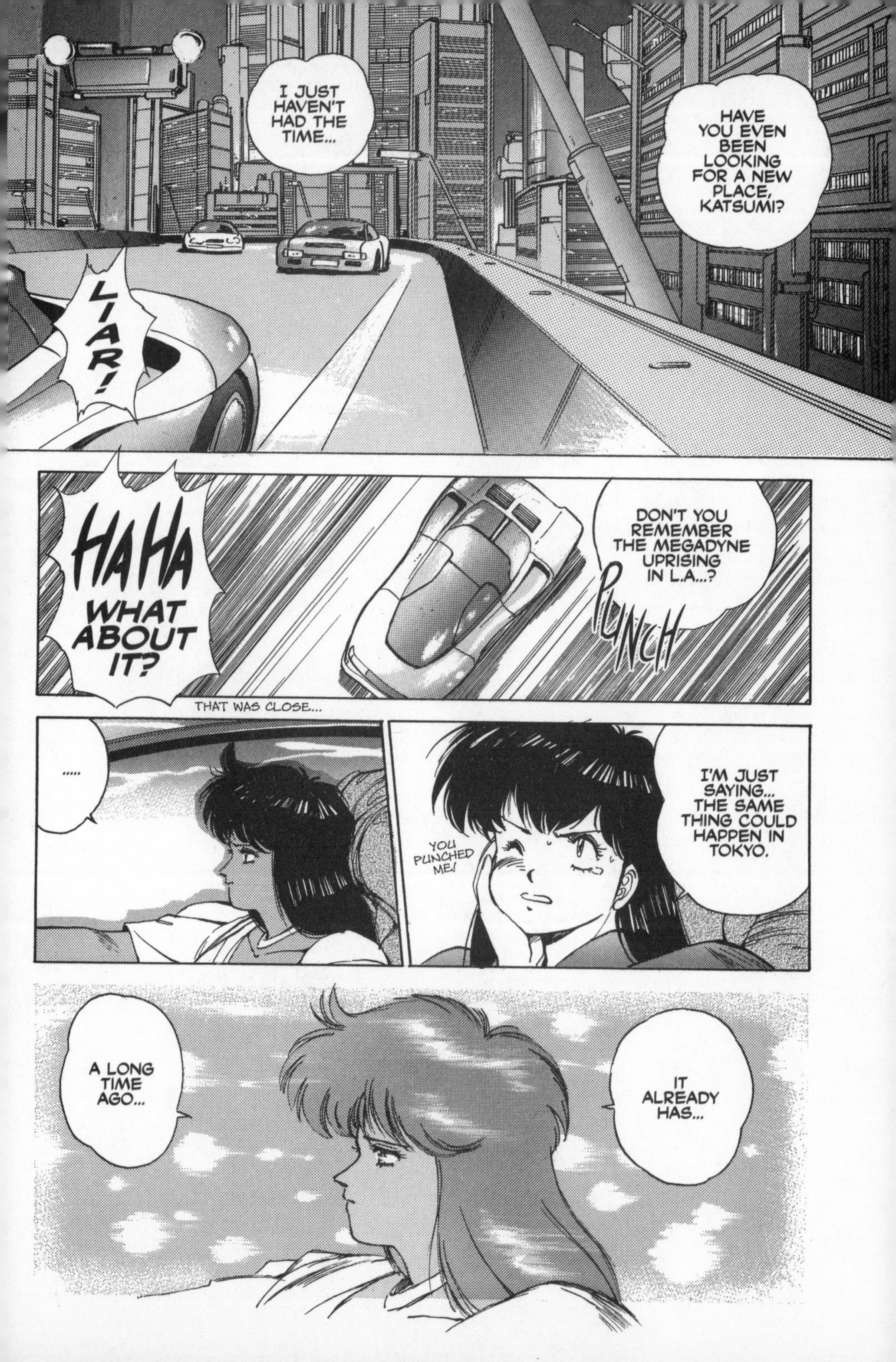
HAVE YOU EVEN BEEN LOOKING FOR A NEW PLACE, KATSUMI?
I JUST HAVEN'T HAD THE TIME...
LIAR!
DON'T YOU REMEMBER THE MEGADYNE UPRISING IN L.A...?
PUNCH
HAHA WHAT ABOUT IT?
THAT WAS CLOSE...
I'M JUST SAYING... THE SAME THING COULD HAPPEN IN TOKYO.
YOU PUNCHED ME!
.....
IT ALREADY HAS...
A LONG TIME AGO...

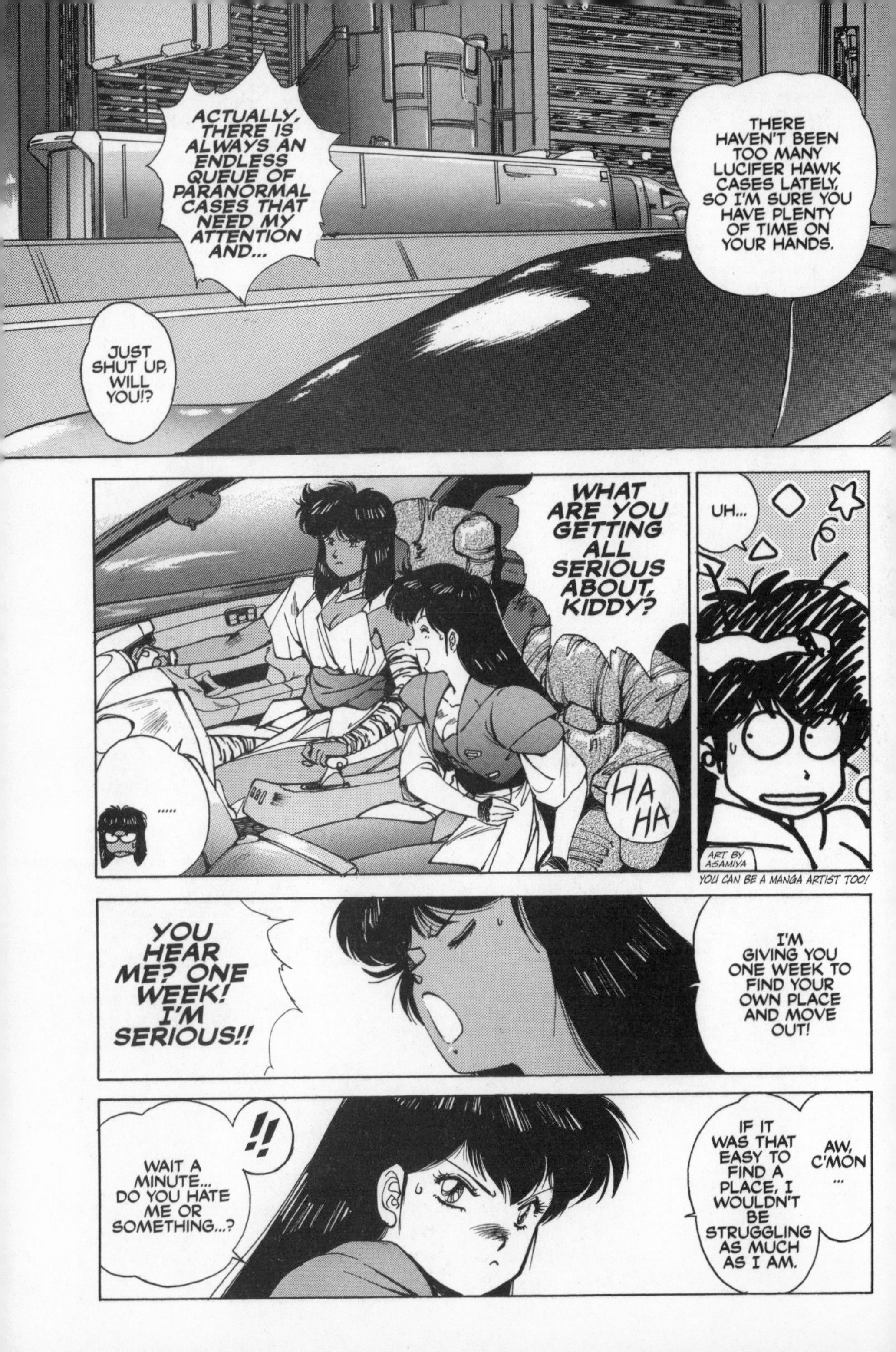
THERE HAVEN'T BEEN TOO MANY LUCIFER HAWK CASES LATELY, SO I'M SURE YOU HAVE PLENTY OF TIME ON YOUR HANDS.
ACTUALLY, THERE IS ALWAYS AN ENDLESS QUEUE OF PARANORMAL CASES THAT NEED MY ATTENTION AND...
JUST SHUT UP, WILL YOU!?
UH...
ART BY ASAMIYA
YOU CAN BE A MANGA ARTIST TOO!
WHAT ARE YOU GETTING ALL SERIOUS ABOUT, KIDDY?
HA HA
.....
I'M GIVING YOU ONE WEEK TO FIND YOUR OWN PLACE AND MOVE OUT!
YOU HEAR ME? ONE WEEK! I'M SERIOUS!!
AW, C'MON ...
IF IT WAS THAT EASY TO FIND A PLACE, I WOULDN'T BE STRUGGLING AS MUCH AS I AM.
!!
WAIT A MINUTE... DO YOU HATE ME OR SOMETHING...?

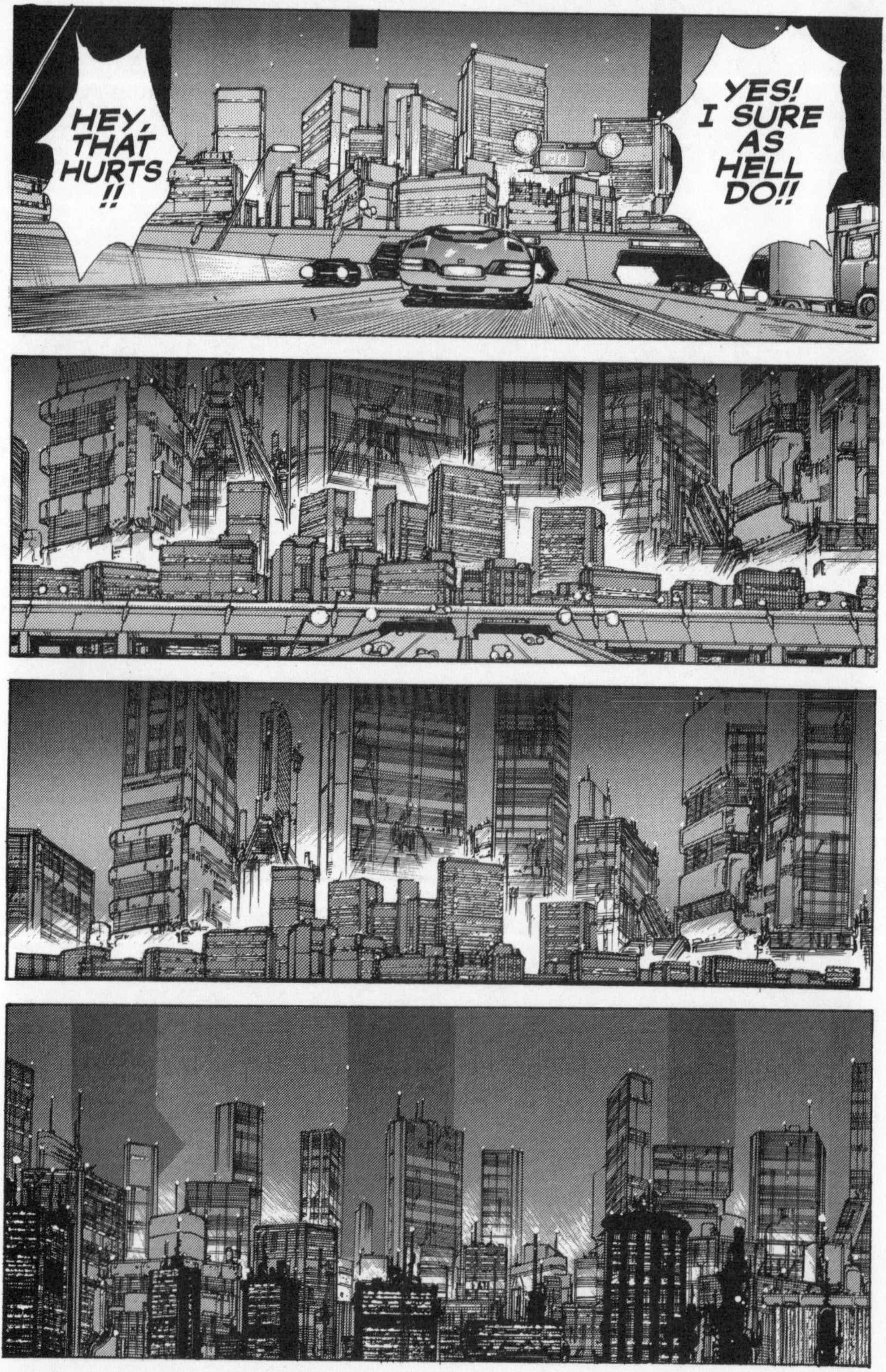
YES! I SURE AS HELL DO!!
HEY, THAT HURTS!!

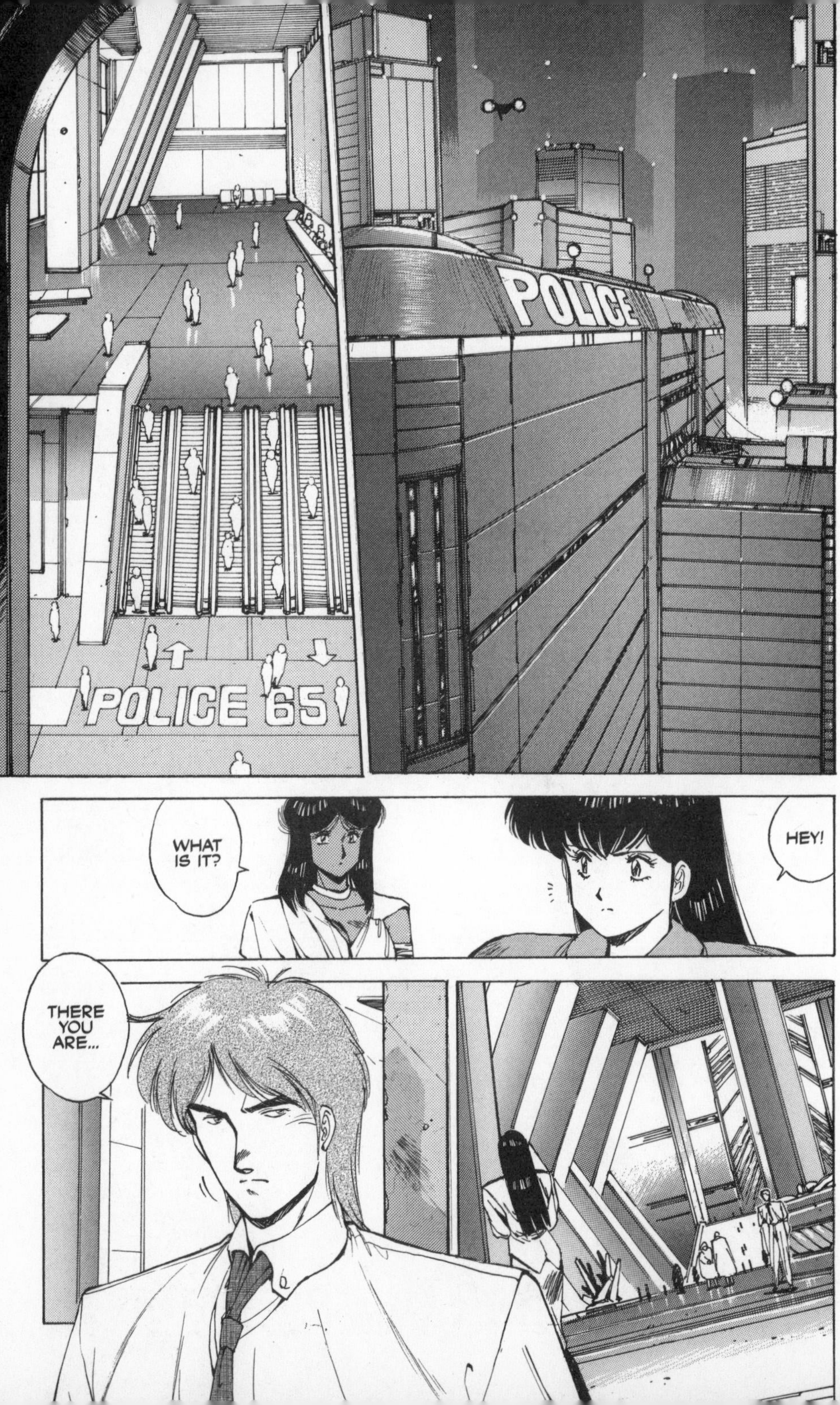
POLICE
POLICE 65
HEY!
WHAT IS IT?
THERE YOU ARE...

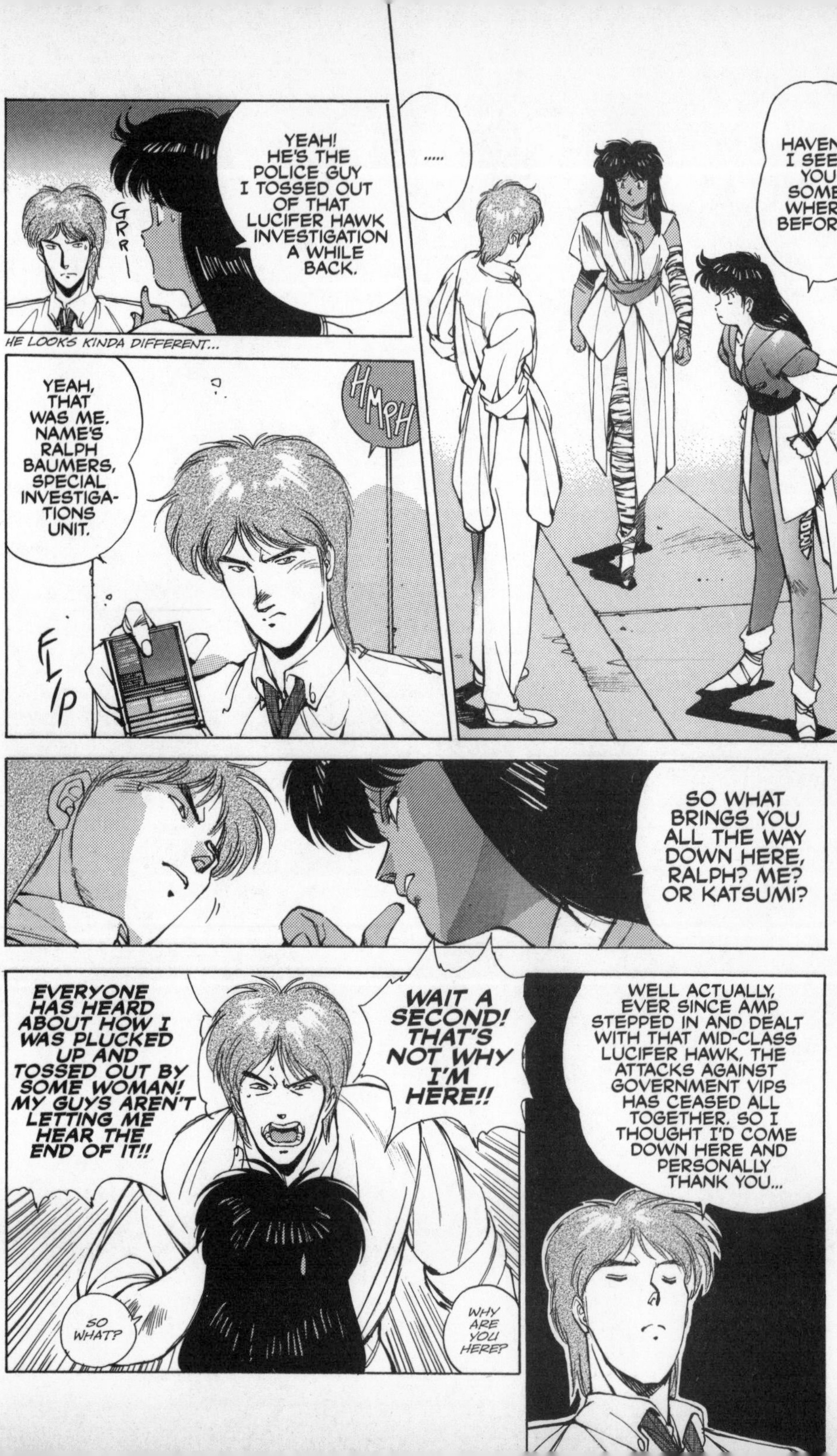
HAVEN'T I SEEN YOU SOME-WHERE BEFORE?
.....
YEAH! HE'S THE POLICE GUY I TOSSED OUT OF THAT LUCIFER HAWK INVESTIGATION A WHILE BACK.
GRRI
HE LOOKS KINDA DIFFERENT...
HMPH
YEAH, THAT WAS ME. NAME'S RALPH BAUMERS, SPECIAL INVESTIGA-TIONS UNIT.
FLIP
SO WHAT BRINGS YOU ALL THE WAY DOWN HERE, RALPH? ME? OR KATSUMI?
WELL ACTUALLY, EVER SINCE AMP STEPPED IN AND DEALT WITH THAT MID-CLASS LUCIFER HAWK, THE ATTACKS AGAINST GOVERNMENT VIPS HAS CEASED ALL TOGETHER. SO I THOUGHT I'D COME DOWN HERE AND PERSONALLY THANK YOU...
WAIT A SECOND! THAT'S NOT WHY I'M HERE!!
EVERYONE HAS HEARD ABOUT HOW I WAS PLUCKED UP AND TOSSED OUT BY SOME WOMAN! MY GUYS AREN'T LETTING ME HEAR THE END OF IT!!
WHY ARE YOU HERE?
SO WHAT?

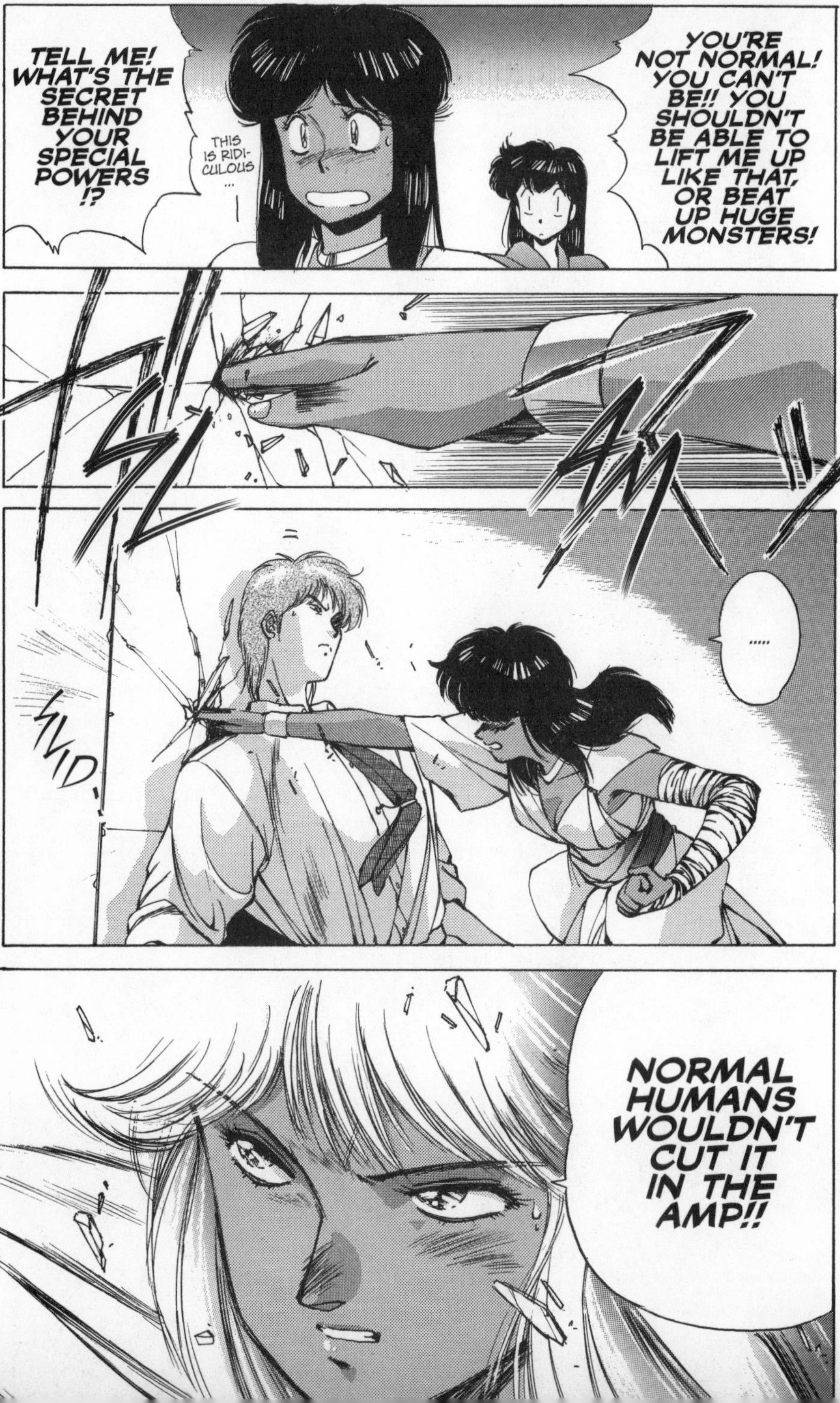
YOU'RE NOT NORMAL! YOU CAN'T BE!! YOU SHOULDN'T BE ABLE TO LIFT ME UP LIKE THAT, OR BEAT UP HUGE MONSTERS!
THIS IS RIDICULOUS ...
TELL ME! WHAT'S THE SECRET BEHIND YOUR SPECIAL POWERS !?
.....
NORMAL HUMANS WOULDN'T CUT IT IN THE AMP!!

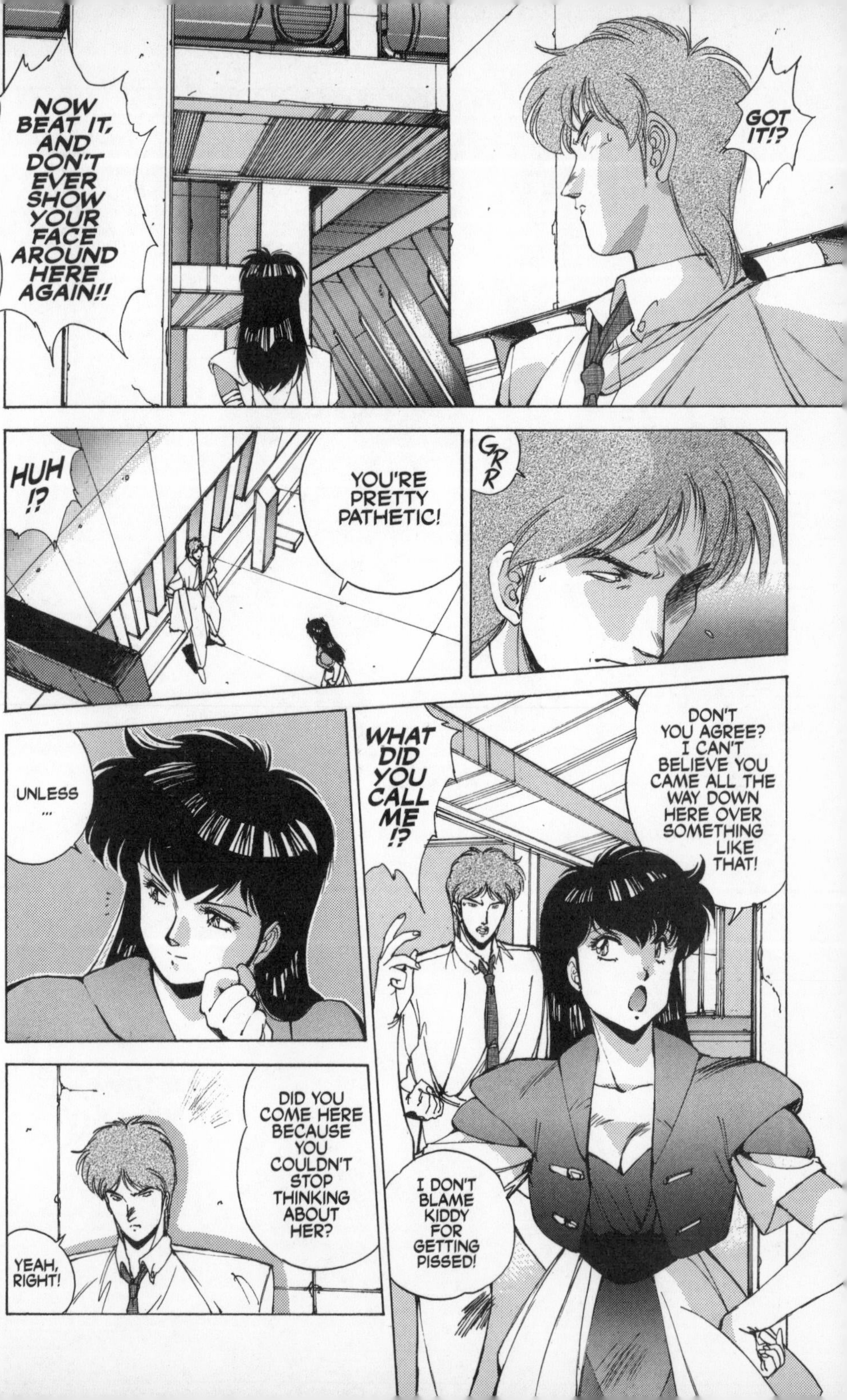
GOT IT!?
NOW BEAT IT, AND DON'T EVER SHOW YOUR FACE AROUND HERE AGAIN!!
GRR
YOU'RE PRETTY PATHETIC!
HUH!?
DON'T YOU AGREE? I CAN'T BELIEVE YOU CAME ALL THE WAY DOWN HERE OVER SOMETHING LIKE THAT!
WHAT DID YOU CALL ME!?
I DON'T BLAME KIDDY FOR GETTING PISSED!
UNLESS ...
DID YOU COME HERE BECAUSE YOU COULDN'T STOP THINKING ABOUT HER?
YEAH, RIGHT!

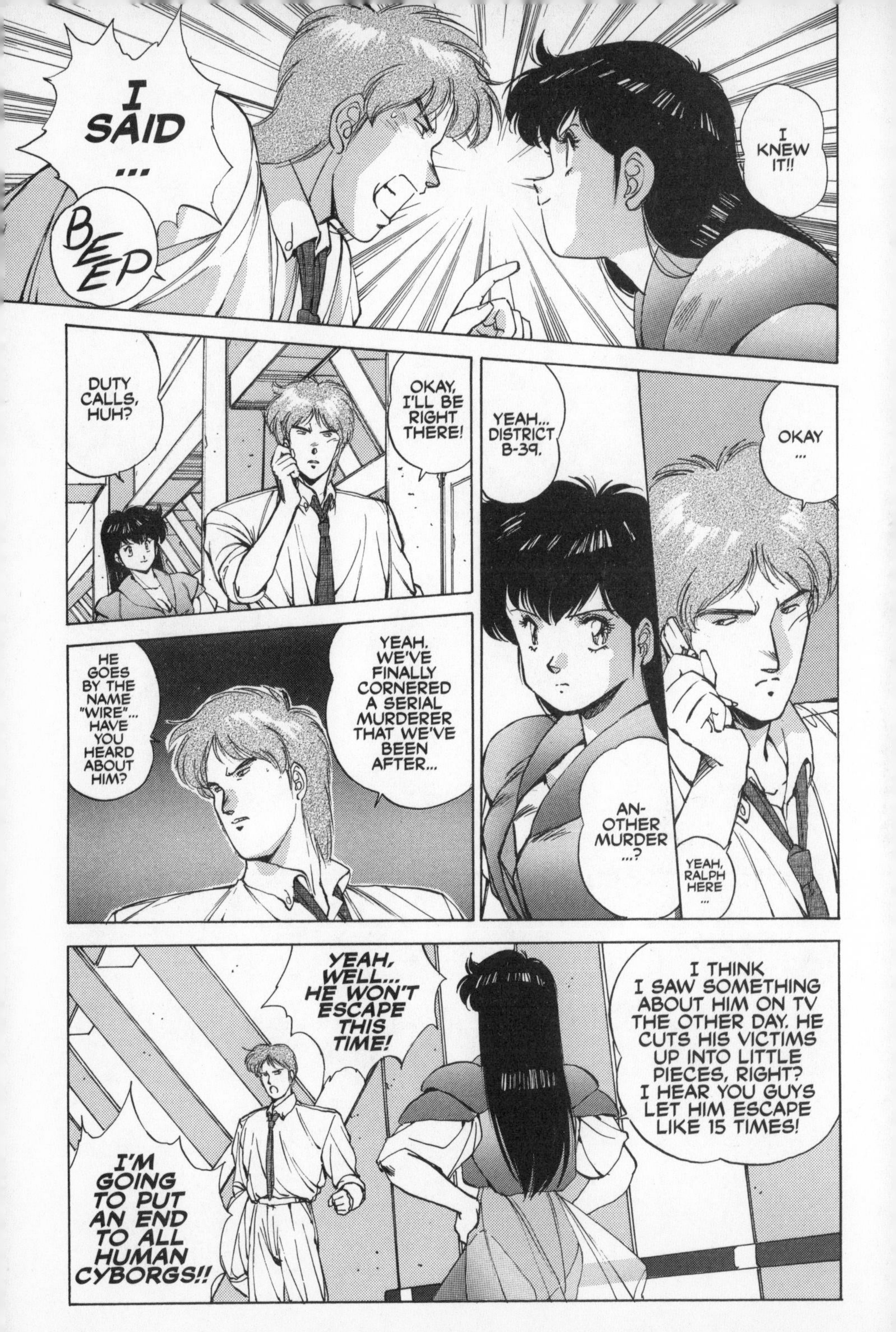
I KNEW IT!!
I SAID ...
BEEP
OKAY ...
YEAH... DISTRICT B-39.
YEAH, RALPH HERE ...
AN-OTHER MURDER ...?
OKAY, I'LL BE RIGHT THERE!
DUTY CALLS, HUH?
YEAH. WE'VE FINALLY CORNERED A SERIAL MURDERER THAT WE'VE BEEN AFTER...
HE GOES BY THE NAME "WIRE"... HAVE YOU HEARD ABOUT HIM?
I THINK I SAW SOMETHING ABOUT HIM ON TV THE OTHER DAY. HE CUTS HIS VICTIMS UP INTO LITTLE PIECES, RIGHT? I HEAR YOU GUYS LET HIM ESCAPE LIKE 15 TIMES!
YEAH, WELL... HE WON'T ESCAPE THIS TIME!
I'M GOING TO PUT AN END TO ALL HUMAN CYBORGS!!

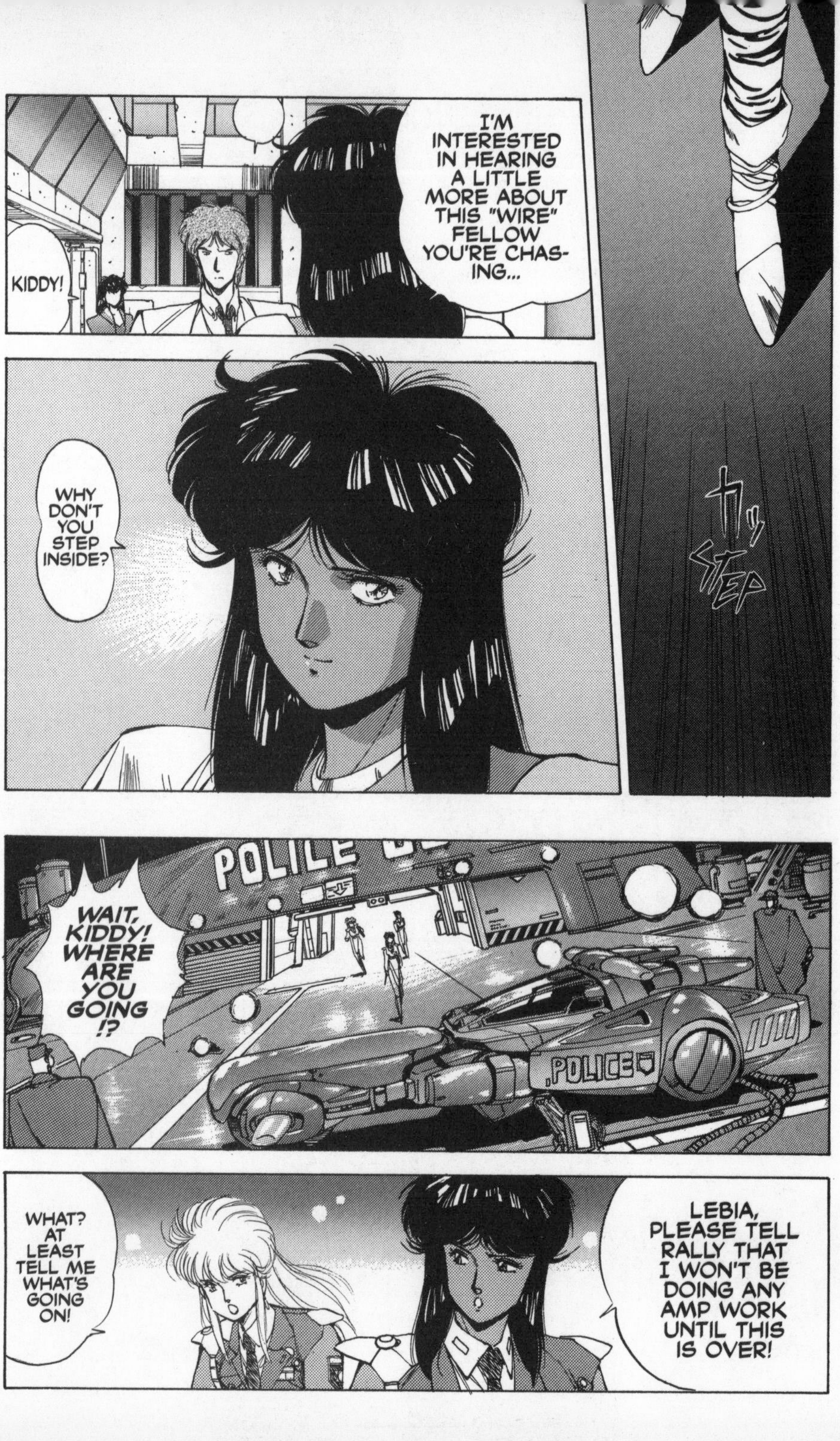
カッ
STEP
I'M INTERESTED IN HEARING A LITTLE MORE ABOUT THIS "WIRE" FELLOW YOU'RE CHAS-ING...
KIDDY!
WHY DON'T YOU STEP INSIDE?
POLICE
WAIT, KIDDY! WHERE ARE YOU GOING !?
POLICE
LEBIA, PLEASE TELL RALLY THAT I WON'T BE DOING ANY AMP WORK UNTIL THIS IS OVER!
WHAT? AT LEAST TELL ME WHAT'S GOING ON!

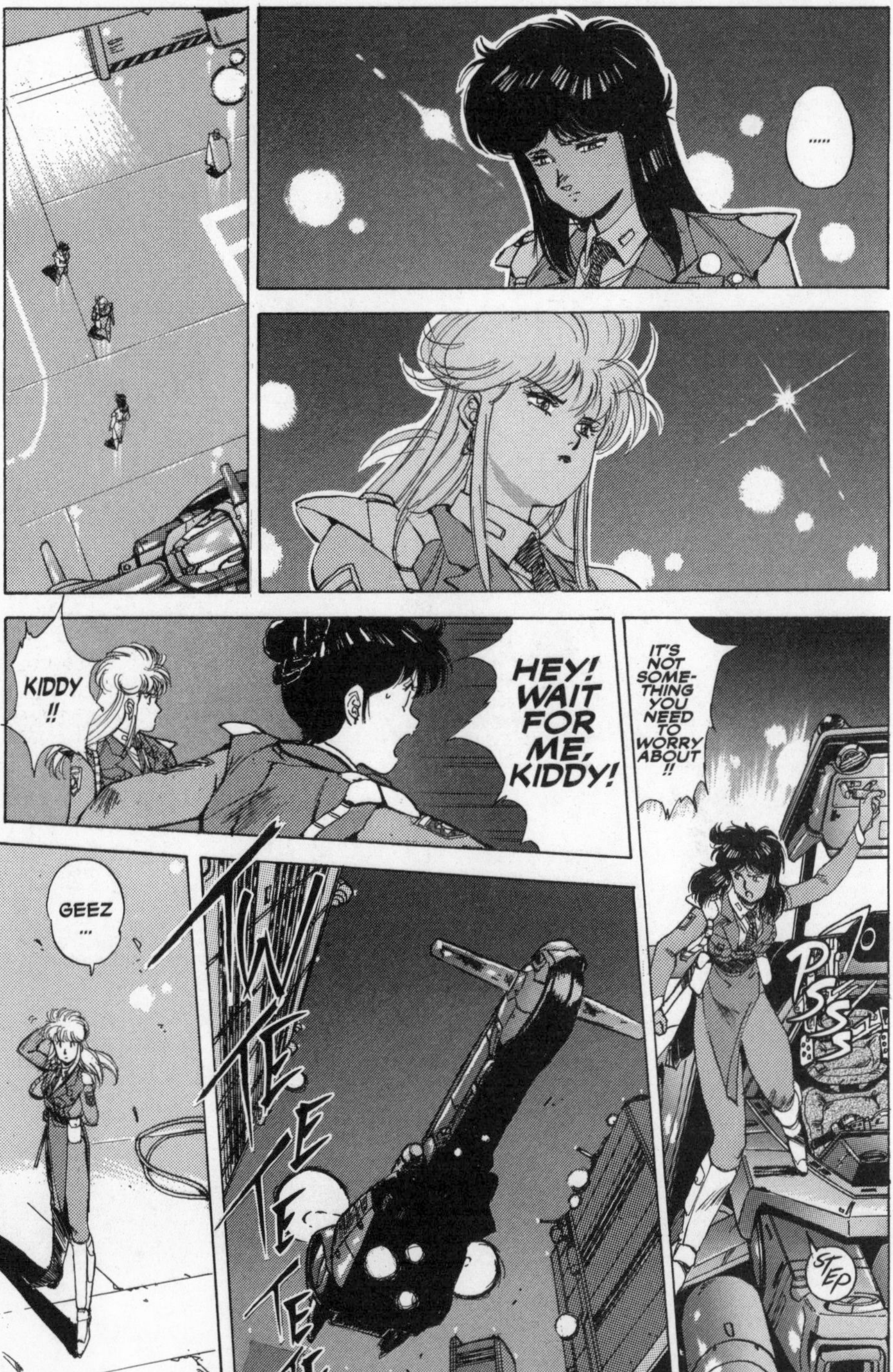
.....
IT'S NOT SOMETHING YOU NEED TO WORRY ABOUT!!
HEY! WAIT FOR ME, KIDDY!
KIDDY!!
PSSS
STEP
TWEEEEEE...
GEEZ ...

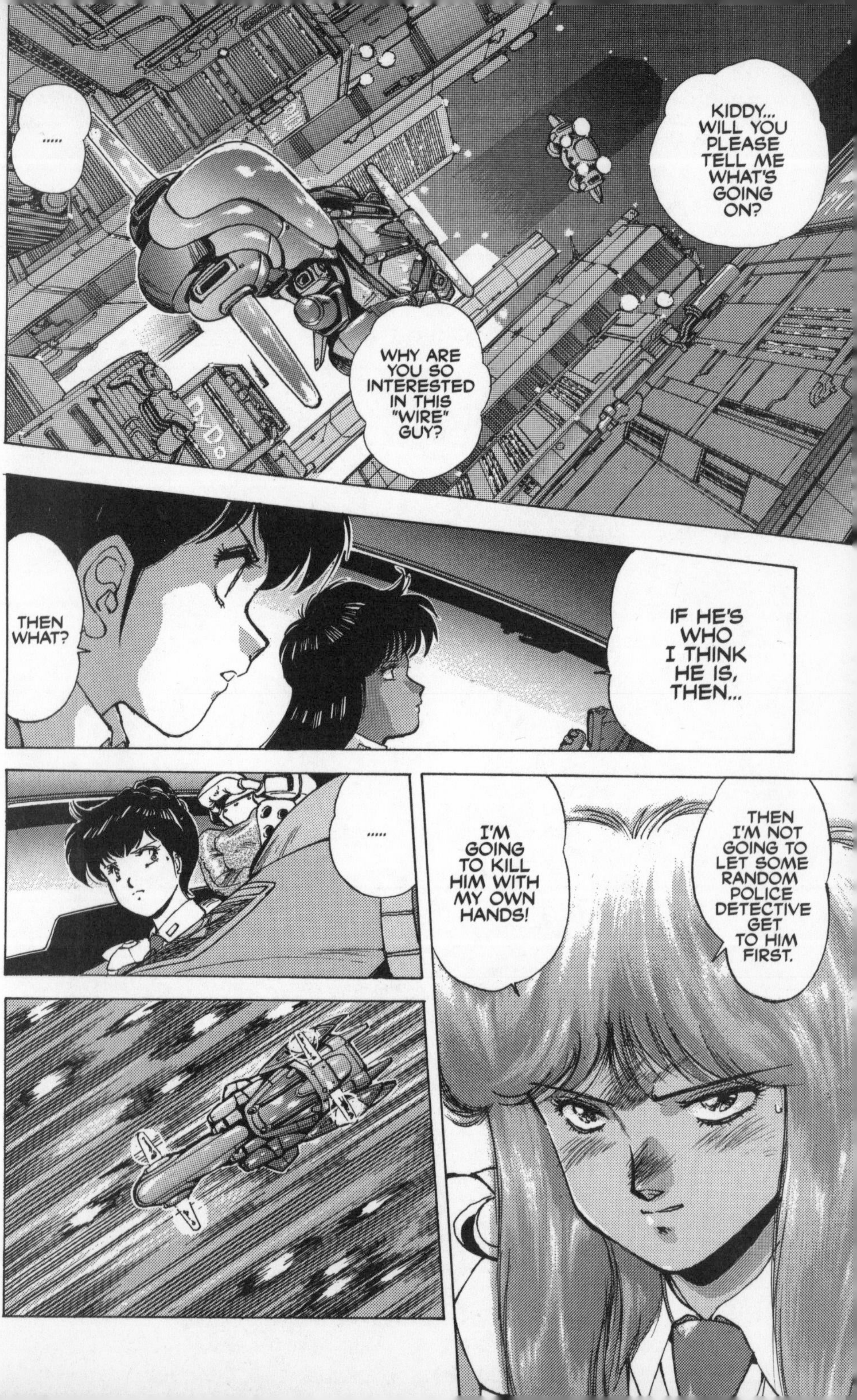
KIDDY... WILL YOU PLEASE TELL ME WHAT'S GOING ON?
WHY ARE YOU SO INTERESTED IN THIS "WIRE" GUY?
.....
IF HE'S WHO I THINK HE IS, THEN...
THEN WHAT?
THEN I'M NOT GOING TO LET SOME RANDOM POLICE DETECTIVE GET TO HIM FIRST.
I'M GOING TO KILL HIM WITH MY OWN HANDS!
.....

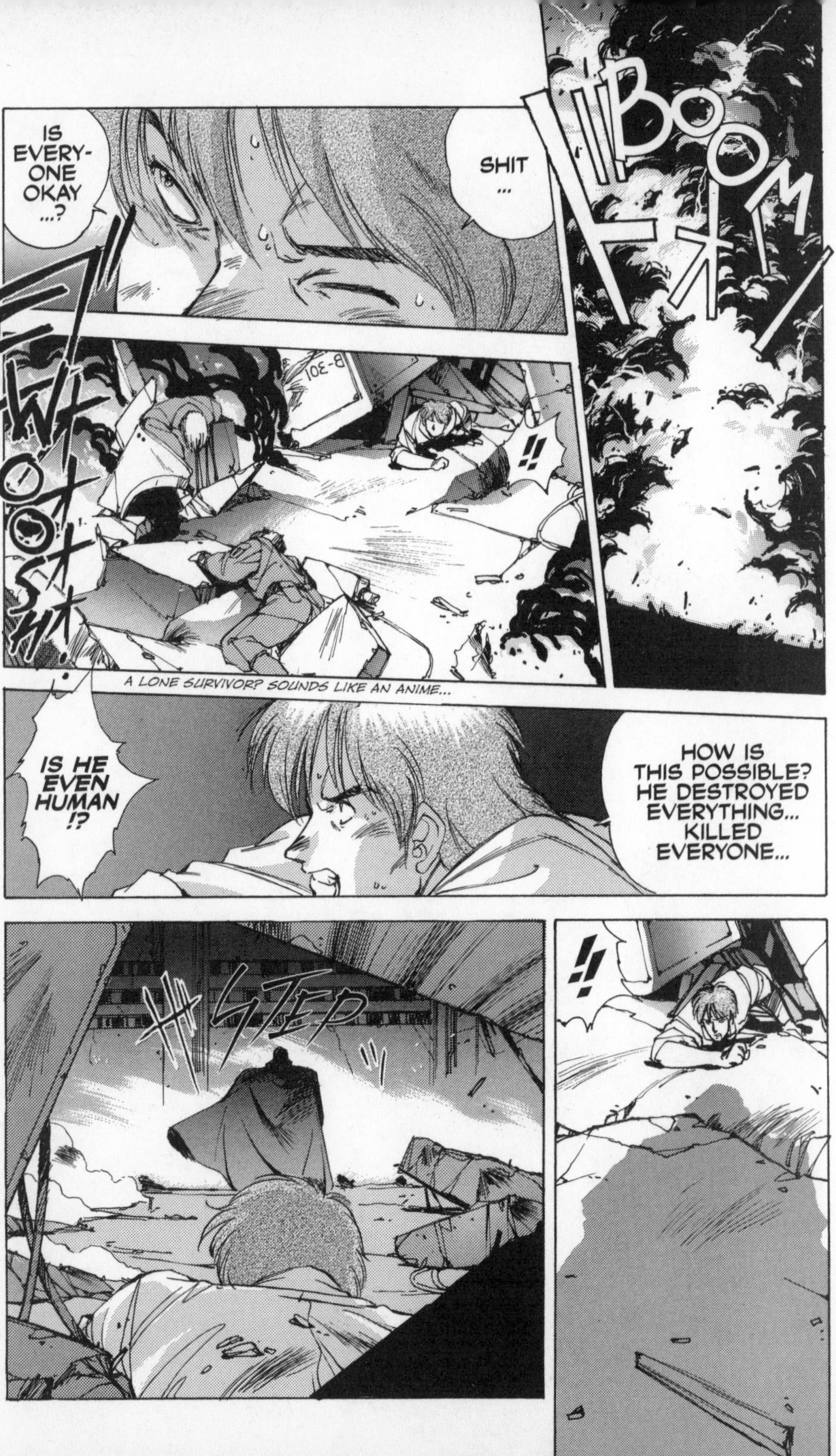
BOOM
SHIT ...
IS EVERY-ONE OKAY ...?
FWOOSH!
!!
A LONE SURVIVOR? SOUNDS LIKE AN ANIME...
HOW IS THIS POSSIBLE? HE DESTROYED EVERYTHING... KILLED EVERYONE...
IS HE EVEN HUMAN !?
!!
STEP

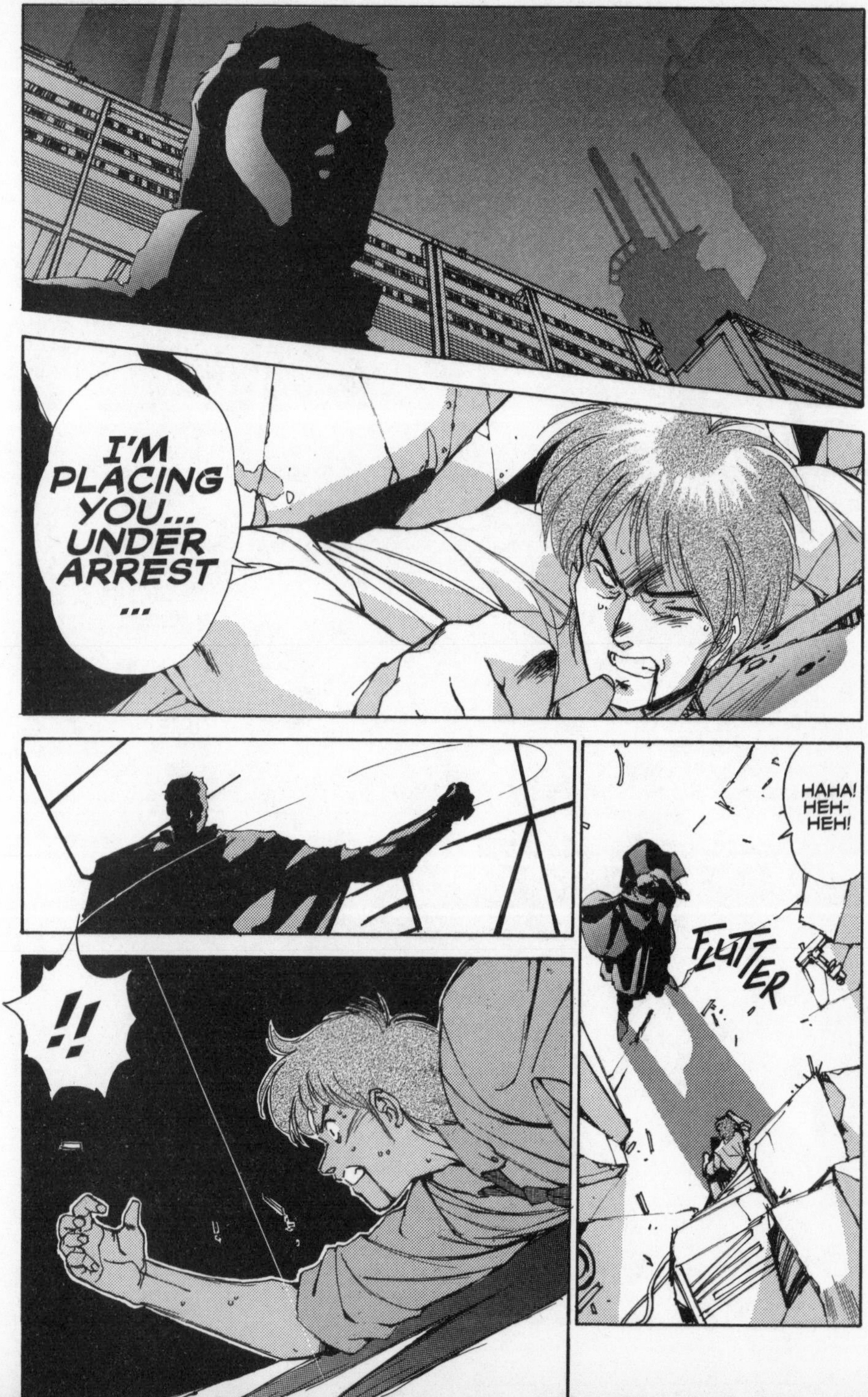
I'M PLACING YOU... UNDER ARREST ...
HAHA! HEH-HEH!
FLUTTER
!!

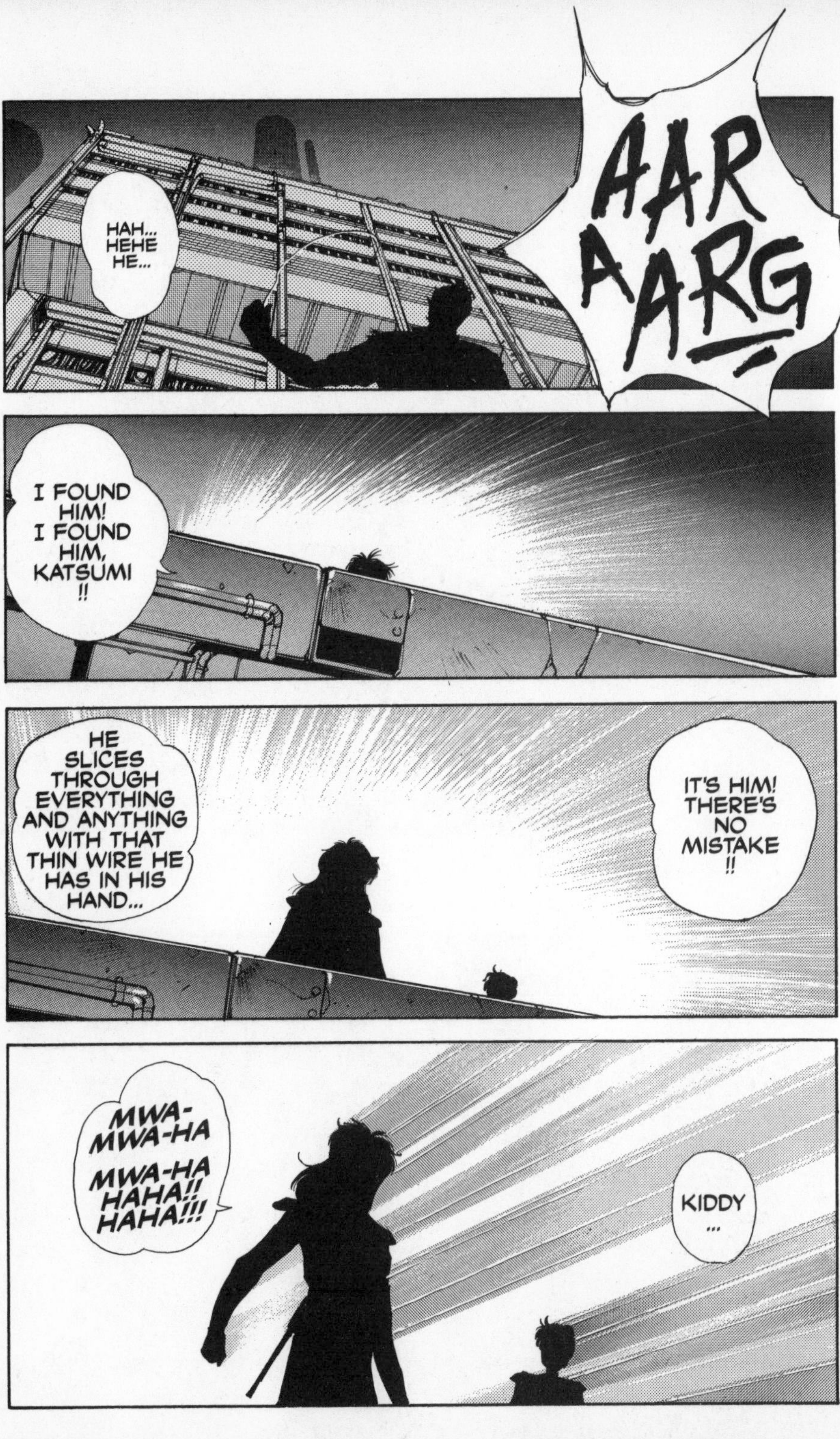
AAR AARG
HAH... HEHE HE...
I FOUND HIM! I FOUND HIM, KATSUMI !!
IT'S HIM! THERE'S NO MISTAKE !!
HE SLICES THROUGH EVERYTHING AND ANYTHING WITH THAT THIN WIRE HE HAS IN HIS HAND...
KIDDY ...
MWA-MWA-HA MWA-HA HAHA!! HAHA!!!

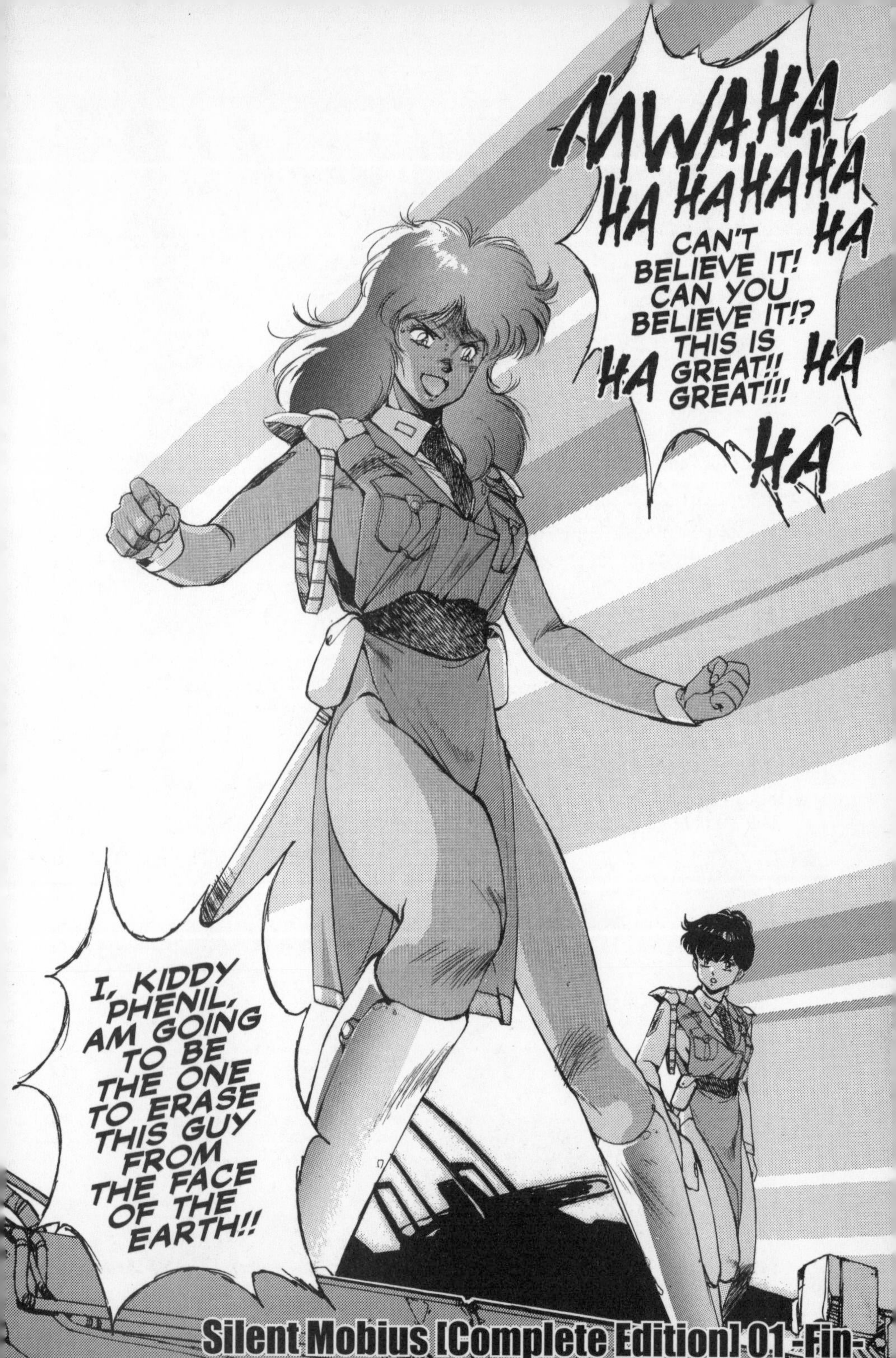
MWAHA HA HAHAHAHA HA
CAN'T BELIEVE IT! CAN YOU BELIEVE IT!? THIS IS GREAT!! GREAT!!!
HA HA
HA
I, KIDDY PHENIL, AM GOING TO BE THE ONE TO ERASE THIS GUY FROM THE FACE OF THE EARTH!!

Silent Mobius [Complete Edition] 01 -Fin-

Silent Möbius

"After finishing the first chapter of the series, I was suddenly overcome with this overwhelming sense of despair and hoplessness. (lol)" - Asamiya

SHIGEMA - Since it hadn't started out as a manga magazine, I think it was able to escape most of the preconceptions and doctrine of other manga magazines. Of all the series it ran, Silent Mobius had the greatest impact on the readers.

ASAMIYA - To be honest, though, after finishing the first chapter of the series, I was suddenly overcome with this overwhelming sense of despair and hopelessness. After all, it took me three months just to draw 32 pages! (lol)

SHIGEMA - It's because he put so much detail into the backgrounds and everything. Most of the recent sci-fi titles have the same basic look, and I really think "the near future" as we see it in modern mangas was based heavily on Silent Mobius. At the time, there basically wasn't any other sci-fi manga that offer such a detailed and high-quality futuristic world. They say "God is in the details," and I think that's so true. Asamiya had paid attention to every little thing about his world. Not to mention the all-female police force was a great idea! (lol)

ASAMIYA - I'm pretty sure it was the first series to star a priestess. (lol)

SHIGEMA - Asamiya managed to incorporate everything that the hardcore fans of the time were looking for: magic, science, and combat! The first chapter showed a magic circle, a massive attack move by one of the main characters, and a girl in her underwear! It had everything! (lol) Their uniforms were designed in great detail, as well. He had prepared for every little thing. Usually, when you build such a complex house of cards like this, it falls apart... but somehow, Silent Mobius worked out its own fragile little balance.

What was it like to draw Silent Mobius?

ASAMIYA - It was like groping around in the dark. One of the things I wanted to do was to allow for a large age range within the main characters. In the first volume, Yuki is still 16, and Rally looks like she could be somewhere in her early 30s... though I will leave that up to the reader to decide. (lol) I thought if the characters covered a wide age range, the readers would have an easier time picking out their favorite character.

Where did you get the idea to do a combat story surrounding a group of women?

ASAMIYA - Actually, it all began as a slapstick comedy-like manga with just Katsumi and Lebia. This was an idea I was working on back when I was still in school.

SHIGEMA - "Dirty Pair" probably has one of the most well-known girl/girl pairings.

ASAMIYA - Right, exactly. This idea was not exactly new or unique. So I thought up an organization that they could belong to. Couple that with my deep respect for women, (they are, after all, the ones who are capable of producing new life) and that's how I ended up with a team composed entirely of women.

I see... and why did you decide to give each character the special abilities that you did?

ASAMIYA - Well, at first you just had Katsumi with her magic, and Lebia with her passion for all things mechanical. They were a very distinct pair who existed at opposite ends of the spectrum. To keep with that line of thought, I tried to make each character unique by giving them... "special abilities," as you called them. Kiddy is the cyborg. Nami is a Japanese priestess, which is basically our version of a shaman. Yuki is a psychic, and Rally is the central figure who sort of brings all of them and their abilities together. Any characters I introduced later on went through a similar thought process.

SHIGEMA - Just like Dirty Pair, which we mentioned earlier, I believe Silent Mobius acts as a foundation for an entire genre. As such, creating a story based around a combat unit comprised entirely of females is a pretty big deal. If Silent Mobius had never existed, I really believe that all of the other titles that came along would have been very different indeed.

In Part 2, we will delve deeper into the secret stories behind the creation of Silent Mobius, and ask about the future of the series. Be sure to check it out!

KIA ASAMIYA

SPECIAL INTERVIEW ~ PART 1

Silent Mobius didn't stop at just a manga. It branched off into different media formats like CDs, novels, movies, etc. Through volume 1 and 2, we would like to share with you this very special interview with author Kia Asamiya, and Kei Shigema, who has closely watched over the evolution of the series. The unknown stories behind the Silent Mobius series, and what the future holds...

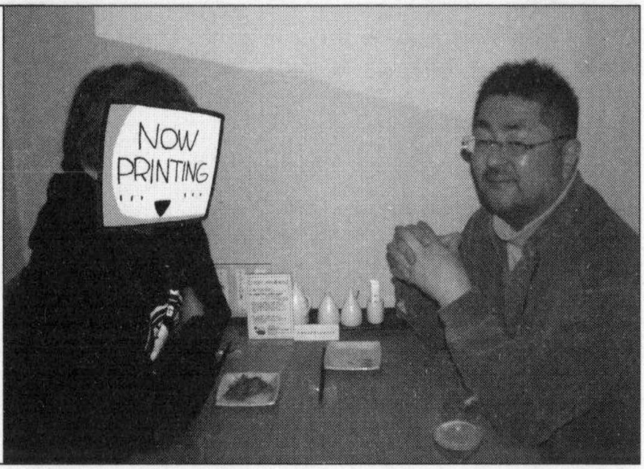
NOW PRINTING

What can you tell me about how you guys met for the first time?

Shigema - At the time, I was working as an editor for Cyber Comics*, but was also dabbling in writing novels for doujinshi. I showed one of my stories to Asamiya's manager, and received an offer to write novels based on that. That one novel carved the path for me becoming a full-fledged writer.
ASAMIYA - It was around the time the first Silent Mobius book was coming out.
SHIGEMA - Yes, that's right. I've been a fan of Kia's since reading his debut title, Shin Seiki Vagrants. Comic Comp*, the magazine that Silent Mobius ran in was... interesting... in more ways than one.

What do you mean by that...?

SHIGEMA - Well, that was the age when they were experimenting with letting animators draw manga. It was the anime era, or in other words, the timeframe when mangas geared toward anime fans started coming out. In the middle of it all, there was Comic Comp, jumping in with both feet. Though if you look at the line-up they had at the time, all of the artists were unknowns... (lol)
ASAMIYA - Yeah, it was a pretty risky line-up. (lol) I still remember those days. The public's response to Comic Comp was iffy at best. Nowadays, the hardcore fans have acknowledged it, and it has becoming something all together new... But at the time, it was a very unique magazine indeed. Comic Comp would only publish series that were of either the heroic fantasy or cyber punk genres. That's why it was generally thought to be for a very specific audience.
SHIGEMA - I guess you could say SF-Fantasy Ryu* from Tokuma Shoten was the real pioneer in that area, but they still had famous artists like Shotaro Ishinomori, among others, in their line-up, which I think helped quite a bit.
ASAMIYA - It was actually a computer magazine originally. They decided to run a little comic series at the end of each issue, which became surprisingly popular. That's how it all began.

NOTES:
***1 [Cyber Comics]**
A comic magazine published by Bandai, Cyber Comics ran several well-known side stories and original titles, including Kidou Senshi Gundam.
***2 [Comic Comp]**
A manga magazine that has its roots in a computer gaming magazine.
***3 [SF-Fantasy Ryu]**
An SF manga magazine published by Tokuma Shoten.

"If Silent Mobius had never existed, I really believe that all of the other titles that came along would have been very different indeed." - Shigema

サイレントメビウス

Silent Möbius

Complete
Edition **02**

KIA ASAMIYA
麻宮騎亜

STUDIO TRON
World Media Carrosseria

UDON

NT MÖBIUS: COMPLETE EDITION VC

The ultimate sci-fi manga continues! In this volume Kiddy confronts the deadly
serial killer known only as "Wire". Meanwhile Katsumi obtains a powerful
weapon – a sword that may actually be self-aware! Plus the girls of the AMP
battle a new type of Lucifer Hawk that threatens the city!

ON SALE NOVEMBER 2009!

サイレントメビウス
Silent Möbius

Story & Art: KIA ASAMIYA

English Translation: M. KIRIE HAYASHI
Lettering: MARSHALL DILLON

UDON STAFF
UDON Chief: ERIK KO
Project Manager: JIM ZUBKAVICH
Managing Editor: MATT MOYLAN
Editor - Japanese Publications: M. KIRIE HAYASHI
Marketing Manager: STACY KING

【サイレントメビウス 完全版 第1巻】
Silent Möbius Complete Edition 01 by Kia Asamiya
Copyright © STUDIO TRON 2006
Originally published in Japan in 2006 by
TOKUMA SHOTEN PUBLISHING CO., LTD.
Published in U.S.A. and Canada by UDON Entertainment Corp
under the license granted by TOKUMA SHOTEN PUBLISHING CO.,LTD.

English language version produced and published by UDON Entertainment Corp.
P.O. Box 5002, RPO MAJOR MACKENZIE
Richmond Hill, Ontario, L4S 0B7, Canada

www.UDONentertainment.com

First Printing: August 2009
ISBN-13: 978-1-897376-21-8   ISBN-10 : 1-897376-21-9
Printed in Canada

WHOOPS

This is the back of the book!

You're looking at the last page, not the first one.

SILENT MÖBIUS is a comic originally published in Japan (known as manga). Traditional manga is read in a 'reversed' format, starting on the right and heading towards the left. The story begins where english readers expect to find the last page because the spine of the book is on the opposite side.

Preserving the original artwork, we've decided to leave the Japanese format intact. Check the examples below to see how to read the word balloons in proper order.

Now head to the front of the book and enjoy SILENT MÖBIUS!